Maurice Blanchot on
Poetry and Narrative

Bloomsbury Studies in Philosophy and Poetry

Series Editors: Rick Anthony Furtak, Colorado College, USA and James D. Reid, Metropolitan State University of Denver, USA

Editorial Board:

Daniel Brown, University of Southampton, UK
Kristen Case, University of Maine Farmington, USA
Hannah Vandegrift Eldridge, University of Wisconsin–Madison, USA
Cassandra Falke, University of Tromsø, Norway
Luke Fischer, University of Sydney, Australia
John Gibson, University of Louisville, USA
James Haile III, University of Rhode Island, USA
Kevin Hart, Duke University, USA
Eileen John, University of Warwick, UK
Troy Jollimore, California State University, USA
David Kleinberg-Levin, Northwestern University, USA
John Koethe, University of Wisconsin–Milwaukee, USA
John T. Lysaker, Emory University, USA
Karmen MacKendrick, Le Moyne College, USA
Rukmini Bhaya Nair, Indian Institute of Technology, India
Kamiyo Ogawa, Sophia University, Japan
Kaz Oishi, University of Tokyo, Japan
Yi-Ping Ong, Johns Hopkins University, USA
Anna Christina Soy Ribeiro, Texas Tech University, USA
Karen Simecek, University of Warwick, UK
Ruth Rebecca Tietjen, University of Copenhagen, Denmark
Íngrid Vendrell Ferran, Goethe University Frankfurt, Germany

Bloomsbury Studies in Philosophy and Poetry explores ancient, modern, and contemporary texts in ways that are sensitive to philosophical themes and problems that can be fruitfully addressed through poetic modes of writing, and focused on questions of style, the relations between form and content, and the conduciveness of literary modes of expression to philosophical inquiry. With a keen interest in the intertwining of poetry and philosophy in all forms, the series will cover the philosophical register of poetry, the poetics of philosophical writing, and the literary strategies of philosophers.

The series provides a home for work on figures across geographical landscapes, with contributions that employ a wide range of methods across academic disciplines, and without regard for divisions within philosophy, between analytic and continental, for example, that have outworn their usefulness. Featuring single-authored works and edited collections, curated by an international editorial board, the series aims to redefine how we read and discuss philosophy and poetry today.

Titles in the series:

Everyday Poetics, by Brett Bourbon
Thought and Poetry, by John Koethe
A Poetic Philosophy of Language, by Philip Mills
Maurice Blanchot on Poetry and Narrative, by Kevin Hart

Forthcoming titles:

Philosophical Fragments and the Poetry of Thinking, by Luke Fischer
A Philosophy of Lyric Voice, by Karen Simecek
Skepticism and Impersonality in Modern Poetry, by Joshua Adams
A Black Poetics of the Everyday, by James Haile III

Maurice Blanchot on Poetry and Narrative

Ethics of the Image

Kevin Hart

BLOOMSBURY ACADEMIC
LONDON • NEW YORK • OXFORD • NEW DELHI • SYDNEY

BLOOMSBURY ACADEMIC
Bloomsbury Publishing Plc
50 Bedford Square, London, WC1B 3DP, UK
1385 Broadway, New York, NY 10018, USA
29 Earlsfort Terrace, Dublin 2, Ireland

BLOOMSBURY, BLOOMSBURY ACADEMIC and the Diana logo are trademarks of
Bloomsbury Publishing Plc

First published in Great Britain 2023
This paperback edition published 2024

Copyright © Kevin Hart, 2023

Kevin Hart has asserted his right under the Copyright, Designs and Patents Act, 1988, to be identified as Author of this work.

2 quotes (p 29 and p 121) from *La Parole en archipel*, René Char © Editions Gallimard, Paris, 1962 – © Editions Gallimard, 1986, pour la présente édition.

1 quote from Argument (*poème pulvérisé*) from *Œuvres complètes*, René Char © Editions Gallimard, Paris 1983

For legal purposes the Acknowledgements on p. x constitute an extension of this copyright page.

Cover image: Mundane Liturgies © Sashanna Hart

All rights reserved. No part of this publication may be reproduced or transmitted in any form or by any means, electronic or mechanical, including photocopying, recording, or any information storage or retrieval system, without prior permission in writing from the publishers.

Bloomsbury Publishing Plc does not have any control over, or responsibility for, any third-party websites referred to or in this book. All internet addresses given in this book were correct at the time of going to press. The author and publisher regret any inconvenience caused if addresses have changed or sites have ceased to exist, but can accept no responsibility for any such changes.

A catalogue record for this book is available from the British Library.

A catalog record for this book is available from the Library of Congress.

Library of Congress Control Number: 2023937741.

ISBN: HB: 978-1-3503-4905-6
PB: 978-1-3503-4909-4
ePDF: 978-1-3503-4906-3
eBook: 978-1-3503-4907-0

Series: Bloomsbury Studies in Philosophy and Poetry

Typeset by Deanta Global Publishing Services, Chennai, India

To find out more about our authors and books visit www.bloomsbury.com and sign up for our newsletters.

In memory:
Monique Antelme
Helen Tartar

Contents

Acknowledgments	x
List of Abbreviations	xii
Note on Citations	xvi
Introduction: Blanchot Encore	1

Part 1 On Poetry

1	Blanchot's Mallarmé	21
2	Blanchot's Hölderlin	38
3	Blanchot's Char	60

Part 2 On Friendship

4	Blanchot's Weil	77
5	The Aggrieved Community	88
6	The Friendship of the No	100

Part 3 On Narrative

7	The Neutral Reduction: *Thomas L'Obscur*	123
8	"Lès-Poésie?": Levinas reads *La Folie du jour*	144
9	Ethics of the Image	157

Part 4 On Being Jewish

10	The Third Relation	177
11	From *The Star* to *The Disaster*	198
12	"The *Absolute* Event of History": The Shoah and the Outside	213

Afterword	233
Bibliography	235
Index	251

Acknowledgments

It is a pleasure to thank all those with whom I have had conversations about Maurice Blanchot over the years, especially Christoph Bident, Yves Bonnefoy, Jacques Derrida, Geoffrey Hartman, Leslie Hill, and Michael Holland, all of whom have been unfailingly generous in sharing their knowledge of Blanchot and twentieth-century French writing in general. When I was teaching at the University of Notre Dame, Alan Padgett, Alain Toumayan, and Henry Weinfield read parts of this book, which is all the better for their kind attentions. Claire Lyu of the University of Virginia read a draft of Chapter 6 and her comments helped me to improve it. I am thankful to William Flesch for sharing with me Blanchot's unpublished letters about Paul de Man and about Blanchot's time writing for *Combat*, and in the same spirit to Jean-Luc Nancy, Claire Nancy, and Leonid Kharlamov for letting me read Blanchot's letter about his political itinerary to Roger Laporte before it appeared in print. I am grateful to Sir Michael Edwards for his advice on my translations of Mallarmé's poems, although he bears no responsibility for the limitations of my ability as a translator of that untranslatable poet. Also, Sir Michael, Patrick Vannier, and Greg Goering kindly investigated the etymology of "Thomas" and advised me as to its possible mistaken origin in Gen. 1: 2. Finally, I wish to acknowledge the vigilance shown by the anonymous readers for Bloomsbury.

This book has been many years in the writing. Parts of it have been given at conferences held in Antwerp, Cerisy, Chicago, Geneva, Melbourne, Pittsburgh, Sydney, and Vienna. Often papers that are not given in full here have offered points of departure for expansions of concerns raised in other papers that have appeared in journals and edited collections. I would like to thank all those who invited me to speak and all those who engaged me in dialogue about Blanchot when I was speaking at conferences.

An earlier version of the first chapter appeared in *Southerly*, 68: 3 (2008) and the text, which was unfortunately garbled, has been corrected; a less elaborated version of the second chapter was published in *The Poesis of Peace: Narratives, Cultures and Philosophies*, ed Klaus-Gerd Giesen, Carool Kersten and Lenart Skof (copyright 2017), reproduced by permission of Taylor and Francis Group; and the third chapter, now slightly recast, was originally published in *Understanding Blanchot, Understanding Modernism*, ed. Christopher Langlois (Bloomsbury, 2018). Chapter 4 appeared, in an earlier form, in *Simone Weil and Continental Philosophy*, ed. A. Rebecca Rozelle-Stone (Rowman and Littlefield, 2017); a shorter version of Chapter 5 was published in *Journal for Continental Philosophy of Religion*, 1: 1 (2019); and I have refreshed my introduction to Blanchot's *Political Writings*, ed. Zakir Paul (Fordham University Press, 2010) to form the sixth chapter. I have added material to my contribution to my edited collection *Clandestine Encounters: Philosophy in the Narratives of Maurice Blanchot* (Notre Dame University Press, 2010) in order to compose the seventh chapter. Chapter 8 consists of a lightly revised version of an essay in *Levinas and Literature*, ed. Michael Fagenblat (De Gruyter, 2020), itself an expansion of the original text in French which appeared in *Maurice Blanchot: La littérature encore une fois,* ed. Sabine Kaufmann (Éditions Furor, 2017). A very early version of Chapter 9, now amplified, first appeared as "Ethics of the Image" in *Levinas Studies* 1 (2005), 119–38, and I would like to thank my friend Jeff Bloechl for inviting me to write it all those years ago. The first version of Chapter 10 originally appeared (in French) in *Blanchot dans son siècle,* ed. Christophe Bident (Parangon, 2009). Chapter 11 first saw the light of day in *Paragraph*, 30: 3 (2007) and has been revised for this volume. Finally, Chapter 12 was published in *Word and Text*, 5: 1-2 (2015) and has since been updated. My thanks to all editors and publishers for kindly granting permission for me to reprint material that had appeared earlier.

For permission to quote from Maurice Blanchot's "Our Clandestine Companion" I am very thankful to the State University of New York Press. For permission to quote from Henry Weinfield's translations of Stéphane Mallarmé, I am grateful to the University of California Press. For permission to quote from René Char, I am obliged to Gallimard. And for permission to quote from Blanchot's *The Infinite Conversation*, I warmly acknowledge the University of Minnesota Press: English translation copyright 1993 by the Regents of the University of Minnesota, and originally published in French in *L'Entretien infini,* copyright 1969 by Editions Gallimard. Although all the chapters in this book were drafted before I met my wife, Sashanna Hart, all of the revisions were completed in the new life she has made possible for me. To her I owe everything. The book was largely revised at "Positive Connection" in Taneyville, Missouri, that admirable facility for advanced research. My thanks to its Director, Dave Stefan.

I offer this book in memory of two great friends of Maurice Blanchot both of whom I have been privileged to know: Monique Antelme, who perhaps was closer to him over a long period than anyone else, and Helen Tartar who, although she did not know Blanchot personally, devoted herself to the publication of his writings in English. I can never read Blanchot without recalling them with admiration and fondness.

Abbreviations

Works by Maurice Blanchot in French:

A	*L'Amitié*. Paris: Gallimard, 1971.
AC	*"Après coup" prédédé par "Le Ressassement eternal."* Paris: Éditions de Minuit, 1983.
Am	*Aminadab*. Paris: Gallimard, 1942.
AM	*L'Arrêt de mort*. Paris: Gallimard, 1948.
C	Pierre Madaule, *Correspondance, 1953-2002*. Édition établie, présentée et annotée par Pierre Madaule. Paris: Gallimard, 2012.
CC	*La Condition critique: articles, 1945-1998*. Ed. Christophe Bident. Paris: Gallimard, 2010.
CI	*La Communauté inavouable*. Paris: Éditions de Minuit, 1983.
CL	*Chroniques littéraires du "Journal des débats," avril 1941- août 1944*. Ed. Christophe Bident. Paris: Gallimard, 2007.
CMP	*Celui qui ne m'accompagnait pas*. Paris: Gallimard, 1953.
CP	*Chroniques politiques des années trente*. Ed. David Uhrig. Paris: Gallimard, 2017.
ED	*L'Écriture du désastre*. Paris: Gallimard, 1980.
EI	*L'Entretien infini*. Paris: Gallimard, 1969.
EL	*L'Espace littéraire*. Paris: Gallimard, 1955.
FP(F)	*Faux pas*. Paris: Gallimard, 1943.
IM	*L'Instant de ma mort*. Paris: Gallimard, 2002.
IQ	*Les Intellectuels en question: Ébauche d'une réflexion*. Paris: Fourbis, 1996.
LS(F)	*Lautréamont et Sade*. Paris: Éditions de Minuit, 1949.
LV	*Le Livre à venir*. Paris: Gallimard, 1959.
LVK	*Lettres à Vadim Kozovoï suivi de La Parole Ascendante*. Ed. Denis Aucouturier. Houilles: Éditions Manucius, 2009.
PA	*Pour l'amitié*. Paris: Fourbis, 1996.
PF	*Le Part du feu*. Paris: Gallimard, 1949.
TH	*Le Très-Haut*. Paris: Gallimard, 1948.

TO (1)	*Thomas l'Obscur: première version* (1941). Paris: Gallimard, 2005.
TO (2)	*Thomas l'Obscur: nouvelle version*. Paris: Gallimard, 1950.
TS	*Thomas le Solitaire*. Paris: Kimé, 2022.
VA	*Une voix venue d'ailleurs: Sur les poèmes de Louis-René des Forêts*. Dijon: Ulysse Fin de Siècle, 1992.

Works by Maurice Blanchot in English translation:

Amin.	*Aminadab*. Trans. Jeff Fort. Lincoln: University of Nebraska Press, 2002.
BC	*The Book to Come*. Trans. Charlotte Mandell. Stanford: Stanford University Press, 2003.
BR	*The Blanchot Reader*. Ed. Michael Holland. Oxford: Basil Blackwell, 1995.
DC	*Desperate Clarity: Chronicles of Intellectual Life, 1942*. Trans. Michael Holland. New York: Fordham University Press, 2014.
DN	*Death Now: Chronicles of Intellectual Life, 1944*. Trans. Michael Holland. New York: Fordham University Press, 2019.
DS	*Death Sentence*. Trans. Lydia Davis. Barrytown, NY: Station Hill Press, 1978.
F	*Friendship*. Trans. Elizabeth Rottenberg. Stanford: Stanford University Press, 1997.
FP	*Faux Pas*. Trans. Charlotte Mandell. Stanford: Stanford University Press, 2001.
IC	*The Infinite Conversation*. Trans. and foreword Susan Hanson. Minneapolis: University of Minnesota Press, 1993.
ID	*The Instant of My Death* bound with Jacques Derrida, *Demeure: Fiction and Testimony*. Trans. Elizabeth Rottenberg. Stanford: Stanford University Press, 2000.
InD	*Into Disaster: Chronicles of Intellectual Life, 1941*. Trans. Michael Holland. New York: Fordham University Press, 2014.
LS	*Lautréamont and Sade*. Trans. Stuart Kendall and Michele Kendall. Stanford: Stanford University Press, 2004.
MD	*The Madness of the Day*. Trans. Lydia Davis. Barrytown, NY: Station Hill Press, 1981.
MH	*The Most High,* trans. Allan Stoeckl. Lincoln: University of Nebraska Press, 1996
OCC	"Our Clandestine Companion," *Face to Face with Levinas*, ed. Richard A. Cohen. Albany: State University of New York Press, 1986, 41-50.

OWM	*The One Who was Standing Apart from Me.* Trans. Lydia Davis. Barrytown, NY: Station Hill Press, 1993.
PW	*Political Writings, 1953-1993.* Trans. and intro. Zakir Paul, foreword Kevin Hart. New York: Fordham University Press, 2010.
SHBR	*The Station Hill Blanchot Reader: Fiction and Literary Essays.* Trans. Lydia Davis et al. Barrytown, NY: Station Hill, 1999.
SL	*The Space of Literature.* Trans. Ann Smock. Lincoln: University of Nebraska Press, 1982.
SNB	*The Step Not Beyond.* Trans. Lycette Nelson. Albany: State University of New York Press, 1992.
TO	*Thomas the Obscure.* Trans. Robert Lamberton. New York: David Lewis, 1973.
UC	*The Unavowable Community.* Trans. Pierre Joris. Barrytown, NY: Station Hill Press, 1988.
VC	*Vicious Circles: Two Fictions and "After the Fact."* Trans. Paul Auster. Barrytown, NY: Station Hill Press, 1985.
VE	*A Voice from Elsewhere.* Trans. Charlotte Mandell. Albany: State University of New York Press, 2007.
WD	*The Writing of the Disaster.* Trans. Ann Smock. Lincoln: University of Nebraska Press, 1986.
WF	*The Work of Fire.* Trans. Charlotte Mandell. Stanford: Stanford University Press, 1995.
WR	*A World in Ruins: Chronicles of Intellectual Life, 1943.* Trans. Michael Holland. New York: Fordham University Press, 2016.
WTC	*When the Time Comes.* Trans. Lydia Davis. Barrytown, NY: Station Hill Press, 1985.

Works by Emmanuel Levinas in French:

AE	*Autrement qu'être ou au-delà de l'essence.* La Haye: Martinus Nijhoff, 1974.
DEHH	*En dévouvrant l'existence avec Husserl et Heidegger.* Paris: J. Vrin, 1994.
DL	*Difficile liberté.* Troisième édition revue et corrigée. Paris: Albin Michel, 1976.
DVI	*De Dieu qui vient à l'idée.* Paris: J. Vrin, 1992.
EE(F)	*De l'existence à l'existant.* Seconde édition augmentée. Paris: J. Vrin, 1993.
EeI	*Éthique et infini. Dialogues avec Philippe Nemo.* Paris: Fayard, 1982.
EN(F)	*Entre Nous: Essais sur le penser-à-l'autre.* Paris: Grasset, 1991.
IH	*Les Imprévus de l'histoire.* Montpellier: Fata Morgana, 1994.

O	*De l'oblitération: Entretien avec Françoise Armengaud à propos de l'œuvre de Sosno.* Seconde édition. Paris: Éditions de la Différance, 1990.
SMB	*Sur Maurice Blanchot.* Montpellier: Fata Morgana, 1975.
TI (F)	*Totalité et infini: Essai sur l'extériorité.* La Haye: Martinus Nijhoff, 1971.

Works by Emmanuel Levinas in English translation:

AT	*Alterity and Transcendence.* Trans. Michael B. Smith. London: Athlone, 1999.
CCP	*Collected Philosophical Papers.* Trans. Alphonso Lingis. Dordrecht: Martinus Nijhoff Publishers, 1987.
DEH	*Discovering Existence with Husserl.* Trans. Richard A. Cohen and Michael B. Smith. Evanston: Northwestern University Press, 1998.
DF	*Difficult Freedom: Essays on Judaism.* Trans. Seán Hand. Baltimore: The Johns Hopkins University Press, 1990.
EE	*Existence and Existents.* Trans. Alphonso Lingis. Corrected edition. Dordrecht: Kluwer, 1988.
EIn	*Ethics and Infinity: Conversations with Philippe Nemo.* Trans. Richard Cohen. Pittsburgh: Duquesne University Press, 1985.
EN	*Entre Nous: Thinking-of-the-Other.* Trans. Michael B. Smith and Barbara Harshav. New York: Columbia University Press, 1998.
GCM	*Of God Who Comes to Mind.* Trans. Bettina Bergo. Stanford: Stanford University Press, 1998.
IRB	*Is it Righteous to Be?: Interviews with Emmanuel Levinas.* Ed. Jill Robbins. Stanford: Stanford University Press, 2001.
ITN	*In the Time of the Nations.* Trans. Michael B. Smith. Bloomington: Indiana University Press, 1994.
NTR	*Nine Talmudic Readings*, trans. and intro. Annette Aronowicz. Bloomington: Indiana University Press, 1990.
OB	*Otherwise than Being or Beyond Essence.* Trans. Alphonso Lingis. The Hague: Martinus Nijhoff, 1981.
PN	*Proper Names.* Trans. Michael B. Smith. Stanford: Stanford University Press, 1996.
TaO	*Time and the Other.* Trans. Richard A. Cohen. Pittsburgh: Duquesne University Press, 1987.
TI	*Totality and Infinity: An Essay on Exteriority.* Trans. Alphonso Lingis. The Hague: Martinus Nijhoff, 1979.

Note on Citations

When I have quoted from an English translation of a work by Blanchot, I give the page number of the translation in parentheses followed by the page number of the French original when it has been collected in a book. If there is any ambiguity, I have supplied an abbreviation from the table of abbreviations given earlier.

Introduction

Blanchot Encore

After returning to Australia from a Fulbright year at Stanford University, I taught high school before beginning doctoral studies. One of my responsibilities at the Geelong College was to take a class to "library hour," which allowed the students to read anything they wished. Teachers could do the same. I remember browsing rather aimlessly along the small selection of books in French. I picked up a collection of essays. I opened it to a piece with a very strange title, "La littérature et le droit à la mort," and was quickly carried along in what seemed to me to be a prose at once philosophically informed while also darkly incantatory. The hour quickly passed, and I took the book home, haunted for days by what I read. The volume had contained only a part of the essay, and no library nearby had any books by the author, someone of whom I had never heard: Maurice Blanchot. I was able to finish reading the essay I had started at the Baillieu Library at the University of Melbourne, which had an unopened copy of *Le Part du feu* (1949); but their holdings of this unnerving author whose prose seemed to look at me, almost within me, and not shift its gaze, were few and far between. It took a long while before I could find much of his writing, and some months before any of his narrative works came my way. In those days, one had to purchase French titles from Blackwell's in Oxford, which took ages to arrive in Australia; there was precious little available in translation; and absolutely no one I knew had heard of him. I had started reading Jacques Derrida while at Stanford—the left-hand side of *Glas* (1974), because I was studying Hegel at the time, and then *De la grammatologie* (1967) and *L'Écriture et la différence* (1967)—and it became clear that Blanchot was important to him. Over the coming months and years, I read all that I could in the time left available from preparing for doctoral studies when I was not teaching secondary classes in English, philosophy, and religion.

Nowadays everything by Blanchot is readily available, including the *première édition* of *Thomas l'Obscur* (1941) and even the draft that led to that novel, *Thomas le Solitaire* (2022), and the main call that tempts one to seek more of his writing comes from Harvard, where a fair number of Blanchot's manuscripts are now held at the Houghton Library. Almost everything has been rendered into English—that first novel and its draft being notable exceptions—sometimes in competing translations, and there is a voluminous secondary literature on him in several languages, which poses a formidable challenge to anyone who wishes to be au courant with what people are thinking about it. There are two *Blanchot Reader*s, one edited by Michael Holland and another by George Quasha. There are the six volumes of the *Cahiers Maurice Blanchot*

(2001–19), essential for any serious reader of the author, as is the exacting *Dictionnaire Maurice Blanchot* (2023), edited by Michael Holland and Hannes Opelez.

The Blanchot I first read seemed to have a deep philosophical culture but not to be a philosopher in the narrow sense of the word. (I had been trained quite strictly in analytic philosophy at the Australian National University and had quietly passed into phenomenology by way of Husserl's *Logical Investigations*.) His literary criticism was nothing like the philological and moral styles of reading I had been taught as an undergraduate; it seemed to be oriented more to the writer than the words on the page—or, rather, to the moment when a writer picks up a pen and is about to lower it and begin forming words. Some of his literary judgments about specific works were perplexing; and, in general, there was an air of intensity and obliqueness to everything he wrote. From what position did he read his favored books? What sort of light, or half-light, did he cast on them? Why were they favored in the first place? And what, in the end, did he tell us about those books? None of these questions could be easily answered at the time, I found. Nor could I be sure why he had constant recourse to the doublet of *mourir* and *la mort*. What I knew, though, is that he was, quite literally, a fascinating writer, one for whom fascination was a theme treated with perspicacity and originality.

That Blanchot was a committed atheist was apparent on almost every page I read, but his was an atheism that was new to me, being nothing like the protest atheism and rational atheism to which I had been exposed while reading philosophy as an undergraduate student. Some of my fellow students had been unimpressed by the traditional proofs for the existence of God—they had the high standards of clarity and rigor set forth by Frege and Russell in the front of their minds—and this experience strengthened them in their indifference to God. I didn't see anything much there by way of proof of divinity, either, but didn't think that, with regard to the *quinquæ viæ* of St. Thomas Aquinas at any rate, they were meant to prove anything. They were explicating in a technical manner the ordinary sense of "God" that was common at the time, especially among educated clerics. As I deepened my familiarity with phenomenology and theology, I came to see that God does not let himself get netted in anything like what we moderns would call a "proof." If anything, to follow that approach is to encounter an implacable barrier that deflects one to search for another way to know God. And that is, I started to see, the dark way of unknowing that the medieval contemplatives recognized as love (*caritas*).

Phenomenology was able to offer a description of this way, in parts lavish and in other parts quite thin, that had opened before me. At first, with reluctance, I embraced the idea that Husserl was largely correct to emphasize description over argument, at least in some areas of human inquiry. Such phenomenological description could be exhausting, even cumbersome, taking account, as it does, of many perspectives, intersubjective as well as subjective, and always at a transcendental level, in a special sense of that elusive word. But it offered something more satisfying than the sort of advanced logical analysis in which I had been tutored as an undergraduate. My long second-year paper formalizing St. Anselm's ontological argument in terms of possible world theory, which at the time I thought well of, began to recede in my mind and to seem very narrow in its manner and unsatisfactory in its conclusions. My argument had led me to rely on Brouwer's axiom, and in retrospect it seemed too frail a thing to bear the burden of eternity. Reading Blanchot showed me two things: there was a sophisticated mode of atheism that was new to me, and there were reasons to be skeptical of the bravado of classical phenomenology.

I viewed Blanchot's atheism, as all the other varieties, through Christian eyes. Even so, I have always thought that atheism must be taken seriously by Christians, especially by theologians. There is reason to distinguish philosophically impressive modes of atheism from the aggressive, but poorly researched, work of the "New Atheists" I would encounter much later. If a theologian were to write in such a loose and untutored manner about the natural sciences, he or she would be rightly laughed at. Yet it seems possible today for a scientist to write prose riddled with conceptual and historical errors that are sternly set against Christian belief and to be taken seriously, at least in some sections of the media. Even though Blanchot's atheism is firmly held, and has intriguing justifications, I saw early on that he also has recourse to a notion of the sacred and, indeed, to several themes in theology, especially in the contemplative or mystical tradition. To document this and weigh it was the burden of an earlier book, *The Dark Gaze: Maurice Blanchot and the Sacred* (Chicago UP, 2004). When I completed that book, I thought that I had written all that I wished to write on this particular author, and I moved on to other topics. However, Blanchot's death, which I mourned more deeply than that of other writers whom I esteemed, set in motion many conferences, special numbers of journals, and lecture opportunities; and I found myself composing more about him. Some of the pieces I wrote, now revised and updated, form the basis of this book. *Blanchot encore*, then; and, in truth, once I returned to his writings, I wanted to spend more and more time with them.

In that earlier book I had recognized Blanchot's criticisms of classical phenomenology, and in some of the chapters in this new book I try to go a little further in that act of acknowledgment. To deal with criticisms of Husserl written in the 1950s or 1960s is a delicate matter, since even careful readers of the philosopher were not in an unassailable position to offer searching criticisms. Much of importance in Husserl, the fabled *Nachlass*, was still unpublished, even in German; and without some of those many volumes one could not be fully aware of the philosopher's emphasis on intersubjectivity, his attention to generative themes, which stress the importance of natural language, and all that he has to say about passivity, especially with respect to sedimentation. Even Derrida's bold and brilliant reading of Husserl in his *Introduction à l'Origine de la Géométrie de Husserl* (1961) and *La Voix et le phénomène* (1967) call for modification, in some respects, by reference to what has appeared so far of the *Nachlass*. Blanchot's case is somewhat different, since unlike Derrida he did not hold (and did not wish to hold) a position in the French tertiary education system. After completing his Diplôme d'Études Supériere at the Sorbonne in 1930, he never sought to write theses or treatises, or to appear in professional philosophy journals, and increasingly was attracted by the prospect of fragmentary writing, which included snatches of narrative as well as aphorisms, glosses, and thoughtful observations. Right through to the late 1960s his critical writings more or less follow the genre of literary journalism as practiced in France, even if, as in *L'Espace littéraire* (1955) and *L'Entretien infini* (1969), he revised what he had first published and organized diverse pieces into a coherent, if troubled, whole. One must seek to find a way of reading

Blanchot that probes his views while also respecting the material limits within which he wrote.

One must also find ways of reading Blanchot's narratives, which I attempt in two chapters of this volume; and this task is more challenging than any other. To be sure, one finds the narrative works crisscrossed by themes some of which are teased out in the critical essays, but those themes in the narratives work in their own ways with respect to character, plot, and situation, if one can evoke that triad in narratives that seek constantly to complicate it. If Blanchot is a "philosophical novelist," as used to be said without too much reflection, he is most certainly not one like Voltaire or Pater or Musil or Sartre. Now I do not accept the antecedent in the previous sentence and in general tend to be wary of using the word "philosophy" without caveat when reading Blanchot's novels and *récits*. It is one thing to bring a deep philosophical culture to the writing of narrative works, and quite another to write philosophy by way of fiction. Also, it is doubtful whether pre-given philosophical positions can motivate characters or stymie action in a narrative. As if that were not sufficient to make us reticent about using the word "philosophy," we need also to keep in mind that Blanchot queries the usual distinctions between philosophy and literature, in both his literary and critical writings. One way in which he does this is by electing the word "philosophical" over the word "philosophy," as he explains in a later essay on his friend Levinas. The philosophical, for him, would be "a questioning so radical that the entire tradition would have to be called forth in its support."[1] Later in the essay, he returns to the word "philosophical" when giving a precise sense of what he values in Levinas's writing. One is always struck, he says,

> by one of his typical procedures: to begin, or to follow out, an analysis (most often, phenomenologically inspired) with such rigor and informed understanding that it seems precisely in this way that everything is said and that truth itself is disclosed—right along, that is, until we get to a minor remark, usually introduced by, e.g., an "*unless*" ["à moins que"] to which we cannot fail to be attentive, which fissures the whole of the preceding text, disturbing the solid order we had been called upon to observe, an order that nonetheless remains important. This is perhaps *the* movement that could properly be called philosophical [*C'est peut-être là le mouvement proprement philosophique*], not by stroke of force or belabored assertion, but a movement that was already Plato's expedient in his dialogues (his probity, and ruse as well). (48)

For Blanchot, the philosophical would be that which undoes an apparent order without simply denying its importance or replacing it with something else.

It was Levinas who introduced Blanchot to phenomenology, a favor returned by Blanchot who led his friend into the equally abundant world of modern French literature, especially Proust and Valéry. "Philosophy would henceforth be our companion day and night," Blanchot writes of his student days in Strasbourg, "even by losing its name [*en perdant son nom*], by becoming literature, scholarship, the lack thereof, or by standing aside" (42). Philosophy loses its proper name and the rights accrued to it over the centuries—the rights to sit in judgment over other discourses, to weigh their rationality, their truth claims, and to expand itself when desired by means of the formula "the philosophy of *x*"—and it does so first of all in becoming the philosophical. One way it does that is in becoming literature when literature constitutes itself as a radical questioning, beginning, no doubt, with received notions of "literature" as variously given by Boileau, Saint-Beuve, the brothers Goncourt, and even Sartre. The same would presumably happen with anthropology, history, literary criticism, politics, psychology, sociology, and so forth. Philosophy becomes a clandestine companion—secret, concealed, working underground—hidden in other discourses in order to question everything more thoroughly than any one discipline will allow, even the discipline that philosophy itself has become. So, when philosophy becomes literature, it does not become anything pure; for literature often has a social and political dimension, itself sometimes hidden. That state of affairs has been amply acknowledged in recent decades. Less broadly recognized is that literature sometimes has a covert philosophical and/or theological dimension; and even when this dimension is elusive, it can still partly organize the text and one's responses to it.

Today, forty-three years since the bright afternoon I came across some pages by Blanchot in a school library, the problem is less that he is read (although, to be sure, he will never be widely read) than that he is not always read well. (Sometimes he is read so perversely that the distinct shape of an axe to grind in the reader's hand becomes apparent.[2]) The puzzlement that I experienced when reading "La littérature et le droit à la mort" for the first time has never entirely gone away, for which I am thankful. Over the years, I have found ways of coming to terms with aspects of it but not wholly eliminating it. I quickly saw that Blanchot is a hedgehog rather than a fox, even if, especially in his last writings, he can seem very foxy indeed. His guiding themes are sometimes expanded or deepened, sometimes by dint of overt or covert dialogues with his contemporaries. They establish new, ever more hidden, vanishing points. Also, we can be surprised by Blanchot pointing us to unexpected moments of coincidence: for example, he indicates that his political views and his theory of writing ultimately converge.[3]

Some of his claims remain, if not opaque, then singular. One of these concerns is the approach of what he calls "the Neutral" or "the Outside" [*le Dehors* or *le dehors*], which he evokes in several ways and to distinct ends. Several of these chapters themselves dilate on the Outside, attempting to understand it and to weigh its significance; and I will say a little about it later in this introduction. I must say now, though, at the outset, that while I think I grasp what Blanchot tells me about it, I find his notion of the Outside less than clear in some respects. For instance, does he have a metaphysically realist or anti-realist understanding of it? Is it a matter of being or of mood—or perhaps the two together? How can one hold, as Blanchot does, that the Outside is beneath time and that one must be attuned to it in order to undergo its trial? Perhaps we should not expect someone who mainly writes literary columns in journals to supply rigorous answers to such questions, but it is odd that many of his readers who work in colleges and universities have not sought clarification. It is also baffling that some readers readily identify *le dehors* with Levinas's notion of the *il y a*: similarities, even overlaps, are not always convergences. Even more, I find it surprising to find a new generation of Blanchot's readers for whom the notion appears to be entirely unproblematic, indeed, for whom the author's works are largely untroublesome and not to be read outside or beyond the parameters he set himself. As a graduate student, I encountered several devout readers of Martin Heidegger, and for them nothing he had written was open to question. It was a "kneeling philosophy." I regret that today some of Blanchot's most fervent admirers also bow, if not kneel, when reading him. A generation or two of clarifying exposition of his writings, especially the volumes of criticism, has perhaps tended to iron out some of the creases in his work—the singularity of his approaches to reading and writing, some of his more counter-intuitive assertions—with the result that one now finds dogmatic Blanchotians, much as one once found emphatic Brownists and Grindletonians. Throughout this book, I try to read Blanchot while keeping in mind the value of his examples to test the generality of his claims and with an eye always on the lookout for counterexamples to recall his claims to their proper limits.

*

The Dark Gaze had a single theme: how Blanchot's reservations about phenomenology were leagued with aspects of the contemplative or mystical tradition in Christianity. Husserl had commended the conversion of the gaze, from the natural attitude to the phenomenological attitude. Were we to accomplish that mental task, Husserl thought, the structures of intelligibility, of things that exist and equally things that are imagined, would be revealed to the one performing the act. Drawing attention to Husserl's uncritical reliance on visuality and light, Blanchot modifies phenomenology so that it can help him answer his overriding question, "How to discover the obscure?"[4] This "obscurity" is what he takes to precede phenomena, that which can never itself enter the light of intelligibility, as phenomena do, and which Blanchot regards as what remains in modernity of the sacred. God and the sacred belong to different orders, he thinks, the former deriving from the One and the latter being the endless approach of what is variously called "the imaginary," "a murmur," "a vacancy," and "a strangeness." We can discern this obscurity in certain prose and poetry, in seeking the everyday, in limit-experiences, and in ordinary suffering. It becomes thematized, to a certain extent, by way of a syntax of "neither-nor," by appeals to "experience" and "mystery" (each set at an angle to the usual sense of the word), by an evacuation of the self, and by an appeal to a fresh way of thinking human relations. Dialogue, so important to Blanchot, ultimately derives, he thinks, from the early Jewish understanding of God being in relation to human beings. In pursuing my theme, I attended mainly to philosophy, psychoanalysis, and mystical theology, both Jewish and Christian. In *Maurice Blanchot on Poetry and Narrative* I remain, as in all my other books, in my little, shifting triangle of philosophy, literature, and religion; for all that, there is more here on politics than in my earlier book, more about poetry, more about the *récits*, and certainly more about Judaism.

The opening section of the book follows Blanchot in his readings of three major poets, each of whom poses immense challenges (as well as pleasures) to readers: Mallarmé, Hölderlin, and Char. In each case, I seek to uncover his investments in each body of work, as well as try to see how his obsessive concerns as a critic are variously shown in his treatment of each writer. These concerns are not those of most literary critics. Nor are they always the sort of things that would animate a philosopher. Certainly, the Outside becomes a dominant concern in this first section. Rather than address it directly and thoroughly here, though, I press onward and somewhat to the side and consider how Blanchot reads Simone Weil. What both attracts him and bothers him in her writing is the sense of religious certitude there (her sense of having been possessed by Christ and her unshakable sense that she loves God), which he thinks should properly be related to the experience of the approach of the Outside. The stakes involving the Outside begin to grow. Curiously, Blanchot does not speak of Weil's politics or of her identification with the working class of Paris and her fellow feeling for the rural poor in the provinces. But it is to politics, especially the notion of the community, to which I turn in the following two chapters. First, I intervene in a long-standing exchange, if that is the word, between Blanchot and Nancy about community. Is Blanchot, as Nancy contends, committed to a Christian or quasi-Christian notion of communion? Not at all, it seems to me. The knot tying Christian and political motifs together occurs quite otherwise in his work, as I try to show. And second, I examine Blanchot's politics more broadly, under the sign of his memorable expression "the friendship of the No." French writers, especially artists, evoke many shades of negation, as any reader of Breton, Bonnefoy, du Bouchet, Char or Ponge will testify; and Blanchot is certainly no exception. Different senses of combat, refusal, and rejection occur in his writings.[5] For him, negation and the neutral must be thought together in an uneasy relation that forbids synthesis.

In the third section of the book, I turn to two of Blanchot's most admired *récits*, *Thomas l'Obscur* (1950) and *La Folie du jour* (1949). The first prompts me to consider what I call "the neutral reduction," namely Blanchot's revision of Husserl's phenomenological reduction. Where Husserl discerns the structures of intelligibility when performing reduction, Blanchot, whose reduction is even more difficult to achieve, yields that which cannot enter the light of intelligibility. Neutrality, here, has nothing to do with impartiality; it has everything to do with an awareness that unity is always a false imposition on a situation and that we are led to the abyss (*tehom*). Having looked at how Blanchot reads other writers, and registered some reservations about what he does, I turn to see how his friend Levinas reads *La Folie du jour* and find that, once again, we view a scene of what amounts to steady confidence in one's own way of proceeding rather than of acknowledgment of another way of thinking or, if you wish, another way of writing. One of the most absorbing exchanges about art and philosophy in mid-century France occurs between Blanchot and Levinas, and in the ninth chapter I attend to it under the sign of "ethics of the image." In some ways, it brings forth several of the motifs that run through the entire book.

Finally, in the fourth section, I extend the theme of ethics in a consideration of what Blanchot calls the "third relation." Usually, we confine ourselves to one or two relations, one of which is dialectical (exemplified by Hegel and Marx in the nineteenth century) and the other of which is based on fusion (and which Blanchot aligns, awkwardly, with mysticism). The third relation opens up a new space of experience for our inspection: it is neither the one nor the other. Perhaps most provocatively, it declines the invitation, proffered by Levinas, of regarding the other person as always speaking to me from a moral height. Blanchot proposes that each of us speaks to the other from on high and we abide in a complex state of double dissymmetry rather than single asymmetry. In the final two chapters, I pick up Jewish themes that were emerging in the fourth chapter. I outline a double reading, of Rosenzweig's *The Star of Redemption* (1921) and Blanchot's *The Writing of the Disaster* (1980). What can these two books, oriented in such different ways to rethink the symbolism of "star," have to say to one another? The penultimate chapter leads me to the last and most painful in the book, a consideration of two themes that cross and re-cross one another in *The Writing of the Disaster*: the Shoah and the Outside. What does this association tell us? What does it not tell us about the darkest moment of the last century?

*

For all his affirmation of the fragmentary, especially in his final writings, and granting that there are one or more evolutions of his critical position over the decades, Blanchot will nonetheless strike the open-minded reader as remarkably coherent in his thought. He offers a relatively small critical vocabulary for our attention and repeats it quite tenaciously throughout his work, sometimes varying its meanings without notice. As indices only, I would point to *désœuvrement, le dehors, expérience, imaginaire,* and *la relation sans relation*. The restricted critical vocabulary, along with an almost obsessive use of it, perhaps explains why it is necessary in the following chapters to return time and again to formulations that Blanchot uses: they need to be examined from different angles and in distinct contexts.

I have already expressed my admiration for the last of Blanchot's tantalizing expressions—*la relation sans relation*—that had come before me under the aegis of the "third relation" and that opens the thought of community, and at this point would add only that his use of the "*X* without *X*" syntax can be enriched and perhaps truly understood only if we trace it back to St. Augustine who used it memorably in his *Literal Commentary on Genesis* when speaking of *mensura sine mensura, numerus sine numero, pondus sine pondere*.[6] For the bishop of Hippo, the divine mode of transcendence compels us to speak of God in this syntax of paradox. He is measure (e.g., of our souls) but is himself without measure, being absolutely singular. He is number (one and three) but without number, for we cannot use arithmetic to resolve the mystery of triune life. And he is weight (for we are attracted ineluctably to him) but is himself without weight, being pure spirit. Of course, Augustine relies heavily on Plato's notion of transcendence here, which we would never expect Blanchot to follow. Instead, Blanchot looks to what runs beneath phenomena rather than over or beyond them and adheres to what Jean Wahl thematized by way of a distinction between transascendance and transdescendance.[7] Levinas adopts the former word to explicate his sense of the other person's moral height, while Blanchot takes the sense of the latter word (without reference to Wahl) in order to indicate how the obscure passes beneath phenomena.[8] By means of this notion, Blanchot criticizes classical phenomenology while paradoxically extending the realm of "phenomenological" description to what precedes any phenomenon.

Just as with *la relation sans relation*, the other expressions I have given can be found in the Western tradition, though, to be sure, not always so prominently as the

X without *X* syntax is in St. Augustine. Perhaps there is no basic word more common than "experience" in writing since the seventeenth century and no word more difficult to pin down. Roger Munier offers a brief and revealing insight into the etymology of the French word "expérience," showing that the radical is the Greek *periri*, "to go through," which is found in the Latin *periculum*, risk or danger. The Indo-European root is *per*, which evokes crossing and test; and there are several Greek derivations, covering the senses of to cross, to go beyond, to go to the end, and limit. Considered in relation to its roots, *expérience*, Munier concludes, "means to endanger."[9] If we follow this train of reasoning, we will regard human experience as a state of having been exposed to peril and doubtless having escaped from it. Nonetheless, Blanchot often conceives it otherwise, in two distinct registers. First, there is the sense of experience as the product of a dialectic in the act of composition. For the writer "institutes between his work [*ouvrage*] and his lucidity [*lucidité*] a movement of composition and of reciprocal development."[10] It is not only a movement but also a labor, one that is "important and complex, a task that we call *experience*" (77; 90). At the completion of this process, the work will have made use of the spirit while serving it, and it will be "absolutely lucid, *if it is the work of lucidity* and *if lucidity is its work*" (77; 91). Never perhaps has Blanchot sounded so Hegelian, and never perhaps has *lucidité* sounded so German. Second, there is the sense of experience as having been put to the test of *désœuvrement* or *le dehors*, having become subject to time as other, in which temporal stagnation comes over us.[11]

Blanchot writes in his criticism and in his narratives about the odd state of *désœuvrement*, the unsettled sense of being untied from a project, of being rendered idle, out of work. It has often been taken to be one of Blanchot's unique words, although it has been used elsewhere in French. Also, it appears in English. Jeremy Bentham, for one, evokes it in his *Chrestomathia* (1816):

> Ennui is the state of uneasiness, felt by him whose mind unoccupied, but without reproach, is on the look out for pleasure: pleasure in some one or more of all shapes; and beholds at the same time no source which promises to afford it: désœuvrement is the state in which the mind, seeing before it nothing to be done, nothing in the shape of business or amusement which promises either security against pain or possession of pleasure, is left a prey to the sort of uneasiness just designated.[12]

Bentham's sense of *désœuvrement* here is readily understood; it is a state of mind most people have experienced at least once or twice. Blanchot asks us to see more in the word as he uses it, though; it points to what used to be called in the 1930s and 1940s— the age of Bataille, Marcel, Sartre, and others—a "metaphysical" situation, something that threatens one's sense of ontological security as a subject. There are occasions when one's work is no more than worklessness, an interruption to a project and to all projects that one might propose. We lose the finality of death (taken as end) and are exposed to the movement of dying (of endlessness without any traction) or, if you wish, of experience as Blanchot explicates it in its second register of meaning.

Bernard Malamud vividly evokes this impression of nothing happening in his historically motivated novel *The Fixer* (1966). There, Yabov Bok (a fictional name for

Manahem Mendel Beilis, although the literary character is freely delineated) is unjustly imprisoned in Tsarist Russia in 1913. His purported crime: killing a child in order to make Passover matzos with Christian blood. The character's grim experience of jail time is evoked:

> Thus the days went by. Each day went by alone. It crawled along like a dying thing. Sometimes, if he thought about it, three days went by, but the third was the same as the first. It was the first day because he could not say that three single days, counted, came to something they did not come to if they were not counted. One day crawled by. Then one day. Then one day. Never three. Nor five or seven. There was no such thing as a week if there was no end to his time in prison. If he were in Siberia serving twenty years at hard labor, a week might mean something. It would be twenty years less a week. But for a man who might be in prison for countless days, there were only first days following one another. The third was the first, the fourth was the first, the seventy-first was the first. The first day was the three thousandth.[13]

Malamud limits himself here to a psychological sense of *désœuvrement* and has nothing of the metaphysical anxiety that Blanchot derives from his early reading of Heidegger, presumably his inaugural lecture at Freiburg, "What is Metaphysics?" (1929). Nor is there anything of the sense that one's work might be the absence of work.

More troublesome, as I have mentioned, is Blanchot's notion of the Outside [*le Dehors*]. What is it? As a placing shot, we might return to *The Fixer* where Malamud evokes "a dirty suffering" that his character must undergo.[14] This, however, is a suffering marked not only by jail time but also by the anti-Semitism of the people of Kiev whose "wild superstition" is responsible for his confinement and the possible bad end of his case.[15] The dirtiness that Blanchot would identify, though, is not a failure of morals, politics, or religion; it is a lack of purity that would be available in closure. Blanchot proposes that moderate suffering is the very means by which we can become aware of the Outside; and it is possible to make fair sense of this without acceding to a secular occult. For when we suffer from insomnia or are ill, we feel as though the arrow of time merely spins. We pass from our usual experience of time to what Blanchot calls "*other* time" or "time as other."[16] Where most of us think of this experience as merely subjective, caused by exhaustion, virus, injury, or merely age, Blanchot regards it as giving us access to a neutral state of affairs that he takes to be the case. It is a phased counterpoint to what some religious persons seek by way of contemplation; it points us to the obscure rather than the transcendent, however, and fascinates us rather than calls for our loving attention.

Another way in which the Outside is introduced is by the figure of people walking the street, in a crowd, or in protest, or under dire threat, such as in the death camps. To do this, Blanchot thinks, is to unmoor oneself from oneself as an "I," one of a kind and governed by a coherent deep interiority; or it is to enter the realm of the everyday, which never truly begins or ends; or it is to speak as one with the mob; or it is to be persecuted as a group in which one's individuality does not matter a jot. Human beings in one of these situations have no viable recourse to an *imago dei* or a *cogito*;

their identities are rendered neutral, and thus they experience the approach of the Outside. Yet also, one might think, a person walking the street sometimes abides in an interior life and does not pay much attention to anyone else, or when participating in *une manifestation* has an eye on breaking loose from the protesters in order to avoid the truncheons or tear gas of the police, or when herded together at Auschwitz or one of the prison camps of the Gulag, or any one of the more recent iterations of those abominations, strives to survive no matter what horrors one must see or even abet.

Blanchot also writes of the approach of the Outside as an indistinct murmur in which words seem to be endlessly sifted. This experience is one to which attentive writers will testify, for it can appear when writing or about to write, that words not only precede one but also have a strange half-life of their own. W. S. Merwin (1927–2019) evokes this eerie sense in his poem "Utterance," testifying that when reading or writing he hears a sigh coming from all human speech.[17] For Blanchot, awareness of this murmur will disperse the work in hand, preventing it from becoming a masterpiece in the classical sense or even becoming a satisfying whole. It is not a matter so much of leaving a work incomplete as interrupting its very possibility of completion. One will become captivated by the approach of the imaginary, which happens, he thinks, when being becomes an image of itself or, as he says in a more heightened way that was common in the age of Kojève and Sartre, when being passes into nothingness. The effect can be varied: it can result in splintered work, such as the later poems of Paul Celan, or in sprawling works that seem to "say everything," such as the novels of the Marquis de Sade.

At issue here is not the making of a memorable visual image, such as we find in these lines from "Upon Julia's Clothes" by Robert Herrick (1591–1674):

Whenas in silks my Julia goes,
Then, then, methinks, how sweetly flows
The liquefaction of her clothes![18]

The point that Blanchot wishes to make is more elusive than anything actually said in this poem and has nothing to do with appreciating this visual image. Instead, he insists that being cannot prevent the possibility of being divided from itself when faced with a human being, of being turned into image. This is not quite what Valéry intends in his elegant observation, "God made everything out of nothing. But the nothing comes through" [*Dieu a tout fait de rien. Mais le rien perce*].[19] For Blanchot is not concerned with a sense of creation wearing thin over time but with the vexed thought that human consciousness affects it to the extent that it can appropriate it and change it significantly. Reflect on the poem I have just quoted. The woman does not offer herself to a reader as flesh, bone, and blood; we do not perceive the color of her dress. Similarly, we do not register first-hand in any sensual manner the movement of the silk she wears. Instead, the being of these things gives itself to us in the poem without primary sensuous being. It manifests itself as language and so seems to vanish before us. We take pleasure as readers in a secondary sensuousness, that of the words and our response to them, especially the choice and placing of the word "liquefaction." No landscape, no object, no phenomenon whatsoever, can resist becoming a poem, a painting, a photograph.

All that is needed is a poet, a painter, or a photographer who decides to apply his or her art to something before him or her. And when that act occurs, we find that the object doubles its mode of being: it remains itself while also generating a new mode of being particular to language, paint, or chemicals on film.

I have given a slightly deflated account of the several versions of the Outside that Blanchot offers, one that allows us to grasp what is perhaps at issue in the notion. If we look attentively at what Blanchot himself says, we will often find a Romantic (or almost Gothic) language that initially distances the Outside from comprehension. When considering art, for instance, he evokes, "the menacing proximity of a vague and vacant outside, a neutral existence, nil and limitless; art points into a sordid absence, a suffocating condensation where being ceaselessly perpetuates itself as nothingness."[20] If this is what poets, novelists, painters, and photographers experience when beginning a work of art, or pausing from its composition to see the next step, it is a wonder that we have any art at all. Faced with this strange claim, we will look back in the history of ideas to see if there are analogues for this perspective. And we shall get further more quickly if we bypass the old question of why there is being instead of nothingness and look to the sense of dread as explored by Kierkegaard and Heidegger. In *The Concept of Anxiety* (1844), Kierkegaard points out that dread comes over us when one conceives one's own endless possibilities. One becomes dizzy at the abyssal prospect.[21] And in "What Is Metaphysics?" (1929), Heidegger adds that it is the very situation of human being to project itself into nothingness and so to ponder one's own demise.[22]

One might say that, for Blanchot, the act of writing prompts what Heidegger calls a fundamental attunement, one of dread. But this would not be right. The dread that comes over Blanchot's artist in the moment of composition is not to do with death but precisely with not being able to die. For the work one is writing is able to survive the author, right from the moment the first word is committed to a page. The shortest sentence, even one that has not the slightest mark of literary genius, contains in its noematic structure one or more aspects of consciousness but does not preserve one's "I."[23] And at any time, during the author's life or after it, the sentence (and the work to which it belongs) can be repeated and, with it, the author's consciousness raised, almost like Lazarus, though only in a ghostly half-life. Authors will commonly testify that one impulse to write is the desire to survive death, albeit in a limited way, to achieve a measure of posthumous fame. But Blanchot goes in the exact opposite direction. To write, he thinks, is to expose oneself to the endlessness of dying; and this accounts for the language of "menacing," "vague and vacant," "sordid," and "suffocating." We are more likely to think of Kafka's "The Hunter Gracchus" with its portrait of the Black Forest hunter who simply cannot win the repose of death than of Horace's boast *non omnis moriar*.[24]

Phenomenologically considered, dying is apprehended as endless because we never experience death. When we think of death, we find ourselves before an ambiguity: death as end and death as dying, as a possibility we must one day grasp (Heidegger), or as an impossibility that approaches us and wears us away (Levinas). All the same, for all intents and purposes, as Blanchot says in an influential remark in *L'Espace littéraire*, the author is dead as soon as the work is complete or at least abandoned.[25] There is a Nietzschean emphasis upon the author instead of the work here, although

Blanchot takes pains to show that there is also an effect apparent in what is written. For as soon as the author is exposed to the movement of dying, he or she will be interrupted in composing the work. To continue writing and produce (one hopes) a literary monument, to participate in the "power and glory" of literature when the ground for such grandeur has been removed, would be a shameful act of inauthenticity for a writer. The work will be dispersed; and, indeed, if the exposure to dying is taken with all due gravity, the author will leave an intransitive text (and not a "work"). This is a justification for Blanchot's approval of poems, stories, and novels that tend to the fragmentary or interminable. Where avant-garde writers and critics are usually half in love with the breaking of form, Blanchot thinks otherwise: form does not primarily interest him, even as a mode of experimentation, for his motivating concerns are ontological (concerned with authorial being), not formal (related to the poem, story, or novel). The negativity that haunts Blanchot is not especially that of admitting the need for formal imperfection (as it is for Bonnefoy, for instance) or of researching formal openings for creativity (Oulipo) but of finding, with Heidegger, a primal sense of negation in nothingness.[26] It is in these terms, then, that we must seek to understand the notion of the Outside: an attunement of dread, to be sure, but one that is oriented to dying, not death.

*

It will be objected with self-evident reason to Blanchot that the duality of *mourir* and *la mort* does not do justice to the variety and wealth of human existence, including the experiences of composing and reading. "Dying" is undoubtedly a profile of living but it is only one among many, and perhaps not the one closest to an author when at his or her desk. The sheer phenomenality of life precedes any act of writing and sometimes informs it in unexpected ways. We can think we have the measure of an author (Hardy, Yeats, Stevens, Hill) and then find ourselves surprised by an unexpected tone, an élan in the writing that we would not have countenanced, and even a confident adventure into a fresh field of human experience, that makes us think again. Given this experience, we might be well advised to retrace the steps that have brought us to ponder *mourir* and *la mort*. Since Heidegger seems to have set some of Blanchot's vanishing points as a critic, even if he puts them to other ends, it is worthwhile to look at the attunements that the German identifies and discusses.

All these attunements—primarily, *Angst* (dread) and *Langeweile* (deep boredom)—fall on the gloomy side of the psychological (or, for Heidegger, ontological) spectrum.[27] *Befindlichkeit*, as Heidegger notes, discloses *Dasein* in its thrownness: it is an inescapable fact that *I* am in the world and that my being must be an issue for me. Sometimes we are attuned otherwise, though: to gratitude, joy, tranquility, or wonder, for instance. Heidegger maintained that philosophy is not to be conducted in a contemplative attitude (*Besinnung, Reflexion*), as Husserl had taught.[28] Instead, being discloses itself more surely in *Angst* or *Langeweile*; and being is the proper theme for thinking. Exceptions suggest themselves, however. G. M. Hopkins's "The Windhover" can be read as consequent to an attunement to ecstasy, one that is at once glorious and frightening, and which manifests the possibility of sanctity.[29] And E. E. Cummings's sonnet "i thank You God" turns on an attunement to sheer delight in an experience of nature understood as creation.[30] Not that all the exceptions are literary. As Jean-Luc Marion has suggested, deep boredom, in which the distinction between being and beings has no purchase on us, is a way in which one passes "beyond being" to regard human existence as a divine gift.[31]

For long stretches of reading Blanchot, it can seem that his critical emphases identify an apparent canon or at least an assembly of writers whose works are exemplary for him. The thought must be treated circumspectly. For one thing, there are various uses of the notion of "canon." There is the canon of works one reads, a slightly different canon that one teaches, and a third canon, which overlaps with these, that identifies an archive one believes should be maintained by the world of the university, the culture, or the State. One might have read Spenser's *The Fairie Queene* (1590) and enjoyed it, have no special desire to read it again, let alone teach it, and yet firmly insist that it is an essential part of the literary archive. For another thing, Blanchot's first writings, right to the end of *Faux pas* (1943), are mostly on books that were sent to him for review. Only with *La Part du feu* (1949) do we find longer essays on writers who have signal importance for him: Char, Hölderlin, Kafka, and Mallarmé, among others. And at no time does Blanchot even suggest that his peculiar, sideways manner of reading literary works is part of a project of evaluation or re-evaluation, as happens with his older contemporary T. S. Eliot. He is less interested in changing the French cultural landscape, or even in producing "literary criticism," especially that favored in the deuxième and troisième cycles of the French education system, than in diagnosing a situation at the most fundamental level of writing. The authors who absorb his interest are those whose writing exemplifies what he takes to be the enabling (and disabling) origin of writing. In this, he resembles Heidegger whose eye was always lured by poets whose poems express what he took to be the essence of poetry or at least come close to doing so. Indeed, when Blanchot writes about reading, he does not speak in the categories of aesthetics or criticism (anatomical, formalist, historicist, moral) but affirms what he calls "the light, innocent Yes" in which one abides while reading.[32]

*

Blanchot encore: a call for more, of course, and very French into the bargain. There can be no more new texts by Blanchot to read, at least none that we know of at the moment. Only drafts, notes, and letters remain to be gathered and studied, and I do not discount the interest of these. Yet there is always a call from the very texts we have to read them again, to try to think along with them once more, and to ponder this enigmatic body of work in new ways. I ask myself as I complete almost eighteen years of further reflection on this author what it is that captivates me in those yellow Gallimard volumes, the white Édition de Minuit volumes, and the slim booklets put out by Fata Morgana and other little presses, on my bookshelf. In some ways, it is the sheer passion and acuity of his engagement with literary and other texts, his willingness to bypass the confines of literary and cultural criticism and draw on philosophy, or anything, in order to read them at a level that is adequate to their elusiveness, richness, or strength. In other ways, it is what he does not actually name but does in so much of his writing: invert our inherited ways of regarding existence, in which God transcends phenomena, and invite us to consider an obscure dimension running beneath them that contests the primacy and power of the divine, including all unity.

One of the main impulses of modernity has been to describe reality (or even explain it) from beneath, as it were, rather than from above: the transcendental, social structures, an immanent dialectic, *la différance*, rhizomes, and so on. Blanchot marks an extreme attempt to do just this. Before modernity, in the worlds of the Greeks and the Romans and the Europe they bequeathed, human beings were referred to contemplation if they wished to gain wisdom. But with the advent and inexorable development of modernity, right up to and including our own time's preoccupation with visuality and simulacra, there is fascination. We live in the age of the image, and we sometimes wonder about the moral problems that beset us in such a time. The means by which we can approach this darkly attractive non-world beneath our own is what he calls first "literature" and then "writing" and then by other names, including "the everyday." As I have said, he feels obliged to limit the authority of phenomenology to talk about reality but, in doing so, extends some of its ambitions. So Blanchot is, among other things, a diagnostician of modern culture and an exemplary figure of what comes after that culture. Whenever I begin to feel close to his thought, as in when he makes more themes available for phenomenological reflection or when he makes me long to read Mallarmé or Proust again and seek for what has eluded me on earlier readings, I realize that I am in fact as far from it as possible in the most important ways. I am a theologian, after all, and I live the contemplative life.

I have always read Blanchot along the grain and against the grain at the same time. I have tried to follow his thought, his passions, and his readings of authors we both love (although not always for the same reasons), and each time I do so I put down one of his books with a greater admiration for the book on which he has commented and for the commentator himself. Blanchot contended that praise has no part in a sound reading, and for him it would not properly motivate an encore. I take the point but cannot take the scruple to be my own. Yet I also read him against the grain, always on the lookout for blind spots in his writings, parts of an *œuvre* that he overlooks because his ideas do not encompass it or even exclude it, ideas that try to reach further than they can ever go, and distinctions that do not do justice to the complexity or bounty of a situation. In doing so, I have learned to read Blanchot better; but the evidence for that claim must be in the chapters that follow, and they too are open to be read with and against the grain.

Notes

1 Maurice Blanchot, *OCC*, 41. Also see Blanchot, "Le 'discours philosophique,'" *CC*, 332–7.
2 For example, Leslie Hill is just in his remark that Jean-Luc Nancy is guilty of a "recidivist misreading" of Blanchot. His strictures on Michel Suyra's *L'Autre Blanchot* are also very much to the point. See his *Nancy, Blanchot: A Serious Controversy* (New York: Rowman and Littlefield, 2018), 243, 211–17.
3 See, for example, Blanchot, "On One Approach to Communism," *F*, 97 (114).

4 See Blanchot, "How to Discover the Obscure," *IC*, 40–8 (57–69). For more detail on Blanchot's relation to phenomenology, see Jérôme de Gramont, *Blanchot et la phénoménologie: L'effacement, l'événement* (Clichy: Éditions de Corlevour, 2011).
5 One might begin to account for these different senses as far back as "On demande des dissidents," *Combat*, 20 (décembre, 1937), *CP*, 477–8.
6 See Augustine, "The Literal Meaning of Genesis," in *On Genesis*, intro., trans. and notes Edmund Hill, ed. John E. Rotelle, The Works of Saint Augustine, 1/13 (Hyde Park, NY: New City Press, 2002), 246.
7 Jean Wahl, *Human Existence and Transcendence*, ed. and trans. William C. Hackett, foreword Kevin Hart (Notre Dame: Notre Dame University Press, 2016), 28.
8 See Emmanuel Levinas, "Reality and Its Shadow," *CCP*, esp. 8–11.
9 See Roger Munier, "Expérience," *Mise en page*, 1 (mai, 1972).
10 Blanchot, *LS*, 77 (90).
11 See my *The Dark Gaze: Maurice Blanchot and the Sacred* (Chicago, IL: University of Chicago Press, 2004), ch. 5.
12 Jeremy Bentham, *Chrestomathia*, ed. M. J. Smith and W. H. Burston, The Collected Works of Jeremy Bentham, gen. ed. J. R. Dinwiddy, 34 vols. to date (1817; Oxford: Clarendon Press, 1983), 20.
13 Bernard Malamud, "The Fixer," in *Novels and Stories of the 1960s*, ed. Philip Davis (New York: The Library of America, 2013), 533.
14 Malamud, "The Fixer," 563.
15 Malamud, "The Fixer," 563.
16 See, for example, Blanchot, "Prophetic Speech," *BC*, 81 (112).
17 W. S. Merwin, *The Rain in the Trees* (New York: Knopf, 1987), 44.
18 Robert Herrick, *Hesperides and Noble Numbers*, ed. Alfred Pollard with pref. A. C. Swinburne, 2 vols. (London: Lawrence and Bullen, 1898), vol. 2, poem 779.
19 Paul Valéry, "Mauvaises pensées et autres," *Oeuvres*, 2 vols., éd. Jean Hytier, Bibliothèque de la Pléiade (Paris: Gallimard, 1960), vol. 2, 907.
20 Blanchot, *SL*, 242–3 (326).
21 Søren Kierkegaard, *The Concept of Anxiety: A Simple Psychologically Orienting Deliberation on the Dogmatic Issue of Hereditary Sin*, ed. and trans. Reidar Thomte in collaboration with Albert B. Anderson, Kierkegaard's Writings, 26 vols., vol. 8 (Princeton, NJ: Princeton University Press, 1980), 61.
22 Martin Heidegger, "What is Metaphysics?," trans. David Farrell Krell, in *Pathmarks*, ed. William McNeill (Cambridge: Cambridge University Press, 1998), 82–96.
23 This became a theme of Derrida's. See, for instance, "Living On," trans. James Hulbert, in *Parages*, ed. John P. Leavey (Stanford, CA: Stanford University Press, 2011), 103–12.
24 See Franz Kafka, "The Hunter Gracchus," trans. Willa and Edwin Muir, in *The Collected Short Stories*, ed. Nahum N. Glatzer (Harmondsworth: Penguin, 1983), 226–30, and Horace, *Carmina* 3: 30.
25 Blanchot, *SL*, 23 (16).
26 See Yves Bonnefoy, "L'Imperfection est la cime," *Poèmes* (Paris: Mercure de France, 1978), 117, and Heidegger, "What Is Metaphysics?," 85–6.
27 See Heidegger, *The Fundamental Concepts of Metaphysics: World, Finitude, Solitude*, trans. William McNeill and Nicholas Walker (Bloomington, IN: Indiana University Press, 1995), §§ 16–38. Heidegger also attends to fright (*Erschrecken*), restraint (*Verhaltenheit*), foreboding (*Ahnung*) and timidity (*Scheu*). See Heidegger, *Contributions to Philosophy (Of the Event)*, trans. Richard Rojcewicz and Daniela Vallega-Neu (Bloomington, IN: Indiana University Press, 2012), § 5.

28 See the discussion of these words by David Carr, *Phenomenology and the Problem of History* (Evanston, IL: Northwestern University Press, 2009), 59–60. Robert Sokolowski favors the word "contemplation" for the stance of the disinterested observer. See, for instance, his *Introduction to Phenomenology* (Cambridge: Cambridge University Press, 2000), 48. Husserl is clear that one must pass from transcendent to immanent contemplation. See Husserl, *Phantasy, Image Consciousness, and Memory (1898–1925)*, trans. John Brough (Dordrecht: Springer, 2005), 202.
29 G. M. Hopkins, "The Windhover," in *Poems*, ed. W. H. Gardner, 3rd ed. (London: Oxford University Press, 1948), 74.
30 E. E. Cummings, "i thank You God for most this amazing," in *Complete Poems*, ed. George James Firmage, 2 vols. (London: Granada, 1981), vol. 2, 663.
31 See Jean-Luc Marion, *God Without Being: Hors-Texte*, trans. Thomas A. Carlson, foreword David Tracy (Chicago, IL: University of Chicago Press, 1991).
32 See Blanchot, *SL*, 196 (258).

Part 1

On Poetry

1

Blanchot's Mallarmé

"Blanchot's Mallarmé": the interlacing of these two proper names could be taken to identify either one relationship among many possible authors or something essential to modern literature. It would be easy to multiply similar doublings, each with a plausible claim to interest readers of Blanchot. Other than Mallarmé, the first literary names that come to mind to pair with Blanchot are Hölderlin, Kafka, and Bataille, although Sade, Lautréamont, Rilke, and Char quickly follow them.[1] Once the list has started to be assembled, the accent seems to shift almost by itself from literature to philosophy, and so we can twin Blanchot with Hegel, Nietzsche, Heidegger or Levinas, or we can go back further into history and name Heraclitus or Socrates, Kant or Kierkegaard, or, looking among Blanchot's younger contemporaries, league Blanchot with Foucault, Deleuze, or Derrida. Reading Blanchot's essays on these diverse authors would confirm what we would have already sensed by reading only two or three pieces, that in the mile, if not in the inch, Blanchot has one big idea rather than many little ideas. If a case is to be made for the relative importance of Mallarmé for Blanchot, or indeed the conjunction of the two names for "modern poetry," it will be based on the continuity and variety of references to his work, and the intensity with which Blanchot identifies an opening of literary space with Mallarmé's poetry and poetics, a space to which he responded faithfully over several decades, in narrative fiction, literary criticism, and fragmentary writing.

Of course, there comes a point in thinking along this line when one is tempted to lose faith in the formulation that has guided us so far. Could it be that we are talking less of Blanchot's Mallarmé than of Mallarmé's Blanchot? For it may seem that, in according such importance to Mallarmé, Blanchot is merely an epigone, that his own work has been programmed by an œuvre that was complete before his birth, and that he continues in narrative and criticism alike insights and ways of writing that were substantially achieved in the period running from the 1860s to the 1890s. The proper name "Blanchot" would therefore stand for a late distillation of Mallarmé; it would be no more than, as Wallace Stevens (one of Blanchot's admirers) puts it, "a great shadow's last embellishment."[2] To be sure, it would then be said in response that his understanding of Mallarmé was not easily reached, that his unfolding of insights and ways of writing was followed by a complex refolding of those same things. His reception of Mallarmé involves a powerful critical reading of the master by Paul Valéry; it is informed by subtle, demanding engagements with Hegel, Nietzsche, and Heidegger; and it has required discernment to see what in Char's poetry extends the inheritance of Mallarmé as well as that of Hölderlin.³ For all that, Blanchot would not mark anything decisive and original in his own writing. He would be, as Harold Bloom implacably maintains, one who speaks to us "only in the accents of a severe belatedness."⁴

Bloom distinguishes in terms of strength Blanchot's narratives, especially the *récit* version of *Thomas l'Obscur* (1950), from his contributions to criticism.⁵ Yet it is far from clear that he is right to diminish the importance of the critical works. For much of the originality that Blanchot ascribes to Mallarmé turns on a reading of the poet that is distinctively his own. It is not to be found in Paul Valéry or Henri Mondor or Yves Bonnefoy or anyone else who writes memorably on the poet. So original is this reading that one finds little or no evidence that others have seen the same things in the poetry and prose that Blanchot has, in part because of the texts that form his reference points in Mallarmé's canon: *Igitur* (1869), "Un coup de dés jamais n'abolira le hasard" (1895), some letters, and the idea of the book. The real question perhaps is not whether we should be talking of Mallarmé's Blanchot instead of Blanchot's Mallarmé but whether Blanchot's Mallarmé bears a close relation of a sort to be determined to Mallarmé. There comes a moment when talk of originality *about* something should be recast as the originality *of* the person doing the talking. Could it be that the questions we assemble under the title "Blanchot's Mallarmé" should properly be set under another heading, "Blanchot's Blanchot"? If so, we would be right to limit Blanchot's achievement as a critic. And yet in the last analysis perhaps "criticism" is not what he does, and for the most part not the sort of practical criticism that Bloom favors.⁶ Levinas is close to the mark when he says of *L'Espace littéraire* (1955) that it is "situated beyond [*au-delà*] all critique [*critique*] and all exegesis."⁷ Blanchot's readings of Hölderlin, Mallarmé, Kafka, and Rilke are not oriented to literary appreciations or evaluations but instead directed to what is involved in encountering the origin of each work. One might revise Levinas's remark to say that Blanchot's mode of reading is anterior to all critique and all exegesis.

The Mallarmé whom Blanchot first brings into focus for us is the subject of a biography, Mondor's two-volume *Vie de Mallarmé* (1941–2). Knowing the Blanchot who wrote in old age, "*The writer, his biography: he died; lived and died,*" and knowing that in writing that line he was keeping faith with his younger self, one might well think that no less favorable genre than biography could have presented itself to the young critic for a reflection on a writer as central to him as Mallarmé.⁸ Yet Blanchot commenced his series "Chroniques de la vie intellectuelle" (1941-44) with some remarks on Mondor's biography, and then wrote separately on each volume of the *Vie de Mallarmé*. The first of the two pieces, "Le biographe connaît le 'genie' et ignore l'"homme"" (avril 23, 1941), begins, "The purest writers are not entirely inside their works; they have existed; they have even lived [*même vécu*]. One must resign oneself to that."⁹ It is the voice of a devout Mallarméan, of someone who knows by heart the poet's evocation of the "pure work" that implies "the disappearance of the poet speaking, who yields the initiative to words."¹⁰ Mondor's achievement will please everyone, Blanchot says, although what most charms Blanchot is that Mondor's is a biography without biography.¹¹ "When we have read it, we perceive that we already knew all that it taught us, and yet we retain the happy feeling of knowing nothing. Our ignorance has remained pure. Such is the real fruit of a perfect erudition and an intelligence completely impregnated with love"

(100; 118). Hard as it is to credit, these sentences are Blanchot's idea of proper praise for Mondor's extensive labors.

This *Vie de Mallarmé* is to be valued in large part for what it does not do. It is thankfully free of anecdotes and crude links between the life and the work, and consequently "does not hide the work" (100; 118). Blanchot continues to praise Mondor for his delicacy and rare achievement when he comes to review the second volume in a piece entitled "Le Silence de Mallarmé" (avril 1, 1942).[12] Nonetheless, he announces there that in this complete and thorough work "the essential point is missing" (103; 121). This is no joke specially prepared for "Poisson d'avril"; he is completely serious. The essential is not missing because Mallarmé did not produce the book he had promised or failed to tell us enough about what it would be like. Nor is it missing because Mallarmé made a secret of it that Mondor could not discover, but because Mallarmé told us nothing about how he wrote. "What was the deliberated work of a poet who refused to keep his poetry from mystery and who succeeded in giving it in all clarity the mysterious power of a spell? What devices did he use? What metamorphoses of language, what secret transformations of words, what births and with what deaths of images did he experiment in his depths?" (106; 124; trans. slightly modified). Of these questions, which Blanchot judges to be fundamental, no one, not even a biographer as discreet and exacting as Mondor, can supply answers.

What interests Blanchot here is not a lost knowledge of how Mallarmé expressed himself, which would have had value for psychological criticism, but of how he created his poems, which would have been a unique contribution to poetics. That this information was never preserved is regrettable because, as we are told in the reflections on the first volume of *Vie de Mallarmé*, the great poet "is above all *the only one* [my emphasis] who has awakened this profound nocturnal assembly, not through verbal drunkenness or fascination but through a methodical arrangement of words, through a very specific awareness of movements and rhythms, through a pure intellectual act" (102; 120). A sharp line is drawn between Rimbaud and Mallarmé, and we are left in no doubt on which side Blanchot stands or with what aspect of Valéry's reading of Mallarmé he is in sympathy.[13] The image of the "nocturnal assembly" evokes Mallarmé's writing by night, the late poem "Un coup de dés," and also the allusion made earlier in the review to Mallarmé's sufferings when composing or not being able to compose. This difficulty is not merely a matter of fatigue. "In reality his torments are of an entirely different order," Blanchot says. "They are much more like the sufferings that certain souls bear in the mystic night. One could say that Mallarmé, through an extraordinary effort of asceticism, opened an abyss in himself where his awareness, instead of losing itself, survives and grasps its solitude in a desperate clarity" (101; 119). Here Mallarmé pondering the abyss in his room at Tournon is edged close to St. John of the Cross undergoing "the dark night of the soul" in his prison cell in Toledo. Yet the two poets, atheist and mystic, do not coincide. Mallarmé does not experience "the flash of an enigmatic revelation" but rather "the extreme point of an entirely conscious meditation" (104; 123). When he touches the night (101; 119) he does not lose himself in a "divine Conception" (101; 120) but dies to himself and becomes, as he says in a letter to Henri Cazalis written on May 14, 1867, "an aptitude that the Spiritual Universe has to see itself and unfold itself through what once was me."[14]

In another early piece that begins by referring to Mondor's books, "Mallarmé et l'art du roman," published on October 27, 1943, Blanchot reflects on the promise of the book, but pushes this reflection away from poetry and poetics to the novel. It is a surprising move, since Mallarmé never mentions in his notes for the book anything about a novel, and even though Blanchot was unaware of all the notes that were to come to light he acknowledges how unlikely talk of the novel is in this context.[15] "It is therefore arbitrarily," he concedes, "that one thinks of the art of the novel when reflecting on the book that Mallarmé dreamed of."[16] Quite so: for everything in Mallarmé has led us to associate the book with poetry. *Littérature* consists of essential words, Mallarmé says, while *reportage* is made of raw or immediate words. Can the novel be literature for Mallarmé? It is unclear, in part because we see the question through the fine veil of Valéry's elegant distinction between poetry as akin to dancing and prose as like walking.[17] Blanchot himself has appeared to agree with this estimation of poetry. In another early piece on the poet (February 24, 1942), he writes that, "The sense of the poem is inseparable from all the words, from all the movements, from all the accents of the poem. It exists only in this ensemble," and one might well think that this is seldom or ever the case with prose.[18] Two counterexamples are adduced, however: Lautréamont's *Les Chants de Maldoror* (1868–90) and Gérard de Nerval's *Aurélia, ou le Rêve et la vie* (1855). Neither example is entirely persuasive, since one can readily imagine each work not having precisely the same words in the same order while fundamentally remaining itself. Meter and rhyme are more exacting taskmasters than prose rhythm is. Yet Blanchot continues with confidence, "it is with reason that we should conceive of the novelist as a possible author of this book and ask him to consider its admirable conditions. Everything will be easy for him, if he truly wants to break with most of his habits and accept an instant of going, with Mallarmé, to the very principles of language."[19] What are these principles of language? And who is the novelist who inherits the ideal of the book from Mallarmé?

If Blanchot was ever at all impressed by Mallarmé's distinction between *parole brute ou immédiate* and *parole essentielle*, he did not remain so. By the time of *L'Espace littéraire* (1955) he found the distinction "crude" while continuing to affirm a doubling at the heart of language.[20] A more enduring principle for Blanchot is that Mallarmé did not conceive language as a system of expression but "as a power of transformation and creation, made to create enigmas rather than to clarify them" (167; 191). The basic principle of language is that it establishes and reveals, and not that it represents and can be used more or less effectively as an instrument of communication. "Language," Blanchot says, "is what founds human reality and the universe" (167; 191). And he adds, "To name the gods, to cause the universe to become discourse, that alone forms the basis of the authentic dialogue that is human reality" (167; 191). Indeed, "our human reality is poetic in its root" and that "language is an absolute, the very form of transcendence" (167; 192). It is striking that Blanchot's Mallarmé sounds here very much like anyone's Heidegger (and almost in the philosopher's own words).[21] Think of statements from Heidegger's essays such as "Language itself is poetry in the essential sense," "language remains the master of man," and "Language speaks."[22] To be sure, "Hölderlin and the Essence of Poetry" (1937) presents the convergence of poetry and the essence of poetry, and some of the ideas just mentioned are incipient in "The Origin of the Work of Art" (the first version of which was delivered as a lecture in 1935). By and large, though, Heidegger was still to formulate these ideas about language and poetry when Blanchot was writing his piece on Mallarmé and the art of the novel.

It is entirely possible that Blanchot was resetting the same late eighteenth- and early nineteenth-century German thought that was to inform Heidegger. Hölderlin was a mutual admiration, while Heidegger devoted himself to Herder's *Abhandlung über den Ursprung der Sprache* (1772), telling his students in 1939 that, "Herder becomes the chief witness of something that just the same stays back, behind him and the German movement."[23] In the 1950s, the decade of *Vortäge und Aufsätze* (1954) and *Unterwegs zur Sprache* (1959), Heidegger will develop his insights into thoughts on poetry, while Blanchot will keep faith with Mallarmé's emphasis on creation and insist himself that creation is not linked to a particular genre, poetry. And so everything that Mallarmé says about language can teach the novelist how to write. Finally, Blanchot, unlike Heidegger, will not seek being. He will be intrigued and disturbed by the Outside, in which being perpetuates itself as nothingness (as an image rather than a phenomenon), and he will attend closely to poetics, understood as the study of the laws of literature and how they can be transgressed.[24]

The novelist who Blanchot imagines inheriting richly from Mallarmé is plainly none other than Blanchot himself whose *Thomas l'Obscur* (the *roman* of 1941) and *Aminadab* (1942) had just recently appeared. He is himself the person of whom he dreams, a "writer, symbol of purity and pride, who would be for the novel what Mallarmé was for poetry."[25] His novels allow us "to glimpse the work that he would desire to make the equal of the absolute," or, more exactly, not the absolute in any idealist sense of the word but the unconditioned approach of the Outside. And yet when Blanchot comes to write about "the pure novel" in a review of that title published on December 4–5, 1943 he evokes Lautréamont not Mallarmé as the author who provides the model for the pure novel.[26] "What is a pure art?," he asks, "An art that seeks to obey an exclusively aesthetic criterion, and which, instead of combing the representation of things with certain laws of sensibility, dispenses with imitation and even with sense-making conventions altogether."[27] At this level of generality, this remark could be a summary of Mallarmé's aesthetics as well as Lautréamont's. Let us therefore return to Blanchot to find more information: "The novel thus does make a serious claim to purity to the extent that its ambition is to create, if necessary, a system that is absolute, complete, indifferent to the usual circumstances in which things exist, constituted by intrinsic relations and capable of sustaining itself without drawing on anything external to it" (264; *CL*, 509). If we weigh each of these words with care, we can see that what seems to have happened. Blanchot's interest in the pure novel has been generated by the ideal of the "literary absolute" of Jena Romanticism, for whom the novel was the literary genre par excellence, and then has been refined by his reading of Mallarmé and Lautréamont.[28] Is this so?

Not quite, for Blanchot begins "Mallarmé et l'art du roman" by quoting a passage from Mallarmé's letter to Paul Verlaine of November 16, 1885, the so-called "Autobiographie," in which he broods on the book in which he gives a detail that has already resonated with Blanchot. What does one find in the book? "The orphic explanation of the Earth, which is *the only* [my emphasis] duty of the poet and the literary game above all others" (165; 189).²⁹ *Thomas l'Obscur*, like much of Blanchot's fiction, is in some ways a retelling of the Orphic narrative, a restatement of the poet's bid to descend into Hades in order to bring back Eurydice and his fatal look back at her before she had left the land of the dead.³⁰ One can see Thomas as an Orpheus and Anne as an Eurydice. As Anne is close to death she opens her eyes, and the narrator comments, "There was in fact no more hope. Anne too had just fallen into this moment of greatest distraction, this snare, this last return of Eurydice, where the dying who have almost vanquished death fall while looking towards what can be seen" [*Il n'y avait plus en effet d'espoir. Ce moment de suprême distraction, ce piège où les mourants qui ont déjà presque vaincu la mort, tombent en regardant, suprême retour d'Eurydice, une dernière fois vers ce qui se voit, Anne aussi venait d'y tomber*].³¹ The theme appears in slight disguise in *Aminadab* when an unnamed young man tells Thomas about the advantages of living underground.³² And the theme is more strongly pronounced in *L'Arrêt de mort* (1948) when the narrator brings the dead J. back to life for a short time.³³

Some of Blanchot's narratives are marked by the Orpheus story both thematically and, like many of the literary works he finds compelling, structurally as well.³⁴ "Le regard d'Orphée," the central text of *L'Espace littéraire*, shows Blanchot reading the story of Orpheus with a light allegorical touch. Thus interpreted, Eurydice is the origin of the work, its inspiration, which Blanchot figures as the whole work given before it is set in words. This work withdraws as the author tries to bring it into the light. Fascinated by the inspiration of the work, the author is drained of all possibility or power with respect to making it a masterpiece in the received sense of the word. He or she is exposed to a "radical reversal" [*renversement radical*] in which what seems eminently possible, the writing of a well-formed piece of literature, yields to the impossible. It is impossible insofar as the work is anterior to the determinate poem or narrative that must be written. And it is also impossible insofar as the work is still to come; it is prophetic, having its meaning ahead of it, not in a future present but in the other time, a time without a vector, of which the approach of the Outside makes us aware.³⁵ Suspended between a past that never was and a future that cannot become present, the work cannot be brought as a whole onto the page. If it comes at all, it can come only when the writer begins to lose the power to say "I," and hence simulates dying, for the work precedes his or her uniqueness. In composition, the origin is forced into a beginning; it is a violence that produces fault lines in the work.³⁶ Art shows us, Blanchot thinks, that human beings are not fundamentally beings of possibility. Not at all: we are marked by the impossible.

To clarify this remark, assess it, and gauge its import, we must turn to *L'Espace littéraire* and look briefly at its argument, which begins with Mallarmé and passes through several stages marked by proper names—Kafka, Rilke, and Mallarmé again—until it comes to Heidegger and only then presents what is surely Blanchot's central claim in all his work, what he calls the "essential situation." Here is the opening of "L'Expérience de Mallarmé":

> When Mallarmé affirms, "I felt the very disquieting symptoms caused by the sole act of writing," it is the last words which matter. With them an essential situation

[*une situation essentielle*] is brought to light. Something extreme is grasped, something which has for its context and substance "the sole act of writing." Writing appears as an extreme situation which presupposes a radical reversal. Mallarmé alludes briefly to this reversal when he says: "Unfortunately, by digging this thoroughly into verse, I have encountered two abysses which make me despair. One is Nothingness" (the absence of God; the other is his own death).[37]

Blanchot seeks to pass from a few words to an essential situation and notes that this situation marks an extreme point. We recall what he said in "Le Silence de Mallarmé," that Mallarmé's dark night is not co-ordinate with revelation but is instead "the extreme point of an entirely conscious meditation." It is a meditation on what is involved in writing that gives Mallarmé his crucial experience, a brushing against the absence of God and a sense of the sourness of dying.[38] The apparent mastery involved in writing verse is subject to a "radical reversal" that places the writer before his or her own death and nothingness after death.

If we shift now to "La littérature et l'expérience originelle," the final section of *L'Espace littéraire*, we find Blanchot once more talking about a radical reversal. He summarizes the complex argument of the entire book:

> But what is art, and what can we say of literature? The question returns now with a particular violence. If we have art—which is exile from truth, which is the risk of an inoffensive game, which affirms man's belonging to the limitless outside where intimacy is unknown, where he is banished from his capability and from all forms of possibility—how does this come about? How, if he is altogether possibility, can man allow himself anything resembling art? If he has art, does this not mean that, contrary to his apparently authentic definition—the requirement which is in harmony with the law of the day—he entertains with death a relation which is not that of possibility, which does not lead to mastery or to understanding or to the progressive achievements of time, but exposes him to a radical reversal? *This reversal*: would it not seem to be the *original experience* [l'expérience originelle] which the work must touch, upon which it closes and which constantly threatens to close in upon art and withhold it? (240-41; 322-23).

Given that human beings have art, and given that art leads us away from possibility, it follows that human beings are characterized not by death as a final possibility to be grasped but by death as the erosion of all possibilities. Such is Blanchot's argument, and it is plainly directed against three philosophers—Hegel, Nietzsche, and Heidegger— each of whom, in his own way, accounts for human beings by way of the possible. The very tip of the argument, though, is aimed at Heidegger's claim in *Sein und Zeit* § 53 that "Death is Dasein's *ownmost* possibility," indeed that death is "the possibility of the impossibility of any existence at all."[39]

And yet Blanchot almost aimed that sharp point of his argument at Mallarmé until he found a way of withholding the blow with a clean conscience. His objection was to the Mallarmé of *Igitur*, or more accurately against the Mallarmé who had dipped into Shakespeare and Hegel and who intended to finish that drama and to have Igitur kill himself and hence claim mastery over death. Listen to Blanchot pondering the thought of an *Igitur* that had been completed along the lines of Hamlet's "To be or not to be" soliloquy: "For if *Igitur* were to be right—if death is true, if it is a genuine act [*acte véritable*], not a random occurrence but the supreme possibility, the extreme moment in which negation is founded and completed—then the negation that operates in words, and 'this drop of nothingness' which is the presence of consciousness in us, the death from which we derive the power not to be which is our essence, also partake of truth" (110; 138). This is a strange series of claims, not least of all because it is hard to know what it means for death to be true or even to be an act (as distinct from an event or a nonevent). Be that as it may, Blanchot takes comfort in the fact that the drama was left dangling for thirty years. "And thereby," he says, "it recovers its meaning. It escapes the naïveté of a successful undertaking to become the force and the obsession of the interminable" (117; 148). Only because *Igitur* is incomplete is it turned toward the impossible, and Mallarmé is saved from the temptation of bringing his thought into line with the possible as promoted by modern European philosophy. It is a curious piece of special pleading, and perhaps only Blanchot could have fashioned it because only he would see its conclusion as converging with the idea of the Outside. "The absence that Mallarmé hoped to render pure is not pure," Blanchot concludes. "The night is not perfect, it does not welcome, it does not open. It is not the opposite of day—silence, repose, the cessation of tasks. In the night, silence is speech, and there is no repose, for there is no position. There the incessant and the uninterrupted reign—not the certainty of death achieved, but 'the eternal torments of Dying'" (118-19; 150).[40]

That well-known quotation from 1914 in Kafka's *Diaries* prompts us to return to the main argument that because we have art, each of us is in a relation not with the possible (death as end) but with the impossible (death as an interminable approach). It must be said that, as stated, the argument is neither valid nor sound. For one thing, no case has been made for a privileged relation between human beings and art. One might argue that, since we have economics, law, mathematics, medicine, science, and technology, among other disciplines, human beings are profoundly committed to possibility. We *can* do things, we tell ourselves, and with very good reason. Perhaps if the writer does lose the power to say "I" when composing, and is therefore placed in relation with dying, there is a link between the writer and dying; but it is not necessarily between human beings and dying. What is it about art that would override the competing claims of other human enterprises? Why would the artist stand for all human beings? More particularly, what is it about art that allows Blanchot to find there a link with death as the impossibility of dying, a connection that we presumably do not find in economics, law, science, and all the other things that occupy our lives?

Answers to these questions will take us quite a way, and we must keep in mind that Blanchot regards literature as exemplary of art in general. His view of language derives from Mallarmé, and in particular from "Crise de vers" (1897): "I say: a flower! And, out of the oblivion where my voice casts every contour, insofar as it is something other than the known bloom, there arises, musically, the very idea in its mellowness; in other words, what is absent from every bouquet."[41] Blanchot adapts this lapidary formulation, so important to Symbolism, and rewrites it in terms of the story of Orpheus and Eurydice: "I say, 'This woman' . . . [and] real death has been announced, and is already present in my language; my language means that this person, who is here right now, can be detached from herself, removed from her existence and her presence, and suddenly plunged into a nothingness in which there is no existence or presence; my language essentially signifies the possibility of this destruction; it is a constant, bold allusion to such an event."[42] Three things are at issue here: the impact of language on someone, the consequence of language for the speaker, and the nature of language itself.

The first element is a variant of an idea that Hegel had when in his first maturity in which Adam on his naming day in Eden destroyed the singularity of individual creatures by naming them and thereby assimilating them to a general class. He lost the full particularity of the purring creature before him when he named it "cat" and gained only a category.[43] Language is linked to finitude, which Blanchot takes somewhat hastily to mean solely temporal finitude. If I say, "This woman," while looking at Furio Piccirilli's garden exhibit "Eurydice," death has not been announced, although finitude has been confirmed. The second element turns on what occurs when I speak or write. Then my consciousness is externalized without me; it exists in language but does not have the being of my selfhood. And so, in speaking or writing—by the time of *L'Entretien infini* (1969) Blanchot will come to settle on the expression *parole d'écriture*—I am attuned not to death as a definitive end of my being but to death as the endlessness of dying or, as he likes to say, "the impossibility of dying."[44]

If we believe what Blanchot says about language, it is always risky to hear him or anyone. Still, let us take our chances and hear him explain himself on language as exposing us to dying:

> Literature is that experience [*La littérature est cette expérience*] through which the consciousness discovers its being in its inability to lose consciousness, in the movement whereby, as it disappears, as it tears itself away from the meticulousness of an I, it is re-created beyond unconsciousness as an impersonal spontaneity, the desperate eagerness of a haggard knowledge which knows nothing, which no one knows, and which ignorance always discovers behind itself as its own shadow changed into a gaze.
>
> One can then accuse language of having become an interminable resifting of words instead of the silence it wanted to achieve . . . this endless resifting of words without content, this continuousness of speech through an immense pillage of words, is precisely the profound nature of a silence that talks even in its dumbness, a silence that is speech empty of words, an echo speaking on and on in the midst of silence. (331-32; 320)

As seen by the author, literature is the experience of having language inescapably orient one toward dying, which cannot be brought within the fold of the possible, and which, even after death, keeps one half-alive, no longer a true self. (The "is," I take it, is that of distribution rather than identity: the author has a special relation with the text but it is nonetheless a text and not an experience.) To write, then, is to be exposed to the peril of being the subject of the dark gaze of one's own consciousness detached from oneself, unable to live and unable to die. And so Blanchot's account of composition is that in writing each author gives us the same sort of mental adventure, an autobiography without autobiography. Not that other people fare any better: "The word gives me the being, but it gives it to me deprived of being. The word is the absence of that being, its nothingness, what is left of it when it has lost being—the very fact that it does not exist" (322; 312). It is as though "Crise de vers" had been pleated tightly into *Sein und Zeit*.

Language then is irreducibly double: it points to death as end and endlessness. "This original double meaning," Blanchot says, "is the source of literature, because literature is the form in which this double meaning has chosen to show itself behind the meaning and value of words" (344; 331). We can see now what Blanchot finally does with Mallarmé's distinction between the brute word and the essential word. An analysis of the literature has revealed that literature is double. It has two slopes, and Blanchot finds Mallarmé on each of them. The first is "meaningful prose," the power of negation, and its aim is "to express things in a language that designates things according to what they mean."[45] And the second, which is the more significant, Blanchot thinks, is poetry. Poets are "interested in the reality of language, because they are not interested in the world, but in what things and beings would be if there were no world" (333; 321). The analysis also shows that this double nature of language cannot be resolved. Language both destroys the singularity of beings and puts us in contact with their absence. Also, though, Blanchot makes the stronger claim that literature attunes us to the Outside, the perpetual passing of being into nothingness.

Let's consider the weaker and the stronger claims with reference to an early, short, and relatively straightforward poem by Mallarmé. What happens with respect to being when I recite "Sainte?"

À la fenêtre recelant
Le santal vieux qui se dédore
Da sa viole étincelant
Jadis avec flûte ou mandore,

Est la Sainte pâle, étalant
Le livre vieux qui se déplie
Du Magnificat ruisselant
Jadis selon vêpre et complie:

À ce vitrage d'ostensoir
Que frôle une harpe par l'Ange
Formée avec son vol du soir
Pour la délicate phalange

Du doigt que, sans le vieux santal
Ni le vieux livre, elle balance
Sur le plumage instrumental,
Musicienne du silence.

[At the window containing
The gilt sandalwood flaking

From the viol that sparkled
Once with flute or mandolin

Is the pale saint displaying
The old book opening at
The Magnificat that flowed
Once at vespers and compline:

In this refulgent monstrance
An angel takes wing at dusk
And comes to light as a harp
Approaching a fingertip

Which, without the old viol
Or crumbling book, balances
On the plumage that she plucks,
A musician of silence.]⁴⁶

When I say these lines out loud, or even quietly to myself, are the window, viol, mandolin, flute, saint, and missal threatened by non being? Only in the sense that the particularity of any window, viol, and so on, is lost, leaving only the generality of window, viol, and the rest. Each item gives me its being but drained of sensuous being. Hence it seems that Blanchot is correct. And yet if I inspect a viol in a music shop, it will give its being to me by way of sensual perception: I can see its shape, hear its body resonate, feel its curves, and smell the varnish on its wood. And when I look at a painting of a mandolin in an art gallery—Vekoslav Karas's "Young Woman with a Mandolin" (c. 1846), say—the instrument gives me its being by way of representation. And the same is true even if "representation" is placed in question, as in Pablo Picasso's "Young Woman and Mandolin" (1932). What Blanchot correctly identifies is the regional ontology proper to literature, although in ignoring all other regional ontologies he makes a hasty induction in saying that literature tells us something special about being. That special truth is that when being presents itself it gives itself as both phenomenon and image, and that the latter indicates a fissure in being. Only when being gives itself in language does it manifest itself as image only. When it gives itself in perception, it manifests itself otherwise.

We may accept the weaker version of Blanchot's claim, then, and not the stronger. And in granting the weaker claim we should note that it has two aspects: a poem names the possible and responds to the impossible. This is not a template for literary criticism; it is an account of the experience of writing a poem: the poet speaks only at the moment of losing the power to say "I." There are several problems with this approach to reading literature in general and reading Mallarmé in particular. First, no regard at all is given to the historical situation of the writer; the evocation of the "original experience" would seem to be Romantic and post-Romantic, although Blanchot nowhere restricts it to this period or argues for Romantic assumptions to be in place in earlier centuries.⁴⁷ Second, although Blanchot prizes those works in which the author has experienced the approach of the Outside, there is no way of telling which ones they are. Those works that present themselves to us as incomplete and even unable to be completed may have been composed by following a particular poetic, not as a consequence of the writer's experience. Third, the experience, if it occurs, is no guarantee of the value of the work; indeed, those poems that appear to be faultless in their formal elaboration—"L'Après-midi d'un faune," for example— may have at least as fair a claim to our admiration as those that are characterized by being fragmentary. And fourth, the attention given to the "original experience" seems to have distracted Blanchot from many of Mallarmé's finest poems, "L'Après-midi d'un faune," to begin with, and others such as the "Hommages et Tombeaux" and "Plusieurs Sonnets."[48]

Now it may be objected that Blanchot does not usually offer himself as a practical critic, and that his reflections on literature are mostly concerned to identify and justify the notion of literary space. Accordingly, he is entirely free to pick and choose among Mallarmé's writings, irrespective of their aesthetic value. This is a reasonable defense. Yet it prompts any reader of Blanchot to put pressure on his more theoretical claims about the anteriority and prophetic nature of the work, namely the impossibility of lodging a poem in the present. Consider a well-known poem by Mallarmé that Blanchot does not cite in his attempt to characterize the original experience:

> Le vierge, le vivace et le bel aujourd'hui
> Va-t-il nous déchirer avec un coup d'aile ivre
> Ce lac dur oublié que hante sous le givre
> Le transparent glacier des vols qui n'ont pas fui!
>
> Un cygne d'autrefois se souvient que c'est lui
> Magnifique mais qui sans espoir se délivre
> Pour n'avoir pas chanté la région où vivre
> Quand du stérile hiver a resplendi l'ennui.
>
> Tout son col secourera cette blanche agonie
> Par l'espace infligée à l'oiseau qui le nie,
> Mais non l'horreur du sol où le plumage est pris.
>
> Fantôme qu'à ce lieu son pur éclat assigne,
> Il s'immobilise au songe froid de mépris
> Que vêt parmi l'exil inutile le Cygne.
>
> [Ah, virginal, vigorous, and beautiful new day,
> Will just a slap of a drunken wing suffice to crack
> This frozen lake that's haunted underneath the frost
> By icy visions of all those flights never dared!
>
> No longer young, a swan recalls his early self,
> Magnificent but now without a hope, quite lost

For never having sung that land where beauty lives
When the flat lassitude of winter shone about.

His neck will wholly shake away that white distress
The world inflicts on anyone who rebuffs its charm,
But not the horror of the ice that holds him tight.

Phantom condemned to this prison by pure lusters,
He braces himself in the cold dream of disdain
Which the swan bears in his fruitless banishment.][49]

Commentators have repeatedly drawn attention to ambiguities in this sonnet. Henry Weinfield, for one, points out that *se délivre* and *secourera* "express their own opposites" and that this "says something about the metaphysical double bind into which the poem is locked."[50] Robert Greer Cohn, for another, argues that *vierge* sets ripples of the erotic through the poem, on the one hand, and a sense of heavenly purity, on the other; while *région* indicates at once the final destination of beauty and ordinary life.[51] None of these ambiguities, however, makes the sonnet fragmentary in any sense; on the contrary, part of its appeal is its elusive unity, one that seems to hover in time to come, waiting for us to arrive.

We do not know what inspired this sonnet, but the inspiration and the poem itself must be distinguished. Catching sight of a swan or a frozen lake could have aroused Mallarmé, and so could the sight of a quivering neck or the sight of a man or woman in exile. The quest for Eurydice, then, would be to contact whatever serves as the prime mover of the poem; and one may readily grant that poets are often prompted into writing by that impossible desire to capture the quoddity of something, the sheer fact that it has existed. However, the sonnet may equally have been inspired by a rhythm, by the idea of a particular rhyme scheme, by a chance combination of words that came into Mallarmé's head, by the ambition to rival Ronsard, or by a combination of these, and none of them fits the allegory of Eurydice and Orpheus that Blanchot proposes. Besides, when composing poetry, Mallarmé wanted, as he says in "Crise de vers," to yield "the initiative to words" (208), and this would indicate another sort of experience than the one that Blanchot calls "original." Indeed, he talks about it with respect to Lautréamont. When he wrote the opening words of *Maldoror*, "Plût au ciel que . . ." [May it please heaven that . . .], Lautréamont hoped that he would one day be the man who will have completed the thought, namely the six cantos of the book.[52] The experience of *Maldoror* was ahead of him, a task that would involve the dialectic of the work to be accomplished and the lucidity of the poet's mind. Similarly, Mallarmé's experience in writing "Le vierge, le vivace et le bel aujourd'hui" was to become the poet who will have written it. To which one might add that the sonnet may speak prophetically, in the sense that it will always offer more meaning to those who read it with care, is doubtless true. But the meaning of the poem is not the same as the poem.

There is reason, then, to doubt Blanchot's insistence that the poem is suspended between a past that was never present and a time still to come. And there is also reason not to expect each and every poem of interest to be a fragmentary work. Mallarmé is exemplary for Blanchot in that he is the very index of the "original experience," although this case can only be advanced on the basis of a few texts, not all of them poems, and with special pleading with respect to *Igitur*. For all its interest, the case blinds Blanchot to some of the very poems that make Mallarmé a great poet. Curiously enough, it is the account of experience offered with respect to Lautréamont that fits Mallarmé's poems the better. It may be that poets write in part to undergo a certain experience, and yet that pathos expiates itself entirely in the writing, and what we are left with is a poem that is silent about its process of composition. Blanchot's Mallarmé is interesting, in the end, not because it tells us much about Mallarmé but because it tells us a great deal about Blanchot, including the sort of information he so badly wanted to know about Mallarmé: how he composed his literary works. In a strange way, *L'Espace littéraire* fills in the gap in *Vie de Mallarmé* that Mondor could not, although it is about Blanchot's poetics, not Mallarmé's, and therefore sends us in another direction than the one we might have wanted to take. In other words, Blanchot's Mallarmé is really Blanchot's Blanchot.

Notes

1 If influences are to be considered, then one would of course think of Jean Giraudoux.
2 Wallace Stevens, "The Auroras of Autumn," in *The Collected Poems of Wallace Stevens* (New York: Alfred A. Knopf, 1954), 419. In a letter to Peter H. Lee dated April 1, 1955, Stevens says, "I love Maurice Blanchot," *Letters of Wallace Stevens*, ed. Holly Stevens (New York: Alfred A. Knopf, 1972), 879.
3 For Blanchot's sense of Valéry's reading, see his "The Myth of Mallarmé," *WF*, 28 (35).
4 Harold Bloom, "Introduction," in *Paul Valéry*, Modern Critical Views (New York: Chelsea House Publishers, 1989), 6. Bloom's claim is that Blanchot is belated with respect to Valéry, not Mallarmé, and he makes no reference to Blanchot in his volume in the Modern Critical Views series, *Stéphane Mallarmé* (New York: Chelsea House, 1987). However, he reprints Blanchot's consideration of *Igitur* in that collection.
5 Bloom includes *Thomas the Obscure*, the *récit* version of 1950, in his catalogue of canonical works at the end of *The Western Canon: The Books and School of the Ages* (New York: Harcourt Brace and Co., 1994), 552.
6 The closest that Blanchot comes to a sustained practice of literary criticism considered as a discourse of evaluation and attention to style is in his many pieces in *Journal des débats*, only some of which are gathered together in *FP*. The others may be found in Blanchot, *CL*. English translations are provided by Michael Holland in four volumes: *InD, DC, WR*, and *DN*. Much of Bloom's career consists of practical criticism, yet he came to prominence for his Freudian literary theory, as exemplified in *The Anxiety of Influence: A Theory of Poetry* (New York: Oxford University Press, 1973).
7 Levinas, "The Poet's Vision," *PN*, 127.
8 Blanchot, *WD*, 36 (61). See his reflections on the writer and biography in "L'Écrivain et le public," *CL*, 94–8 (*InD*, 107–12).
9 Blanchot, "The Silence of Mallarmé," *FP*, 99 (117). The first remarks on Mondor's book appear in "Les peuples meutris . . .," *CL*, 13–14 (*InDr*, 11). We need to distinguish Blanchot's direct claims about a writer not referring to his or her life and

what one can discern in his own *récits*. On this theme, see Christophe Bident, *La vie versée dans les récits (vers le nom de Blanchot)* (Genève: Furor, 2021).
10. Stéphane Mallarmé, "Crisis of Verse," in *Divagations*, trans. Barbara Johnson (Cambridge, MA: Harvard University Press, 2007), 208.
11. "Le Silence de Mallarmé" in *FP* joins together versions of the reviews of each volume of *Vie de Mallarmé*. The second paragraph of "Le biographe connaît le 'génie' et ignore l'homme'" is omitted in *Faux pas*, thereby giving the reader the impression that Blanchot is fainter in his praise than he actually is. For a different estimation of Blanchot's tone at this point, see Leslie Hill, "Blanchot and Mallarmé," *MLN* 105, no. 5 (1990): 897.
12. The first column and a bit of "Le Silence de Mallarmé" have been dropped from the essay of that title in *FP*.
13. Also see, with respect to distinctions between Mallarmé and Valéry, "Les *Mauvaise Pensées* de Paul Valéry," *CL*, 271–7 (*DC*, 188–95).
14. See Mallarmé, *Correspondance, 1862–1871*, ed. Henri Mondor and Jean-Pierre Richard (Paris: Gallimard, 1959), 242.
15. The notes for the book appeared long after Blanchot's review, however. See Jacques Schérer, *Le "Livre" de Mallarmé* (Paris: Gallimard, 1957).
16. Blanchot, "Mallarmé and the Art of the Novel," *FP*, 166 (190–1). Trans. modified.
17. See Mallarmé, "Crisis of Verse," 210 (368), and Valéry, "Poetry and Abstract Thought," in *The Art of Poetry*, trans. Denise Folliot, intro. T. S. Eliot, The Collected Works of Paul Valéry, ed. Jackson Mathews, 15 vols., vol. 7 (Princeton, NJ: Princeton University Press, 1958), 70.
18. Blanchot, "Is Mallarmé's Poetry Obscure?" *FP*, 108 (127).
19. Blanchot, "Mallarmé and the Art of the Novel," 166 (190–1).
20. Blanchot, "Mallarmé's Experience," *SL*, 39 (38). Also see "By Means of a Violent Division . . .," *F*, 148 (171).
21. See Heidegger, "Hölderlin et l'essence de la poésie," trans. Henry Corbin, *Mésures* 3 (1937): 120–43.
22. Heidegger, *Poetry, Language, Thought*, trans. Albert Hofstadter (New York: Harper and Row, 1975), 74, 146, 192.
23. See Johann Gottfriend von Herder, "Treatise on the Origins of Human Language," in *Philosophical Writings*, trans. and ed. Michael N. Forster (Cambridge: Cambridge University Press, 2002), and "Fragments on Recent German Literature (1767–8) [excerpts on language]," 64. Also see Heidegger, *On the Essence of Language: The Metaphysics of Language and the Essencing of the Word, Concerning Herder's Treatise "On the Origin of Language,"* trans. Wanda Torres Gregory and Yvonne Unna (Albany, NY: State University of New York Press, 2004), 35.
24. On laws of literature, see Blanchot, "Paradoxes sur le roman," *CL*, 115–20 (*InD*, 131–7).
25. Blanchot, "The New Novel," *FP*, 186 (212).
26. Later, in 1949, Blanchot will say that *Maldoror* is "a model of this kind of literature that does not entail a model," *LS*, 77 (91).
27. Blanchot, "The Pure Novel," *WR*, 264 (*CL*, 509).
28. On the notion of the "literary absolute" see Philippe Lacoue-Labarthe and Jean-Luc Nancy, *The Literary Absolute: The Theory of Literature in German Romanticism*, trans. Philip Barnard and Cheryl Lester (Albany, NY: State University of New York Press, 1988). A full discussion of Blanchot's early thoughts on the novel would include reference to Horace Walpole's *The Castle of Otranto* (1764), which he admired. See his

"Le Roman Noir," *CL*, 578–82, "The Gothic Novel," *DN*, 68–72. Also see his essay "Le roman, œuvre de mauvaise foi," *Les Temps modernes*, no. 19 (avril 1947), 1304–17.

29 Mallarmé, "À Paul Verlaine," *Oeuvres complètes*, éd. Bertrand Marchal, Bibliothèque de la Pléiade, 2 vols. (Paris: Gallimard, 1998), vol. 1, 788.

30 In a letter to Evelyne Londyn of 22 avril, 1978, Blanchot writes about her proposal to consecrate an essay to the theme of the Orpheus story in his narratives, "le sujet . . . me semble très justifié: *L'Arrêt de mort*, *Celui qui ne m'accompagnait pas*, *Au Moment voulu* et aussi, d'une manière désespérante (peut-être, mais peut-être non) *Le Dernier homme* ou *L'Attente l'oubli* sont portés par ce mouvement . . . et les réflexions théoriques sur Orphée, dans *L'Entretien infini*, sont, à mon sens, infiniment plus restreintes," "L'Orphique chez Blanchot. Voir et Dire," *French Forum* 5, no. 3 (1980): 261. Interestingly, Blanchot does not include *Thomas l'Obscur* in his list. For an early comment on Orpheus, though, see Blanchot, "Oeuvres poétiques," *CL*, 268 (*DC*, 184). The passage is not included in "Poésie involontaire" in *FP*.

31 Blanchot, *TO* (1), 287. Blanchot also reflects on the relation of being seen and dying in "Des diverses façons de mourir," *CL*, 632–6 (*DN*, 132–6).

32 See Blanchot, *A*, 186 (212).

33 See Blanchot, *DS*, 20–30 (36–52).

34 It should be noted that *Le Très-Haut* (1948) traces in its own way the story of Orestes. See Michel Foucault, "Maurice Blanchot: The Thought from Outside," in Foucault, *Maurice Blanchot: The Thought from Outside* bound with Maurice Blanchot, *Michel Foucault as I Imagine Him*, trans. respectively by Brian Massumi and Jeffrey Mehlman (New York: Zone Books, 1990), 39.

35 See Blanchot, "The Beast of Lascaux," *VE*, 41.

36 See Blanchot, *SL*, 241 (323). The idea of the anteriority of the artwork to the artist is foreshadowed in "Oeuvres poétiques." Also see "The Beast of Lascaux," 12.

37 Blanchot, *SL*, 38 (37). Blanchot quotes Mallarmé's letter to Cazalis in late April 1866, *Correspondance 1862–1871*, 207.

38 I take it that Blanchot intends the *complete and utter* absence of God from reality—that there never was a God in the first place—namely atheism, and not the absence of God as the peculiar way in which he is present from time to time.

39 Heidegger, *Being and Time*, trans. John Macquarrie and Edward Robinson (Oxford: Basil Blackwell, 1973), 307. See Blanchot, "The Work and Death's Space," *SL*, 96 (119).

40 See Franz Kafka, *Diaries 1914–1923*, ed. Max Brod (New York: Schocken Books, 1965), 77.

41 Mallarmé, "Crisis of Verse," 210.

42 Blanchot, "Literature and the Right to Death," *WF*, 322–3 (313).

43 See G. W. F. Hegel, *System of Ethical Life (1802/3) and First Philosophy of Spirit (Part III of the System of Speculative Philosophy 1803/4)*, ed. and trans. H. S. Harris and T. M. Knox (Albany, NY: State University of New York Press, 1979), 221–2.

44 See Blanchot, "Literature and the Right to Death," 328 (317). For the expression "parole d'écriture," see *EI*, the subtitle to section one, "La Parole plurielle," in the contents page.

45 Blanchot, "Literature and the Right to Death," *WF*, 332 (321).

46 Mallarmé's poems are taken from *Oeuvres complètes*, éd. Henri Mondor et G. Jean-Aubry, Bibliothèque de la Pléiade (Paris: Gallimard, 1945). In order to give a fuller sense of the French, I offer Henry Weinfield's translation, which preserves rhyme, in his collection, Stéphane Mallarmé, *Collected Poems* (Los Angeles, CA: University of California Press, 1994):

> At the window frame concealing
> The viol old and destitute
> Whose gilded sandalwood, now peeling,
> Once shone with mandolin or flute,
>
> Is the Saint, pale, unfolding
> The old, worn missal, a divine
> Magnificat in rivers, flowing
> Once at vespers and compline:
>
> At the glass of this monstrance, vessel
> Touched by a harp that took its shape
> From the evening flight of an Angel
> For the delicate fingertip
>
> Which, without the old, worn missal
> Or sandalwood, she balances
> On the plumage instrumental,
> Musician of silences. (43)

47 Bloom extends Romanticism back to Homer and forward to Hart Crane. See his "The Internalization of Quest Romance," in *Ringers in the Tower: Studies in Romantic Tradition* (Chicago, IL: University of Chicago Press, 1971), 3.

48 Michael Holland develops a similar insight along different lines. See his fine essay, "From Crisis to Critique: Mallarmé for Blanchot," in *Meetings with Mallarmé in Contemporary French Culture*, ed. Michael Temple (Exeter: University of Exeter Press, 1998), 97.

49 Again, I offer Weinfield's translation of the poem by way of giving a fuller sense of the original:

> The virginal, vibrant, and beautiful dawn,
> Will a beat of its drunken wing not suffice
> To rend this hard lake haunted beneath the ice
> By the transparent glacier of flights never flown?
>
> A swan of former times remembers it's the one
> Magnificent but hopelessly struggling to resist
> For never having sung of a land in which to exist
> When the boredom of the sterile winter has shone.
>
> Though its quivering neck will shake free of the agonies
> Inflicted on the bird by the space it denies,
> The horror of the earth will remain where it lies.
>
> Phantom whose pure brightness assigns it to this domain,
> It stiffens in the cold dream of disdain
> That clothes the useless exile of the Swan. (67)

50 See Mallarmé, *Collected Poems*, 215.
51 Robert Greer Cohn, *Toward the Poems of Mallarmé*, expanded ed. (Los Angeles, CA: University of California Press, 1980), 126, 130.
52 See Blanchot, *LS*, 77 (91).

2

Blanchot's Hölderlin

Let us assume that we have a body of work—poetry, drama, essays, letters, a novel, and translations—that we call "Hölderlin," and let us assume also that we can revolve it all in our minds. One by one its aspects would come before us, and over time we would view many profiles of these aspects. Some readers might say that Hölderlin is finally given to them in a manifold of profiles, and it is easy to see what they would mean. They would grasp Hölderlin's individual works, of course, but also they would comprehend the work as a whole in terms of the genres he uses, through his characteristic themes, and with respect to his language, his rhythms, and his preferred forms. By way of association, they would see the work now in relation to Pindar and Sophocles or Klopstock and Schiller, and now in relation to George, Rilke, Celan, and René Char, or, in our own day, in conversation with Geoffrey Hill, Gustaf Sobin, or, as surprising as it might seem, John Ashbery.[1] Also by way of association, they would see Hölderlin emerge in his various maturities in an overlapping sequence: the novel *Hyperion* (1792–9), his early odes and epigrams (1797–9), the three versions of *Der Tod des Empedokles* (1798–9), the later odes (1798–1803), the hymns (1799–1805), the elegies (1800–1), *Die Trauerspiele des Sophokles* (1804), the Pindar fragments and commentaries (1805), and the last poems (1807–43). In the same manner, they would see Hölderlin in groups of themes, most likely starting with "Poetry and Philosophy," because, after all, the poet is linked from the beginning and forever with Greek thought, with Kant, with Hegel and Schelling, and, since the 1930s, with Heidegger.[2] Needless to say, that last name would also bring in tow the array "Poetry and Politics," and in parts it would be darkly shaded. Doubtless too our admirers of the poet would see him in another arrangement, "Poetry and Religion," for Hölderlin, a student at the Tübingen *Stift*, has long been regarded as a *poeta theologus* and even a *sacer vates*. Greek and Hebrew elements would come into view, as would the hard words of the "default of God" and much else besides.

Blanchot's quest as a reader of literature is "to find out what the fact that the poem, the song, exists really signifies."[3] He is clear that it does not signify anything in the realm of aesthetics. Appeals to the aesthetic, he thinks, conceal the disruptive movement of writing rather than reveal anything telling about it. Instead, he wishes to make us see Hölderlin as surely within the field of "Poetry and Religion" as within "Poetry and Philosophy," and this is not because he is an apologist for religion, as other contemporary admirers of Hölderlin are: Hans Urs von Balthasar and Jean-Luc Marion, for example.[4] On the contrary, Blanchot is a radical and consequent atheist, his atheism not revolving around theism like a dark moon but rather preceding the distinction between the two and questioning the unity presumed in both terms ("God" and "man").[5] Nor does he wish to make a small claim, that some of Hölderlin's poems are religious in one or another sense of the word.[6] Not at all: he makes a big claim, somewhat to the side of the small claim, that all Hölderlin's poems involve the sacred or the holy. (I shall use both words interchangeably as translations of *das Heilige*.[7]) "Religion" is bracketed. All literature draws on the sacred, or whatever is left of the sacred, Blanchot argues, although Hölderlin does so in an exemplary manner. Accordingly, we are not talking about an argument for minor literature ("devotional poetry" or even "religious poetry") but about literature as such and its future. At the same time, though, Blanchot dismisses the very idea of there being a wholeness to Hölderlin, in all his works or even in just the one poem, that could be given to us through imaginative variation of the sort I have entertained. No sooner does he name Friedrich Gundolf in his early essay "La parole 'sacrée' de Hölderlin" (1946) than he acidly observes that the critic "took care to ruin his study from the beginning by recalling that a poem is a whole" (111; 115). On the contrary, for Blanchot a poem has no unity in which it subsists or that properly supervenes with respect to it; and if he rejects the idea of a whole as early as *Le Part du feu* (1949) he will come, by the time of *L'Entretien infini* (1969), to contest in the name of "writing" all unity, wholeness, and totality in whatever guises they assume.[8]

Blanchot remains close to Heidegger's reading of Hölderlin both in his selection of poems to discuss and at times in his language that echoes the phrasings of the German thinker in the essays gathered in *Erläuterungen zu Hölderlins Dichtung* (1st ed., 1951) and in courses of the 1930s and 1940s: "Hölderlins Hymnen ('Der Rhein' und 'Germanien')" (Winter, 1934–5) and "Hölderlins 'Andenken'" (Summer, 1942). "The Sacred is the shining power that opens to the sacred all that its shining attains," Blanchot writes, with Heidegger's ink flowing from his pen.[9] At the same time Blanchot detaches himself from Heidegger: he is alert to the motif of exile in poetry, to poetry as exile, rather than to poetry arising from the *Heimat* and establishing one there.[10] That Heidegger writes of un-truth as wandering is of course correct, but the wandering that leads to exile is of another order than the one that Heidegger discusses.[11] It is not a matter of a flight "from the mystery to what is readily available, onward from one thing to the next" but the very nature of the poetic condition: to write is to be exiled, to belong "to the outside," a notion that, as we shall continue to see, comes to bear significant conceptual freight.[12] It is in terms of his distance from Heidegger as well as in his closeness to him that Blanchot writes of Hölderlin while drawing on a religious vocabulary. He uses a received lexicon ("the gods," "revelation," "sacred," "sacrifice") that Hölderlin himself takes from Judaism, Paganism, and Christianity, a lexicon that is appropriated by Heidegger and put to his own ends, and one that is redirected by Blanchot to his own ends, which are as unorthodox as Hölderlin's and Heidegger's but in quite other ways.

On four occasions Blanchot writes at length about Hölderlin. First, in conversation with a then-recent issue of the review *Fontaine* devoted to French translations of the poet and two of his most eminent critics, he proposes to specify the nature of the poet's "'sacred' speech," the quotation marks indicating his prudential distance from the convictions of both the poet and the thinker.[13] Second, responding to Karl Jaspers's *Strindberg und van Gogh: Versuch einer pathographischen Analyse unter vergleichender*

Heranziehung von Swedenborg und Hölderlin (1949), he attends to the question of Hölderlin's madness. Third, in a study of the poet's itinerary, he seeks to discern "the mystery of the God's departure" in the poetry.[14] And, finally, with a backward glance at his first interest, he tries to rethink what "sacred" might mean for literature and for us. This is the sequence from *Le Part du feu* (1949*)* to "La Folie par excellence" (1951) to *L'Espace littérature* (1955) to *L'Entretien infini* (1969). These essays are not the only places where Blanchot refers to Hölderlin, and not the only occasions when the pressure of the poet's thought can be felt.[15] It is true that René Char becomes increasingly an exemplary poet for Blanchot, yet it is no less true that one or more profiles of Hölderlin stand behind the figure of Char, including the figure of the poet as prophet. And if it is true that Hölderlin marks for Blanchot one vanishing point in poetry, in what poetry can and really must say to us today, it is equally true that Mallarmé marks another.[16]

Blanchot learns slightly different things from Hölderlin and Mallarmé, however, although both occur in the difficult and painful field of modern religious experience. Mallarmé taught Blanchot a great deal about how the felt absence of God could lead one to the "pure novel," a work of fiction that could come about only through the insights of Mallarmé's atheistic mysticism.[17] Those insights are a counterpart in literature of what St. John of the Cross's "the dark night of the soul" is for Christian spirituality.[18] Blanchot learned from Mallarmé that there is a link between self-sacrifice and literature. For a writer to touch the night may not be the same as for a mystic to lose himself in "a divine Conception" but it is to reach "the extreme point of an entirely conscious meditation," one that associates literature and an endless movement of dying that denies any possibility of there being a unified self.[19] From Hölderlin he learned something else, a lesson that comes from another place, that the sacred must be retained if there is to be art, including poetry as art. And yet, against Hölderlin, he also maintained that one may not pass in any direction between "sacred" and "whole," and indeed that the sacred—or, better, the "Sacred"—is what disrupts the whole.

*

Let us take this lesson and counter-lesson as our starting point. "It is well known," Blanchot says, "that Hölderlin profoundly linked god and man, each needing the other, with only poetic existence ensuring the truth of their union" (116; 120). This god, or more properly these gods, do not exist *a se*, as the Christian God does. In the Christian vision, at least according to St. Thomas Aquinas, our relations with God are real, *relatio realis,* although God's relations with us are unreal, *relatio rationis tantum*. We depend ontologically on the Creator, but the Creator does not need to have created anything in order to enjoy all possible perfections as God.[20] For Hölderlin, though, the gods are secondary to nature, φύσις: even "the sacred Father," the highest of the gods, would languish without the poets and without people reading them. In "Der Mütter Erde" Hölderlin writes,

> Denn wenn er schon der Zeichen genug
> Und Fluthen in seiner Macht und Wetterflammen

> Wie Gedanken hat der heilige Vater,
>   unaussprechlich wär er wohl
> Und nirgend fänd er wahr sich unter den Lebenden wieder
> Wenn zum Gesange nicht hätt ein Herz die Gemeinde.
> [For while he has sufficient signs
> And floods at his command and flames of thunder
> Like thoughts, the holy Father cannot be spoken of
> And nowhere would he find himself among the living
> If the community had no heart for song.][21]

It is the poets who enable the Father to be properly praised (i.e., celebrated), and so keep him in relation with mortals, and yet the poet requires a community to read and recite his poems. The lines bespeak either a smooth or a vicious circle. If all is well—if the community sings the poet's words, and the gods are one with us—the circle may well continue endlessly, enriching all who participate in it, and, if so, a *Volksreligion* will be founded and elaborated. Yet if the circle breaks, if the people find themselves without gods, the old ones having become incredible and the new ones not yet having revealed themselves, then the community will not sing the poet's words, and the poet cannot praise the gods. This is of course the situation in which Hölderlin found himself: "in dürftige Zeit," in a thin time, as he says in "Brod und Wein"; and the only way out of this circle, the sole way for Hölderlin to be a poet, Blanchot argues, is for him to "exist as a presentiment of himself," to be ahead of himself and his age.

Now we might take this affirmation of the poet to be a doctrine of poetic or even religious genius. Only the poet, the truly creative person, lives prophetically! There is a sense in which Blanchot could subscribe to this proposition, for he considers the poet to speak prophetically of the Outside, the non-place where being passes endlessly into image, which will interest us later.[22] Yet Blanchot prefers another explanation of how the poet can reach into the future, an explanation that is entirely paradoxical. The poet already abides in time to come because the poem not only stretches ahead but also precedes him, and he conforms himself to the poem. One can unravel this paradox by appealing to different Greek sources. One can point to Plato's argument in book ten of *The Republic* (esp. 596b) and in *Cratylus* 389b that the craftsman sees the εἶδος of what he creates in his soul, or one can refer to a quite traditional notion of inspiration: the poem is given to the poet and remains unjustified by any appeal to the principle of sufficient reason, certainly any principle of sufficient *historical* reason. Also, the poem is always ahead of itself insofar as all its meanings are never to be gathered in any present. I may read "Heimkunft" every year of my life, and each time I may write a commentary on it, one that is each year to be succeeded by a longer account of the subtleties, heights, and depths of the elegy. At no time, though, can I say that I have exhausted the poem, for it is always possible that new relations between its figures and tropes can be discerned, new links between this elegy and other poems by Hölderlin, hidden paths from "Heimkunft" to odes by Pindar, as well as to poems still be to be written and indeed experiences that may illuminate facets of the elegy in utterly unexpected ways. Thoroughly reasonable, and completely in tune with contemporary secular criticism, this kind of explanation is precisely *not* what Blanchot offers us.

"Hölderlin's entire work," he tells us, "bears witness to the awareness of an anterior power surpassing the gods as well as men, the very one that prepares the universe to be 'completely whole'" (119; 122).

So Blanchot allows Hölderlin's commitment to the All, and to the wholeness of the All, to come before us, front and center. "To be one with all—that is the life of the divinity, that is the heaven of man," Hyperion writes to Bellarmin in the poet's early epistolary novel, but of course Blanchot cannot agree with him or any of the Romantics who yearn for the All or the One.[23] He may acknowledge the "joyful movement" of inspiration affirmed there and also the "desire for death" latent in Hyperion's words, yet it is the wholeness of the All, and the possibility of fusion with it, that he seeks to expose as delusive.[24] Before he critically engages with the All, however, Blanchot looks over his shoulder to Heidegger who determines that this prior wholeness is "das Heilige," the holy or the sacred. Several poems could have served as proof texts— "Patmos," "In Lieblicher Bläue . . .," and even, perhaps, "Der Einzige" among them—but we are turned to read or re-read some lines in the unfinished Pindaric hymn "Wie Wenn am Feiertage . . ." (1799) in the context of Heidegger's elucidation of that poem. This is, Heidegger testifies, "the purest poem on the essence of poetry," and it is one that in 1946 had just been translated into French by Joseph Rivan.[25] The lines have become well known in discussions of poetry and philosophy as well as in poetry and religion:

> Jezt aber tagts! Ich harrt und sah es kommen,
> Und was ich sah, das Heilige sei mein Wort.
> Denn sie, sie selbst, die älter denn die Zeiten
> Und über die Götter des Abends und Orients ist,
> Die Natur is jezt mit Waffenklang erwacht,
> Und hoch vom Aether bis zum Abgrund nieder
> Nach vestem Geseze, wie einst, aus heiligem Chaos gezeugt,
> Fühlt neu die Begeisterung sich,
> Die Allerschaffende wieder.
> [But now day breaks! I waited and saw it come,
> And what I saw, the holy be my word.
> For she, herself, older than the ages
> And higher than the gods of West and East,
> Nature is now awake among the clang of weapons,
> And from high Ether down to the depths,
> Following the old laws, born, as once, from holy Chaos,
> Feels the new enthusiasm,
> The all-creating once again.] [26]

"What is the Sacred?" Blanchot asks, and right away gives Heidegger's answer: "the immediate that is never communicated but is the principle of all possibility of communication" (120, 123).[27] No contestation *of* the sacred is considered, only one *within* the sacred.

Blanchot does not disagree with Heidegger when he looks to Hölderlin's commentary on Pindar ("Das Höchste") where we are told that the immediate is impossible for mortals just as it is for immortals. The Sacred is not a property of the gods but precedes them, the gods being, for the Greeks, the highest beings in the cosmos and not beyond it.[28] The Sacred is not Chaos, as Heidegger surmises. Blanchot clearly marks his disagreement with the German thinker, for Chaos is nocturnal, he says, and there is nothing of the night, nothing of Novalis's *Hymnen an die Nacht* (1800), say, in Hölderlin. Mallarmé is Blanchot's poet of the night, the poet of the dark nights of Tournon, and Hölderlin is his poet of the morning. (We might wonder how to square Blanchot's insistence on Hölderlin as a poet of the morning with the German's lines about the "heiliger Nacht" ["holy night"] in "Brot und Wein" or the "heil'ger Nacht" in "Lebenslauf" ("Grössers wolltest auch du") and elsewhere.) The Sacred "is the day," Blanchot adds, "but anterior to the day, and always anterior to itself" (121; 124). So we have another paradox, a very important one to Blanchot, one that makes him into who he is, but before I try to make sense of it, I would like to explore an alternate path that could have been followed in explicating these lines from "Wie Wenn am Feiertage . . . ." It is one that takes us away from Blanchot for a while only to return him to us in a sharper focus, one informed by the nature of the θεωρός and the relation of sacrifice to the sacred.

*

It is important to recognize, as Heidegger does, that the poem is framed by a holiday: a holy day, feast day, or festival.[29] Just as the countryman sees that his vines are safe the morning after a storm, so too the poets are lightly embraced by nature. When nature seems to be sleeping, in winter for example, the poets may seem sad, yet they are nonetheless divining the presence of the All. Hölderlin, the presumptive "I" of the poem, has been waiting for the daybreak on a holy day, even if it is an ordinary day regarded by virtue of its presence as holy. We remember how in ancient Greece a πόλις would send a man as a representative to a distant festival, and this person, the θεωρός, would witness the event and participate in it. On coming back home, he would tell his people what he had seen, but on returning might find himself changed by what he has seen and done. If so, he would be no longer entirely one with his people. We remember too how Plato in the parable of the Cave in book seven of *The Republic* thought of the philosopher as θεωρός, as a person who, through the practice of dialectic, achieved insight into the Forms, saw the truth of being, and returned to tell his countrymen about it only to be rejected by them.[30] Plato has internalized the arduous journey to another place in order to participate in a festival. In "Wie Wann am Feiertage . . ." Holderlin also interiorizes the role of the θεωρός but in terms of the poet, not the philosopher.[31] He waits reverently, perhaps right where he is, for the day to break, sees the holy coming, the light that reaches over the horizon just before the sun appears, and rejoices in its advent.[32] He accepts the role of witnessing it: "das Heilige sei mein Wort." The poetry he shall write from now on will not actually say the holy in so many words (he does not write "das Heilige *ist* mein Wort") but, in adopting the optative mood, he prays that the poetry will preserve the mystery of nature as a mystery, preserve its immediacy, and communicate it indirectly, not translate it into other terms.

For Hölderlin, the poetry to be written by him precedes composition in that it is the silent mystery of nature that shall be artfully gathered in individual poems. At the same time, the poet lives ahead of himself by dint of what he has witnessed. He lives now in order to be the man who will have written those poems and thereby testified to the wordless mystery that has been revealed to him. As Heidegger notes, this poetry will be the "hymn *of* the holy" (98; my emphasis), and because the holy is the All it can bring forth endless poems if the poet is strong enough to write them. The poet is charged with a hard task: not to speak the holy directly, for it would annul itself in losing its immediacy, but to preserve the unsayable mystery of the holy in his own words that speak of phenomena. In talking of particular, ordinary things—vines and storms, mountains and fields, rivers, and the homeland—the poet must also allow the holy immediately to communicate itself beneath, within, and around those very words. We can say, as a placing shot, that the poet must sacrifice himself, including his personal themes as poet, in order to allow the sacred to speak silently through his poems. Poetry, then, will be oriented to θεωρία, the rapt contemplation of the All, and will be offered to the community to which the poet belongs.[33] If the community accepts the words of the poet, they will sing his words; if they refuse those words, then the "tender and infinite relations" of mortals and gods, mediated without mediation by the poet, will be broken.[34] Note that in speaking of holiness, the poet does not necessarily say anything about the gods; for the holy is what appears, and not the gods, who remain distant in this meager time.

For Heidegger, "Wie Wenn am Feiertage . . ." is pure in that it speaks clearly of the essence of poetry. As Paul de Man rightly observes, Heidegger needs Hölderlin to be a witness to the coming of being. He, the thinker, "is not so sure that he has seen Being and, in any case," de Man says a little archly, "he knows that he has nothing to say about it beyond the fact that it conceals itself. Yet he does not intend to give up discourse since it is still his intention to collect and found Being by means of language."[35] In other words, Heidegger needs a θεωρός to come home to Germany from Greece to give witness to the coming of Being that he has experienced there. "There must be someone," de Man continues, "of unquestionable purity, who can say that he has traveled this route and seen the flash of illumination. One such person is enough, but there must be one. For then, the truth, which is the presence of the present, has entered the work that is language" (253). Of course, the poetry does not *say* the holy, as Heidegger wishes; it can communicate it only obliquely and silently, and although de Man does not take this path one might argue that this obliqueness justifies in principle Heidegger's exegetical procedures in reading Hölderlin.

It may be that de Man insists overly that Heidegger must *make* Hölderlin declare that poetry *says* the holy. Why? Because if one looks aside, to Heidegger's lecture course in the winter semester of 1942–3, just three years after writing his commentary on "Wie Wenn am Feiertage . . .," we find an alternative way of thinking about the matter. Here is Heidegger reflecting on a thought of Parmenides in the following manner:

> Sight into the unconcealed transpires first, and only, in the disclosive word. Sight looks, and is the appearing self-showing that it is, only in the disclosive domain of the word and of telling perception. Only if we recognize the original relation

between the word and the essence of Being will we be capable of grasping why, for the Greeks and only for them, to the divine (τὸ θεῖον) must correspond the legendary (ὁ μῦθος). This correspondence is indeed the primordial essence of all analogy (homology), the word "ana-logy" taken essentially and literally.[36]

A little later, speaking of the plastic arts, he tells his students,

> The statue and the temple stand in silent dialogue with man in the unconcealed. If there were not the *silent word* [schweigende Wort], then the looking good as sight of the statue and of the features of its figure could never appear. (116; Heidegger's emphasis)

It is entirely possible that Heidegger credits Hölderlin with saying the "silent word" in his poems, the word that the words of an ode, elegy, or hymn can indicate without actually pronouncing it. Heraclitus would have been in the background of Heidegger's thinking here (and remains so for Blanchot as well): "The lord whose oracle is in Delphi neither speaks out nor conceals, but gives a sign."[37] And of course the idea of poetry speaking a silent word has become familiar in contemporary poetics. Consider Octavio Paz, who states the idea without leaning very heavily on either philosophical or religious language: "The Word has its roots in a silence *previous* to speech—a presentiment of language. Silence, *after* the Word, is based on a language—it is an embodied silence. The poem is the trajectory between these two silences—between the wish to speak and the silence that fuses the wishing and the speaking."[38]

*

It is one thing to debate how to read Hölderlin and another to ponder what of Hölderlin to read, indeed what counts as "Hölderlin." Heidegger's poet is a man of morning knowledge, and de Man, who stealthily follows the thinker step by step, like a patient hunter walking in the footprints of his prey, does not question this. Without doubt, Hölderlin speaks of the holy as a gaiety, even if amid our tragedy joy is sometimes expressed by way of mourning. We lament the passing of the gods and anticipate with hope and joy those who will come. Nonetheless, poetry will preserve holiness in this distressed time, and holiness is the very ether of the gods. When they reveal themselves once more, perhaps in an utterly unexpected manner, the poets will have preserved the medium of revelation, and the people will be ready to receive the revelation if they have sung the poems. In more modest ways, both T. S. Eliot and Karl Rahner offer versions of the same position within orthodox Christianity.[39]

Yet is Hölderlin so sanguine, even in his witnessing of the holy? It is significant that Heidegger excludes from the text of the ode the fragmentary lines at the end of the poem as textually established by Friedrich Beissner:

Des Vaters Stral, der reine versengt es nicht
Und tieferschüttert, die Leiden des Stärkeren
Mitleidend, bleibt in den hochherstürzenden Stürmen

> Des Gottes, wenn er nahet, der Herz doch fest.
> Doch weh mir!
> [The Father's ray, the pure one, will not scorch it
> And deeply shaken, suffering with him
> The stronger, the heart remains firm
> In the high storms of the god when he comes near.
> But woe is me!]⁴⁰

The poet as θεωρός is changed by what he experiences, and sometimes finds himself woefully inadequate to what he witnesses. So fully does Hölderlin identify himself with the role of receiving the holy and communicating it in his poems that he sees himself, in the draft's final lines, as "Den falschen Priester," the false priest, who has been burnt by the divine and can at best sing "the warning song."⁴¹

How far we have come from "Des Morgans" where the approach to the gods is made in all innocence and without the slightest sense of things going awry. "Komm nun, o komm, und eile mir nicht zu schnell, / Du goldner Tag, zum Gipfel des Himmels fort!" ["Come now, o come, not overly quickly / Golden day, hasten to the peaks of heaven"], Hölderlin sings, and then, later, says, gloriously, "Des frohen übermüthigen du, dass er / Dir gleichen möchte" ["At my happy high spiritedness, [you smile] / In him wanting to resemble you"]. It is that smile at "frohen übermüthigen" that is severely denied in the last stanzas of "Wie Wenn am Feiertage . . .." And yet we have not come far from *Der Tod des Empedokles*. In the first version of the play, we hear Hermokrates talk of Empedokles:

> Es haben ihn die Götter sehr geliebt.
> Doch nicht is er der Erste, den sie drauf
> Hinab in sinnenlose Nacht verstoßen
> Vom Gipfel ihres gütigen Vertrauns,
> Weil er des Unterschieds zu sehr vergaß
> Im übergroßen Glück, und sich allein
> Nur fühlte.
> [The gods loved him dearly
> But he's not the first one whom they thrust
> Into the senseless night, fallen
> From the heights of their trust, because
> He overly forgot the difference [between them]
> In his good fortune, feeling
> Only for himself.] ⁴²

Taken together, *Der Tod des Empedokles* and "Des Morgans" illustrate the motif from Empedocles with which Hölderlin closely identified, Φιλίαν καὶ Νεῖκος, love and strife.

It is difficult to interpret the final lines of "Wie Wenn am Feiertage . . ." with any confidence, not knowing how they would have fitted into the poem were it completed, but once we place them in context, we can get some idea of what is being said:

> Und sag ich gleich,
> Ich sei genaht, die Himmlischen zu schauen,
> Sie selbst, sie werfen mich tief unter die Lebenden
> Den falschen Priester, ins Dunkel, daß ich
> Das warnende Lied den Gelehrigen singe.
> Dort
> [And let me say right away
> That I came near to look at the Heavenly Ones,
> And they themselves cast me down, down
> Beneath the living, cast me down
> Me, the false priest, into the dark,
> So that I may sing the warning song to those who will hear.
> There][43]

The poet witnesses the holy and seeks to go further, to approach the gods themselves, but the right time for their self-revelation has not yet come, and the divine beings remain far from all mortals, including poets, and cast Hölderlin down as punishment for his presumption at seeking to see them or even name them. Now he is lower than ordinary mortals. The proper religious role of the poet is that of the participation of the θεωρός; for as a self-appointed priest, actively mediating between mortals and gods, he can only be a failure.

Why does the image of the priest even occur to Hölderlin as something he could plausibly adopt as a figure for himself as poet? It follows generally from his understanding of Oedipus. "The *intelligibility* of the whole," he writes of *Oedipus Tyrannos*, "rests primarily on one's [ability to] focus on the scene where Oedipus interprets the saying of the oracle *too infinitely*, and is tempted into *nefas*."[44] And Hölderlin notes, "right afterwards [Oedipus] speaks in priestly fashion" (103). The idea of the poet as priest also follows, more particularly, from the answer that Heinse, the dedicatee of "Brot und Wein," supposedly gives to the question "wosu Dichter in dürftiger Zeit?" ("who wants poets at all in lean years?"):

> Aber sie sind, sagst du, wie des Weingotts heilige Priester,
> Welche von Lande zu Land zogen in heilige Nacht.
> [But they are, you say, like the winegod's holy priests,
> Who roamed from place to place in the holy Night.][45]

I pause to note that Hölderlin says, "wie" ("like"): the poets are *like* the priests of Dionysius and are not priests themselves. Still more pressingly, Hölderlin thinks of the figure of the priest because of the lines in "Wie wenn am Feiertage..." about Semele, the priestess of Zeus.

Ovid beautifully tells the story of Semele in *Metamorphoses* 3: 308–12. In Hölderlin's words, "da sie sichtbar / Den Gott zu sehen begehrte, sein Bliz auf Semeles Haus / Und die göttlichgetroffne gebahr, / Die Frucht des Gewitters, den heiligen Bacchus" ["when she longed to see / The god himself, visible, his lightning fell on Semele's house

/ And the one struck by the holy one gave birth / To the fruit of the thunderstorm, to holy Bacchus"]. What Hölderlin omits is precisely Juno's plot against Semele, her disguising herself as an old woman and telling the young woman to ask Jove, who had already promised her anything, to appear as he really is, with "his bright three-forkèd mace." As Juno well knows, the mere sight of Jove will kill Semele, even if he brings his "second mace," which has "less fierceness, lesser might." Yet it is far more likely that Hölderlin had in mind the opening lines of Dionysus's first speech in Euripides's *The Bacchæ* than the more complete and elegant narrative of Ovid.[46] He is entranced by the rhythm of Euripides's lines. Dionysus begins,

> Ἥκω Διὸς παῖς τήνδε Θηβαίαν χθόνα
> Διόνυσος, ὃν τίκτει ποθ' ἡ Κάδμου κόρη
> Σεμέλη λοχευθεῖσ' ἀστραπηφόρωι πυρί·

In Hölderlin's rendition, we read,

> Ich komme, Jovis Sohn, hier ins Thebanerland,
> Dionysos, den gebar vormals des Kadmos Tochter
> Semele, geschwängert von Gewitterfeur.[47]

> [I am Dionysius, the son of Zeus,
> come back to Thebes, this land where I was born.
> My mother was Cadmus' daughter, Semele by name,
> midwived by fire, delivered by the lightning's blast.][48]

And of course, Euripides's audience would have known that Semele was the priestess of Zeus.

Even if we prefer Ovid's fuller narrative to Euripides', the outcome is the same. Even Zeus's second mace is too much for Semele. As Arthur Golding renders Ovid's lines:

> She, being mortal, was too weak and feeble to withstand
> Such troublous tumults of the heavens, and therefore out of hand
> Was burnèd in her lover's arms.[49]

There is no trickery for Hölderlin, however; his downfall is brought about solely by hubris. Now he is to warn the people that in this thin time, the late Enlightenment, it is not propitious to approach the gods or to seek to name them. The tryst of Semele and Zeus brings forth wine; the "fruit" of Hölderlin's misjudged encounter with the gods is the very poem we read, along with other poems by him, and its incompleteness is a sign of the damage that too much illumination can make. The most that a poet can do is to preserve the holy in his song; it cannot be rendered as ὁ μῦθος. Of course, it would be difficult for Heidegger to include these fragmentary lines in his understanding of the hymn. For him, "being is prior to all beings, for they owe what they are to being. And the gods likewise: to the degree that they *are*, and however they are, they too all stand *under* 'being.'"[50] It makes sense for Heidegger for the poet to bespeak the holy, but it would be difficult for him to explain how the gods, beings, are experienced as *higher* than being. Only the Christian God is higher or beyond being, ὑπερουσία, and Hölderlin and Heidegger agree that the Christian God has withdrawn from the Earth.

*

It is hard to see either Semele or Hölderlin as sacrificing themselves according to Christian models of redemptive sacrifice. To understand what is at issue for Hölderlin and Blanchot, we must ponder tragic sacrifice, and keep in mind that neither Aristotelian nor Hegelian notions of tragedy are fitting for the poet. Schelling's concept, as sketched in the tenth of the *Philosophische Briefe über Dogmatismus und Kritizismus* (1795), is closer to what Hölderlin has in mind. "Greek tragedy honored human freedom; it was the *honor* due to freedom. Greek tragedy honored human freedom, letting its hero *fight* against the superior power of fate. In order not to go beyond the limits of art, the tragedy had to let him succumb. Nevertheless, in order to make restitution for this humiliation of human freedom extorted by art, it had to let him *atone* even for the crime committed by fate."[51] In Hölderlin's own terms, as he writes about *Oedipus*:

> Tragedy resides in this: that the immediate God, wholly one with man (for the god of an apostle is less immediate but is the highest the understanding is capable of, in the highest spirit), that an infinite enthusiasm infinitely, which is to say in antithesis, in consciousness that cancels out [*aufhebt*] consciousness, and sacramentally departing from itself, apprehends itself, and the god, in the shape of death, is present.[52]

Tragedy, here, is religious rather than aesthetic or ethical. That the suffering Hölderlin sees himself as an Oedipus figure is clear from his letters to Casimir Ulrich Böhlendorff in December 1802 ("consumed in flames—we expiate the flames which we could not tame," "I may say that Apollo has struck me").[53] The poet grasps himself as poet, as truly inspired, in drawing close to death.

The motif of this sort of sacrifice surfaces from time to time in Hölderlin's own poems. *Der Tod des Empedokles* offers several instances where one witnesses the mutual engagement of pain and joy.[54] Consider, above all, however, these demanding lines from "Der Rhein":

> Denn weil
> Die Seeligsten nichts fühlen von selbst,
> Muß wohl, wenn solches zu sagen
> Erlaubt ist, in der Götter Nahmen
> Theilnehmend fühlen ein Andrer,
> Den brauchen sie; jedoch ihr Gericht
> Ist, daß sein eigenes Haus
> Zerbreche der und das Liebste

> Wie den Feind schelt' und sich Vater und Kind
> Begrabe unter den Trümmern,
> Wenn einer, wie sie, seyn will und nicht
> Ungleiches dulden, der Schwärmer.
>
>   [For since
> The most blessed do not feel of their own accord,
> Another, if such a thing be right to say,
> Must feel in their name; they need that man.
> But their judgment is that he shall break
> His own house and curse like an enemy
> Those he most loves, and bury his father and child
> Under the rubble, if he wants to be like them [the gods]
> Denying unequal things, the enthusiast.][55]

We may well wonder what it means to feel vicariously. Compassion and empathy might be candidates for an answer, but can one feel these things for the gods? Could the Greeks do so? In "Der Rhein" Hölderlin seems to figure the poet's role by way of empathy, of passing from the inside to the outside, but in his essay on the ground of Empedocles, he says something quite different: "Precisely because he expresses the deepest inwardness, the tragic poet denies altogether his individuality, his subjectivity, and thus also the object present to him; he conveys them into a foreign personality, into a foreign objectivity."[56] Could it be that vicarious feeling "in the name of the gods" is true inwardness? That could at least be an understanding of what the θεωρός takes away from the festival.

We have seen that in "Wie Wenn am Feiertage . . ." Hölderlin is punished by the gods for seeking to be a priest, and that the figure of the priest is inappropriate to the poet. Not reading the fragmentary end of the hymn, Blanchot denies that there is a punishment for hubris, and focuses on the sacrifice of Hölderlin as poet. Thus in "La Folie par excellence" we read,

> We must say this once again: it is not excess that the gods punish in the man who becomes the mediator; it is not punishment for an offence that sanctions his ruin, but the poet must be ruined in order that in and through him the measureless excess of the divine might become measure, common measure; this destruction, moreover, this effacement at the heart of language is what makes language speak, and causes it to be the sign *par excellence*. "That which is without language, in him becomes language; that which is general and remains in the form of the unconscious, in him takes the form of the conscious and concrete, but that which is translated into words is for him what cannot possibly be stated (*Empedocles*)."[57]

Sacrifice, for Blanchot, is tragic but not punitive; the poet is ruined by having to render the measureless in measure, the ineffable in meter. If one thinks (for Hölderlin) of Kant on the aesthetic idea, one also thinks (for us) of Marion urging us to think of revelation, saturation to the second degree, being received in the mode of counter-experience.[58]

Above all, though, sacrifice for Blanchot is not redemptive. The poet is no priest and redeems nothing through his sacrifice, and even his authority as a poet is expiated in the writing of the poem. We are used to thinking of redemptive sacrifice rendering something sacred. Here, though, it is tragic sacrifice that brings about the sacred. The poet waits for dawn to break and makes himself available to receive what he cannot bear, and it is that "beginning, the origin," that is "the point where the Sacred communicates and founds itself in the firm resolve of language" (123). That Blanchot passes over the punishment for hubris may make us wonder if his theory of sacrifice is drawn from Hölderlin.

As early as one of his regular columns in *Journal des débats*, "Oeuvres poétiques" (1942), Blanchot had written,

> The poet, careful as he may be to use a technique for which his most conscious 'I' is necessary, tries to sacrifice [*tend à sacrifier*] that which constitutes the limit, boundary, pleasure without risk, consciousness of this 'I.' By putting into play his personal gifts, he proceeds to an existence in which this word *personal* no longer has any meaning. '*Je est un autre*' [I is an other], said Rimbaud.[59]

Not that Blanchot draws this theory of sacrifice from Rimbaud rather than Hölderlin. It is grounded, rather, in the speculations of Georges Bataille, specifically in his account of the nexus of communication and sacrifice, and was adapted by Blanchot as a general view, one that he had sufficiently made his own by the time he introduced *Faux pas* (1943): "The writer is summoned by his anguish to an actual sacrifice of himself" [*L'écrivain est appelé par son angoisse à un réel sacrifice de lui-même*] (5; 13). The theory of sacrifice that Blanchot ventures is articulated in terms of theories of contestation and communication.[60]

Let us interrupt Blanchot meditating on an aspect of Bataille's *L'Expérience intérieure* (1943): "Contestation, experience, communication are narrowly defined terms—to say no more. Contestation is the calling into question of a particular and limited being, and it is also, consequently, an effort to break this particularity and these limits . . . . Communication thus begins being authentic only when experience has stripped existence."[61] Communication, here, is neither verbal nor nonverbal; rather, it is fusion with what is, amounting to a loss of self, as in death, and—following Laure's speculations—is held to be sacred.[62] That Bataille's ideas were refined in conversation with Blanchot is evident from reading *L'Expérience intérieure*, where Bataille credits his friend with pointing out that in experience authority must expiate itself.[63] At any rate, for Blanchot we see that the poet, in trying to resolve an intolerable tension, sacrifices or—more accurately—*contests* himself in the writing of a poem. Whatever authority he has been given by the gods is expiated in the writing of the poem, and the poem communicates the holy without recourse to ὁ μῦθος. And so we have "sacred" speech in Hölderlin's poetry, a speech that is justified not by the poet's authority or his individual concerns but that stands outside all personality and all dialogue; it comes from the anteriority of the holy and points to a time to come in which the gods may reveal themselves, which means that it has no ground in the present.[64]

*

At the time of "La parole 'sacrée' de Hölderlin" (1946) Blanchot figures "sacred" speech solely by way of contestation and communication. If we move ahead, though, to *L'Espace littéraire* (1955) we hear him speaking in slightly different terms:

> When art is the language of the gods, when the temple is the house where the god dwells, the work is invisible and art unknown. The poem names the sacred, and men hear the sacred, not the poem. And yet the poem names the sacred as unnamable; in this silence it speaks the unspeakable . . . The poem shows, then; it discloses, but by concealing, because it detains in the dark that which can only be revealed in the light of darkness and keeps this mystery dark even in the light which the dark makes the first dawn of all. The poem is effaced before the sacred which it names; it is the silence that brings to the word the god that speaks in silence—but since the divine is unspeakable and ever speechless, the poem, through the silence of the god which it encloses in language, is also that which speaks as poem, and shows itself, as a work, at the same time that it remains hidden.[65]

In hearing Blanchot here we also overhear Heidegger, the thinker of "The Origin of the Work of Art" (1935) and of the "silent word," and we hear the word "sacred" pronounced without quotation marks because Blanchot is speaking of the Greeks, and not Hölderlin, of a world in which τὸ θεῖον is indexed to ὁ μῦθος. Notice that there is no talk of sacrifice here, only of the sacred. And yet, as we shall see, sacrifice has not dropped out of the picture altogether. Notice too that the sacred is not held in suspense anymore. If we ask ourselves what happens in the passage from "sacred" to "'sacred,'" we have only to read on for a few more pages for Blanchot to ask the same question in his own way:

> Why is art so intimately allied with the sacred? It is because in the relationship between art and the sacred, between that which shows itself and that which does not . . . the work finds the profound *reserve* which it needs . . . What will become of art, now that the gods and even their absence are gone, and now that man's presence offers no support? . . .. And where will art find, *elsewhere than in the divine, elsewhere than in the world* [ailleurs que dans le divin, ailleurs que dans le monde], the space [*l'espace*] in which to base and to withhold itself? (233; 310-11; my emphasis)

The answer, Blanchot tells us, is "the experience of the origin" (233; 311); this origin is the "elsewhere," yet to go there is not to encounter plenitude, the sudden communication of the dawn that is the Sacred as evoked in "La Folie par excellence." On the contrary, in *L'Espace littéraire*, art "indicates the menacing proximity of a vague and vacant outside, a neutral existence, nil and limitless; art points into a sordid absence, a suffocating condensation where being ceaselessly perpetuates itself as nothingness" (242-3; 326). The poet, in seeking the origin of the poem, grasps image rather than being, not as an accidental mistake but as a constitutive error of writing, for being gives itself in art only as image. Not *an* image, but *image*. Being and truth are withheld, and indeed the desired wholeness of the poem, if there was one to begin with, is shattered by the experience of vacancy rather than fullness.

When Blanchot turns to characterize this situation, he does so in terms taken directly from Hölderlin. "Do we have art?" Blanchot asks, and then responds to his own question:

> The poet is the one who, through his sacrifice, keeps the question open in his work. At every time he lives the time of distress, and his time is always the empty time when what he must live is the double infidelity: that of men, that of the gods—and also the double absence of the gods who are no longer *and* who are not yet. The poem's space is entirely represented by this *and*, which indicates the double absence, the separation at its most tragic instant. But as for whether it is the *and* that unites and binds together, the pure word in which the void of the past and the void of the future become true presence, the "now" of dawn—this question is reserved in the work. (247; 332)

These are difficult sentences, and they call for interpretation along two paths.

1. As we know, for Hölderlin the gods have turned away from mortals; it is a hard lesson he learns from Sophocles's tragedy *Oedipus Tyrannos*, namely the teaching of the caesura. In pain, we mortals must also turn away from the gods. "Nämlich es reichen / Die Sterblichen eh an den Abgrund," we are told in the second version of "Mnemosyne": "Namely the mortals / Reach the abyss in any case." Our touching of the abyss is a mimetic act of infidelity and is what Hölderlin calls the "categorical reversal." The poem abides in a double space, between mortals and gods, and between the old gods and the gods who may one day come. With respect to this first space Blanchot says, "Hölderlin maintains the purity of the sacred realm left empty by the double infidelity of men and gods. For the sacred is this very void, the sheer void of the interval which must be kept pure and empty according to the ultimate requirement 'Preserve God with the purity of what distinguishes'" (245 n. 7; 330 n. 1).[66] The Sacred then has passed from immediacy to interval, from the incommunicable allowing communication to take place to the holding apart and together of a space between gods and mortals, an interval that is *neutral* precisely because it is neither that of the gods nor mortals.

2. The poem's space, Blanchot tells us, is represented by the "and" between the gods who are no longer and the gods who are to come. Is this "the *and* that unites and binds together?" If so, this "and" would stand for "religion," which, as Blanchot tells us much later, in *L'Écriture du désastre* (1980), is, as his friend Levinas says, "that which binds, that which holds together."[67] Yet it is possible, he implies, that there is another relation than one that binds, a relation that would not be religious at all: "a non-bond which disjoins beyond unity—which escapes the synchrony of 'holding together,' yet does so without breaking all relations or without ceasing, in this break or in this absence of relation, to open yet another relation" (64). If this is so, the sacrifice of the poet in the writing of a poem, the "most tragic instant," would open a space that is sacred but not religious, and the sacred for us (though not for the Greeks) would be indexed to the third relation. Would an artist be able to draw on this sense of what remains of the sacred, rather than on religion (even a religion of art), in order to make art? That

is exactly the question that Blanchot poses, and the question, he thinks, that abides in the artwork itself. Whether a Romantic or post-Romantic poem can be art, as Pindar's odes are art, turns on the question of the sacred being posed in it, and doubtless not being fully answered by the poem itself. Art for us is not the Jena "literary absolute" in which philosophy is tucked into literature but is rather the question of the sacred that is posed in all rigor but that awaits an answer.[68]

Blanchot's affirmation of the sacred in Hölderlin, centered on tragic sacrifice, makes no reference to the role that Christ plays in the poetry. "Hölderlin's Christology will not be found where those who squeeze the text look for it; perceivable only as a water-mark, it is dissolved throughout the existential statement as a whole, and can be most powerfully felt when directly contradicted by the framework inside which it is stretched."[69] Such is von Balthasar's assessment, and it is entirely correct. To be sure, Hölderlin is no orthodox Christian: he incorporates the revelation of the Christ into the Greek theophanies that preoccupy him. In "Der Einzige" he calls Christ "Mein Meister und Herr!" ["My Master and Lord"] and "mein Lehrer!" ["my Teacher!"]; but in the end Christ remains "Der Halbgott" ["the demigod"], as Hölderlin says in "Patmos." How could one not ascribe Arianism to him? For Marion, to be sure, there are richer though more elusive Christian resources in Hölderlin's poems. It is in the default of the divine, the Frenchman thinks, that we find the very question of how God manifests himself. That manifestation turns on distance: the Father must withdraw for us to see Him in and through the incarnation of Christ. We read Hölderlin well, Marion thinks, when we see in his poems that "withdrawal" is "the most radical mode of presence for God."[70] One may or may not agree with Marion. Yet it is plain that Blanchot bypasses "Der Einzige," "In Lieblicher Bläue . . . ," and "Patmos" and the other poems on which Marion draws to make his case.

The poet's sacrifice, for Blanchot, is his act of holding himself between mortals and gods, between the old gods and the new gods, maintaining "the extreme limit of suffering."[71] We have art if we can draw upon the Sacred, but we do not have the "now," the immediate that is the Sacred, only the neutral space that the poet's tragic sacrifice *renders* sacred. Is this sufficient for art? Or do we need the sacred to be looped into religion in order to have art? We do not know. Of course, if we reflect on what Blanchot has said about the Outside and wish to assimilate it to the neutral space of the Sacred, we have a problem, for the language about the one ("sordid absence," "suffocating condensation") does not square with the language about the other ("purity"). And yet the "experience of the origin," which generates the dark language about the Outside, seems to be Blanchot's answer to the pressing question as to the relation between art and the sacred. The "elsewhere" he seeks is the origin of the poem. No satisfactory solution is possible in the terms offered in *L'Espace littéraire*, and so we must pass to Blanchot's last discussion of Hölderlin in *L'Entretien infini*. That occurs in "Le Grand Refus," Blanchot's long and patient engagement with the poet Yves Bonnefoy who, like Hölderlin, but in a completely different manner, prizes the relation of poetry and the "now" in his early essays gathered in *L'Improbable* (1959) and throughout his poetry, beginning with *Du mouvement et de l'immobilité de Douve* (1953).

There can be no dialectical rethinking of immediacy, Blanchot insists, nor can it be thought by way of mystical fusion. He accepts Hölderlin's statement that "*the immediate is for mortals as well as for immortals, strictly speaking, impossible*," and responds by saying that, if this is so, "it is perhaps because impossibility—a relation escaping power—is the form of relation with the immediate."[72] Here we find Blanchot shifting the center of gravity of Hölderlin's statement, seeking to make the immediate (and hence the Sacred) into what he calls "the third relation" or "the neutral relation." The only relation one can have with the Outside is neutral; but how can we discover this obscure region, when it is beyond the realm of phenomena? There is an attunement to it, Blanchot suggests, and that is suffering, "The present of suffering is the abyss of the present, indefinitely hollowed out and in this hollowing indefinitely distended, radically alien to the possibility that one might be present to it through the mastery of presence" (44; 63). In suffering, "we are delivered over to another time—to time as other, as absence and neutrality; precisely to a time that can no longer redeem us, that constitutes no recourse" (44; 63). If the poet sacrifices himself or herself, it is the suffering that comes of this act that leads him or her to the Outside and that stalls one there in fascination, in relation with "the *ungraspable that one cannot let go of*" (45; 65), that is, being passing endlessly into image. Immediate presence, then, is "presence as Outside" (46; 66) or, as he glosses the statement (revolving and even reversing "presence" in order by his lights to be more precise), presence as "a neutral, an empty or an infinite presence" so that "The immediate as non-presence, that is to say, the immediately *other*" (440 n. 7; 66 n. 2). Of course, suffering is not the preserve of the poets; and so anyone can pass from the phenomenal world to the non-world of the Outside, and so "discover the obscure." Yet we cannot name this obscurity; we can only respond to it. The self-sacrifice of the poet can be saved only if his or her sacrifice, his or her response to the Outside, is regarded as exemplary. The writing of poetry is a model of experience as such.

What remains of the Sacred exists without religion, Blanchot thinks, and it breaks up the unity and wholeness that religion has traditionally offered. Blanchot's Hölderlin has no Christian moment, as we may well have surmised; he has no religious moment, either. Sacrifice for him is entirely tragic which, for Blanchot, means that it is endless contestation with no redemption in play, a contestation that shatters the manifold of profiles that give us the unity of "Hölderlin." Heidegger's Hölderlin is the θεωρός of Being. Blanchot's Hölderlin is the θεωρός of the Outside.

Notes

1 See Geoffrey Hill, "Little Apocalypse: Hölderlin: 1770–1843," in *Selected Poems* (London: Penguin, 2006), 18. The impress of Hölderlin on Hill goes far beyond this short lyric, needless to say. Also see Gustaf Sobin, *Collected Poems*, ed. Esther Sobin et al., intro. Andrew Joron and Andrew Zawacki (Greenfield, MA: Talisman House, 2010). John Ashbery's ways of drawing on and displacing Hölderlin in some of his poems have not yet been detailed. Two poems in particular that could be approached with Hölderlin in mind are "Evening in the Country," in *The Double Dream of Spring* (New York: Ecco Press, 1976), 33–4, and "Poem at the New Year," in *Hotel Lautréamont* (New York: Alfred A. Knopf, 1992), 83.

2. On the relation of Hölderlin to Kant, less well known than the other philosophical relations, see Jean-Luc Nancy, "Hyperion's Joy," in trans. Christine Laennec and Michael Syrotinski, *The Birth to Presence*, trans. Brian Holmes et al. (Stanford, CA: Stanford University Press, 1993), 58–81.
3. Blanchot, "The 'Sacred' Speech of Hölderlin," *WF*, 114 (118). Also see, "Note," *IC*, xi (vi).
4. See Hans Urs von Balthasar, *The Glory of the Lord: A Theological Aesthetics*, 7 vols., vol. 5: *The Realm of Metaphysics in the Modern Age*, trans. Oliver Davies et al. (Edinburgh: T. and T. Clark, 1991), 298–338, and Jean-Luc Marion, *The Idol and Distance: Five Studies*, trans, and intro. Thomas A. Carlson (New York: Fordham University Press, 2001), §§ 8–12.
5. Blanchot observes, "We carry on about atheism, which has always been a privileged way of talking about God," which may be true of some atheists, but the atheism that he affirms is not merely a denial of theism. See his *WD*, 92 (145).
6. For a study that reads Hölderlin in this way, see Martin F. A. Simon, *Friedrich Hölderlin, The Theory and Practice of Religious Poetry: Studies in the Elegies* (Stuttgart: Hans-Dieter Heniz, Akademischer Verlag Stuttgart, 1988).
7. Needless to say, various distinctions may be drawn between "sacred" and "holy" but to impose any one of them here would skew the poems under consideration.
8. Blanchot, *IC*, xii (vii).
9. Blanchot, "The 'Sacred' Speech of Hölderlin," 119 (122).
10. See Blanchot, *SL*, 237–9 (318–21).
11. See Heidegger, "On the Essence of Truth," *Pathmarks*, ed. William McNeill (Cambridge: Cambridge University Press, 1998), 150–2. Also see his *Introduction to Metaphysics*, trans. Ralph Manheim (New Haven: Yale University Press, 1959), 92.
12. Blanchot, *SL*, 237 (318).
13. Blanchot's text is a review essay that refers to four pieces in *Fontaine*, 54 (1946): Hölderlin's "Tel qu'en un jour de fête," trans. Joseph Rivan, 199–205, Heidegger's "L'hymne 'Tel qu'en un jour de fête,'" trans. Joseph Rivan, 206–35, Hölderlin, "Dix letters," trans. Denise Naville, 256–9, and Rainer Maria Rilke, *À Hölderlin*, trans. Jean Wahl, 260–2.
14. See Blanchot, "Le Tournant," *Nouvelle Nouvelle Revue Française* 25 (1955): 110–20, and "Hölderlin's Itinerary," *SL*, 274–6 (371–4).
15. See, for example, Blanchot, "Hölderlin," *L'Observateur* 17, 3 août 1950, 19.
16. See the first chapter of this volume.
17. See Blanchot, "The Pure Novel," *WR*, 261–8 (*CL*, 506–13).
18. It should be noted that Blanchot had attempted to translate some of St. John of the Cross's verse into French. See *C*, 70.
19. Blanchot, "The Silence of Mallarmé," *FP*, 101, 104 (120, 123).
20. See Thomas Aquinas, *Summa theologiæ*, 1a, q. 13 art. 7, c; 1a, q. 28, art. 1, ad 3; 1a, q. 45 art. 3, *On the Power of God*, trans. Lawrence Shapcote (1932; rpt. Eugene, OR: Wipf and Stock, 2004), 1, q. iii, iii, and *Truth*, 3 vols., trans. Robert W. Mulligan (1954; rpt. Indianapolis, IN: Hackett Publishing Co., 1994), 1, q. 4 art. 5, *responsio*.
21. All quotations from Hölderlin are taken from *Sämtliche Werke*, ed. Friedrich Beissner, 15 vols. (Stuttgart: W. Kohlhammer Verlag, 1952). For another English translation, see Michael Hamburger, trans., *Friedrich Hölderlin: Poems and Fragments* (London: Anvil Press, 1994), 401.

22 See Blanchot, "Prophetic Speech," *BC*, 79–85 (109–19). Also see "The Beast of Lascaux," *VE*, 41 (57).
23 Hölderlin, *Hyperion or The Hermit in Greece*, trans. Ross Benjamin (Brooklyn: Archipelago Books, 2008), 12.
24 See Blanchot, "Hölderlin's Itinerary," *SL*, 269 (363).
25 Heidegger, "Hölderlin and the Essence of Poetry," in *Elucidations of Hölderlin's Poetry*, trans. Keith Hoeller (New York: Humanities Books, 2000), 61. For other French translations of the poet, see Hölderlin, *Oeuvres*, trans. Philippe Jaccottet (Paris: Gallimard, 1967).
26 For another English translation, see Hamburger, *Friedrich Hölderlin*, 395.
27 See Heidegger, "As on a Holiday . . .," *Elucidations of Hölderlin's Poetry*, 85, 90, 94. Note that Heidegger observes, "that the holy is entrusted to a mediation by the god and the poets, and is born in song, threatens to invert the essence of the holy into its opposite. The immediate thus becomes something mediated," 94. Blanchot does not cite the second sentence. See "The 'Sacred' Speech of Hölderlin," 120 (123).
28 On this theme, see Robert Sokolowski, *The God of Faith and Reason: Foundations of Christian Theology*, 2nd ed. (Washington, DC: Catholic University of America Press, 1995), esp. ch. 2.
29 See Heidegger, "Remembrance," *Elucidations of Hölderlin's Poetry*, 126–8.
30 See Andrea Wilson Nightingale, *Spectacles of Truth in Classical Greek Philosophy: "Theoria" in its Cultural Context* (Cambridge: Cambridge University Press, 2004), ch. 2.
31 See Gregory Nagy, "Early Greek Views of Poets and Poetry," *The Cambridge History of Literary Criticism*, 9 vols., vol. 1: *Classical Criticism*, ed. George A. Kennedy (Cambridge: Cambridge University Press, 1989), 28.
32 On the motif of waiting, see Heidegger, *Hölderlin's Hymn "The Ister,"* trans. William McNeill and Julia Davis (Bloomington, IN: Indiana University Press, 1996), 55.
33 See Heidegger, *Plato's "Sophist,"* trans. Richard Rojcewicz and André Schuwer (Bloomington, IN: Indiana University Press, 1997), 44. Also see *Parmenides*, 147.
34 Hölderlin, "On Religion," in *Essays and Letters on Theory*, ed. Thomas Pfau (Albany, NY: State University of New York Press, 1988), 92.
35 Paul de Man, "Heidegger's Exegeses of Hölderlin," in *Blindness and Insight: Essays in the Rhetoric of Contemporary Criticism*, 2nd ed. rev. (London: Methuen, 1983), 253.
36 Heidegger, *Parmenides*, trans. Richard Rojcewicz and André Schuwer (Bloomington, IN: Indiana University Press, 1992), 114.
37 G. S. Kirk and J. E. Raven, *The Presocratic Philosophers: A Critical History with a Selection of Texts* (Cambridge: Cambridge University Press, 1962), 211. Also see Blanchot, *IC*, 31 (44).
38 Octavio Paz, "Recapitulations," in *Alternating Current*, trans. Helen R. Lane (London: Wildwood House, 1974), 69.
39 See T. S. Eliot, "The Social Function of Poetry," in *The Complete Prose of T. S. Eliot: The Critical Edition*, gen. ed. Ronald Schuchard, 7 vols., vol. 6: *The War Years* (London: Faber and Faber / Baltimore: The Johns Hopkins University Press, 2021), 639–52, and Karl Rahner, "Poetry and the Christian," in *Theological Investigations*, 23 vols., vol. 4: *More Recent Writings*, trans. Kevin Smyth (London: Darton, Longman and Todd, 1974), 357–67.
40 For another English translation, see Hamburger, *Friedrich Hölderlin*, 399.
41 On this neglected aspect of the poem, see Jennifer Anna Gosetti-Ferencei, *Heidegger, Hölderlin, and the Subject of Poetic Language: Toward a New Poetics of Dasein* (New York: Fordham University Press, 2004), 101–2.

42 For another English translation, see *The Death of Empedocles: A Mourning Play*, trans. and intro. and notes David Farrell Krell (Albany, NY: State University of New York Press, 2008), 45.
43 For another English translation, see Hamburger, *Friedrich Hölderlin*, 399.
44 Hölderlin, "Remarks on 'Oedipus,'" *Essays and Letters on Theory*, 102. Also see on this point Philippe Lacoue-Labarthe, "The Caesura of the Speculative," in *Typography: Mimesis, Philosophy, Politics*, ed. Christopher Fynsk and intro. Jacques Derrida (Cambridge, MA: Harvard University Press, 1989), 233.
45 For another English translation, see Hamburger, *Friedrich Hölderlin*, 271.
46 The draft of the poem follows Hölderlin's manuscript translation of the opening of *The Bacchæ*. See David Constantine, *Hölderlin* (Oxford: Clarendon Press, 1988), 119.
47 Hölderlin, *Sämtliche Werke*, vol. 5, 41.
48 David Grene and Richard Lattimore, eds., "The Bacchæ," in *The Complete Greek Tragedies*, 9 vols., *Euripides 5* (Chicago: The University of Chicago Press, 1959), 155.
49 Ovid, *Metamophoses*, trans. Arthur Golding, ed. Madeleine Forey (London: Penguin, 2001), Book 3, *ll*. 387–9.
50 Heidegger, "On the Essence and Concept of φύσις," *Pathmarks*, 184.
51 F. W. J. Schelling, "Philosophical Letters on Dogmatism and Criticism," *The Unconditional in Human Knowledge: Four Early Essays, 1794–1796*. trans. Fritz Marti (Lewisburg, PA: Bucknell University Press, 1980), 193.
52 Constantine, trans., "Notes to *Antigone*," in *Hölderlin's Sophocles: Oedipus and Antigone* (Highgreen, Tarset: Bloodaxe Books, 2001), 116.
53 Hölderlin, *Essays and Letters on Theory*, 150, 152. For the idea that the sacrifice is national, a view that goes back to Friedrich Wolters, see Joseph Suglia, *Hölderlin and Blanchot on Self-Sacrifice* (New York: Peter Lang, 2004), 51.
54 See Hölderlin, "Becoming in Dissolution," *Essays and Letters on Theory*, 98.
55 For another English translation, see Hamburger, *Friedrich Hölderlin*, 436–7.
56 Hölderlin, "The Ground for 'Empedocles,'" *Essays and Letters on Theory*, 52.
57 Blanchot, "Madness *par excellence*," trans. Ann Smock, *BR*, 124.
58 See Immanuel Kant, *Critique of Judgement*, trans. James Creed Meredith (Oxford: Oxford University Press, 1969), 175–6, and Marion, *Being Given: Toward a Phenomenology of Givenness*, trans. Jeffrey L. Kosky (Stanford, CA: Stanford University Press, 2002), 215–16. For more detail on revelation, see Marion, *D'ailleurs, la révélation* (Paris: Grasset, 2020).
59 Blanchot, "Involuntary Poetry," *FP*, 133 (155). The passage in question first appeared in "Oeuvres poétiques," *Journal des débats*, 9 décembre 1942, 3.
60 Bataille's understanding of sacrifice was developed over several decades. A signal text is the well-known essay "Hegel, la mort et le sacrifice," (1955) *Oeuvres complètes*, 12 vols. (Paris: Gallimard, 1970–88), vol. 12, 326–45, but the theme of sacrifice is announced as early as "Sacrifices" (1936), the text that accompanies artwork by André Masson. See *Oeuvres complètes*, vol. 1, 87–96.
61 Blanchot, "Inner Experience," *FP*, 40 (51). Trans. modified.
62 See Jeanine Herman, trans., *Laure: The Collected Writings* (San Francisco, CA: City Lights Books, 1995), 37–94.
63 See Georges Bataille, *Inner Experience*, trans. and intro. Leslie Anne Boldt (Albany: State University of New York Press, 1988), 53.
64 Blanchot speaks of René Char in the same terms. See his "The Beast of Lascaux," *VE*, 41–42 (57–8).
65 Blanchot, *SL*, 230 (307).

66 Also see Blanchot, *SL*, 272 (368).
67 Blanchot, *WD*, 64 (106).
68 See Blanchot, "The Athenaeum," *IC*, 351–9 (515–27), and Philippe Lacoue-Labarthe and Jean-Luc Nancy, *The Literary Absolute*.
69 Balthasar, *The Glory of the Lord*, 5, 320.
70 Marion, *The Idol and Distance*, 89.
71 Blanchot, *SL*, 274 (371).
72 Blanchot, "The Great Refusal," *IC*, 38 (54).

3

Blanchot's Char

In 1953, one of his *anni mirabiles* for critical writing, Blanchot turns to René Char on two occasions, each time making a very large claim for his significance.[1] In the April of that year in "La Bête de Lascaux" he heralds him as "a poet linked with our destiny," and two months later in "Où va la littérature?" he is deemed to be, like Hölderlin, "Poet of the poet, poet in whom the possibility, or impossibility, of singing is made song." Char's poetry "answers" the German's poetry over a century later, we are told, and in this contemporary Frenchman's writing we find "a form of experienced time [*durée*] very different from the time that simple historical analysis grasps."[2] On the first occasion Char is allied with Heraclitus, and his poetry is approached by way of the *Phaedrus*, while on the second occasion he is introduced with reference to Heidegger's elucidations of Hölderlin. The poetry is bookended by major philosophers at the dawn and evening of the West. Blanchot will value other French poets over the course of his long life, including Yves Bonnefoy and Louis-René des Forêts, but among his contemporaries Char will always have a privileged place, and not for purely literary or literary-historical reasons.[3]

Nowhere in "La Bête de Lascaux," for instance, does Blanchot turn an appeal to the "primitive" art of the cave, which had been open to the public since 1948, into a case for Char as an exemplary modernist poet.[4] Char's collaborations with Braque, Kandinsky, Klee, Matisse, Miró, and Picasso, now all secure figures in the canon of modernist visual art, are nowhere mentioned.[5] At no time does he point to Char's schooling in surrealism, a movement he greatly prizes, as a prime credential for his standing in the pantheon of the avant-garde or as a representative of what we would tend to call these days "late modernism."[6] And he never dilates on formal concerns in Char's poetry—his lack of interest in *la facture des vers françois* as prized by the Parnassians, his taste for *vers libre* and the prose poem (and even short prose texts), and so on—as distancing him from symbolism, *l'art pour l'art*, and other literary movements that preceded him.[7] Rather, Blanchot figures Char by way of the philosophical, ancient and modern, the political, and with reference to the sacred.

Blanchot's reading of Char takes place in a context far broader than literary history, indeed far more capacious than literature, a category he will increasingly distrust, and wider even than history, which he regards Char's poetry as puncturing so as to indicate something neither truly ancient nor truly modern, a ceaseless hollowing of being as it becomes image in the act of writing, which he will name "the Outside" [*le Dehors*].[8] I note again that Blanchot does not say "an image"; he has no commitment to imagism, unlike modernists such as Eliot and Pound in their first maturities, but is concerned with image as the state in which beings seem to disappear when captured by art, a borderless realm that fascinates us. "Our destiny," if we are mid-century French speakers, is to follow Char so that we may experience the approach of the Outside and thereby overcome any mistaken commitments to "being" or "unity" that we may hold. More than this is in play, as will become evident, but for now let us see how this is thought to happen.

*

Blanchot prefaces "La Bête de Lascaux" with a central lyric from the sequence of the same name, "La Bête innommable." What appears to Char in the figure of the so-called unicorn in Lascaux is a "mother fantastically disguised/ Wisdom, eyes full of tears." Yet what first appears to Blanchot in reading Char's lyric poem is a particular sort of speech, one that is impersonal, which Socrates identifies in the *Phaedrus*.

A written speech merely offers "the appearance of wisdom [δοξόσοφοι], not true wisdom [σοφίας]," Socrates insists, because it allows people to recite compositions by others and so seem "to know many things, when they are for the most part ignorant and hard to get along with, since they are not wise but only appear wise."[9] So writing can readily be abused, especially by Sophists, and can impair one's ability to learn. When used properly, as Socrates urges in a story about the invention of writing by Theuth in Thebes, Upper Egypt, it serves to remind oneself of something, not to replace memory (*Phaedrus*, 275a). It remains an external prompt, not an internal process. Truth itself turns on what is written in the soul of the learner, which knows to whom it should speak and to whom it should not speak (276a–b). Blanchot also tells us that Socrates "rejects no less forcefully—but with more reverence—another impersonal language, the pure speech that seeks to articulate the sacred" (37; 52). "Prophetic utterances" came from the oak at Dodona, Socrates says; it is the oldest of Greek oracles. He then observes to Phaedrus of those who went to listen to it: "The people of that time, not being as wise [σοφοῖς] as you young folks, were content in their simplicity [εὐηθεία: 'foolishness'], to hear an oak or a rock, providing only that it spoke the truth; but to you, perhaps, it makes a difference who the speaker is and where he comes from, for you do not consider only whether his words are true" (275 b–c). And Phaedrus, who had cast doubt on the authenticity of Socrates's story of the invention of writing, now agrees with Socrates about the dangers of written speech. He also accepts the rebuke: if something is true, it is true regardless of who says it.

Of course, Socrates is being ironic when he says that Phaedrus and his friends are "wise" and that their forebears enjoyed a state of "simplicity." Léon Robin's translation from the Greek, on which Blanchot relies, has Socrates say, "You others, you moderns [*les modernes*], want to know who it is who is speaking and what country he comes from."[10] More important, though, is that Blanchot misunderstands Socrates almost entirely. As he reads the lines, Socrates says, "We are no longer... the kind of people who are content to listen to the voice of the oak or the stone [*Nous ne sommes plus... de ceux qui se contentaient d'écouter la voix du chêne ou celle d'une pierre*]," and infers from this reading that "everything that is said against writing would serve, as well, to discredit the recited speech of the hymn [*l'hymne*]" (37). Yet Socrates is not contrasting the modernity of Athens with the primitive belief in the oracle that one finds in Homer and perhaps long before him. Nor is he saying anything about religious hymns, presumably the Homeric hymns to the gods or something like them.[11] Hymns might have been recited at religious ceremonies at Dodona, but for Socrates the place is important for the oracles uttered there in response to bronze tripods hanging from branches of the oak tree (and so murmuring when the wind caresses the tree). Instead, Socrates is doing two things. First, as we have seen, he is saying that truth is truth, no matter where it comes from and no matter who declares it. And second, he is obliquely recalling that the priestesses in a state of ecstasy orally communicate the truths of the god.[12] The allusion to Dodona and not to a mystery cult such as the one at Eleusis probably goes by way of the story, preserved by Herodotus, that the priestesses there were originally from Thebes in Upper Egypt.[13]

Char feels kinship with Heraclitus, Blanchot recalls, and the final lines of "La Bête innommable" might remind us that he was known in antiquity as the weeping philosopher. The association with Heraclitus allows Blanchot to pass to Fragment B 93: "The Lord whose oracle is in Delphi [not Dodona, note] neither indicates clearly nor conceals but gives a sign" [ὁ ἄναξ οὗ τὸ μαντεῖόν ἐστι τὸ ἐν Δελφοῖς οὔτε λέγει οὔτε κρύπτει ἀλλὰ σημαίνει].[14] Socrates desires language to be human and dialogic, not to come from an unknown origin, which is precisely what oracular language is. There are times, especially in *L'Entretien infini*, when Blanchot will insist on a more radical dialogue between human beings than one finds in Socrates, and will value Char's commitment to fragmentary writing, but here, as in his earlier piece on the poet, he gravitates to oracular speech, which he will use to give substance to the claim that Char's verse is "linked with our destiny."[15] The oracular utterances at Dodona were not hymns; they were mostly replies in the positive or negative to questions written on a tablet, and consequently not quite the same as the famously ambiguous oracles at Delphi. In freely associating Dodona and Delphi, Blanchot pushes what we know of Dodona further than is warranted: "Voice of the oak, rigorous and closed language of aphorism [*aphorisme*]. . ." (51). Thus, oracle converges on aphorism, doubtless by way of Heraclitus's dark fragments. (Yet we remember Char telling us in *Seuls demeurent* (1938–44) "The oracle no longer has me as its vassal" and wonder what the status of the remark would be for Blanchot.[16])

To be sure, some of Char's poetry is intensely aphoristic—we think of "Afin qu'il n'y soit rien changé," "Partage formel," *Feuillets d'Hypnos* and "Rougeur des martinaux," and, well after the appearance of "La Bête de Lascaux," *L'Âge cassant* (1965)—and individual sentences in lyrics and prose poems alike are also angular, incisive, and have the air of the absolute. Yet Char's remarks have no kinship with aphorisms, epigrams, or maxims that state moral principles or that sparkle with pithy social wit, as one finds in La Rouchefoucauld and Chamfort. The connection between oracle and aphorism allows Blanchot to comment on the two at one and the same time. He does so by way of an unusual understanding of "prophet" [προφήτης]:

> The language in which the origin speaks is essentially prophetic. That does not mean that it dictates future events [*les événements futurs*]; it means that it does

not rely on something that already exists—neither on an already accepted truth nor on a language that has already been spoken or verified. It announces, because it begins. It indicates the future [*l'avenir*], because it does not yet speak: language of the future [*du futur*], insofar as it, itself, is already like a future language [*un langage futur*], which anticipates itself, finding its meaning and legitimacy only ahead of itself, that is to say fundamentally unjustified. (41-42)

Prophetic language, in this sense, will remain important to Blanchot. Four years later, with André Neher's *L'Essence du prophétisme* (1955) in mind, he will consecrate an essay to its role in Judaism and will comment on its dialogic structure.[17] God speaks to the prophet who then speaks imperiously to the people or a king.[18] One might well think that the same is true in Greek religion: the god speaks to a priestess who then delivers an oracle. Yet Blanchot insists instead on the oracle's grounding in an unknown origin, a murmuring of the sacred tree, and relates it to the "closed language of aphorism" (51; 67). When responding to prophecy in Judaism, and unmooring it from positive revelation, Blanchot cites Rimbaud and Claudel; when speaking of Dodona, and bracketing belief in the Olympian deities, he invokes Char and retains talk of oracles. For all these poets, no doubt, "the chance of the poem is to be able to escape prophetic intolerance" (46; 62). How that chance is concretely played out in the three poets is left unclear, but it is claimed that it occurs in an exemplary manner with Char.

Prophetic speech presumes nothing, Blanchot thinks; it speaks from a space it opens by itself and that can thereafter be occupied by other speech. As soon as Blanchot begins to clarify this oracular speech, however, he quietly starts to view Greece through a specific German lens. He evokes "the most tender break of day in which all the violence of a first clarity is declared" (46; 61-2), and if we know our Blanchot, we think inevitably of Hölderlin's "Wie wenn am Feiertage. . . , " as discussed in the previous chapter. The relevant lines read, "Jezt aber tagts! Ich harrt und sah es kommen, /Und was ich sah, das Heilige sei mein Wort."[19] In "Le Grand Refus" (1959) Blanchot takes Hölderlin to be wishing that his speech be holy. It is not holy now—it does not offer itself as the transcription of a private revelation, say—but it opens a space in which the holy may be witnessed. As we are told earlier, this prophetic speech says nothing at all, but in a sovereign gesture, "makes this silence into the finger imperiously pointing toward the unknown" (46; 62).

Can modern poetry resemble oracular speech? It is written, of course, and therefore silent until read aloud. But can it indicate the unknown? Marina Tsvetaeva witnesses that some poetry, Pasternak's, opens a new future. "For in reality he isn't yet," she writes: "a babbling, a chirping, a clashing—he is all Tomorrow!—the choking cry of a baby, and this baby is the World."[20] Yet Char's poetry, for Blanchot, is not merely originating fresh literary possibilities in this world but is orienting us to the sacred (or, perhaps better, something that mimes the sacred). And here, for Blanchot, the sacred is not that which calls for veneration or worship; it has no power to redeem us; it has nothing to do with Magdalenian rites in the cave; and it is not quite *mysterium tremendum et fascinans*. It is not the "holy night" of Hölderlin's "Brot und Wein" but the spectral "*other* night" in which absence appears.[21] It does not transcend the world but attracts us from an imaginary point that the world covers over (including "world" as the thesis of the natural attitude). Nonetheless, it is unknown in a highly particular sense of the word. It is not simply the future, which is not yet known but will be known one day. Nor is it the sense familiar to us in Descartes, namely of those things that exceed the capacity of the human mind but that, because of our limits, give us a negative certainty of them.[22] It exercises no power.[23] Rather, it is that which the known and the ordered have long hidden.

Is this how Char sees things? In part, yes. "How can we live without the unknown in front of us," he asks in the "Argument" of *Le Poème pulvérizé* (1945–7). The poetry to be written after the war will reject Parnassian perfection and surrealist freedom equally; it will not celebrate the deeds of the *maquis*; it will be a new poetry, without a literary model, yet one that remains answerable to the world he sees and feels. The "Argument" ends, "*Born from the call of becoming and from the anguish of retention, the poem, rising from its well of mud and stars, testifies, almost silently, that there was nothing in it which did not really exis*t [qu'il n'était rien en lui qui n'existât], *in this rebellious and solitary world of contradictions*."[24] A poem consists of worldly things, Char thinks, but not the ordered world of the κόσμος. Yet when Blanchot reads it, admiring its "furious ascension," it conjures the Heraclitean, primal Chaos, which precedes order.[25]

Blanchot relies on the Platonic interpretation of Heraclitus developed in *Theatetus* 152a–160e. The obscure philosopher of Ephesus can be read, perhaps more strongly, as a thinker of the deep unity of opposites, not primal flux; and in his poetry Char is sympathetic to this reading, as is apparent in his talk of "les loyaux adversaires" in *Fureur et Mystère*, which undergirds the imagery of hunter and hunted, man and woman, which runs throughout his writing. A more appropriate figure, given Blanchot's design, would be Cratylus who, according to Aristotle, was so committed to the idea that everything flows [πάντα ῥεῖ] that he "ended by thinking that one need not say anything, and only moved his finger."[26] That said, Blanchot follows Char very closely, right down to alluding to *Le Poème pulvérizé* in the context of his poetry as a whole. "This work has the force of the impersonal, but it is to the faithfulness of a unique destiny that it summons us, a tense but patient work, tempestuous and still, energetic, concentrated in on itself, in the explosive brevity of the instant, a power of image and affirmation that 'pulverizes' the poem and yet keeps the slowness, the continuity, and the understanding of the uninterrupted" (47; 63).

Three things need to be brought to the surface here:

1. For Blanchot, as for Bataille, the sacred is consequent on sacrifice: in the act of writing Char yields his empirical "je," and so, in a way, exposes himself to death, in order to let the sacred announce itself through him. "For isn't the writer dead as soon as the work exists?" he asks rhetorically in "La Solitude essentielle" (1953), then adds that after writing the author has "an impression of being ever so strangely out of work" [*l'impression d'un désœuvrement des plus étranges*].[27] These remarks, and many others like them, serve to remind us that Blanchot tends to draw distinctions in an extreme manner, and that he frequently overdramatizes his main insights. Put less theatrically, the act of writing produces a poem, and the poem is itself and not the presence of the author or even a representation of what he actually thinks or feels: one ends up saying things in a

poem of which one had not been conscious before it was composed. One begins writing as a "je" and is deflected into an "il," and this would be the case even if one were writing a narrative or a dramatic monologue: who the pronoun stands for does not matter. (Husserl would say that the sense of dislocation of self occurs because of awakenings brought about by way of passive genesis in the very act of writing.[28] And if we follow him, we have no reason to distinguish the "je" and the "il" quite so sharply.) If the emphasis on art and being derives from Heidegger, the insistence on sacrifice harkens back to Henri Hubert and Marcel Mauss; and the elaboration of the theory, quite unlike anything one finds in Anglophone literary modernism, goes by way of Greece, specifically the figure of Orpheus.[29]

2. This self-sacrificial act turns on a particular construal of the creative act, which Blanchot reprises later in the essay. "The work," he says, is "the struggling intimacy of irreconcilable and inseparable moments," which he calls "communication." This sense of communication is an unusual and complex one; it is reached by linking Heidegger and Laure, and it cuts its figure against the ordinary use of the word: the felicitous transmission of linguistic statements.[30] Instead, it is an attempt to reach beyond death to the sacred, which occurs in risking the apparently solid "je" in writing. The sacred, in this sense, is what Bataille (perhaps looking back to Rimbaud) calls "*the impossible,*" since it exceeds our realm of possible experience. It goes without saying that we have no reason to think that Char would completely agree with Bataille on this point. Certainly, he uses the same language, but at least in his later writings the sense is quite different: "The impossible, we never reach it, but it serves us as lantern."[31] With regards to *Le Poème pulvérisé*, Char says (specifically of composing "J'habite une douleur"), "I seized my head as one takes a chunk of salt and literally pulverized it."[32] What Blanchot sees as occurring in the poem, Char figures as having taken place mentally.

At any rate, Blanchot adapts Bataille's idea in thinking of a particular moment in literary composition. In the act of writing there is a moment when the "je" is establishing the work in hand yet is, at the same time, being shadowed by the "il"; it is a time in which the "je" asserts its power to create, as though from nothing, and the creation itself, in coming into being, renders the writer increasingly powerless. This is communication, understood as the struggle between "the measure of the work that established a certain power and the measurelessness or excess of the work that strives toward impossibility."[33] (Char puts the same thing more memorably in "Impressions anciennes" when he says, simply, "To create: to exclude oneself" and also in "À la santé du serpent" when, I take it, he addresses the poem he is writing: "My love, it hardly matters that I have been born: you become visible just where I vanish.")[34] It is worth taking a moment to step back and explicate Blanchot's overly condensed expression.

In writing, Blanchot maintains, Char loses his empirical "je" but rather than dying produces a poem in which, *stricto sensu*, no living person speaks. It is not being that "speaks" in it but the Outside that murmurs just beneath, as it were, what we conventionally take to be the author's voice, this author who is born only in and through the poem. This murmur is the neutral "il" that has vanquished the authorial "je," and it is called a murmur and not a voice because what has been written turns on primary and secondary passive syntheses made in language: it seems as though one's consciousness is speaking without reference to oneself.[35] The "experience" in play is not anything represented by an aphorism, a number of verses, or several lines of a prose poem; instead, the poem is itself experience, a passage for the author from one state to another, from "je" to "il," and an exposure to peril. There is a formal issue also in play, for the struggle is between a poem's drive toward a definite form, and the limitlessness from which it draws: the realm of image, which of course has no borders, in which sensuous or abstract being is hollowed out. If a poet retains mastery over his or her composition, if one does not remain open to what might come to be said by acceding to the imaginary point that becomes clearer as the "il" takes over and that fatally attracts then dismisses the "je," one might produce what could be taken to be a masterpiece but it would have foreclosed on the unknown.[36] Of course, the question arises how a reader could ever know what has happened in the composition of a poem. It is usually hard enough for a poet to know it himself or herself. Yet there is often a sense of surprise when one reads what one has composed: "Is that what I have really thought or felt?" Blanchot often appeals to writers, familiar with the psychology of composition, more than to practical critics who respond solely to the words of a poem before them.

3. Char writes that poetry's purpose is "to make us sovereign by impersonalizing us"; poetry touches upon "la plénitude."[37] Yet Blanchot approaches the matter otherwise. The sacred is encountered in the impersonal speech of the "il" which, unlike the one who says "je," occupies neither space nor time; it is neither internal (a "subject") nor external (another person). Hence the equivalent expressions "Neutral" and "Outside." Recall the *récit* of 1953, *Celui qui ne m'accompagnait pas*: "A speech? And yet not a speech, barely a murmur [*à peine un murmure*], barely a shiver, less than silence, less than the abyss of emptiness: the fullness of emptiness, something that one can't silence, occupying all of space, uninterrupted and incessant, a shiver and already a murmur, not a murmur, but a speech, and not just any speech, but distinct, appropriate: within my reach."[38] The sacred (or that which mimes it) is always anterior, never able to become a phenomenon like the burning bush or the Transfiguration. Yet poetry can open a relationship with the sacred.[39] Plato's attribution to Heraclitus of a primal flux is a figure for it, to be sure, but it is better to recognize it as *désœuvrement*, the state of being rendered idle, drawn toward the non-world of image, precisely by the triumph of the "il."[40]

*

A decade after writing "La Bête de Lascaux," Blanchot returns to *Le Poème pulvérisé* but in a new spirit, with other things to see there. The first essay, "René Char et la pensée du neutre" (1963), passes from attention to the sacred and phenomenology to the thought of the Outside, while the second one, "Parole de fragment" (1964), embodies his and Char's distaste for de Gaulle and the politics of the Fifth Republic. When revised for inclusion in *L'Entretien infini* (1969), this second essay also resonates with the irruption of *les événements de mai*.[41] The background for "Parole de fragment" is plain: Blanchot had written "La Perversion essentielle" (1959), a fierce reflection on the Algiers putsch of May 1959, to which Char had responded, expressing his agreement.[42] What galls most about the power play is that it embodies "perverted values of the sacred": de Gaulle as the savior of France.[43] (One might note that Napoléon played a similar role in the previous century.)

In the first essay Char's question is repeated: "How to live without the unknown in front of us?" An answer comes after the quotation: "Research—poetry, thought—relates to the unknown as unknown." The terms of the answer, especially in the final version of the essay, deserve close attention: "This relation discloses the unknown, but by an uncovering that leaves it under cover; through this relation there is a 'presence' of the unknown; in this 'presence' the unknown is rendered present, but always as unknown... This relation will not consist in an unveiling... The unknown will not be revealed, but indicated."[44] We have heard a version of this argument before, in "Comment découvrir l'obscur?" (1959), the second part of Blanchot's engagement with Bonnefoy, in which the question of the relation between the sacred and poetry is explored.[45] If the first part takes its clue from Hölderlin's insight in "Wie wenn am Feiertage. . ." that the sacred precedes manifestation, the second part broods on how poetry is experience of that anteriority, a relationship with the Outside or the "obscure."[46] Now, in passing from Bonnefoy to Char, we find a strengthened emphasis that phenomenology, even broadly considered, reaches a limit in considering the unknown.[47] The poetic word does not manifest being but points to the Outside, which is no longer coded as the sacred. (The influence of Derrida's deconstruction of full presence in the mid-1960s is apparent in the placing of "presence" in scare quotes in *L'Entretien infini*.[48])

"To write and to read this poem," Blanchot says in the second essay, "is to accept bending our listening to language toward the experience of a certain breaking up, an experience of separation and discontinuity."[49] His remarks are partly directed against those French readers of Char who have found his fragmentary writing after the war frustrating.[50] These people are mistaken, Blanchot thinks, in part because they bring aesthetic categories to a work that fundamentally resists them. A fragmented poem "opens another manner of accomplishment—the one at stake in writing, in questioning, or in an affirmation irreducible to unity" (308; 452). We read poetry not for the consolation afforded by the beautiful or certain versions of the sublime but in order to grasp better how to be in relation with one another without those relations turning on the "je" as a center of power; and the best model is not of belonging to the homeland, as one finds in Heidegger (and later in Beda Allemann), but rather of being in exile from it.[51] Char's poetry asserts "a new relation with the Outside" (308; 452), in which neither the Same nor the Other absorbs the binary term. To be sure, this poem appears "like a block to which nothing seems able to attach" but then, reversing the train of his reasoning in "La Bête de Lascaux," he says that it is a "strange misunderstanding" to think that Char writes aphoristically, for the aphorism—he appeals to the etymology of the word [ὁρίζων]—"is closed and bounded: the horizontal of every horizon" (308; 452) and Char's poetry is nothing if not open to the unknown (or, as Char would more likely say, the mystery of "the people of the fields").[52] Blanchot likes to quote Char's beautiful line about poetry being the realized love of desire that has remained desire.[53] Even the most polished poem still remains in a relation of longing for what has inspired it; it is a process as well as a thing.

The Outside can only approach us; it never appears. Yet we discern it in many aspects of life: art, communism, everyday life, image, and the sacred. Talk of the sacred is quietly replaced in "Parole de fragment" by a fresh sense of the political. What Blanchot now values is the spatial arrangement of *Le Poème pulvérizé*: it "accepts disjunction or divergence as the infinite center from out of which, through speech, relation is to be created: an arrangement that does not compose but juxtaposes, that is to say, leaves each of the terms that come into relation *outside* one another, respecting and preserving this *exteriority* and this distance as the principle—always already undercut—of all signification" (308; 453). And once more Blanchot evokes Heraclitus, this time as Char's brother in thought, two thinkers of "Difference" separated by over two millennia. An analogy is proposed between difference in nature and in society, although the ground of the analogy is nowhere specified.

We must not forget the word "destiny" that resounds frequently in Blanchot. Doubtless he recalls Heraclitus's Fragment 119: ἦθος ἀνθρώπῳ δαίμων (a person's character is his fate [divinity]), but the word rings also for Char in language and in France alike.[54] In "Comment découvrir l'obscur?" we are told that "Destiny" is "that which diverts from every destination and that we are seeking to name more directly in speaking of the *neutral*."[55] Let us keep this in mind when reading a few lines from "La Perversion essentielle." Blanchot evokes Charles de Gaulle as Symbol, "the visible presence of a great absent nation," who stands apart from power until René Coty (1882–1962), last president of the Fourth Republic, appeals to him to become prime minister, which de Gaulle accepts on the condition of being given extraordinary powers, including the power to draft a new constitution:

> From this experience arose the consciousness of a sovereignty of exception that coincided, during the dramatic hours of the void, with the essential presence of the national destiny. What is characteristic here is the manifestation of this void: in 1940, nothing was more pathetic and more obvious; where France had been, there was nothing more than the void, and beyond this void of history, the almost visible, almost perceptible Destiny, as the very prophecy of her salvation. De Gaulle has held onto the horror [*hantise*] of this void, but also its intimate knowledge and the feeling of its necessity. He inscribed it into the Constitution. He made it legal in a way. For France to raise herself into a Destiny and for the power that represents her to become a sovereignty of salvation, she must become conscious of this void, which, owing to its institutions and its divisions, does not cease to threaten her.[56]

If we step back from "La Perversion essentielle" and the two later essays on Char, we can make out what Blanchot urges his readers to think. To escape the grim politics of the Fifth Republic, that dark apparent destiny of France, we must turn to Char's poetry as marking the true destiny of France: a society marked by an openness to experience, to openness itself, and to the other in all its modes. It is unknown in the sense that the political, as envisaged here, has no precedent.

To return to the main argument: The wisdom at issue in "La Bête innommable," Blanchot believes, repeats the oracular language of Dodona. One does not have to go so far as to say that the unicorn is a "fantastically disguised" image of Gaea or Rhea who, some believe, was worshipped at Dodona before Zeus was connected with the cult. All that is required is to twin the passing of the wind through the sacred oak tree with the rustling of the Outside, that "murmuring where nothing lets itself be heard" (50-51; 66–7). The pre-historical beast depicted at Lascaux is an image of the Outside, covered over by generations of people who lack genuine wisdom; the tears of Wisdom, like those of Heraclitus, testify to our irretrievable loss of a consoling reality that is stable and unified, underwritten by a sense of the sacred that points to the gods or god. Char does this in the very writing of his poetry, Blanchot argues, and he even sees this conception of poetry rendered as a theme in some of the poems. The Outside is neither ancient nor modern, although Blanchot thinks, like Foucault, that a few writers have only recently become attuned to it.[57] There is no need to appeal to Char as a hero of the *maquis*. He is a poet of France's authentic destiny, a time to come that announces itself as unknown.

*

We are now in a position to understand what Blanchot has in mind when he says that Char's poetry "makes rise up before us a form of experienced time [*durée*] very different from the time [*la durée*] that simple historical analysis grasps."[58] It is time as image, time as fascination. And we can also see Blanchot's deeper investment in Char as a French prophet. But we have yet to explain what is in play when he says that Char "answers" Hölderlin [*lui répond*]. One could do this by way of a close reading of "Pour un Prométhée saxifrage," which is written "En touchant la main éolienne de Hölderlin," and which asks, "What is reality without the wrenching energy of poetry?"[59] More economical, though, would be to follow the link between the two poets provided by Heidegger, as Blanchot himself almost suggests, and in doing so we can gain a fuller understanding of Char's achievement and why it cannot be contained by modernity and less so by an aesthetic-historical category such as modernism.

The principal commentary by Heidegger that Blanchot has in mind is "Hölderlin und das Wesen der Dichtung," first given as a lecture in Rome in 1936, published the same year in *Das innere Reich*, and eventually gathered in *Erläuterungen zu Hölderlins Ditchtung* (1951). Heidegger chooses Hölderlin, over and above arguably greater poets, to illuminate the "essence" [*Wesen*] of poetry. This is not an essence that would have universal, timeless pertinence, as if we could exfoliate Hölderlin's odes and then find what is essential to Homer's epics, Petrarch's lyrics, or Shakespeare's tragedies. Instead, Heidegger maintains that Hölderlin's poems provide "anew" the essence of poetry and in doing so determine a new age. "It is the time of the gods who have fled *and* of the god who is coming."[60] One will notice with disquiet that Heidegger edges Hölderlin toward the politics of culture that was so loudly and darkly pronounced in Germany in the 1930s. At the same time, his ostensible concern is otherwise, and is indicated by two quotations, one from "Brot und Wein" and the other from a Pseudo-Hölderlin, "In lieblicher Bläue": "wozu Dichter in dürftiger Zeit" and "Voll Verdienst, doch dichterisch, wohnet der Mensch auf dieser Erde." The "time of need" is to be met, if at all, only by "dwelling poetically on the earth," that is, by standing before the gods. If this seems to be cultural nostalgia, it is not how Heidegger sees things. In a commentary on "Der Rhein" we are told, "Hölderlin is not the Greek world, but the future of the Germans."[61]

Heidegger nowhere specifies the linguistic extent of this divine interregnum, and we might well doubt if Emily Dickinson, G. M. Hopkins, and Alexander Pushkin, among others, experienced it to any great extent. Can one detect it in Wallace Stevens, Paul Celan, Federico García Lorca, or Eugenio Montale? Perhaps so—but in its specifics, barely, and at times not at all—and never with the pathos that weighs in Heidegger's meditation on art and in the final pages of Blanchot's *L'Espace littéraire*. That tonality seems to be specifically German, although for Blanchot it spills over into French, where it is reset, for he hears Mallarmé, Rimbaud, and of course Char speaking in its key. He is not wrong to do so, for in "Seuil" Char memorably evokes "l'abandon du divin" as a sense of a huge crack appearing in a dam (a metaphor for the human being).[62] In "Brot und Wein" Hölderlin evokes poets, like the priests of Bacchus, wandering from land to land. This is plainly not the case with Char who remains rooted in his beloved Vaucluse. Instead, one finds in Char's poetry, Blanchot urges, a place where one can dwell, not in peace and contentment but in the grip of fascination.

That the natural world of the Vaucluse rivets Char is evident: we need only read "Quatre fascinants."[63] Blanchot goes further, however, seeing in the poetry—or at least some of it—an attraction to the Outside, the last vestige of the sacred in human history, in Char's poetry; and once one succumbs to its allure one loses hold of the fullness and direction of time. Rather, one lives the emptiness and stagnation of image: not exactly *la durée* as Henri Bergson conceived it but *la désœuvrement* as Blanchot diagnoses it.[64] Char responds to Hölderlin precisely by making his "sacred speech" ever more explicit, by living as a poet *avant le Dehors*. He is situated, for Blanchot, both in the space between the divine's turn away from human beings and our turn away from the divine, which is the opening of modernity, and also in the space between the loss of the old gods and the arrival of the new.[65] The old gods spoke through the rustling of the sacred oak at Dodona, and the last god, who attracts us to the non-world of image, murmurs in Char's poetry.

*

Blanchot seems to need Char in much the same way as Heidegger needed Hölderlin. Each poet supplies a sacred scripture for the thinker to explicate and find there his own views glowing with "an alienated majesty."[66] Heidegger's Hölderlin became a symbol for a new Germany, for a *vaterländische Umkehr*, and the same is true of Blanchot's Char with respect to France. In order to do that, of course, one must be selective in one's reading. Lautréamont and Rimbaud are dropped from Char's heritage, leaving Hölderlin behind and having him on center stage. The great fragmentary poem of *Le Poème pulvérizé* is surely "Le Météore du 13 août," yet the others are not written in that way and have powers of different kinds. More generally, if one reads Char in the mile as well as the inch, one finds a great many fine poems that play no role in Blanchot's construction of him, and that are arguably his main legacy. I am thinking of, among many others, poems that recall folk lyrics ("Quatre fascinants," "Quatre âges"), expansive love poems ("*Lettera amorosa*"), and other lyrics in verse and prose, such as "Congé au vent," "Sur le volet d'une fenêtre," "Compagnie de l'écolière," "La Sorge,"

"L'Amoureuse en secret," "Le Martinet," "Le Bois de l'Epte," "Redonnez-leur," "Qu'il vive!," "Le Vipereau," "Allegeance," and "Les Inventeurs."

Char saw the pertinence of Blanchot's criticism of his work, and we can perhaps discern the lineaments of his admiration of his friend in a poem he dedicated to him, "Le Partenaire mortel."[67] I read the poem to be about composition regarded as an erotic struggle between the poet (male) and the inspiration of the poem (female). Yet Char is also responding to composition as Blanchot conceives it. There are people whose secret "lies deep in the very secret of life," he writes. "They approach it. It kills them. But the future they have stirred with a whisper foresees them and creates them. Oh maze of extreme love!"[68] Here we can hear a lyrical echo of some lines in Blanchot's first essay on Char: "Inspiration is not the gift of a secret or a word granted to someone already present; it is the gift of existence to someone who does not yet exist."[69] An unusual echo, it reverses part of what it repeats. For Char, the secret that animates Blanchot and his writing, narrative as well as critical, is close to the secret of life itself, which I take to be, for Blanchot, the Outside. To approach it directly, as Orpheus does with Eurydice, who is the inspiration of his poetry, is to lose it; and, as we have seen, to produce a new work is an act of self-sacrifice. It bespeaks extreme love. Although the poem is actually spoken by no one, its very articulation gives birth to a new person: the poet. And this particular poet, author of "Le Partenaire mortel," is for Blanchot the one who gives birth to hope for another France, one who breaks decisively with the politics of the Fifth Republic. Yet when Blanchot reads Char he also finds confirmation of his own thoughts on composition and the Outside. For some, reading might well be a "light, innocent Yes," but for Blanchot it is not always an entirely innocent activity.[70]

Notes

1 Blanchot had written on Char earlier. See his "René Char," *Critique* 5 (octobre 1946): 387–99; "René Char," *WF*, 98–110 (103–14). The essay is an unimpressed review of Georges Mounin, *Avez-vous lu Char?* (Paris: Gallimard, 1946).
2 Blanchot, "The Beast of Lascaux," *VE*, 40 (55), and "The Disappearance of Literature," *BC*, 198 (269). "La Bête de Lascaux" was first published in *Nouvelle Nouvelle Revue Française* 4 (avril 1953): 684–93, without the quotation of "La Bête innommable," and "Où va la littérature?" in *Nouvelle Nouvelle Revue Française* 7 (juillet 1953): 98–107, with the reference to Char on p. 102. Blanchot had associated Char and Hölderlin a year beforehand in "L'Art, la littérature et l'expérience originelle," *Les Temps modernes* 79 (mai 1952): 2210, which was reprinted in *EL*, 277–333.
3 See the dedication to *Le Livre à venir* that Blanchot makes to Bonnefoy in 1959 and also his warm remarks of 18 octobre, 1983 in Yves Bonnefoy, *Correspondance*, vol. 1, édition établic, introduite et annotée par Odile Bombarde et Patrick Labarthe (Paris: Les Belles Lettres, 2018), 329 n. 42. That Bonnefoy had mixed feelings about Blanchot's criticism is evident in his correspondence. See, in particular, his letter to Pierre Torreilles of 25 novembre, 1959, *Correspondance*, 329.
4 Blanchot's interest in Lascaux, oriented by Bataille's study of the cave, continued. See his "Naissance de l'art," *Nouvelle Nouvelle Revue Française* 35 (novembre 1955): 923–33, translated as "The Birth of Art," *F,* 1–11 (9–20).

5 On Char's collaborations with visual artists, see Rosemary Lancaster, *Poetic Illumination: René Char and his Artist Allies* (Amsterdam: Rodopi, 2010).
6 See Blanchot, "Reflections on Surrealism," *WF*, 85–97 (90–102).
7 Yet Char is perfectly capable of writing formal verse. See, for example, "Complainte du lézard amoureux," in *Oeuvres complètes*, intro. Jean Roudaut, Bibliothèque de la Pléiade (Paris: Gallimard, 1995), 294.
8 For Blanchot's reservations about aestheticism and its relations with literature, see *IC*, xi (vi).
9 Plato, *Phaedrus*, 275a–b, in Harold North Fowler, trans. *Euthyphro, Apology, Crito, Phaedo, Phaedrus*, intro. W. R. M. Lamb, Loeb Classical Library (Cambridge, MA: Harvard University Press, 1914).
10 See Léon Robin, ed., *Platon*, Édition de la Pléiade (Paris: Gallimard, 1944).
11 See Apostolos N. Athanassakis, trans. and intro. *The Homeric Hymns*, 2nd ed. (Baltimore, MD: The Johns Hopkins University Press, 2004). Other hymns may well have been performed, but most likely not Orphic hymns, most of which come centuries after Plato. See Athanassakis and Benjamin M. Wolkow, trans., and intro., *The Orphic Hymns* (Baltimore, MD: The Johns Hopkins University Press, 2013).
12 See Homer, *Illiad*, 16, 233–5. For Dodona, see Walter Burket, *Greek Religion*, trans. John Raffin (Oxford: Basil Blackwell, 1985), 114.
13 A. D. Godley, trans., *Herodotus*, 4 vols., Loeb Classical Library (Cambridge, MA: Harvard University Press, 1981), vol. 2, 54–7.
14 See René Char, "Heraclitus d'Éphèse," *Oeuvres complètes*, 720–1, and T. M. Robinson, trans., *Heraclitus: Fragments: A Text and Translation with a Commentary* (Toronto: University of Toronto Press, 1991), 57.
15 See Blanchot, *IC*, 73–4 (103–5), and for his association of Char and the fragmentary, "The Fragment Word" in the same volume, 307–10 (451–5). Also see "René Char," 106 (110).
16 Char, *Oeuvres complètes*, 133. All translations from Char's poetry are my own.
17 Indeed, Blanchot will study Neher's work intently. See Éric Hoppenot, *Maurice Blanchot et la tradition juive*, avant-propos Éric Marty (Paris: Éditions Kimé, 2015), 188–97, 485–507.
18 See Blanchot, "La Parole prophétique," *Nouvelle Nouvelle Revue Française* 48 (janvier 1957): 283–92. It appears in English as "Prophetic Speech," *BC*, 79–85 (109–19). The references to Rimbaud and Claudel may be found at 85 (119) and 84 (117) respectively.
19 All quotations from Hölderlin are from the *Sämtliche Werke*, as specified in the previous chapter. For an English translation of this passage, see Hamburger, trans., *Friedrich Hölderlin*, 395. Also see Blanchot, "The 'Sacred' Speech of Hölderlin," *WF*, 111–31 (115–32). The placing of the comma in the second line is controversial, and one might contest the translation of "das Heilige sei mein Wort."
20 Marina Tsvetaeva, "Downpour of Light: Poetry of Eternal Courage," *Art in the Light of Conscience*, trans., intro. and notes Angela Livingstone (Cambridge, MA: Harvard University Press, 1992), 23.
21 Blanchot, *SL*, 163 (213). See Hölderlin, *Friedrich Hölderlin*, 270.
22 See René Descartes, "Rules for the Direction of the Mind," *The Philosophical Works*, 2 vols., trans. Elizabeth S. Haldane and G. R. T. Ross (Cambridge: Cambridge University Press, 1972), vol. 1, 28. Marion develops this train of thought in his *Negative Certainties*, trans. Stephen E. Lewis (Chicago: Chicago University Press, 2015).
23 See Blanchot, "René Char and the Thought of the Neutral," *IC*, 302 (445).

24 Char, *Oeuvres complètes*, 246. We can get a clearer idea of Char's sense of *Le Poème Pulvérisé* by reading his glosses on the poems, which first appeared in *Arrière-Histoire du Poème pulvérizé* (Paris: John Hughes, 1972) and is now in the *Oeuvres complètes*, 1291–7.
25 See Char, *Oeuvres complètes*, 189.
26 Aristotle, *Metaphysics,* 1–9, trans. Hugh Tredennick (Cambridge, MA: Harvard University Press, 1933), 1010a.
27 Blanchot, "La Solitude essentielle," *Nouvelle Nouvelle Revue Française* 1 (janvier 1953): 78 (*SL*, 23).
28 On passive genesis, see Husserl, *Analyses Concerning Passive and Active Synthesis: Lectures on Transcendental Logic*, trans. Anthony J. Steinbock (Dordrecht: Kluwer Academic Publishers, 2001), esp. 119.
29 See Heidegger, "The Origin of the Work of Art," in *Poetry, Language, Thought*, trans. Albert Hofstadter (New York: Harper, 1971), 71, and Henri Hubert and Marcel Mauss, *Sacrifice: Its Nature and Functions*, trans. W. D. Halls, foreword E. E. Evans-Pritchard (Chicago, IL: University of Chicago Press, 1981). Blanchot's "Le Regard d'Orphée" is contemporary with "La Bête de Lascaux"; it was published in *Cahiers d'art* 28, no. 1 (1953): 73–5. See "Orpheus's Gaze," *SL*, 171–6 (225–32).
30 See Heidegger, "The Origin of the Work of Art," 71, and Laure (Colette) Peignot, "The Sacred," *The Collected Writings*, esp. 45.
31 Char, *Oeuvres complètes*, 766.
32 Char, *Oeuvres complètes*, 1294. Also see "La Bibliothèque est en feu," *Oeuvres complètes*, 378.
33 Communication is a common theme in Bataille, especially in the early 1940s when, most likely, he elaborates on Laure's thoughts on the subject. See, for example, *Guilty*, trans. Bruce Boone, intro. Denis Hollier (Venice: The Lapis Press, 1988), 139. Blanchot takes up the idea in "L'Œuvre et la communication," *Nouvelle Nouvelle Revue Française* 12 (décembre 1953): 1064–71 (*SL*, 198–207).
34 Char, *Oeuvres complètes*, 744, 265.
35 See Blanchot, "Literature and the Right to Death," trans. Lydia Davis, *WF*, 331 (320).
36 On the imaginary point, see Blanchot, "Encountering the Imaginary," *BC*, 7 (14).
37 Char, *Oeuvres complètes*, 359.
38 Blanchot, *OWM*, 66–7 (125–6).
39 See Blanchot, "How to Discover the Obscure?" *IC*, 40–8 (57–69).
40 See Blanchot, "Heraclitus," *IC*, 85–92 (119–31). Also see in the same volume his distinction between the narrator's voice and the narrative voice in "The Narrative Voice (the 'he,' the neutral)," 379–87 (556–67). For Levinas on the *il y a*, see his *EE*, 57–64.
41 See Blanchot, "René Char et la pensée du neutre," *L'Arc* 22 (1963): 9–14, and *EI*, 439–50. Also see his essay "Parole de fragment," which first appeared in Italian translation as "La parole en arcipel," in *Il Menabò* 7 (1964): 156–9, the journal being the sole publication under the sign of the *Revue Internationale*. One of Blanchot's hopes for this venture was the leaguing of far left-wing politics and fragmentary writing. The essay was modified and appeared as "Parole de fragment," in *L'Endurance de la pensée: Pour saluer Jean Beaufret* (Paris: Plon, 1968), 103–7. (Blanchot's essay was dedicated to Levinas in order to mark his concerns about Jean Beaufret's reputed denial of the death camps.) Later, the same piece, recast again, and without the dedication, appeared in *EI*, 451–8. On the *Revue*, see ch. 6.
42 See Blanchot, "La Perversion essentielle," *Le 14 Juillet* 3 (1959): 18–20, and Char, "Note à propos d'une deuxième lecture de 'La Perversion essentielle,' in 'Le 14 juillet' 1959," *Oeuvres complètes*, 744–5.

43 Blanchot, "The Essential Perversion," *PW*, 13.
44 Blanchot, "René Char and the Thought of the Neutral," *IC*, 300 (442).
45 See Blanchot, "Comment découvrir l'obscur?" *Nouvelle Revue Française* 82 (novembre 1959): 867–79. The piece was included *EI*, 57–69.
46 See Blanchot, "How to Discover the Obscure?" *IC*, 46 (66).
47 Blanchot will propose a new mode of reduction to mark his difference from Husserlian phenomenology. See my essay "Une réduction infinie," *Cahiers de l'Herne* (2014), Blanchot special issue, ed. Dominique Rabaté and Éric Hoppenot, 323–8.
48 See Blanchot, *IC*, 452 n. 16 (255 n.). Also see Derrida, *Resistances of Psychoanalysis*, trans. Peggy Kamuf et al. (Stanford, CA: Stanford University Press, 1998), 61–2.
49 Blanchot, "The Fragment Word," 308 (452).
50 A dissenting minority still contents Char's preeminence in modern French poetry. See, for example, François Crouzet, *Contra René Char* (Paris: Les Belles Lettres, 1992).
51 See Beda Allemann, "Le retounement natal dans l'œuvre de Hölderlin," *Recherches et débats du centre catholique des intellectuels français*, n.s. 24 (1958): 183–99.
52 Char, *Oeuvres complètes*, 217.
53 Char, "Partage formel," *Oeuvres complètes*, 162. Also see Blanchot, "The Great Refusal," *IC*, 47 (68).
54 Blanchot claims that language has a destiny in "Literature and the Right to Death," 328 (317). See Robinson, *Heraclitus*, 69.
55 Blanchot, "How to Discover the Obscure?" 47 (67).
56 Blanchot, "The Essential Perversion," 11.
57 See Michel Foucault, "Maurice Blanchot: The Thought from Outside," in Blanchot and Michel Foucault, *Foucault / Blanchot*, trans. Brian Massumi and Jeffrey Mehlman (New York: Zone Books, 1990), and Foucault, *The Order of Things: An Archeology of the Human Sciences* (New York: Random House, 1994), 384.
58 Blanchot, "Where is Literature Going?" 198 (269).
59 Char, *Oeuvres complètes*, 399.
60 Heidegger, "Hölderlin and the Essence of Poetry," in *Elucidations of Hölderlin's Poetry*, trans. Keith Hoeller (Amherst, NY: Humanity Books, 2000), 64.
61 Heidegger, *Hölderlin's Hymns "Germania" and "The Rhine,"* trans. William McNeill and Julia Ireland (Bloomington, IN: Indiana University Press, 2014), 231. Also see Heidegger, *Hölderlin's Hymn "The Ister,"* trans. William McNeill and Julia Davis (Bloomington, IN: Indiana University Press, 1996), 54.
62 Char, "Seuil," *Oeuvres complètes*, 255.
63 Char, *Oeuvres complètes*, 353–4.
64 See Henri Bergson, *Time and Free Will: An Essay on the Immediate Data of Consciousness*, trans. R. L. Pogson (London: Allen and Unwin, 1910), 100–10.
65 See Blanchot, *SL*, 247 (332–3).
66 Ralph Waldo Emerson, "Self-Reliance," in *Essays: First Series* (New York: A. L. Burt Co., 1900), 48.
67 For a somewhat different account of Blanchot's and Char's readings of one another, see Alain Milon, "Maurice Blanchot, lecteur de René Char?" in *Maurice Blanchot, de proche en proche*, éd. Éric Hoppenot et coordonné Daiana Manoury (Paris: Éditions Complicités, 2008), 209–20.
68 Char, "*Oeuvres complètes*," 363. The dedication does not appear in the *Oeuvres complètes*.
69 Blanchot, "René Char," 99 (104).
70 See Blanchot, *SL*, 196 (258).

Part 2

On Friendship

4

Blanchot's Weil

In the July and August of 1957, the *Nouvelle Nouvelle Revue Française* published two related commentaries by Blanchot: "Simone Weil et la certitude" and "L'expérience de Simone Weil."[1] Later, in 1969, the two pieces were united, retitled as "L'Affirmation (le désir, le malheur)," to form the fourth chapter of the second part of *L'Entretien infini*, which bears the subtitle, "L'expérience-limite." The placing of the essay is significant: after a reflection on Pascal, "La Pensée tragique" (1956), and before an important essay on Judaism, "Être juif" (1962).

So Blanchot's essay on Weil appears, in its final form, as a passage between the Jansenist author of the probabilistic argument for living a good Christian life (the famous or infamous "wager"), on the one hand, and with Judaism, understood as the opening of speech between human beings and God, on the other. Weil finds herself situated between two conversation partners with whom she has little sympathy. Blanchot ends his thoughts on Pascal by evoking the *Deus absconditus* and wondering if the idea of a deity who does not allow himself to be known is mystical, dialectical, or tragic; and he begins his meditation on being Jewish by noting (unfairly) that Weil closed her eyes to the ordeal that the Jews underwent in the Second World War. Another dialogue partner who remains unnamed throughout is Georges Bataille to whom we owe the idea of the limit-experience, which is probed in the ninth chapter of the second part. Blanchot refers in passing to Weil at other times in his writings, but our focus must be his detailed 1957 essay and its place in *L'Entretien infini* over a decade later.[2] And yet we need also to ponder those moments when Blanchot learns from Weil without explicitly naming her, the lessons sometimes being received according to the horizon of the reader rather than the intentions of the one being read.

It is worth noting, right at the start, what aspects of Weil do not appear under Blanchot's intense gaze. Perhaps most astonishingly for someone as interested in politics and the political as Blanchot, nothing is said about Weil's left-wing political activity in the 1930s, her direct experience of affliction in factory work, her reflections on oppression and liberty, and her rejection of political parties. Nor is any notice taken of Weil's reflections on the anticipations of Christianity she finds in writings by the ancient Greeks. Also bypassed is Weil as a writer, especially her adoption of aphoristic (or is it fragmentary?) writing, most notably in *La Pesanteur et la grâce* (1947). There could hardly be comments on her views of science, or on her poems and her unfinished play, *Venise sauvée*, since none of this material was available in 1957. Blanchot tended not to rewrite his pieces in the light of new publications, although he revised his commentaries on occasion so that they might be consistent in their vocabulary and themes.[3] Almost single-mindedly in "L'Affirmation (le désir, le malheur)," he follows the threads of certitude and experience in Weil's books (not her articles), taking the first word in a less technical sense than one finds in philosophers such as Duns Scotus and John Henry Newman. Hers is a thought that is "strangely surprised" [*étrangement surprise*] by its readers, he says. We pass through cosmetic contradictions and surface tensions and come upon what Weil truly thinks suddenly and unexpectedly; we elicit its truths unawares or without warning; but also it is unprepared for the assaults that some readers make on it. Weil speaks from a position of authority, and yet her speech is oddly unguarded. The gap between these two things provides Blanchot with his point of entry into her writing.

*

Weil is reproached, Blanchot reminds us, for a lack of coherence in her work: "one must become uprooted, one must take root; God is perfectly absent, he is the only presence; the world is evil, the order of the world is the good itself."[4] A case can assuredly be made for the consistency of her thought, and it can be made along very different lines. Blanchot stresses the persistence of her atheism, even after her personal experience of Christ in 1938, and although he readily accepts the deep influence of Plato on her ideas, he does not figure the unity of that thought by way of "religious metaphysics," as Miklos Vetö was to do shortly after the appearance of *L'Entretien infini*.[5] Yet those readers who dismiss Weil because she seems to change her mind about important things read her badly. She gainsays herself not so much, as Blanchot surmises, because of "the inevitable opposition of thoughts" (106; 153) but because she follows a particular way of thinking. "Method of investigation: as soon as we have thought something, try to see in what way the contrary is true."[6] Blanchot is uninterested in harmonizing Weil's thought and attends, rather, to the tone and manner in which her claims are made. "What is surprising [*Ce qui surprend*] . . . is the quality of the affirmation and the transparency of the certitude" (108; 156).

Believers and nonbelievers alike, Blanchot thinks, tend to proceed by questioning. It is what he often called, when younger, *la contestation*. Commenting on Bataille's *L'Expérience interieur* (1943), he observes that in the past querying the workings of the world has often led to an "absolute beyond" but that this situation has changed: "it is the very fact of existence that is now called into question" first of all by reason, to be sure, but the mind soon fills itself with anguish when everything is contested. Accordingly, we cannot remain at the level of discourse but must pass from thought to action, with no assured horizon of knowledge before us.[7] "This state, a state of violence, of tearing apart [*d'arrachement*], of abduction, of ravishing, would in every respect be similar to mystical ecstasy if it were disengaged from all the religious presuppositions that often change it and, by giving it a meaning, determine it" (39; 49). Weil had only apparently been taking another course than the one Bataille and Blanchot felt called to explore in the last year of her life. "Affirming is often for Simone Weil a way of questioning or a way of testing" (108; 156); it is a mode of effacing herself before the truth.[8] All the certainties one holds about life and identity, which for Blanchot are concentrated in the power of the "I," must be renounced, his Weil says, in order to gain certitude. For Bataille and Blanchot, this certitude is nonreligious "ecstasy"; for Weil, Blanchot implies, it must be experience of Christ. Yet for Blanchot Weil misunderstands her own experience, and what "experience" is, though not as badly as some Christian mystics do.

If we move ahead quickly, we can readily see what Blanchot has in mind about Weil's certitude. She rejects "all forms of power, even spiritual power," we are told, but not in order to yield to a greater power, the divine, for she clearly sees that the Christian God "is not the All-Powerful that our idolatry hastens to adore so we can adore the power in ourselves" (115; 167). Instead, Weil's God is "the absolute renunciation of power: he is abdication, abandon, the consent to not being what he could be, and this in the Creation as well as in the Passion" (115; 167). What then "tore her from herself" [*l'a arrachée à elle*] if not herself or God? The answer: "this tearing itself" [*l'arrachement même*] (115; 167). Blanchot surprises Weil by making her say something she never actually says—"she does not quite (but very nearly) give it this form" (115; 167)—namely, that a movement of self-effacement, a desire to abandon the "I," is what "sustains her entire life and her entire thought" and grants her certitude (115; 167). Plainly, Weil is being received in the context of the limit-experience, but we must not abide with this insight and must listen to something easily overlooked, how the self-effacement is characterized. "There is in us something that must be called divine," Blanchot tells us, "something by which we already dwell close to God" (115; 167). To understand this "something" we must retrace our steps.

*

Blanchot draws a strict distinction between certitude and faith. Weil's experience of certitude "does not even give her faith" (107; 154); "this certitude is too lofty and too certain to be an object of faith" (111; 161); and her affirmation "eludes the obscurities of faith" (114; 165). One might add that Weil possesses not only religious faith but also religious insight, for much of her reflection on religion turns not so much on things to be believed as on things that are thought and practiced.[9] The Pythagoreans are an object lesson here. More generally, there can be little doubt that Weil came to have *fides qua*, the subjective pole of faith, but her last years are consumed with tormented worries about *fides quæ*, the doctrinal content of faith.[10] One cannot have certitude in the Catholic sense of the word without the two poles being in harmony, and since Weil was unable honestly to achieve this spiritual condition, she could not enter the church. The certitude Weil enjoyed was of another order: it came from direct contact with Christ.[11]

No doubt Weil did not wish to be baptized for a range of reasons: because of the church's many declarations of *anathema sit*, which deny spiritual truths she prized and which were held by those outside the fold; because of the church's tendency to demand loyalty, much as a political party does; and finally her sense, consonant with being a philosopher, that to be Catholic one must have a definite idea of exactly what must be believed and what must not be believed.[12] Yet one must also keep in mind her testimony that when reciting George Hebert's "Love" (3) in 1938 "Christ himself came down and took possession of me" and that when saying the *Pater noster* in Greek "Christ is present with me in person, but his presence is infinitely more real, more moving, more clear than on that first occasion when he took possession of me."[13] These statements accord with what theologians call "supernatural certitude," a conviction of truth that is unshakable because it relies on divine revelation, even if it is, in this case, a private revelation (and one that has not been investigated by the Church). Nonetheless, let Blanchot's distinction stand, if only for ease of exposition, and let us continue.

Weil's reformulation of Pascal's wager is well known, as is her claim that it is "greatly preferable" to the original.[14] Blanchot claims to find no less than three new versions of the wager, presumably all written in 1942, and prefers the third one, which he condenses as follows:

> If I avert my desire from the things of this world, as being false goods, I have the absolute, unconditional certainty of being in accord with truth...
>
> To turn away from them—that is all... But—it will be asked—does this good exist? What does it matter? the things of this world exist, but they are not the good... And what is this good? I have no idea—but what does it matter? It is that whose name alone, if I attach my thought to it, gives me the certainty that the things of this world are not goods... But is it not ridiculous to abandon what exists? By no means, if what exists is not good and if what perhaps does not exist is the good. But why say "what perhaps does not exist"?... It makes no sense to say the good exists or the good does not exist; one can only say: the good. (315-16)

Blanchot sees two striking things here. First, there is the pivotal role of desire, one so strong as to turn away from each and every created thing. Plainly, it shares some qualities with *la contestation*, although it also opens onto de-creation. Second, there is the power of the word "good," which does not even need to refer to any metaphysical state of affairs in order to remain potent. (Doubtless Weil, always a Platonist, is thinking, in her own way, of the good as beyond being, ἐπέκεινα τῆς οὐσίας, as ventured in *Republic* 509b.)

That Weil generally held the views in her wager, at least in her last years, is evident, for a version of them, limited to the question of personal immortality, is commended to Jean Posternak in Spring, 1937. (The very idea that the "I" might survive endlessly would be distasteful to her.[15]) That letter was written after her experience in a chapel of the Basilica of Santa Maria degli Angeli, just beneath Assisi: she senses an absolute conviction that she must kneel and pray.[16] Of course, we must not lose sight of Weil's method of investigation, a relevant (although undated) instance of which is offered in the *Cahiers*: "I am absolutely certain [*tout à fait sûr*] that there is a God, in the sense that my love is not illusory. I am absolutely certain that there is not a God, in the sense that I am absolutely certain that there is nothing real which bears a resemblance to what I am able to conceive when I pronounce that name, since I am unable to conceive God."[17] *Deus semper maior*. God, she adds, presumably in case we miss the theological point, "is not an illusion" (127). Her version of Pascal's wager is not a statement that would properly belong in a doctrine of God; it is an exercise in apologetics, no doubt, while also a spiritual exercise, for it trains the soul to attend solely to the good and not to glorify the "I," always a lie and always spoken by sin, by figuring it as in a special relationship with an all-powerful higher being.[18] If Blanchot edges us to regard Weil's thought as "tragic" because it abides in an "extreme tension between contraries," we may demur; for those contraries do not grip one in a vice but rather awaken one to an endless contemplation of the absolutely singular God.[19] Contradiction here is, as she says, "like a pair of pincers, so that through it direct contact may be made with the transcendental sphere of truth beyond the range of the human faculties."[20] The tragic element of Weil's life and thought is admirably put in a letter to Maurice Schumann in 1943: "I feel an ever increasing sense of devastation, both in my intellect and in the center of my heart, at my inability to think with truth at the same time about the affliction of men, the perfection of God, and the link between the two."[21]

Together the stress on desire and the power of the word "good" indicate essential features of Weil's thought. We see that her religious sense is profoundly Platonic, with no adhesion of Aristotle, which places her at a distance from traditional Catholic understandings of the being of God. We also see, with Blanchot, that for her "true knowledge is surnatural [*surnaturelle*]," which is largely so in her final years (115; 166). Yet he notices an ambiguity in the word *surnaturelle*, as it organizes her theological epistemology. On the one hand, a person can be approached by the *surnaturelle* (Christ takes possession of her), while, on the other hand, nothing other than the natural is needed in order to approach it (attention, desire, obedience, and renunciation). That Weil writes of Grace is well known—it is one of the main burdens of *La Pesanteur et la grâce*, for example—and Blanchot is attentive to it, noting that, for her, there is an immense distance between the mortal and the eternal. "Apparently nothing less than grace will diminish this frightening distance between we who know nothing of the Good and can do no more than desire it, and the 'reality' of the Good" (112; 162). He turns to a particularly eloquent passage to illustrate her understanding of Grace:

> Over the infinity of space and time, the infinitely more infinite love of God comes to possess us. He comes at his own time. We have the power to consent to receive him or to refuse. If we remain deaf, he comes back again and again like a beggar, but also, like a beggar, one day he stops coming. If we consent, God puts a little seed [*une petite graine*] in us and he goes away again. From that moment God has no more to do; neither have we, except to wait.[22]

If when reading these sentences we recall St. Bernard of Clairvaux on the coming of the Word, or Lope de Vega's haunting sonnet "Qué tengo yo que mi amistad procuras," we also register something very unusual in her Christian vision, if that is what it is: the withdrawal of God so that Grace may do its work unaided as the soul practices humility.[23] This seems to render Grace a finite act, and veers away from the orthodox view that it needs to be preserved in the believer, and indeed that the believer's very acceptance of Grace needs to be sustained by the deity.

The unease an orthodox Catholic will feel on reading these lines will perhaps increase if we continue to follow Weil's essay beyond where Blanchot's quotation ends: "A day comes when the soul belongs to God, when it not only consents to love but when truly and effectively it loves. Then in its turn it must cross the universe to go to God. The soul does not love like a creature with created love. *The love within it is divine, uncreated* [incrée]; *for it is the love of God for God that is passing through it. God alone is capable of loving God*" (133; my emphasis). One can link Weil's thought here to that well-known crux in Peter Lombard's *Sentences*, vol. 1, distinction 17, when he proposes, with some support from Augustine, that our love for one another *is* the Holy Spirit and is therefore uncreated.[24] Aquinas resists the idea. At first, when young, he distinguishes how we love God effectively (uncreated love) and how we love God formally (created love) and insists that God does not love us as we love him.[25] Later, in the *Summa theologiæ*, he affirms that human love is created.[26] Yet Lombard was never condemned for his view. What was denounced, however, is a theological position that preceded and succeeded Lombard and that can easily be confused with his claim (*Denz.* 401, 444). I am thinking of Gnosticism as inflected by the Cathari in Languedoc, who continued the ancient teaching that the spirit is an uncreated spark or seed, and this is the relevant reference for the passage in question.

Weil's sympathy for the plight of the Cathari under Simon de Montfort and her admiration of aspects of their culture are amply documented, and we know that she thought that being a Cathar in her day was not a live option, even though a revival of interest in their civilization was desirable.[27] Care must be taken, though, not to allow her enthusiasm for the Cathari to render her a committed Gnostic or even to credit her with a broad and deep knowledge of the religion. Scholarship on the Cathari was not to begin in earnest until after her death.[28] To be sure, there are times when Weil elevates Manicheans over Catholics, and there are elements of her thought that recall Cathari beliefs.[29] For instance, she tends to use Greek culture, especially Pythagoras and Plato, much as Christians use the Old Testament as adumbrating the revelation of Christ; and her negative remarks on some of the Hebrew Scriptures are notorious.[30] One can also evince views she proposes that, if not of Gnostic inspiration, are at least consistent with it. She figures an immense gulf between the created order and the divine order, and frequently construes the mundane world as abandoned by God.[31] Also, she writes of the role that Grace can play in "completely destroy[ing] the 'I.'"[32] These claims can appear Gnostic, for most Christian writers would speak rather of offering the "I" to God; and yet there are moments when one hears similar things in St John of the Cross and Jean-Pierre de Caussade (yet also in François Fénelon).[33] It must always be remembered that Gnosticism has fermented within religious beliefs more than it has been affirmed as a particular religious belief itself.

Certainly, Weil does not affirm a dualism between the soul and the body, which is a major tenant of Gnosticism. Early and late, she stresses the importance of the body. In one of her first writings, she reduces the imagination to the body; later, she laments the early modern division between mind and body; and after her religious turn she greatly prizes the incarnation, and even attests the physical effects of Grace.[34] That said, she places little emphasis on the bodily resurrection of Christ, focusing instead on the Cross. (Nowhere does she seek to reconcile her devaluation of the resurrection with her certainty that Christ becomes present to her.) At no time does she propose a duality of God and a demiurge, and she plainly understands human beings to have only one "indestructible attribute," *ens creatum*.[35] And yet she plainly says that there is an "uncreated part of every creature."³⁶ Unlike the Cathari, however, she honors the sacraments and regards beauty as a path to God.³⁷ Other evidence is ambiguous. For example, she translates επιούσιος in the Lord's Prayer as "supernatural," which accords with the practice of the Cathari. Yet Jerome does the same when rendering Matt. 6: 11 as *panem nostrum supersubstantialem da nobis hodie.* (He translates Luke 11: 3 as *panem nostrum quotidianum da nobis hodie.*) In general, it might be said that Weil's thought incubates certain Gnostic elements that incline her to prize some Cathari beliefs as well as to regret the loss of their culture.

Blanchot remarks on the significance that the name of God has for Weil. Then he makes a surprising leap, wondering if she "came under the influence of the Jewish religious traditions—particularly that of the Cabala—for which the secret name of God is the object of a special reverence and can even, through the contemplation and combination of letters, ecstatically engage us in the divine mystery" (110; 159). A little later he introduces Isaac Luria who, drawing on Gnostic sources, makes the πνεῦμα central to his Kabbalah. To be sure, only the High Priest in Jerusalem knows the vowels in the most sacred name of God, *Shem HaMeforash*, and would say it only once a year on entering the Holy of Holies on Yom Kippur. Lurianic Kabbalah develops the idea of the most sacred name to be kept apart from the ears and mouths of the impure. One need not go past the Hebrew Scriptures, however, to find many passages in which the name of God is hallowed (e.g., Ezek. 36: 23, Neh. 9: 5, and Micah 4: 5); and the power of the divine name is also declared in the New Testament (John 17: 6, 26, for instance) and becomes a theme in patristic theology: Pseudo-Dionysius the Areopagite, for one, extolls the Good as the first of the divine names.³⁸ Where there is reason to associate Weil and Lurianaic Kabbalah is in her teaching of *tzimtzum* in which the Creation is viewed as coming about by God's contraction of himself. This is what Blanchot has in mind when speaking of Weil's God in terms of "the absolute renunciation of power" in Creation as well as in the Passion. For Weil affirms the teaching without using the word.³⁹ Yet the divine contraction need not be read as an abandonment of what is thereby created; it can be appreciated as God's way of allowing created beings to have a space in which to develop and to form relations with him. Weil elects a particularly bleak reading of the teaching.

We are now in a position to appreciate Blanchot's central claim, that Weil does not tear herself from herself nor does God tear her away from herself but that what rips her into pieces is "this tearing itself" (115; 167). "All the certitude comes together here," we are told.

> There is in us something that must be called divine, something by which we already dwell close to God [*nous demeurons déjà auprès de Dieu*]: it is the movement by which we efface ourselves, it is abandon—the abandonment of what we believe to be, a retreat outside ourselves and outside everything, a seeking of emptiness through the desire that is like the tension of this emptiness and that, when it is the desire for desire (then a surnatural desire), is the desire of emptiness itself, emptiness desiring (115; 167).

Blanchot affirms Gnosticism more surely than Weil, although, to be sure, his version of it bears little resemblance to what the Cathari held. The πνεῦμα is not a spark of the uncreated deity but is rather the desire that recognition of the Outside, the non-world of image, awakes in us no longer to say "I."

*

Losing the power to say "I" is a strong motif in Weil's writing. It stems from the mental power granted to the "I" in the Cartesian tradition that came to her from Maine de Biran by way of Alain: "I have power, therefore I am [*Je puis, donc je suis*]," she writes in an early essay.[40] One has only to open *La Pesanteur et la grâce* to see what she makes of this tradition: "We possess nothing in the world—a mere chance can strip us of everything—except the power to say 'I' [*le pouvoir de dire je*]. That is what we have to give to God—in other words, to destroy. There is absolutely no other free act which it is given to us to accomplish—only the destruction of the 'I' [*la destruction du je*]."[41] Elsewhere, one sees another slant of light fall on the proposition: "Let the 'I' disappear in such a way that Christ, thanks to the intermediary formed by our soul and body, himself goes to the help of the neighbor."[42] And, lest we misunderstand, she says, "One must not be *I*, but still less must one be *We*."[43]

When we turn to Blanchot we find him referring to "those who have lost the power to say 'I' [*celui qui a perdu le pouvoir de dire 'Je'*]" in "Réflexions sur l'enfer" (1954), gathered in *L'Entretien infini*, but the idea behind it was formed far earlier.[44] The loss of selfhood, of "being in nothingness itself," appears vividly in *Thomas l'Obscur* (1950); in *L'Espace littéraire* (1955) we find the insight that in writing the *je* becomes *il*; and, later, in *Le Pas au-delà* (1973) we are told, "Everything must efface itself, everything will efface itself."[45] Where Weil uses the expression to denote the evacuation of selfhood before God, Blanchot uses it to refuse the idea of the "subject" in post-Cartesian thought, to insist that the "I" is no more than an "abbreviation that one could call canonical," and to shift attention from the individual subject to the community, understood as an archipelago rather than as a self-contained unity.[46] Behind his claims there abides Sartre's rejection of the transcendental "I" in *La Transcendance de l'ego* (1936).[47]

One could track other motifs prominent in Weil's writing that Blanchot absorbs and redirects. I will attend to just two:

1. "The name of God," for instance, is taken up in *Le Pas au-delà* in a manner that points to what one might call "gnostic atheism." There is a hidden corridor that leads to this discussion from the commentary on the reserve needed in naming God in *L'Entretien infini*.[48] God's name, Blanchot announces in the later text, exceeds language, but not in the sense that "Good" as one of the divine names does. Instead, the name of the hyper-transcendent deity disappears on entering language: its absolute singularity is lost in the play of words that are only ever relatively singular. We seek that absolutely singular and secret name as a "cure" for language, which can never name that singularity; and yet, for Blanchot, there is nothing to name.[49]
2. Affliction is another motif of importance to both writers. For Weil, inner affliction renders human life "impossible"; our quest for the good, and our very desire, is impossible: neither can be satisfied. Yet this very situation is needed in

order to bring us to God.⁵⁰ Things are quite different for Blanchot. "In the space of affliction," he tells us, "we have very close to us, and almost at our disposition, all that religion, in inverting it, projected up into the heavens. We are not above but beneath time: this is eternity."⁵¹ It is the Outside that runs "beneath time" and that we experience in times of affliction when time occurs without event and when we lose our world. When we pass from this world to the Outside we lose relation with the possible and can only respond to the endless passing of being into nonbeing (image) he calls "the impossible."⁵²

We see in Blanchot's reading of Weil something entirely characteristic of his cast of mind. Her experiences that are usually called "mystical" are, for him, truly not of what transcends the mundane world but what runs beneath it, detected only in and through language; her focus on attention is less on the good than, when seen properly, by way of her careful use of language; and her intense love of God is in fact a mode of atheism, even though she observes that "Every atheist is an idolater."⁵³ Limit-experience dissolves the beyond, for Blanchot, and yet Weil affirms God as prior to the world, as loving it without cause, as pure "attention without distraction."⁵⁴ Like all critics, Blanchot reads his author within his own horizon: her certitude is properly to be found in limit-experience, not in contact with the objective sphere of the truth or the descent of Christ into her soul.⁵⁵ In reading Blanchot we are likely to be surprised that he is so very sure that experience of the Outside is the only thing that ultimately guarantees certainty, especially when limit-experience eliminates the "absolute beyond." We will not be surprised to find him a consistent atheist, but that he does so on Gnostic grounds is another matter entirely and one that has not been remarked.

Notes

1 Blanchot, "Simone Weil et la certitude," *Nouvelle Nouvelle Revue Française* 55 (juillet 1957): 297–310, and "L'Expérience de Simone Weil," *Nouvelle Nouvelle Revue Française* 56 (août 1957): 165–79.
2 See, for example, Blanchot, "Prophetic Speech," *BC*, 84 (116), *IC*, 47, 53, 139 (67, 76, 207) and *WD*, 6 (16).
3 See Simone Weil, *Sur la science* (Paris: Gallimard, 1966) and *Poèmes, suivis de "Venise sauvée"* (Paris: Gallimard, 1968). The two-part essay on Weil is hardly revised, however.
4 Blanchot, "Affirmation (desire, affliction)," *IC*, 106 (153).
5 See, in particular, Miklos Vetö, *The Religious Metaphysics of Simone Weil*, trans. Joan Dargan (Albany, NY: State University of New York Press, 1994), 2. The book appeared in French in 1971. It should be noted that Weil declines to speak of her sense of the Christ by way of "mystical experience." Her reservations about such experiences evidently were given in her *lycée* class in Roanne in 1933–4. See her *Lectures on Philosophy*, trans. Hugh Price, intro. Peter Winch (Cambridge: Cambridge University Press, 1978), 171. Yet also see her more positive affirmation in *The Need for Roots: Prelude to a Declaration of Duties towards Mankind*, trans. Arthur Wills, pref. T. S. Eliot (London: Routledge, 2002), 274–5. For Weil, the mystical is best approached by way of contemplation, which she styles as attention, rather than experience.

6 Weil, *Gravity and Grace*, intro. and postscript Gustave Thibon, trans. Emma Crawford and Mario von der Ruhr (New York: Routledge, 2002), 102.
7 Blanchot, "Inner Experience," *FP*, 38 (48). For the importance of *la contestation*, see Kevin Hart and Geoffrey Hartman, eds., *The Power of Contestation: Perspectives on Maurice Blanchot* (Baltimore, MD: The Johns Hopkins University Press, 2004), esp. ch. 8.
8 Blanchot's modifier "often" should be noted, especially in the light of an early essay by Weil such as "Science and Perception in Descartes," in *Formative Writings 1929–1941*, ed. and trans. Dorothy Tuck McFarland and Wilhelmina Van Ness (London: Routledge and Kegan Paul, 1987), 21–88.
9 See Rush Rhees, *Discussions of Simone Weil*, ed. D. Z. Phillips and assisted by Mario von der Ruhr (Albany, NY: State University of New York Press, 2000), 64.
10 Weil's final confession of faith may be found in her *Gateway to God*, ed. David Raper with the collaboration of Malcolm Muggeridge and Vernon Sproxton (New York: Crossroad, 1982), 62–5.
11 See Weil, "Forms of the Implicit Love of God," in *Waiting for God*, trans. Emma Crawford, intro. Leslie A. Fiedler (New York: Capricorn Books, 1959), 209.
12 See Weil, *Letter to a Priest* (New York: G. P. Putnam's Sons, 1954).
13 Weil, "Spiritual Autobiography," *Waiting for God*, 69, 72.
14 Weil, "New York Notebook," in *First and Last Notebooks*, trans. Richard Rees (London: Oxford University Press, 1970), 157. Also see *The Need for Roots*, 247.
15 See Weil, *Gravity and Grace*, 37.
16 See Weil, *Seventy Letters*, trans. and ed. Richard Rees (London: Oxford University Press, 1965), 87.
17 Weil, *The Notebooks of Simone Weil*, 2 vols., trans. Arthur Wills (London: Routledge and Kegan Paul, 1956), vol. 1, 127.
18 For the "I" as a lie, see *First and Last Notebooks*, 132, and for sin saying "I," see *Notebooks*, vol. 1, 126.
19 See Blanchot, "Tragic Thought," *IC*, 99 (141).
20 Weil, *Oppression and Liberty*, trans. Arthur Wills and John Petrie, intro. F. C. Ellert (Amherst, MA: The University of Massachusetts Press, 1973), 173.
21 Weil, *Seventy Letters*, 178.
22 Weil, "The Love of God and Affliction," *Waiting for God*, 133.
23 See St. Bernard of Clairvaux, *On the Song of Songs*, 4 vols., vol. 4: *Sermons 67–86*, trans. Irene Edmonds, intro. Jean Leclercq (Kalamazoo, MI: Cistercian Publications, 1980), 74. 2. 5, and Lopa de Vega, *Poesía selecta*, ed. Antonio Carreño (Madrid: Ediciones Cátedra, 1984), 326.
24 See Peter Lombard, *The Sentences*, trans. Giulio Silano, 4 vols, vol. 1: *The Mystery of the Trinity* (Toronto: Pontifical Institute of Medieval Studies, 2007), distinction 17, ch. 1. Also see Augustine, *De trinitate*, 8.5.12.
25 See Thomas Aquinas, *In I Sent*. d. 17 art. 1 *responsio*, *In 1 Sent*. d. 17 (*Lectura Romana*), q. 1 art. 2, *responsio*, *Summa theologiæ*, 1a q. 20 art. 2 *responsio*.
26 See *Summa theologiæ* 2a-2æ q. 23 art. 2 *responsio*.
27 See, for instance, Weil's letter to Déodat Roché, *Seventy Letters*, 129–31, *Letter to a Priest*, 37, and "Forms of the Implicit Love of God," 161–2. For a consideration of the Languedoc culture that flourished between the Cathari and the Catholics, also see *Écrits historiques et politiques* (Paris: Gallimard, 1960), ch. 4 and 5.
28 For early studies of the Cathari, see Charles Schmidt, *Histoire et doctrine de la secte des cathares ou albigeois* (Paris: J. Cherbuliez, 1849), Edmond Broeckx, *Le Catharisme*:

Étude sur les doctrines, la vie religieuse et morale, l'activité littéraire et les vicissitudes de la secte cathare avant la croisade (Hoogstraten: J. Haseldonckx, 1916), Hans Söderberg, *La religion des cathars: Étude sur le gnosticisme de la basse antiquité et du Moyen âge* (Uppsala: Almqvist and Wiksells Boktr., 1949) and Zoé Oldenbourg, *Le bûcher de Montségur: 16 mars 1244* (Paris: Gallimard, 1959). The *Cahiers d'études cathares* begins publication in 1949, and the *Bibliographie du chararisme languedocien*, ed. Pierre de Berne-Lagarde, appears in 1957 from the Institut des études cathares in Toulouse. The number of books on the topic increases in the 1960s, rises sharply in the 1970s, and then continues to escalate.

29 See, for example, Weil, *Notebooks*, vol. 2, 352, *Gravity and Grace*, 30.
30 See, for instance, Weil, *Letter to a Priest*, 64, and *Gravity and Grace*, 159–63.
31 See Weil, "New York Notebook," 103.
32 Weil, *Gravity and Grace*, 27.
33 See, for instance, St. John of the Cross, "The Dark Night of the Soul," in *Collected Works*, trans. Kieran Kavanaugh and Otilio Rodriguez (Washington, DC: ICS Publications, 1991), Jean-Pierre de Caussade, *Self-Abandonment to Divine Providence*, trans. John Beevers (New York: Image, 1993), and François Fénelon, *Oeuvres de Fénelon: Archevêque-duc de Cambrai*, nouvelle éd. revue et corrigée avec soin, 10 vols. (Paris: L. Tenré et Boistre fils aîné, 1822), vol. 5, 156–7.
34 See Weil, "Science and Perception in Descartes," 87; "Pre-War Notebook," *First and Last Notebooks*, 38, 84; *Notebooks*, vol. 1, 225.
35 See Weil, "New York Notebook," 283.
36 Weil, "New York Notebook," 103. Also see *Gravity and Grace*, 38.
37 See Weil, *Letter to a Priest*, 44.
38 See Dionysius the Areopagite, *The Divine Names*, iv.
39 See Weil, "Forms of the Implicit Love of God," 145.
40 Weil, "Science and Perception in Descartes," 59.
41 Weil, *Gravity and Grace*, 26.
42 Weil, *Notebooks*, vol. 2, 358.
43 Weil, *Notebooks*, vol. 1, 298.
44 Blanchot, "Reflections on Hell," *IC*, 173 (259).
45 Blanchot, *TO*, 100 (116) *SL*, 26 (21); and *SNB*, 53 (76). I analyze the motif of losing the power to say "I" in *The Dark Gaze*, ch. 4.
46 Blanchot, *SNP*, 4 (12). For the shift to community, understood in Blanchot's sense, see "The Relation of the Third Kind: Man without Horizon," *IC*, 71 (101).
47 For an English translation, see Jean-Paul Sartre, *The Transcendence of the Ego: An Existentialist Theory of Consciousness*, trans. and intro. Forrest Williams and Robert Kirkpatrick (New York: Hill and Wang, 1960), 38–42.
48 See Blanchot, "Affirmation (desire, affliction)," *IC*, 119 (173).
49 See Blanchot, *SNB*, 48 (69).
50 See Weil, *Gravity and Grace*, 94–7.
51 Blanchot, "Affirmation (Desire, Affliction)," *IC*, 120 (175).
52 See Blanchot, "How to Discover the Obscure," *IC*, 48 (68). Blanchot refers to this chapter in "Affirmation (desire, affliction)," *IC*, 446 n. 7 (174 n.).
53 Weil, "New York Notebook," 308.
54 Weil, "New York Notebook," 141.
55 See Weil's remarks on certainty in her letters to Father Perrin, *Waiting for God*, 64, and to Joë Bosquet in 1942, *Seventy Letters*, 141.

5

The Aggrieved Community

One of the most remarkable politico-philosophical dialogues in the twentieth century concerns the nature of community. Does "community" contain an ineradicable memory of "communion," and thereby inevitably have conceptual ties to Christianity, if not (to shift categories very dramatically) to fascism? Or can the word, rather, indicate a new way of being in common, one that became briefly visible in the communist experiment, understood first as the appearing of the truth of democracy before it collapsed under the weight of ideology and militarism?[1] Maurice Blanchot and Jean-Luc Nancy have brooded on these questions with one another in mind.[2] Does this pondering constitute a dialogue? The question is difficult to answer, partly because Blanchot finds hidden complications in the very idea of dialogue and partly because Nancy, himself a thinker of dialogue, well attuned to it as both errant and a mode of sharing, largely conducts his response after Blanchot's death, finding decisive motifs of the older man's early right-wing political commitments in his later left-wing thought, motifs that presumably lie at the heart of their different understandings of community.[3]

In February 1983 Nancy published a long essay at the invitation of Jean-Christophe Bailly in an issue of *Aléa* that was dedicated to the theme of "La Communauté, le nombre." This is "La Communauté désœuvrée."[4] Since one of Blanchot's signature words, *désœuvrée*, is in the title, and since the thoughts of Blanchot's close friend Georges Bataille on community animate the essay, it could not be a great surprise that Blanchot would write a response to it. (The exact value of the word "response" here will need to be weighed.) This is *La Communauté inavouable* (1983). In 1986 Nancy published *La Communauté désœuvrée*, which contains a slightly revised version of the original essay as its first chapter; and then there is a long pause in the conversation, at least between the two main parties.[5] Nancy publishes *La Communauté affronté*, which was commissioned as an introduction to an Italian translation of *La Communauté inavouable*, in 2001, and thereafter *Maurice Blanchot, passion politique* (2011), a commentary on a hitherto unpublished letter or *récit* written by Blanchot about his early political itinerary in 1984. Finally, there follows *La Communauté désavouée* (2014), a critical reading of *La Communauté inavouable*.[6]

This dense exchange invites many questions about the relations of democracy and community, about the memory of communion in community, about what communism opened for humankind to contemplate about the possibilities of our being in common, about the nature and effectiveness of political conversion, about the relations of community and the sacred, about the relations of literature and politics, and about what dialogue means when conducted if the idea of the human subject has been called radically into question. Here I will follow only one thread, and only for a little while: Nancy's claim that, despite his affirmation of a community unregulated by a reference to unity, Blanchot is committed to a notion of communion, indeed a Eucharistic community.

*

Nancy insists time and again that Blanchot's *La Communauté inavouable* is a response to his essay. He tells us that Blanchot "expressly set [his book] up to resonate" with his article, although later this is put more circumspectly: the essay provides "the occasion" for Blanchot's reflections.[7] Later, though, Nancy regains his boldness, saying that, "Blanchot's book was thus *written from beginning to end* as a response or rejoinder—in many ways, as a riposte—to the text I published in *Aléa*" [my emphasis], and he stars himself as "the first person obligated" in any examination of Blanchot on community.[8] That the "response" is not merely a difference of opinion is evident: Blanchot "undoubtedly disapproved of the way I had read Bataille," Nancy tells us, and also that he "felt diminished [*démuni*] before this judgment that was more authoritative" than his own.[9] This disapproval pivots on Blanchot reminding his readers of Bataille's work on community in the 1930s and 1940s, which Nancy does not consider; but it is worth keeping in mind the younger man's carefully nourished grievance over the decades, right down to a sense of "intimidation" he finds in Blanchot's little book.[10]

Blanchot begins *La Communauté inavouable* with a reference to Nancy's essay, which should be read with care: "In the wake [*À partir*] of an important text by Jean-Luc Nancy, I would again like to take up a reflection, *never in fact interrupted although surfacing only at long intervals, concerning the communist exigency. . .*" [my emphasis].[11] Thereafter, one finds two reservations about Nancy's reading of Bataille, two admiring allusions to his thought, an injunction, not restricted to Nancy, that we must continue to think about community, and a line from another essay by Nancy quoted as an epigraph to a slightly recast consideration of Marguerite Duras's *La Maladie de la mort*.[12] Nancy admits that Blanchot "wasn't wrong" to be aggrieved when reading his account of Bataille, for he had indeed avoided mentioning the years of *Contre-attaque* and *Acéphale*. The "limit-situation" does not interest him, as it had Bataille and Blanchot before and during the War, and the Bataille of the 1950s had abandoned "all affirmation that could have been called 'communist.'"[13] Given that the second part of the little book, the section devoted to Duras, was written before Nancy's essay appeared, it is difficult to see how the whole book could have been written "from beginning to end" with Nancy in mind; indeed, the final forty-two pages of the French text are exclusively concerned with Duras and Levinas and make no allusion to Nancy.[14] So Nancy overstates the extent to which Blanchot responds solely to his essay, and gives insufficient credence to the history of Blanchot's writing on communism and on behalf of left-wing causes. What then motivates the grievance that seems to animate Nancy's writings about *La Communauté inavouable*?

Putting aside Nancy's personal reaction to the book—the felt sense of diminishment and intimidation in the face of a powerful text by a major writer in which his understanding of Bataille is brought into question—the answer is not hard to find. He tells us that "the meaning" of Blanchot's response "extended back much further in his life," that it "bears witness to a profound fidelity to his earliest ambitions," by which he means the older man's memory of his youthful and "aristocratic" "right-wing anarchism," a memory that has been kept in play with another dimension of his political thought, one that is "democratic, rebellious in the name of a law of justice beyond all law."[15] It would be, it seems, Blanchot's political past that silently organizes his present political thinking, and which leads him to slight Nancy. To which the younger man responds, well after the older man's death, and thereby ensuring that he can have the last word, by reminding us that Blanchot had a past in which he rejected democracy in favor of alternatives promoted by the far right.[16] Indeed, not only did Blanchot express disenchantment with democracy in the 1930s but also he decreed it to have lost its radiance in the early 1980s.[17] Blanchot and Nancy: not quite a community of friends, but an aggrieved community, asymmetrical in volume of response over time and, in addition, with each having different reasons for irritation or resentment.

*

In *Maurice Blanchot: Passion politique* Nancy notes that Blanchot's reflections on community go in a different, even opposing, direction from his own, and it is striking that Nancy points to how Blanchot "made a 'communion' spring up from the dark ground of community" [*faisait surgir dans le fond obscur de la communauté une 'communion'*].[18] This is not how we usually think of the later Blanchot, who is guided, as he says at the beginning of *L'Entretien infini*, by "an anonymous, distracted, deferred, and dispersed way of being in relation, by which everything is brought into question—and first of all the idea of God, of the Self, of the Subject, then of Truth and the One, then finally the idea of the Book and the Work."[19] Listening to these words, it would be very hard to see a "communion" emerge as something that Blanchot endorses, but let us look to see what he actually says in *La Communauté inavouable*.

First of all, Blanchot asks, is it not the case that community is strictly "outside intelligibility" [*dehors de l'entente*], and his reason for posing the question is straightforward: community, as he conceives it, cannot be avowed because it has a property that cannot be common to any group or gathering.[20] This property is foundational, not accidental; for at the ground of community we do not find a relation between Same and Same but between Same and Other (or, more strictly, as we will see, Other and Other).[21] Another person is irreducibly other, as Blanchot learned from Levinas, and this alterity indicates an inability for sharing to take place: accordingly community implies the absence of community. In establishing this initial difficulty in even defining "community," Blanchot speaks of the relation with the other person by way of "dissymmetry," as we would expect him to, if we have read his responses to Levinas's *Totalité et infini* in *L'Entretien infini*.[22] Later in *La Communauté inavouable*, though, Blanchot will speak instead of "asymmetry" being at the heart of community; and this slight change of vocabulary is not without interest, as we shall see in a moment.

Blanchot's caveat about whether "community" can be understood has different senses and functions in parts of his text that are not all that far from one another. At first, we take it as a characteristic index of the radical nature of his questioning; the new "way of being in relation" resists the usual categories of understanding intersubjective bonds. Thereafter, however, we are asked to notice that the notion of community, as rigorously formulated, is inherently unstable and so communities cannot survive for long; they fall back into communions of Same and Same. Communities tend to be small, Blanchot freely acknowledges. "The community," he says, "seems to propose itself as a tendency towards a *communion*, even a fusion, that is to say an effervescence assembling the elements only to give rise to a unity (a super-individuality) that would expose itself to the same objections arising from the simple consideration of the single individual, locked in his immanence."[23] Sharing cannot take place for long in a community as Blanchot conceives it because he thinks in terms of Same and Other rather than being in common. Inevitably, though, those in a community may come to think of themselves in less radical ways, as citizens or members or individuals, and when this happens community slides toward communion.

If Blanchot appears to draw from Levinas here, it is not a simple borrowing but a significant readjustment. As we know from *L'Entretien infini* he does not affirm that the moral height of the other person is a phenomenological given. Instead, he argues that intersubjective space curves upward in both directions: I am above the other person, and at the same time he or she is above me. Hence for Blanchot intersubjective relations turn, strictly, on Other and Other, a pivot that calls into question each party as a subject. The vigilance required in for this situation to be maintained doubtless renders community small and temporary. Democratic societies are necessarily marked, for Blanchot, by a failure of community: they simply cannot sustain a relation of Other and Other and must fall back into relations of Same and Other or even Same and Same. This does not make Blanchot antidemocratic, however, nor does it make him anti-communist. On his model we can always glimpse the possibility of a communism beyond any "real communism," as Nancy puts it, one that would be short-lived, to be sure, but nonetheless potent.[24] The community *désœuvrement* springs from communion and falls back into it while leaving a memory of community. His prime example of this explosive, short-lived community is May 1968.

Now Blanchot does not affirm the value of this communion to which any community is perpetually exposed, and from which it springs, and he shields Bataille from all criticism that suggests he allowed or admired social fusion. In doing so, he notes that Bataille's "non-religious quest for an ecstatic experience" did not implicate him in any thought of social fusion.[25] Indeed, contestation requires exposure to another person, and "inner experience" is never something that could be undergone alone; it involves communication with another. Ecstasy presupposes "a community" (18; 35), not a communion; it presumes the otherness of another person, for only otherness can contest my self-understanding as a unified subject. In explaining this view Blanchot borrows from Levinas, not from Bataille: he writes of "breaking with few words the impossibility of Saying [*l'impossibilité du Dire*] which the unique trait of experience seems to contain."[26] As the etymology of the word suggests, "expérience" presumes breaking with what is known and possible and exposing oneself to what is unforeseeable, unknown, and perhaps perilous (and hence coded as "impossible").[27]

The ethical relation of the one to the other begins, Levinas says, in a structure of responsibility that is prior to intentional consciousness.[28] So while Blanchot indicates the fragility of community, its tendency to break down after only a short period, he does not affirm or defend communion in any sense, and certainly not by way of social fusion. There is reason, then, not to accept Nancy's implication that Blanchot remains committed to a notion of communion.

Is Nancy correct, though, to suggest that there is some "christic" dimension to Blanchot's thought about community?[29] An examination of Blanchot's earliest writings suggests nothing hidden or secreted, no commitment to *communitas perfecta* or to *Gemeinschaft*, and no important adhesion to the Catholic teachings he received as a child.[30] Let us take a step back, however, and ask, first, whether there is a theistic dimension to Blanchot's mature thought. What founds community, Blanchot argues, is "my presence for another who absents himself by dying."[31] This relation, he says, subsists in the *vous* form, not the *tu* form, and is one of "asymmetry." We might gloss "asymmetry" here along Levinasian lines, that is, by way of the transcendence of the dying person: he or she speaks to me in the tone of command because he or she is another, and always speaking from a position of height with respect to me. Yet we know what Blanchot himself would say about this gloss. Asymmetry presumes the ethical height of the other person, as Levinas says in *Totalité et infini*, and this transcendence, Blanchot insists, must be understood without reference to God.[32] Blanchot's words are that the affirmation of the other must be maintained "independently of the theological context in which [the affirmation of the other person] presents itself."[33] On reflection, he acknowledges that neither "theological" nor "context" would be acceptable to Levinas: "theological" would not be appropriate because Levinas does not presume any phenomenality of revelation or, for that matter, make existential statements about God, and "context" is out of place because the face of the other is held to signify καθ' αὑτὸ, outside any and all context.[34] How something can signify outside any context is neither explained nor, I think, able to be explained.

And yet Blanchot keeps both words, and he does so, I take it, in order to mark the theistic implication of "asymmetry." When Levinas says, "All true discourse is discourse with God" Blanchot immediately recasts it to mean discourse between men. It is as though he fears that, despite Levinas's insistence on the face signifying καθ' αὑτὸ his friend is involving not only the face of the other person but also God, and so forming a context that is theological. In order to neutralize any possibility of God being implied or presumed in the new "way of being in relation" Blanchot replaces "asymmetry" with "dissymmetry," Same and Other with Other and Other: I and the other person exist in Riemannian space, as it were, each transcendent with respect to the other. A casual reading of *La Communauté inavouble* might find a theistic assumption in the *founding* of community that is not present in the *account* of community, which turns on dissymmetry. Yet if we read *La Communauté inavouble* alongside *L'Entretien infini* we will not find that at all. The asymmetry at issue turns on the fact that someone is dying *now*, and not on the God whose trace we may traverse in approaching another person.

Could there be, however, what Nancy calls a "christic" element in Blanchot's sense of community, a memory of communion, even a Eucharistic communion? It would take a long time to give an adequate answer to this question, for we would have to examine minutely the values that "sacrifice" and "substitution" have in Bataille, Blanchot, and Levinas. Given that Nancy is focusing the question for us, we would also have to be attuned to his understanding of Christianity, which would not be likely to withstand the scrutiny of a theologian, especially a specialist in Christology.[35] More, we would have to see how Jewish notions of sacrifice and Christian notions of atonement have been brought into these writings. By no means can we rest with an Anselmian theology of vicarious representation as being *the* Christian understanding of satisfaction or atonement. One must take care when thinking "Eucharist" and "communion" together, for there is no clear fusion of the faithful that takes place in the celebration of the Eucharist. The sacrament of the altar is a sacrificial offering that is shared by the community, yet in partaking of it the community finds itself in a complex temporality, being referred back to the Passion and forward to the Banquet of Heaven. Memory and anticipation, modes of presentification rather than presencing, divide any present moment in which a fusion might be thought to take place.

If we look closely at what Blanchot writes in *La Communauté inavouble* we find that he proposes a theory of substitution. Yet it is not vicarious representation or anything like it; nor is it anything that points to the necessity or value of a communion. He stresses two "essential traits": "the community is not the restricted form of society, no more than it tends toward a communitarian fusion," and "it differs from a social cell in that it does not allow itself to create a work and has no production value as aim."[36] The community has no point unless it is "the service to others [*autrui*] unto/in death, so that the other does not get lost all alone, but is filled in for [*suppléé*] just as he brings to someone else [*un autre*] that supplementing [*suppléance*] accorded to himself."[37] The purported end of community is that *each member* reenacts the community's founding moment. As Blanchot sums up his position, "Mortal substitution is what replaces communion" [*La substitution mortelle est ce qui remplace la communion*].[38] There is no unique, vicarious sacrifice, for him, only an endless serial substitution, and far from offering a christic sense of communion Blanchot offers a *non-christic* explanation of *community*. Nancy goes to considerable lengths to avoid seeing this point. Perhaps the most extreme of them concerns his attempt to make Blanchot into a Christian. Let us see how this happens.

"Assuredly," Blanchot writes, "there exists an abyss no theoretical deceit can bridge between the impotent power of what one cannot refer to except by that so easily misunderstood—the people (do not translate it as *Volk*)—and the strangeness of that antisocial society or association, always ready to dissolve itself, formed by *friends* or *couples*."[39] This would clearly be the case if one sought to compare the State with two lovers, yet, as Blanchot points out, it is possible to discern a way of thinking of "the people" without invoking the State. Nancy reads this passage in a remarkably ungenerous spirit: "Why bring up the possibility of deceit unless it is because one knows that it is highly probably that the reader wants to uncover a deceit or because one knows that one is already implicated in one?"[40] The answer is plain enough: because it is common to bridge the abyss by an appeal to unity. The State is one, and the lovers are one. Now the lovers are for Blanchot a community, Other and Other. The people can be regarded in a similar manner; their situation resembles "the gathering of the children of Israel in view of the Exodus if they had gathered while at the same time forgetting to leave."[41] The scene is of a people who are never able to put down roots in the Same, a people who glimpse the possibility of living a plural, mobile, and deferred way of being. Nancy draws a different conclusion: "one should discern here the evocation of a fantasmatic (an originary [*ultra-primitif*]) Christianity prior to Judaism."[42] Not at all: what is noticed here is what Blanchot calls a "communism. . . always beyond communism."[43]

*

None of this is to say, of course, that Blanchot does not speak of the sacred and sacrifice in his discussions of literature. He does so repeatedly, almost obsessively at times. In *L'Espace littéraire* he asks, "Why is art so intimately allied with the sacred?"[44] His answer is that the two are joined together at a very deep level, in the one movement of disclosure and concealment. Art turns on appearing, while the sacred is the principle of such manifestation, always anterior to manifestation.[45] The sacred is neither subject nor object but neutral.[46] Consequently, it may approach us yet never be reached. Positive religions, he implies, have always mistaken the neutral for the sacred; and yet it would be a mistake simply to deny the sacred, since to do that would be to take away "the profound *reserve*" that art needs. The writer is always involved in an act of self-sacrifice: at the extreme moment of composition, his or her "I" is renounced, leaving only the anonymity of the third person.[47] Is there a relation to this talk of the sacred and sacrifice and what Blanchot proposes in his political writing, especially about community?

There is such a relation, and it is at the heart of Nancy's brief discussion of Blanchot's political "conversion" from the far right to the far left. The word came up first in a letter that Philippe Lacoue-Labarthe sent to Blanchot on July 6, 1984 in which he talked about a proposal for a special number of *Cahiers de l'Herne* to be consecrated to Blanchot and mentioned Blanchot's "political conversion."[48] In *Maurice Blanchot: Passion politique* Nancy tells us that this "conversion" was "internal to Christianity" because he retained the notion of the infinite and "something of absolute transcendence."[49] Now to appeal to the infinite need not tie one to Christianity. Levinas also invokes the infinite, directly from Descartes, yet puts it to use in an ethics that is deeply informed by Judaism. And one can readily point out that, for Blanchot, the word "transcendence" is one that he rejects, although, to be sure, he attends to what he calls the "dead transcendence" that one finds in Kafka and, I presume, in other modern literature.[50] If Blanchot retains anything of transcendence it is not "absolute transcendence" but rather a particular form of what Wahl calls "transdescendance," in which the neutral is always anterior to phenomena.[51] Modernity has many exhibits of transdescendance, not least of all Derrida's quasi-concept, "la différance." Nancy's claim that Blanchot's political "conversion" is "internal to Christianity" is hard to justify, in part because he makes Christianity so vast a fuzzy set, one that includes atheism, that it is difficult to see what would not be internal to it. Needless to say, we can recognize forms of "Christian atheism," but these do not seem to converge with the views to which Blanchot subscribes. Without attention to examples and counterexamples that would clarify his view, it is hard to know what Nancy means here.

Also contained in *Maurice Blanchot: Passion politique* is a letter from Dionys Mascolo written to Philippe Lacoue-Labarthe in 1984. It is clear that Lacoue-Labarthe had invited Mascolo to contribute to the special number of *Cahiers de l'Herne* and had spoken of Blanchot's "conversion" and of his "exemplary itinerary" from the right to the left of politics. Mascolo contests this sense of Blanchot's change of heart with regard to politics. There is nothing exemplary in Blanchot's itinerary; on the contrary, Mascolo deems it singular, for Blanchot deduces "*the necessity of communism*" from "*the existence of literature.*" I take it that Mascolo has in mind Blanchot's review of his book *Le Communisme, révolution et communication ou la dialectique des valeurs et des besoins* (1953). Blanchot ends that piece in the following way:

> It is undoubtedly the task of our age to move toward an affirmation that is entirely *other*. A difficult task, essentially risky. It is to this task that communism recalls us with a rigor that it itself often shirks, and it is also to this task that "artistic experience" recalls us in the realm that is proper to it. A remarkable coincidence.[52]

Blanchot returns time and time again to aspects of this claim, speaking at first of "literature" and then later of "writing," even "prophetic writing" and the "erotic" (with respect to Robert Musil's *The Man without Qualities* (1930)).[53] He speaks of "everyday speech" and its relation to the neutral, which is "entirely *other*," neither a subject nor an object; and there is no doubt that Mascolo is right to suggest that, on the basis of all he knew, Blanchot's political change of heart cannot strictly be regarded as an example of anything.

And yet there is perhaps more to say on the topic. For it was ten years later, in *L'Instant de ma mort* (1994), when Blanchot wrote in another way about what might well be construed as a "conversion" with regard to political views. I am thinking of the passage when the narrator recalls standing before a firing squad. At this stage of the narrative, he believes them to be Germans, and he has every reason to think that he is about to be executed:

> I know—do I know it—that the one at whom the Germans were already aiming, awaiting but the final order, experienced then a feeling of extraordinary lightness [*un sentiment de légèreté extraordinaire*], a sort of beatitude [*une sorte de béatitude*] (nothing happy, however)—sovereign elation? The encounter of death with death?
>
> In his place, I will not try to analyze. He was perhaps suddenly invincible. Dead—immortal. Perhaps ecstasy. Rather the feeling of compassion for suffering humanity, the happiness of not being immortal or eternal.[54]

It turns out, however, that the soldiers are not Germans but Russians; they belong to the Vlassov army and allow the young man to escape. He does so, hiding for some time, and then returns to see that the land has been burned and three young sons of farmers had been "slaughtered" [*abattus*].[55] The Château, where the young man lived, had not been burned down "Because it was the Château."⁵⁶ Then a change is registered: "No doubt what then began for the young man was the torment of injustice. No more ecstasy; the feeling that he was only living because, even in the eyes of the Russians, he belonged to a noble class."⁵⁷

Several things are worth noting in these two passages. First, the young man seems to experience a non-theistic ecstasy: his death will not render him immortal, except in the trivial sense that he will no longer be mortal. Already, however, this "ecstasy" is modified into "the feeling of compassion for suffering humanity." Thereafter, once he returns and sees what has happened, all ecstasy is disowned, and there is no further talk of compassion. Instead, he experiences "the torment of injustice": he has been spared death by dint of his social class while others of a lower class have been murdered. *L'Instant de ma mort* is a complex text in which, as Derrida and Lacoue-Labarthe have shown, testimony is given by way of a narrative that has autobiographical moments.⁵⁸ What seems to be offered here is the narrative of a conversion from one form of life to another, and that this is recognized by the narrator to turn on an affirmation of social justice. It should be noted, though, that the narrator and the young man form a community, each other than the other. The narrator at once knows what the young man knew yet does not know it, now being other than him: "I know—do I know it—..." [*Je sais — le sais-je —. . .*].

Is there an affirmation here by the young man of something that is "entirely *other*?" It is hard to say: he experiences "a feeling of extraordinary lightness, a sort of beatitude," which might well be regarded as "entirely *other*," although the allusion to "a feeling" and "sort of" introduces caveats. And he is made to experience "the torment of injustice," which may well point him to a way of thinking about the political order that, for him at the moment, is "entirely *other*" and that will get fleshed out only as late as *L'Entretien infini* and *La Communauté inavouable*. Yet all this is done in a narrative that seems to turn on an experience of conversion, a turn toward another way of thinking of society and the distribution of justice. Mascolo had no idea at the time of writing to Lacoue-Labarthe that *L'Instant de ma mort* would be written. Even if he had read it, though, he would surely have underlined that here too there can be no question of anything exemplary in this sort of political conversion. It is an abandonment of what Nancy calls "aristocratic" "right-wing anarchism," presumably grounded in limit-experience, and an endorsement of what he barely glimpsed at the time: a communism beyond communism, one that is of itself irreducible to communion but that inevitably slides back to "real communism," fascism, or even democracy.

Notes

1 See Jean-Luc Nancy, *The Truth of Democracy*, trans. Pascale-Anne Brault and Michael Naas (New York: Fordham University Press, 2010), 30.
2 Note should be made of an early attempt to think community as being in common: Eugen Fink, "Ontological Problems of Community," trans. Michael R. Heim, in *Contemporary German Philosophy*, 2 vols. (University Park, PA: The Pennsylvania State University Press, 1983), vol. 2, 1–19. Fink's important essay was read in German

at a conference held in Cologne in July 1953 and appeared in Spanish translation in 1956.
3. For Blanchot on dialogue, see his "Interruption (as on a Riemann surface)," *IC*, 75–9 (106–12), and for Nancy on dialogue, see his "Sharing Voices," trans. Gayle L. Ormiston, *Transforming the Hermeneutic Context: From Nietzsche to Nancy*, ed. and intro. Gayle L. Ormiston and Alan D. Schrift (Albany, NY: State University of New York Press, 1990), esp. 226–47.
4. Nancy, "La Communauté désœuvrée," *Aléa* 4 (février, 1983): 11–49.
5. Nancy, *La Communauté désœuvrée* (Paris: Christian Bourgois, 1986), translated into English as *The Inoperative Community*, ed. Peter Connor and trans. Peter Connor et al., foreword Christopher Fynsk (Minneapolis, MN: University of Minnesota Press, 1991).
6. Nancy, *La Communauté affronté* (Paris: Galilée, 2001), trans. as "The Confronted Community," trans. Amanda Macdonald, *Postcolonial Studies* 6, no. 1 (2003): 23–36; *Maurice Blanchot: Passion politique, lettre-récit de 1984 suive d'une lettre de Dionys Mascolo* (Paris: Galilée, 2011), and *La Communauté désavouée* (Paris: Galilée, 2014), trans. as *The Disavowed Community*, trans. Philip Armstrong (New York: Fordham University Press, 2016). Also see Nancy's interview with Mathilde Girard, "Reste inavouable," *Lignes: Les Politiques de Maurice Blanchot, 1930–1993*, mars 2014, 155–76. Leslie Hill supplies a full account chronology of the "exchange," in his *Nancy, Blanchot*, 247–52. Also relevant is the dossier "Questions ouvertes à Jean-Luc Nancy: Autour de *La Communauté désavouée*," *Cahiers Maurice Blanchot* 4 (hiver 2015/2016): 88–150.
7. See Nancy, "The Confronted Community," 27, and *Maurice Blanchot*, 31.
8. Nancy, *The Disavowed Community*, 5, 4.
9. Nancy, *The Disavowed Community*, 10, 12.
10. See Nancy, *The Disavowed Community*, 90 n. 6. Nancy takes the idea of intimidation from Michel Surya's *Sainteté de Bataille* (Paris: Éditions de l'éclat, 2012), 93. For Surya, however, the ascription of intimidation is affirmative.
11. Blanchot, *UC*, 1 (9). As Hill observes, however, "community" is not a word that is thickly in evidence in Blanchot's earlier writings. See his *Nancy, Blanchot*, 52.
12. See Blanchot, *UC*, 4, 7, 10, 19, 23, 29 (13, 18, 23, 38, 43, 51).
13. Nancy, *The Disavowed Community*, 10.
14. Nancy admits that the note to his essay in the original article on Duras must have been added when Blanchot was correcting the proof of the article. See *The Disavowed Community*, 28.
15. Nancy, *The Disavowed Community*, 58, x, 60.
16. That Blanchot wrote a considerable amount of political journalism for far right-wing political organs, some of it quite violent in its rhetoric, is well known. It is worth remarking that Nancy nowhere quotes or cites any of this material in support of his view of the far-right Blanchot as "aristocratic" in his "right-wing anarchism."
17. See Nancy, *The Disavowed Community*, 22. He cites Blanchot's "Intellectuals Under Scrutiny," trans. Michael Holland, *BR*, 221 (*IQ*, 19).
18. Nancy, *Maurice Blanchot*, 31.
19. Blanchot, *IC*, xii (vii).
20. Blanchot, *UC*, 1 (9).
21. See Blanchot, *UC*, 3 (12). Blanchot uses the words *Même* and *Autre*.
22. Blanchot, *UC*, 12 (25); see *IC*, ch. 5–7.
23. Blanchot, *UC*, 6–7 (17).

24 See Nancy, *The Disavowed Community*, 2.
25 Blanchot, *UC*, 7 (18).
26 Blanchot, *UC*, 18 (35).
27 See the discussion of the etymology of "expérience" in the introduction to this book.
28 See Levinas, "The Ruin of Representation," *DEH*, 111–21.
29 Nancy, *Maurice Blanchot*, 31.
30 For more detail, see Hill, *Nancy, Blanchot*, ch. 2.
31 Blanchot, *UC*, 9 (21).
32 See Levinas, *TI*, A3, and Blanchot, *IC*, 50 (71).
33 Blanchot, "Knowledge of the Unknown," *IC*, 56 (80).
34 See Blanchot, *IC*, 441 n. 2 (80 n. 1).
35 See, for example, these two passages: "Christianity has had only two dimensions, antinomical to one another: that of the *deus absconditus*, in which the Western disappearance of the divine is still engulfed, and that of the god-man, *deus communis*, brother of humankind, invention of a familial immanence of humanity, then of history as the immanence of salvation," and "Fascism was the grotesque or abject resurgence of an obsession with communion; it crystallized the motif of its supposed loss and the nostalgia for its images of fusion. In this respect, it was the convulsion of Christianity, and it ended up fascinating modern Christianity in its entirety," Nancy, "The Inoperative Community," 10, 17. Could one plausibly say that a religion as culturally, historically, theologically and philosophically complex as Christianity "has had *only two* dimensions" [my emphasis]? Can one responsibly say that "modern Christianity *in its entirety*" was fascinated by fascism" [my emphasis]?
36 Blanchot, *UC*, 11 (24).
37 Blanchot, *UC*, 11 (24).
38 Blanchot, *UC*, 11 (24).
39 Blanchot, *UC*, 33 (57).
40 Nancy, *The Disavowed Community*, 35.
41 Blanchot, *UC*, 33 (57).
42 Nancy, *The Disavowed Community*, 37.
43 Blanchot, *IC*, xii (viii).
44 Blanchot, *SL*, 233 (310).
45 See Blanchot, "The 'Sacred' Speech of Hölderlin," *WF*, 119, 122 (122, 125).
46 See Blanchot, "The Detour Towards Simplicity," *F*, 193 (220).
47 See, for example, Blanchot, *FP*, 5 (13).
48 Philippe Lacoue-Labarthe, *Ending and Unending Agony: On Maurice Blanchot*, trans. Hannes Opelz (New York: Fordham University Press, 2015), quoted by Aristide Bianchi and Leonid Kharlamov on p. 4. Blanchot uses the expression "une sorte de conversion" in his letter to Laporte, *Passion politique*, 61.
49 Nancy, *Maurice Blanchot*, 38.
50 See Blanchot, *SNP*, 27 (41) and "Reading Kafka," *WF*, 7 (15).
51 See Wahl, *Human Existence and Transcendence*, 28.
52 Blanchot, "On One Approach to Communism," *F*, 97 (114).
53 See Blanchot, "Prophetic Speech" and "Musil" in *BC*.
54 Blanchot, "The Instant of My Death," *ID*, 5 (11).
55 Blanchot, *ID*, 7 (13).
56 Blanchot, *ID*, 7 (13).
57 Blanchot, *ID*, 7 (15).

58 Surya goes to considerable lengths to discredit the historical reliability of this encounter with the Vlassov army on the basis of letters that Blanchot wrote about it at quite different times to Jean Paulhan (July 5, 1944) and Roger Laporte (November 18, 1982) and which appeared in the *Cahier de l'Herne* devoted to Blanchot (2014), 157 and 104 respectively. (There are other letters about the event, most notably to Jacques Derrida (July 20, 1994), Maurice Nadeau (April, 1977) and Pierre Prévost (November, 1944) about the same event with varying degrees of specificity.) He does so both in the "Envoi" to *L'Autre Blanchot* (2015) and especially in *À plus forte raison: Maurice Blanchot, 1940–1944, Suivi de deux lettres de Jean-Luc Nancy* (Paris: Éditions Hermann, 2021), part 2. His argument bypasses how one's experience is represented to others in manifolds of profiles and how epistolary selves and addressees are formed in correspondence: the sort of thing that Derrida analyzes so well in his "Telepathy," *Psyche: Inventions of the Other*, 2 vols., vol. 1, ed. Peggy Kamuf and Elizabeth Rottenberg (Stanford, CA: Stanford University Press, 2007), 226–61. Also, it overlooks Blanchot's memory as an older man and his reticence in writing about himself: that he dramatizes fictional events in his *récits* is apparent, but he tends to under-dramatize himself. Of course, there is no compelling reason to think that the account in *L'Instant de ma mort* offers a complete and historically accurate description of all that "really happened." The line between historical fact and fiction is troubled here as in other *récits* by Blanchot. For example, Bident suggests that the event might have occurred on June 20, 1944, rather than in the July of that year. See his *Maurice Blanchot*, 522 n. 5.

6

The Friendship of the No

Blanchot was always a political writer, and although over his lifetime his politics changed radically, from the far right to the far left and then somewhat to the side of the far left, he remained constant in his rejection of party and in his affirmation of dissidence. When, in 1986, Levinas was reminiscing with François Poiré about his close friend, the first thing he said is that when they met as undergraduates at Strasbourg, "I had the impression of an extreme intelligence, of an aristocratic cast of mind," and the second is that Blanchot was, "Very distanced politically from me during that epoch, he was monarchist . . .."[1] Extreme intelligence and, as we shall see, extreme politics: the combination is volatile, regardless of whether the politics are on the right or the left. Levinas goes on to say of his friend that, "He experienced the occupation in an extremely heightened and painful way . . . he also experienced 1968 in an extraordinary manner" (29). Levinas and Blanchot vowed friendship shortly after they met, a vow that was never broken on either side. Nor was the vow of friendship that Blanchot must have made early on to the "No," for it sustained him throughout his political itinerary, in the grim years leading up to the Vichy régime, the occupation of France by the *Wehrmacht*, as well as when the Fourth Republic was dissolved in 1958, when *les événements* of May 1968 irrupted, and when, not so very long after the student-worker uprising, some members of the French far left upset Blanchot by supporting Palestine over Israel.

As an author, the young Blanchot begins to come into focus for us as a journalist committed to the right, even at times the far right. He was one of those men who reached adulthood during what Emmanuel Mounier ironically called the time of *le désordre établi*, the established disorder, in which fascism and communism were both vying for supremacy in a world in which France seemed weak and impotent, threatened by an impending war it could not win. Only a spiritual, national revolution could save France. In one of Blanchot's first pieces, "Les pensées politiques de M. Paul Valéry," published in *La Revue française* in August 1931, he reviewed the great poet's *Regards sur le monde actuel* (1931). Blanchot noted how, for Valéry, the word "political" is seductive, and "excites considerable scruples and distaste in the author's mind," and that history "is nothing but a *horrible mélange*."[2] Blanchot takes exception to what he sees as Valéry's endorsement of amnesia as a political virtue, and sees his image of Europe as a monster, a Hippogryph or a Siren, or indeed a horror with many heads, like Cerberus or the Hydra, each with its own thoughts. "Europe will never have had the policy [*la politique*] which its thought demands," writes Valéry.[3] To which Blanchot says yes and no, for some European countries have no policies at all. What frightens Blanchot is the specter of *Homo Europaeus*, a creature like Aristide Briand who risks having no politics or thought and thereby attains only mediocrity. Valéry's elegant, almost weary reflections on the world today remain too fuzzy for the young Blanchot, too unaware of the need to remember what has happened, and too unconcerned with saving France in a world in which Europe is not so much "a balance of weaknesses" as a tragic play of weakness (France) and growing strengths nearby.[4]

Blanchot's own political views are more readily seen in another of his first pieces, "Comment s'emparer du pouvoir?," published in *Journal des débats* also in August 1931. He reviewed the Italian Curzio Malaparte's much discussed *Technique du coup d'état* (1931).[5] There Malaparte argued that, "the problem of the conquest and defense of the State is not a political one . . . it is a technical problem"—a matter of knowing when and how to occupy the telephone exchanges, control the water reserves and the electricity generators, and so on—and also taught the hard lesson that a revolution can wear itself out in strategy.[6] Critical of Hitler and Mussolini, Malaparte was removed from the Partito Nazionale Fascista and exiled, first in Lipari and then, more comfortably, in Ischia. Blanchot argued against Malaparte in his review that revolution is not always or entirely a matter of technique. Some revolutions are embedded in a prior politics, as was the case with the 1917 Russian overthrow of Czarist autocracy. Yet there is also the possibility of a revolution that comes about through "the bad politics of governments," and then the revolution must presumably itself create a new politics.[7]

That latter situation had been more or less the case since the First World War, Blanchot judged, pointing disparagingly to the premiership of Aristide Briand and the presidency of Raymond Poincaré.[8] Things did not improve over the years between the two wars. For all their policy differences, the governments of Pierre Laval and Edouard Daladier, and the *Front populaire* alliance of Léon Blum, could merely form pacts and sign treaties with nearby countries and do nothing decisive to strengthen France.[9] Far from helping to secure France, Blum's government was infiltrated by agents from Moscow.[10] Not that committed anti-communists were especially needed, for the position was insufficiently radical. In general, the young Blanchot thought, a government is only as good as its ability to enforce the rule of law, and accordingly a weak government in unstable times must be overthrown for the good of the country. Besides, Blanchot asked himself, why pay taxes to a coterie of private interests pretending to govern the country?[11] The League of Nations was no help; its muzzy internationalism could bring no clarity to the situation in France, since only force and the willingness to use it when needed create clarity in politics. A revolution must come, and it must come from French dissidents. Only "national ideas" give youth the hope they need, he said in 1933, and each day, he surmised, events bring the national, spiritual revolution closer "and make it more necessary."[12]

On the nationalist, far-right wing though he surely was, at no time did Blanchot align himself with fascism. His nonconformism in that regard was absolute. His preoccupation was preserving France against the threats of German rearmament and Soviet expansionism, against liberal ineffectiveness, and the encroachments of international socialism. There was no point in looking to Hitler: all he could give German youth was "a new religion" that was a "perverted nationalism," namely that of a superior race.[13] Fascism promoted an affirmative sense of "neither-nor" ("neither right nor left"), a fusion of elements from each side of politics achieved in a supposedly higher synthesis; but Blanchot took "neither-nor" in a negative sense, criticizing both the left and the right as pungently as he could.[14] He communicated his message in diverse, scattered, and at times irreconcilable ways. He wrote for the then generally respectable conservative paper *Journal des débats* as well as (and usually more fiercely) for short-lived nonconformist organs that ventured much further out on the right wing of politics than the readers of the venerable paper were easy with. Some of these organs were Catholic nationalist papers that attracted the young intellectuals who had broken with the royalist movement Action Française (condemned by Pius XI in 1926) and who formed La Jeune Droite: *Réaction, La Revue du Siècle* (renamed *La Revue du XXe Siècle* in 1934) and *La Revue universelle*.

Other papers to which he also contributed were even more extreme in their nationalist fervor: *Le Rempart, Combat,* and the nationalist syndicalist *L'Insurgé*. His pieces for these ephemeral publications are striking, at once independent and inflammatory in tone. If at times Blanchot may be found supporting the parliament, at other times he calls for its overthrow; he looks to democracy only to the extent that diplomacy can still save France.[15] His faith in parliament is intermittent, at best. In the June of 1933 when he expresses hope in diplomacy he also asserts, in another place, that national revolution is France's only chance of salvation.[16] In 1936 he is heard insisting that public salvation can be achieved only through terrorism.[17] If the thought seems extreme, we should note that he is alluding to the Comité de salut public established by Robespierre during the Terror which sought to defend the young Republic against domestic and foreign enemies. The ultimate aim is to protect France, not overthrow it; but there is much at risk before that aim can be fulfilled.

It is important to point out that Blanchot denounces what he calls, in no uncertain terms, "the barbaric persecutions of the Jews," and that he does so as early as May 1, 1933.[18] Does the young Blanchot publish reviews and commentaries in papers that run articles with anti-Semitic leanings? Yes, he does. Would it have been possible at the time to write for a right-wing paper, broadsheet, or periodical without appearing near such odious material? No, it would not: a certain level of anti-Semitism was everywhere and was widely tolerated. More than that, anti-Semitic slurs could easily be inserted into any text offered for publication. When we read an article signed by Blanchot denouncing "Juifs émigrés" and "Juifs déchaînes" shortly after Hitler re-militarized the Rhine, we must pause before speaking of xenophobia and anti-Semitism and weigh the very likely possibility of editorial interference in his piece.[19] For the remarks do not square with other comments he makes at the time about the Jews. Of course, no one can be completely sure of this at this late stage, which is one reason why silent pre-publication modification can be so damaging to a writer; and, if there was editorial intrusion, we might ask ourselves why Blanchot continued to write for the press after experiencing such crude tampering with his prose. He says himself that when *L'Insurgé* ran a foul anti-Semitic article he immediately worked with Thierry Maulnier to have the paper closed down.[20] Perhaps he was prepared to tolerate some editorial intervention but not outright anti-Semitism. Whatever the reasons for his silence in 1936, though, we have no reason to assume that his silence was the same as Heidegger's, which is of another character entirely.²¹ We know that Heidegger knew about the death camps; we do not know that Blanchot wrote of "Juifs émigrés" and "Juifs déchaînes."

Did Blanchot himself make anti-Semitic remarks? Not as such, although, to be sure, he included Jews in his tirades against all people whose influence threatened France, namely that "holy alliance" of "Soviet, Jewish, Capitalist interests," a coalition that he deemed to be "anti-national" and "anti-social."²² Did he publish in the anti-Semitic, fascistic paper *Je suis partout*? No, he did not; and in fact, that horrid paper denounced him to the Gestapo as well as finding his first novel, *Thomas l'Obscur* (1941), objectionably Jewish.²³ In the interview from which I have already quoted, Levinas says, "I must mention especially that he saved my wife during the war while I was in captivity" (29). At considerable personal risk, Blanchot had hidden Raïssa Levinas in his apartment in Paris. It is also worth mentioning that Marguerite Blanchot, the author's sister, helped his friend Paul Lévy, owner of first *Le Rempart* and then the outspoken *Aux écoutes*, avoid being caught by the Gestapo.²⁴ It is difficult to imagine that Blanchot himself was not involved in this good work. Given that the Germans would have known Lévy's direct and sustained criticisms of Nazism, including an editorial for *Le Rempart* entitled "La peste hitlérienne," they were looking for him for one reason, and for one reason only.²⁵

If we listen to Blanchot's political rhetoric in 1937, toward the end of his time as a right-wing journalist, we can hear one politics that fades away and another that will remain, albeit transformed. In *L'Insurgé* he repeats the refrain that to be French now is to be against France from within its borders.²⁶ His last pieces appear in *Combat*, the monthly directed by Jean de Fabrègues and Thierry Maulnier (not the later clandestine paper of the same title associated with Albert Camus). In "La France, nation à venir," published in *Combat* in November 1937, he laments that, "The spiritual mission of France is not to be France but to assure the triumph of Marxism or Fascism in Spain."²⁷ And in "On demande des dissidents," his final piece for *Combat*, published in December 1937, he provides his last word on how social energies can best be mobilized in France. He begins by deploring the fact that once there were dissidents in the country, but they cannot be found any longer, and he concludes by outlining what a true dissident is and why we need them:

> In reality what counts is not being above parties but of being against them. It is not to take that vulgar slogan "neither right nor left," but to be really against the right and against the left. One can see in these conditions that the true form of dissidence is of abandoning a position without ceasing to maintain the same hostility with regard to the contrary position or rather of abandoning the position in order to accentuate this hostility. The true communist dissident is someone who leaves communism not in order to find common ground with capitalism but in order to define the true conditions of the struggle against capitalism. In the same way, the true nationalist dissident is someone who neglects traditional formulas of nationalism, not in order to seek reconciliation with internationalism but in order to fight internationalism in all of its forms, including the economy and the nation itself. These two examples of dissidence seem to us each as useful as the other. But they seem equally rare. We need dissidents.²⁸

Combat continues to appear through to July 1939 but without the help of Blanchot who, so far as we can tell, stops writing political journalism. Or, to put the matter more exactly, he stops *signing* political journalism. He continues as *rédacteur en chef* of the *Journal des débats* and *Aux écoutes* until 1940, and presumably writes unsigned editorials.

What Blanchot stops expressing, then presumably drops, though neither simply nor all at once, is the nationalist fervor for securing France by way of a revolution and the distaste for international solutions to national political problems.[29] And what remains is the negative cast of the neither-nor attitude: not just neither Marxism nor fascism (a matter of indifference to him, it would seem, in the November essay) but a principled and sustained critique of all parties and all positions. To be sure, in "On demande des dissidents" this relentless critique is needed in order to save France from almost certain peril. Later, however, the style of critique he calls on dissidents to embody will be put to other ends. It would be a mistake to infer that Blanchot simply stops writing about politics in order to compose literature and write about it: he had been reviewing literary books since June 1931, writing a novel since 1931 as well, and composing short stories since 1935. Yet in 1938 he stops writing about current political events, perhaps out of a recognition that editorial interference was unavoidable. In 1939 he publishes only one article, a piece on Gérard de Nerval.[30] He writes a column, "Chronique de la vie intellectuelle" for the then Pétainist *Journal des débats* from April 1941 to August 1944, and publishes a second novel, *Aminadab*, in 1942.

Does *L'Arrêt de mort* (1948), his fourth narrative, indirectly tell us what Blanchot was doing in 1938? "These things happened to me in 1938," he says in the opening sentence, "I feel the greatest uneasiness in speaking of them."[31] We too should have the greatest uneasiness when reading Blanchot's narratives, especially when being invited to identify first-person narration and autobiography. For Blanchot misaligns facts and narratives at the very moments when we are most likely to anticipate personal revelations. "The only date I can be sure of is the 13th of October—Wednesday, the 13th of October," the narrator tells us; but, as Christophe Bident points out, there was no such day in 1938 (the 13th fell on a Thursday that year), although there was such a day in 1937.[32] Perhaps the personal events described in *L'Arrêt de mort* took place in 1937 and run parallel to the political events of 1938, above all the Munich agreement about the Sudetenland, dated September 29 and signed the following day. ("Since September I had been living in Arcachon. It was during the Munich crisis" (4, 11), we are told in *L'Arrêt de mort*.[33]) We know that Blanchot was in a sanatorium at Cambo-les-Bains, near the Spanish border, being treated for tuberculosis sometime in the late 1930s; perhaps it was over the summer and early autumn of 1937, giving him an opportunity to reflect on his life and political commitments and perhaps also to work on *Thomas l'Obscur*. On September 22, 1937, he would have turned thirty: a time to take stock of things.

At any rate, at some point before, during, or just after the war, Blanchot moved from the far right toward the left. The first definite sign of this change is his involvement in *Actualité* (1946), which he edited with Georges Bataille and Pierre Prévost. In late 1937 he had been against the Spanish Republic, and certainly against Blum's ineffective support for it.[34] Now, though, he was for *L'Espagne libre*. In his contribution to the journal, a belated review of Malraux's novel about how the Republicans fought the fascists in Spain, *L'Espoir* (1937), Blanchot affirmed "hope always has the same name: liberty."[35] This change in political allegiance was by no means publicly known or even well known in the French intellectual world. For one thing, Blanchot retreated to the village of Èze in the south of France from the end of 1946 to 1957, almost the whole time of the Fourth Republic, making sporadic trips to Paris, and it was in Èze that he wrote some of his finest narrative and critical work, including the *récit* version of *Thomas l'Obscur* (1950), *Au Moment voulu* (1951), *Celui qui ne m'accompaignait pas* (1953), *L'Espace littéraire* (1955), *Le Dernier homme* (1957), along with major essays later to appear in *L'Entretien infini* (1969) and *L'Amitié* (1971). The essays he publishes just after the war are placed in journals with quite different political associations from those he favored before the war: *L'Arche*, *Cahiers de la Pléiade*, *Critique*, *Les Temps modernes*.

It was only in 1958 when Dionys Mascolo founded the anti-Gaullist journal *Le 14 Juillet* that he received a letter from Blanchot in which the former right-winger announced what then must have seemed to be a complete *volte face*. "After the publication of the first number," Mascolo says in an interview, "Maurice Blanchot, who had not said a word about politics since the war, sent me a letter that bowled me over: 'I want to tell you that I agree with you. I refuse all the past and accept nothing of the present.'"[36] It is not quite true to say that Blanchot had not uttered a political word since the war. In December 1953 he had favorably reviewed Mascolo's *Le Communisme* (1953) in *La Nouvelle Revue française*.[37] Yet there is no denying the directness of Blanchot's comment in his letter of 1958.

*

What made Blanchot change his political position so radically? Was it the events of 1937–8? Were there other events? Did it happen all at once or over a period of years?

We know from the previous chapter that on July 20, 1944, he testified in a *récit* to narrowly avoiding being executed by the Vlassov army.[38] As he faced the firing squad, the young Blanchot (as remembered by the older writer) "experienced then a feeling of extraordinary lightness, a sort of beatitude (nothing happy, however)—sovereign elation?"[39] The soldiers allowed him to escape while their lieutenant was distracted. Only later, when he returned to the scene, did he discover that three young men had been slaughtered, presumably in vengeance for his escape. "No doubt what then began for the young man was the torment of injustice. No more ecstasy; the feeling that he was only living because, even in the eyes of the Russians, he belonged to a noble class" (7; 15). One might see Blanchot's final change of political allegiance occurring in that very moment in which he *feels* the full force of injustice. And yet it must have been enmeshed in a prior decision, for he speaks of himself being in the Maquis and of his comrades managing to distract the lieutenant, the very event that allowed him to escape summary execution. It was on July 10, 1940, he tells Maurice Nadeau, that he was present at the sitting of the Assemblée Nationale when power was handed over to Marshall Pétain and the Third Republic ended that he made a political decision.

> At that moment, I realized that Europe and perhaps the world were surrendering to the worst. My decision was immediate. Come what may, our duty was to keep alive centers of resistance in France, intellectual ones if nothing else. That was how I met Georges Bataille, and also became involved in clandestine activity which I have never spoken about, and shall not speak about here.[40]

Is this decision what effects Blanchot's passage from the right to the left of politics? Not if one takes him at his word in his letter to Nadeau of April 17, 1977. For then he says about his early right-wing journalism,

> I shall not defend the texts that I saw fit to publish at that time. There can be no doubt that I have changed. As far as I can tell, I changed under the influence of writing (at the time, I was writing *Thomas the Obscure* and *Aminadab*), and also through my knowledge of events (at the time I was working on a paper whose proprietor was a Jew, and we were visited by many German-Jewish émigrés).[41]

Blanchot recalls here his days of working for Paul Lévy for the weekly satirical paper *Aux écoutes*. That was between 1933 and 1940. In 1941 he was involved with Jeune France, as well as engaged in talks with Pierre Drieu La Rochelle concerning the possibility of becoming editor of an entirely literary *Nouvelle Revue française*, which came to nothing. "Let me be blunt," he reports himself as saying to Drieu, "I cannot invite people to contribute to a journal in which I would not myself want to be published."[42] Does this indicate a political change of view on Blanchot's part? Not necessarily: the right-wing Blanchot was always firmly against collaboration in any form. What is striking in the letter to Maurice Nadeau from which I have quoted is not only that Blanchot attributes his political change to *writing*, along with "knowledge of events," but also that he evokes writing *before* mentioning Lévy or the émigrés. As we have seen, Blanchot started writing what was to become *Thomas l'Obscur* in 1931, interrupted his drafts of it to write two stories, "Le Dernier mot" (1935) and "L'Idyll" (1936), and stops writing right-wing journalism in 1938.[43] Recalling his experience of writing in the 1930s, he tells us that composing "Le Dernier mot" was "an attempt to short circuit the other book that was being written [*Thomas l'Obscur*], in order to overcome that endlessness and reach a silent decision."[44] The writing of *Thomas l'Obscur*, he says, led him to encounter "in the search for annihilation (absence) the impossibility of escaping being (presence)—which was not even a contradiction in fact, but the demand of an endlessness that is unhappy even in dying" (64). The silent decision, I take it, is "the renunciation of the roles of Teacher and Judge—a renunciation that is itself futile" (65).

None of these reflections on writing *Thomas l'Obscur*, *Aminadab*, "L'Idylle" or "Le Dernier mot," quite explains how the experience of writing narrative fiction can precipitate a shift from the right wing to the left wing of politics. It could happen only for a singular personality. (It plainly did not happen with Brasillach or Céline.) Only in later texts by Blanchot does it become clear. Consider, for example, his proposal in May 1993 to intervene in the *fatwā* declared against Salman Rushdie by Ayatollah Khomeini. "To write is, through passivity, to place oneself already beyond death—a death which fleetingly establishes a search for the Other [*l'Autre*], a relation without relation to others [*autrui*]."⁴⁵ In writing, then, two things become apparent. The first is that there is no substantial "I": the sense of a deep self is revealed to be an illusion by the "demand of an endlessness" that comes with writing.⁴⁶ And the second is that one becomes aware of the other person in the strangeness of a relation without relation. I am related to the other person not by way of dialectical engagement or by way of fusion but solely by a relation that exceeds both of those possibilities.⁴⁷ There may not be an "I" in a metaphysical sense but there is one in a moral and political sense: individuals have responsibilities that they must discharge.

Blanchot makes the point even more clearly in his "Note" to *L'Entretien infini* (1969). "Writing," he says there,

> passes through the advent of communism, recognized as the ultimate affirmation . . . . Writing thus becomes a terrible responsibility. Invisibly, writing is called upon to undo the discourse in which, however unhappy we believe ourselves to be, we who have it at our disposal remain comfortably installed. From this point of view writing is the greatest violence, for it transgresses the law, every law, and also its own.⁴⁸

How can one's act of writing point to communism that exceeds any government and warms our desire for greater justice? The answer, given in the previous chapter, bears repetition. Because writing, not speech,

> seems to devote itself solely to itself as something that remains without identity, and little by little brings forth possibilities that are entirely other: an anonymous, distracted, deferred, and dispersed way of being in relation, by which everything is brought into question—and first of all the idea of God, of the Self, of the Subject, then of Truth and the One, then finally the idea of the Book and the Work (xii).

It is doubtful that these formulations were in Blanchot's mind in the mid-late 1930s; it would take another decade and a half before they started to come into focus.

There is no doubt that he changed his vocabulary over the years, giving more prominence to writing over speech in the 1960s, for example.⁴⁹ The extent to which his meetings with German-Jewish émigrés while working for Paul Lévy gave him a sense of the moral elevation of the other person is also hard to say. We are looking back in hindsight with lenses ground by Blanchot, Derrida, and Levinas. Certainly in 1960, in the one interview that Blanchot ever gave, on the *Déclaration sur le Droit à l'Insoumission dans la Guerre d'Algérie*, he says that he signed the declaration "as a writer" and then goes on to specify "not as a political writer, nor as a citizen involved in political struggles, but as a nonpolitical writer led to comment on problems that essentially involve him."⁵⁰ This is not what one would expect of a major act of political defiance; but it makes sense if one understands that for Blanchot the act of writing places one in relation with other people, a relation without relation or, as he sometimes says, a neutral relation. One does not have to be an engaged or committed writer to be political, as Sartre taught in *Qu'est-ce que la littérature?* (1948). One simply has to be a *writer* who is aware of being in relation with others and therefore of being responsible for what happens to them.[51] As early as 1946, Blanchot was speaking of the hyper-responsibility of the writer in terms that resonate with the "Note" of 1969: the writer is responsible, he says, "to the laws he recognizes, before those he does not recognize, before others that he is alone in recognizing, and also before that absence of law which his work [*œuvre*], where imposture necessarily predominates, deludes him into considering essential."[52] Transgression of the law may be essential to the writer, but so too is responsibility to the law.

*

In *Le Pas au-delà* (1973) Blanchot writes, "Tout doit s'effacer, tout s'effacera" [Everything must efface itself, everything will efface itself].[53] In the margin of a letter to Roger Laporte about his early political life he writes, "Tout s'efface, tout doit s'effacer." What has passed, he says to Laporte, is without importance. And yet, if we look elsewhere in Blanchot, we find another wisdom. In a comment on automatic writing in *L'Espace littéraire* (1955) Blanchot sympathetically puts the surrealists' position as follows, "Everything must become public. The secret must be violated. The dark must enter into the day, it must dawn. What cannot be said must nevertheless be heard: Quidquid latet apparebit. Everything hidden: *that* is what must appear. And not with the anxiety of a guilty conscience, but with the insouciance of happy lips."[54] Blanchot quotes here from the Requium Mass where we hear, "*Judex ergo cum sedebit, quidquid latet, apparebit, nil inultum remanebit*" [When the judge sits, what is hidden will be revealed, nothing will remain unavenged]. In 1986 Mascolo wrote to Blanchot about a letter from Robert Antelme that he had discovered; it had been written shortly after their mutual friend's return from Dachau. Should it be published? he asked Blanchot. And Blanchot replied by quoting his own view, *quidquid latent apparebit*, adding, in his own words, "*Rien ne doit, rien ne restera caché*" [Nothing must, nothing will, remain hidden].[55] Blanchot's reflections on his early political life run between two limits: his conviction that he should have no public role as a writer and his understanding that all decisions and acts will come to light and be judged.

In his letter to Laporte Blanchot alludes to his principle of letting each express himself according to his responsibility. Yet responsibility is linked to memory. After speaking of the injustice of apartheid, he writes, "I do not only recall these awful facts so that they do not erase themselves from memory, but so that their memory should make us more aware of our responsibility."[56] We must remember in order to be fully responsible. Most of all, we must remember the Shoah. "Once again I transcribe what was written at Birkenau and which escapes memory as it escapes thought, by way of warning from which no thoughts and no memories are free: 'Know what happened here. Do not forget. And yet you will never know.'"[57] It is the transmission of that injunction to know, and for those who have not known horror to know only within limits, that is important. One must live within that memory and forge one's own sense of responsibility for it. "It comes down to each one to remain (or to fall) in the face of the event: the event beyond answer, beyond questions. That is the pact."[58] It is a covenant made with those murdered in the death camps, and a covenant made with his friend Levinas and with all Jews.

If infinite responsibility marks Blanchot's later political life, so does infinite contestation. He keeps the idea of infinite contestation, the relentless questioning of positions, from his early days but rather than it leading to national revolution, as he believed at the time of writing his last piece for *Combat*, he comes to think of it as indicating a communism beyond party: a demand for justice that is (and always shall be) beyond the declarations and actions of the Parti Communiste Français, for example. Readers of Blanchot's literary criticism will be familiar with his insistence that art too is endless contestation.[59] Consider this remark from "The Great Reducers" (1965):

> Literature is perhaps essentially (I am not saying uniquely or manifestly) a power of contestation: contestation of the established power, contestation of what is (and of the fact of being), contestation of language and of the forms of literary language, finally contestation of itself as power. It constantly works against the limits that it helps fix, and when these limits pushed back indefinitely, finally disappear in the knowledge and happiness of a truly or ideally accomplished totality, then its force of transgression becomes more denunciatory, for it is the unlimited itself, having become its limit, that it denounces by the neuter affirmation that speaks in it, which always speaks beyond.[60]

And when he lays out the grounds for the *Revue Internationale*, a few years before writing "The Great Reducers," he tells us much the same thing: "art is infinite contestation, contestation of itself and contestation of other forms of power—and this not only in simple anarchy, but in the free quest for original power that art and literature represent (*power without power*)."[61] And before writing either these pieces, in 1953, he had already recognized that political and artistic contestations derive from one source:

> It is undoubtedly the task of our age to move toward an affirmation that is entirely *other*. A difficult task, essentially risky. It is to this task that communism recalls us with a rigor that it itself often shirks, and it is also to this task that "artistic experience" recalls us in the realm that is proper to it. A remarkable coincidence.[62]

Indeed, criticism and "inner experience" are also forms of infinite contestation, and they too mark out "our age" as one that is seeking to affirm the "entirely *other*."[63] That irreducible otherness, experienced by the writer as "the demand of an endlessness," is what he will increasingly call the Outside or the Neutral. Its approach will be his main concern in the years to follow, whether it be in literature, fostering international communication in the *Revue Internationale*, or in taking to the streets in May 1968.

*

It is by no means clear what a full compilation of Blanchot's political writings would look like. Such an edition would have to include, first, all the right-wing journalism of the 1930s. It would also have to include *La Communauté inavouable* (1983), and a fair number of additional texts, some of them substantial essays (e.g., "Intellectuals under Scrutiny,"), some of them quite short, and some of them letters to journals.[64] Should one include his reflections on Michel Foucault and his reviews of books on communism? Should one include the essays in *L'Entretien infini* (1969) that arise from May 1968 and fragments from *L'Écriture du désastre* (1980) that discuss Auschwitz? Should one include "L'Idylle," *L'Arrêt de mort, Le Très-Haut*, "La Folie du jour," and perhaps other narrative writings? Doubtless; and doubtless there are more writings of political interest, some of which are visible—letters to Kosovoï and Mascolo, for example—and others that may one day come to light, including letters to Derrida, Jabès, and Levinas. (There is a brief, unpublished correspondence about the "de Man affair," and, as already indicated, a long, intriguing letter to Laporte about his early political life.) Blanchot seldom appeared "on the street" in demonstrations; not every cause moved him to act. And he never drew attention to himself on the street when protesting against the war in Algeria or in May 1968. "When a number of us took part in the May 1968 movement," he writes,

> they hoped to be preserved from any ambition in the singular, and in a way they succeeded, through not being singled out for attention, but treated in the same way as everyone else, the strength of the anti-authoritarian movement making it almost easy to forget all particularity, and impossible to distinguish between young and old, the unknown and the too well-known, as if, despite the differences and the incessant disputes, each person recognized himself in the anonymous words inscribed on the walls and which, in the end, even when on occasion they were the result of a collective effort, never declared themselves the words of an author, being of all and for all, in their contradictory formulation.[65]

Yet from his last home on the Place des Pensées in Le Mesnil Saint-Denis, some 47 kilometers outside Paris, he was constantly involved in the affairs of his day. He was, as Christophe Bident puts it so happily in the subtitle of his biography of Blanchot, our "invisible partner."

This invisible partnership might plausibly be seen to begin in 1958, with Blanchot already seasoned in his leftist views, protesting against France's involvement in Algeria, and shortly thereafter in the hope that a new journal, the *Revue Internationale*, can bring writers together in a project of intense political and literary significance. It would include the tracts that Blanchot wrote, and left unsigned, during May 1968 as well as reflections relating to them. And it would give us a number of texts to do with the "Heidegger affair," Judaism, and other political concerns of the eighties and nineties. Some of these late political texts speak for themselves: they are expressions of solidarity, cries for justice, warnings not to forget the horror of the Shoah. Others are highly nuanced pieces: "Reading Marx," for instance, which is surely the best short essay ever written on the father of communism. In many of these pieces Blanchot's thoughts about anonymous speech and fragmentary writing come to fore, and I will say something about these before commenting on a couple of specific issues.

The *Manifeste des 121*, Blanchot tells us, "was never a question of stylistic research, but on the contrary of speaking as if anonymously in order to attain the simplicity of a just solution," and in his letter to Sartre of December 2, 1960, he evokes "a certain anonymous community of names."[66] He insists that *Comité*, the organ of Le Comité d'action étudiants-écrivains, will feature only anonymous texts. "Anonymity not only aims to remove the author's right of possession over what he writes, nor even to impersonalize him by freeing from himself (his history, his person, the suspicion attached to his particularity), but to constitute collective or plural speech: a communism of writing."[67] Anonymity is achieved, then, by affirming plural speech. This is not a dialogue and not a complex conversation among several people but a contestation of unity. It is a theme of *L'Entretien infini*, where Blanchot keeps insisting that plural speech is "intermittent, discontinuous," and does not represent a point of view, or even several points of view, so much as establish a space of the "between" and open up "a relation of infinity."[68] This new relation ("the third relation": neither dialectic nor fusion) is the sheer otherness that marks a change of epoch, a revolution that will fundamentally change how human beings relate to one another, no longer as subjects.[69] If we are tempted to say that the affirmation of the third relation is less of a political statement than a critique of metaphysics, being based on rejecting the One, then Blanchot will want us to say that it is a critique fraught with political consequences; and if we also say that it is less of a political statement than an assault on the Abrahamic faiths, for God is One, then Blanchot will ask us to acknowledge that it is also a political critique of those faiths and their heritages. Communism too is brought under this contestation of unity, at least to the extent that some of its advocates believe in dialectical meaning and insofar as its positions on the events of the day can be called into question. That was the case with the *Déclaration*, Blanchot thinks, and it will be the case time and again.

Plural speech is one way of approaching the fragmentary, which is at the heart of Blanchot's impossible politics. Consider what he says about the writings he wants for *Comité*: "Thus the texts will be fragmentary: precisely to make the plurality possible (a non-unitary plurality), to open a place for it and at the same time never arrest the becoming itself."[70] "Communism of writing" depends therefore on the fragmentary. This notion should not be confused with the fragment valued by Novalis and Friedrich Schlegel, still less with the aphorism, epigram, and the maxim of writers such as Chamfort, La Rochefoucauld, and Vauvenargues. These short literary forms contain their centers within themselves and reveal them in a burst of insight or a sudden glitter of wit about politics, love, or literature. Fragmentary writing, on the other hand, has no center within itself, and strictly has no center at all: it abides in a shifting relation of texts which in principle can always be extended. (It is always a possibility, one that Blanchot darkly acknowledges, that fragmentary writing, if sufficiently supplemented, can freeze and become a counter-system.[71]) In short, Blanchot's idea of literary communism is of a writing, an "aphorisms of thought, rather than of style," that would enable a break with present times to declare and affirm itself.[72] It would be what he calls a "disaster," a wandering away from a fixed star that has served as a guiding light. "Truth is nomad," he says in his presentation of the *Revue Internationale*.[73]

Someone might object that all this talk of rupture and fragmentary writing seems very remote from political life as we live it in the United States—voting in elections, lobbying our representatives in Congress, as well as our president—and that affirming something entirely *other* might be entirely irresponsible. Blanchot would reply with understanding of this response and perhaps not a little impatience as well. He would say, first, that this explosive affirmation of new, plural relations can at best be lived momentarily—in *les événements* of May 1968, for instance—and that it can only indicate a horizon to which we should move, a justice that is beyond any institutionalized justice (but one that is neither divine nor ideal).[74] Contestation may still have revolution as its aim; it is a communist revolution, though, not a nationalist one, and it affirms a communism that has not yet seen the light of day. ("There is no good nationalism," the leftist Blanchot states.[75]) And he would tell us, second, that we should continue to rally around causes of defiance, even at the risk of affirming a transitory unity or union. For all its commitment to difference and dispersion, Blanchot's politics is also pragmatic. It is worth remembering that in November 2002, his last political act was to express solidarity with the "Not in Our Name" appeal that was launched in New York against the US Government's response to the 9/11 attacks.[76] In leftist politics we must always speak two languages at the same time, one dialectical and one neutral, which is his inflection of the French distinction between *la politique* and *le politique*.[77] For Blanchot, it is the language of *le politique*, the political, that guides how we should engage in *la politique*, politics, the contestation of settled positions, the decision not to accept complaisantly the advances in liberty that we have made over the decades and centuries. *La politique* is the "No" that opens the future in which there will be justice, but before one says that single decisive syllable one must first hear the murmur of the Outside, which informs *le politique*. And if someone were to object to this language of the murmur of the Outside, Blanchot would probably respond by saying it is no more than a figure for the mental grasping of the third relation.

Equally, though, one could say, with Derrida (who learned a great deal from Blanchot about the political as well as the literary) that it is a structure of double affirmation ("Yes, yes") which opens what is to come. If the murmur of the Outside inclines one to say "No" to injustice whenever it confronts us, the whisper of *la différance* nudges one to say, "Yes" to each and every prior affirmation in justice, no matter where it is found. It was in saying "Yes" to democracy that the ancient Greeks left us a heritage that we can make our own only by joining our "Yes" to theirs. Democracy that was once a male prerogative is now something shared by male and female voters only because something deemed essential in democracy has been re-affirmed. In part this difference between Blanchot and Derrida is a matter of style, not substance, for they wish to say fundamentally the same thing. Blanchot avows the friendship of the No, and Derrida writes on the politics of friendship, which includes, as it happens, a critique of the unexamined fraternalism at the heart of Blanchot's political writings.[78] None of this is said to suggest that Blanchot and Derrida converged exactly in their sense of politics and the political. If Blanchot lived May 1968 with passion, regarding it as unique, as an *"explosive communication"* that affirmed itself "beyond the usual forms of affirmation," Derrida was more distant, more reserved, more nuanced, in his response, for he simply did not believe in historical ruptures.[79] Yet he admired

Blanchot and valued his political work. I well remember him telling me one evening in Melbourne, Australia, that once in 1968, when Blanchot was visiting him at the École Normale Supérieure, Blanchot leaned over toward him and said, "with a religious intensity in his voice, 'Would you ever write a *tract*?'" Derrida told me that he explained to Blanchot that he could never write in that genre and that he preferred to analyze texts in a differentiated manner and not to make direct pronouncements or political interventions, to which Blanchot listened closely and silently before leaving. Derrida then said to me, "To think! He must then have been writing those tracts for *Le Comité d'action étudiants-écrivains*. They are some of the finest political tracts ever written."

"It is undoubtedly the task of our age to move toward an affirmation that is entirely *other*." Blanchot wrote those words in 1953. If we take this remark in the frame of literature and philosophy, first in terms of post-Enlightenment horizons of thought (Marx, Nietzsche, and Freud), then by way of experiments with the forbidden (Sade, Hölderlin, Lautréamont, Bataille), then in modern literature (Mallarmé, Kafka, Char, Beckett), and finally contemporary philosophy (Heidegger, Levinas, Derrida), we can see what he has in mind, even if the adverbs ("undoubtedly" and "entirely") now seem extreme. The age is more modest, as Lacoue-Labarthe says with the second half of the last century in mind.[80] Yet to the extent that Blanchot was thinking of a communist revolution, even one not countenanced by the Soviet Union, Cuba, or China, we must say that the age decided otherwise. The second half of the twentieth century marks a retreat from communism, first in Europe and Russia and then, in a more complex way, in China. True, at the same time we find a rethinking of community and friendship, but it is one that remains in the seminar room and does not take to the street.[81] It was the World Wide Web and then Social Media that was unforeseen and "other," and that was able to join all manner of people in a way that is neither dialectical nor achieved by fusion, and that has had all manner of political consequences, negative as well as positive, that are still in flux and that still require patient examination and vigilance. "Our age" happened differently than Blanchot thought it would. If he saw, rightly, that Christianity would come to live a greatly diminished life in Europe, he did not foresee its rapid rise in China, the flourishing of Islam, and conceive the affirmation of Allah as the One who is entirely other. Yet when May 1968 came, he recognized that something extraordinary had taken place, something that was in deep accord with what he had had in mind in 1953.

Yet while May 1968 saw Blanchot at an ecstatic height in his political life, that life was soon to end, at least in its main lines. Within a year of May 1968 Levinas received a letter from Blanchot, in which the writer of tracts for *Comité* explains, in Levinas's words, why "He separated himself from his revolutionary friends when they opted against Israel." I quote from the end of the letter, which is all that Levinas gives us, directly after Blanchot has said that the 1968 revolutionaries were not anti-Semitic and even that anti-Zionism is not anti-Semitic:

> it is as though Israel were put in peril by ignorance—yes, an innocent ignorance perhaps, but from now on gravely responsible and deprived of innocence—put in danger by those who want to exterminate the Jew because he is a Jew and by those

who are completely ignorant of what it is to be Jewish. Antisemitism will now have as allies those who are as if deprived of antisemitism?"[82]

In 1984, in an essay brooding on the Dreyfus Affair and its lasting significance, Blanchot observed, "From the Dreyfus Affair to Hitler and Auschwitz, the proof is there that it was anti-Semitism (along with racism and xenophobia) which revealed the intellectual most powerfully to himself: in other words, it is in that form that concern for others obliged him (or not) to abandon his creative solitude."[83] The essay is a testimony of what Blanchot himself had done: after 1968 he had revealed himself to himself, and understood himself within his limits and the limits of his time, in terms of laws of responsibility that he would not transgress. In a letter to Bernard-Henri Lévy written in September 1989, a time of debate over the church's decision to close down a Carmelite convent in a former storehouse for holding Zyklon-B gas at Auschwitz, Blanchot chose to end his letter by addressing the murdered Jews rather than Lévy: "You who are now dead, you who died for us and often because of us (because of our shortcomings), you must not be allowed to die a second time, and silence must not mean that you sink into oblivion."[84] The Blanchot who for many years had been revealed to himself, as it were, by death as dying, by the loss of the power to say "I," now sees himself in terms of responsibility to the Jewish dead.

Also in that essay of 1984, "Les Intellectuels en question," Blanchot had noted that when the intellectual, the writer, "makes up his mind and declares himself, he suffers perhaps irreparable damage. He absents himself from the only task that matters to him" (217; 38). What is that task? It is "to utter the unexpected" [*la parole inattendue*] (217; 38). Blanchot's letter to Levinas was the saying of an unexpected word, and all that he said after he posted it was a sequence of unexpected words. Intellectuals, he once wrote to Sartre, become aware of their peculiar power; it is a "power without power": not a power to vote on bills or to sign Presidential memos or anything of the sort. It is the power, rather, to contest power wherever it comes, but not to do so as a knee-jerk reaction. Thought is required, hard thought, the thought that looks neither to the dialectic nor to fusion. The word that counts, he thinks, is the unexpected word, a word perhaps from left field, a word not always recognized or wanted by the political left but needed all the same.

Notes

1 Jill Robbins, ed., "Interview with François Poiré (1986)," *IRB*, 29.
2 Paul Valéry, *Reflections on the World Today*, trans. Francis Scarfe (London: Thames and Hudson, 1951), 7, 10. The English translation is of an expanded and selective version of *Regards sur le monde actuel* (1931).
3 Valéry, *Reflections on the World Today*, 26.
4 Valéry, *Reflections on the World Today*, 27.
5 See Blanchot, "Comment s'emparer du pouvoir?" *Journal des débats*, août 18, 1931, 1. The piece is signed "M.B.," not "M.Bl.," yet the identification by Michael Holland seems accurate. Blanchot's early political writings are assembled in *CP*. I shall give page numbers to the complete versions of these short pieces.

6   Curzio Malaparte, *Coup d'État: The Technique of Revolution*, trans. Sylvia Saunders (New York: E. P. Dutton and Co., 1932), 250, 18.
7   Blanchot, "Comment s'emparer du pouvoir?" *CP*, 36–9.
8   See Blanchot, "Réquisitoire contre la France," *L'Insurgé* 1 (janvier 13, 1937): 4, *CP*, 393–5.
9   See Blanchot, "La guerre pour rien," *Combat* 3 (mars 1936): 42, *CP*, 368–71, and "Après le coup de force germanique," *Combat* 4 (avril 1936): 59, *CP*, 372–6. Also see "Blum provoque à la guerre," *L'Insurgé* 12, mars 31, 1937, 4, *CP*, 427–9, esp. the final paragraph.
10 See Blanchot, "Le Caravansérail," *Combat* 10 (décembre 1936): 171, *CP*, 388–92.
11 See Blanchot, "La Révolte contre le pouvoir," *Le Rempart* 40 (mai 31, 1933): 1, *CP*, 175–7.
12 Blanchot, "La Révolution nécessaire," *Le Rempart* 62 (juin 22, 1933): 3, *CP*, 218–20.
13 Blanchot, "La Vraie Menace du Troisième Reich," *Le Rempart* 69 (juin 29, 1933): 3, *CP*, 234–6.
14 On the formulation "neither right nor left," see Zeev Sternhell, *Ni droite ni gauche: L'idéologie fasciste en France* (Paris: Seuil, 1983). I agree with Leslie Hill in his interpretation of this matter. See his *Blanchot: Extreme Contemporary* (London: Routledge, 1997), 40–1, and *Nancy, Blanchot*, 42.
15 See, for example, Blanchot, "La Vraie Menace du Troisième Reich," 3, *CP*, 236, esp. the final paragraph.
16 See Blanchot, "La Révolution nécessaire," 2, *CP*, 218–20.
17 Blanchot, "Le terrorisme, méthode de salut public," *Combat* 7 (juillet 1936): 106, *CP*, 376–80.
18 Blanchot, "Des violences antisémites à l'apothéose du travail," *Le Rempart* 10 (mai 1, 1933): 3, *CP*, 134–6.
19 Blanchot, "Après le coup de force germanique," *Combat* 4 (mai 7, 1936), *CP*, 372, 373. David Uhrig in his editorial commentary on this article in *CP* speaks of "le caractère xenophobe de cette remarque" and also of "le propos antisemite" in the second comment. He does so, however, without showing due awareness of editorial intervention in the 1930s. To write for a paper, even today, is to risk having one's prose and indeed one's views changed by a subeditor without consultation, and things were far worse in the pressured years of the 1930s. Hill offers a thorough and judicious analysis of the likelihood of such interference in his *Blanchot politique: Sur une réflexion jamais interrompue* (Genève: Furor, 2020), 157–68. He quotes from a letter partly on *Combat* that Blanchot wrote to William Flesch on May 26, 1988, and which I have read in whole, in which Blanchot says, "on allait jusqu'à modifier mes textes, jugés trop antinazis, même par le gouvernement [sic]," 169. The extent of this interference is vague and is likely to remain so. Yet Hill's argument for editorial tampering with respect to the offensive expressions is a strong one. He draws attention to various problems with Uhrig's editorial work in *Blanchot politique*: see, in particular, 255, 265, 448.
20 See "Two Letters to Maurice Nadeau," trans. Michael Holland, *Paragraph* 30, no. 3 (2007): 19, where Blanchot writes of closing down *L'Insurgé* "the moment it allowed an article with a hint of anti-semitism in it to appear." In Blanchot's letter to Laporte the piece is called "détestable."
21 See Surya, *L'Autre Blanchot* for this argument. Also see Hill, *Blanchot politique*, ch. 7. On different modes of silence, see my "Ambassadors and Votaries of Silence," *Poetry and Revelation: For a Phenomenology of Religious Poetry* (London: Bloomsbury, 2017), ch. 12.

22 Blanchot, "Le terrorisme, méthode de salut public," 106, *CP*, 378. Of course, it may well be that there was editorial interference here as well.
23 See Blanchot, "Two Letters to Maurice Nadeau," 18. See the unsigned review of the novel in *Je suis partout* 534 (octobre 18, 1941): 8. Earlier, the paper had two special issues, "Les Juifs" and "Les Juifs et la France," each of which is fiercely anti-Semitic.
24 See Paul Lévy, *Journal d'un exilé* (Paris: Grasset, 1949), 30.
25 See Lévy, "La peste hitlérienne," *Au Temps des grimaces* (Paris: Nagel, 1948), 111–15. This editorial is dated juillet 21, 1936. Several other pieces that were published in the 1930s would have angered the Germans and repay close attention and yield interesting comparisons with Blanchot's political journalism of the time.
26 Blanchot, "La seule manière d'être Française," *L'Insurgé* 23 (juin 16, 1937): 4, *CP*, 458, "Nous, les complices de Blum. ...," *L'Insurgé* 2 (janvier 20, 1937): 4, *CP*, 398.
27 Blanchot, "La France, nation à venir," *Combat* 19 (novembre 1937): 132, *CP*, 473.
28 Blanchot, "On demande des dissidents," *Combat* 20 (décembre 1937): 155, *CP*, 477–8.
29 Attention should be drawn to Blanchot's article "La politique de Sainte-Beuve," *Journal des débats* (mars 10, 1942): 1–2. The article is examined by Jeffrey Mehlman, "Pour Sainte-Beuve: Maurice Blanchot, 10 March 1942," in *Maurice Blanchot: The Demand of Writing*, ed. Carolyn Bailey Gill (London: Routledge, 1996), 212–31. The essay comes after a letter by Blanchot, addressed to Roger Laporte, in which Blanchot castigates himself very severely for even mentioning the name of Maurras at this time. Mehlman reprinted his essay in his collection, *Genealogies of the Text: Literature, Psychoanalysis, and Politics in Modern France* (Cambridge: Cambridge University Press, 1995), 174–94. Also see his essay "Blanchot at *Combat*: Of Literature and Terror," in *Legacies: Of Anti-Semitism in France* (Minneapolis, MN: University of Minnesota Press, 1983). See Blanchot's comment in *LVK*, 74.
30 See Blanchot, "Un essai sur Gérard de Nerval," *Journal des débats* (juin 22, 1939): 2.
31 Blanchot, *DS*, 1 (7).
32 See Bident, *Maurice Blanchot: A Critical Biography*, trans. John McKeane (New York: Fordham University Press, 2019), ch. 14. Bident explores the hypothesis that the first part of *L'Arrêt de mort* is a double narrative, personal events of 1937 and public events of 1938. Also see his remarks on the date of J's death in his *La vie versée dans les récits*, 68.
33 The passage runs, "Depuis les mois de septembre, je faisais un séjour à Arcachon. J'y éstais seul. C'étaient les jours troubles de Munich."
34 See Blanchot, "La France, nation à venir."
35 Blanchot, "*Days of Hope* by André Malraux," trans. Michael Holland, *Paragraph* 30, no. 3 (2007): 11.
36 Aliette Armel, "Un itinéraire politique," *Magazine littéraire* 278 (juin 1990): 40. Also see Blanchot, "For Friendship," *PW*, 134–43 (*PA*), and Mascolo, *Entêtements* (Paris: Éditions Benoît Jacob, 2004). One can get an idea of what it would be to agree with Mascolo by reading his piece in Jean-Paul Sartre, Bernard Pinguad, and Dionys Mascolo, *Du rôle de l'intellectuel dans le mouvement révolutionnaire* (Paris: Eric Losfeld, 1971), 41–50, reprinted in *Entêtements*, 165–75. Also see the two DVDs, *Autour du Groupe de la Rue Saint-Benoît de 1942 à 1964: L'Esprit d'insoumission*, produit et realize par Jean Mascolo et Jean-Marc Turine (Benoît Jacob Vidéo, 2002).
37 See Blanchot, "Dionys Mascolo: *Le Communisme*," *La Nouvelle Revue française* 12 (décembre 1953): 1064–71. Blanchot reprinted the review with slight changes in *A*.

38 See Blanchot's letter to Vladim Kozovoï for mai 28, 1982, in his *LVK*, 73, and Derrida, "A Witness Forever," trans. Charlotte Mandell, *Nowhere without No*, ed. Kevin Hart (Sydney: Vagabond Press, 2003), 47.
39 Blanchot, *ID*, 5 (11). Also see the previous chapter.
40 Blanchot, "Two Letters to Maurice Nadeau," 19.
41 Blanchot, "Two Letters to Maurice Nadeau," 19. In his later life, Blanchot was sharply critical of his earlier political self. See "A Letter," trans. Leslie Hill, *Maurice Blanchot: The Demand of Writing*, 209-10. Also see the letter quoted by Bernard-Henri Lévy, *Adventures on the Freedom Road: The French Intellectuals in the Twentieth Century*, trans. and ed., Richard Veasey (London: The Harvill Press, 1995), 318.
42 Blanchot, "For Friendship," *PW*, 136 (15). In a letter to Flesch dated décembre 10, 1988, Blanchot adds a detail to this story, namely, that Drieu said that Blanchot could have a free hand as editor so long as he published only purely literary texts. To which Blanchot says that he responded, "But there are no purely literary texts." (He served as secretary for a brief period, not editor.) Yet see Pascal Fouché's counter claim in his *L'Edition française sous l'Occupation, 1940-1944*, 2 vols. (Paris: Bibliothèque de Littérature Contemporaine, 1987), vol. 2, 80, and Jean Paulhan, *Choix de lettres*, vol. 2 *(1937-1945)* (Paris: Gallimard, 1992), 280. These last two claims form the basis of Mehlman's case against Blanchot, which Blanchot consistently rejects. Finally, see in this regard, Steven Ungar, *Scandal and Aftereffect: Blanchot and France since 1930* (Minneapolis, MN: University of Minnesota Press, 1995), ch. 5, esp. 116.
43 Blanchot gives the starting date of 1932 in his note to the *récit* version of *TO (2)*. In his letter to Laporte he says "without doubt" that he had started to write narrative prose since 1930. *Thomas le Solitaire* seems to have been commenced in 1931.
44 Blanchot, "After the Fact," *VC*, 64 (*AC*, 93).
45 Blanchot, "The Inquisition Destroyed the Catholic Religion. ...," trans. Michael Holland, *Paragraph* 30, no. 3 (2007): 43.
46 For a full discussion of this view, see my *The Dark Gaze*, ch. 4.
47 See Blanchot, "The Relation of the Third Kind *(man without horizon)*," *IC*, esp. 66-7 (94-5).
48 Blanchot, "Note," *IC*, xii (viii). Also see Blanchot's remarks on narrative writing as to journalistic writing in *SNB*, 2 (9). Blanchot makes the same point toward the end of his letter to Laporte.
49 See on this Derrida, *Resistances of Psychoanalysis*, 61.
50 Blanchot, ["It is as a writer"], *PW*, 26.
51 For a late instance of Blanchot holding this view, see his "Our Responsibility (On Nelson Mandela)," *PW*, 168-9.
52 Blanchot, "Intellectuals are Always Guilty," trans. Michael Holland, *Paragraph* 30, no. 3 (2007): 12.
53 Blanchot, *SNB*, 53 (76). It is worth noting that Laporte wrote an essay on Blanchot entitled, "Tout doit s'affacer, tout s'effacera," *Études* (Paris: P.O.L., 1990), 51-62.
54 Blanchot, *SL*, 187 (247).
55 See "Correspondance D. Mascolo—M. Blanchot," *Lignes* 33 (1998): 210. The book that resulted from the correspondence is Mascolo, *Autour d'un effort de mémoire: sur une lettre de Robert Antelme* (Paris: M. Nadeau, 1987).
56 Blanchot, "Our Responsibility," *PW*, 169.
57 Blachot, "Writing Committed to Silence," *PW*, 172.
58 Blanchot, "Writing Committed to Silence," *PW*, 172.

59 On the various senses of "la contestation," see *The Power of Contestation: Perspectives on Maurice Blanchot*, ed. Kevin Hart and Geoffrey Hartman (Baltimore, MD: The Johns Hopkins University Press, 2004).
60 Blanchot, "The Great Reducers," *F*, 67 (80).
61 Blanchot, ["The Gravity of the Project"], *PW*, 58.
62 Blanchot, "An Approach to Communism (Needs, Values)," *F*, 97 (114).
63 See, for example, Blanchot, "What is the Purpose of Criticism?" *LS*, 5 (13), "Inner Experience," *FP*, 39–40 (50).
64 See Blanchot, "Intellectuals Under Scrutiny," *BR*, 206–27 (*IQ*).
65 Blanchot, "Intellectuals Under Scrutiny," 224 (*IQ*, 60). Also see his remarks in *Michel Foucault as I Imagine Him*, bound with Foucault, *Maurice Blanchot: The Thought from Outside*, 63. Mascolo refers to Blanchot as an "angel" of May, 1968, in an interview with Marianne Alphant, "Une présence secrète," *Libération* 28 (janvier, 1984): 23, and that the import of May weighed heavily on Blanchot is apparent in a letter he wrote to Marguerite Duras on 13 octobre 1968. See Bernard Alazet et Christiane Blot-Labarrère, dir., *Marguerite Duras* (Paris: L'Herne, 2005), 55. Finally, for an overview of Blanchot's actions in May, 1968, see Jean-François Hamel, *Nous sommes tous la pègre: Les années 68 de Blanchot* (Paris: Éditions de Minuit, 2018).
66 Blanchot, "Maurice Blanchot to Jean-Paul Sartre," *PW*, 36.
67 Blanchot, "*Comité*: The First Issue," *PW*, 85.
68 Blanchot, *IC*, 156 (234), 8 (9).
69 Kristin Ross observes that "the political subjectivity that emerged in May was a *relational* one, built around the polemics of equality: a day-to-day experience of identifications, aspirations, encounters and missed encounters, meetings, deceptions, and disappointments," *May '68 and its Afterlives* (Chicago, IL: The University of Chicago Press, 2002), 11.
70 Blanchot, "*Comité*: The First Issue," *PW*, 85.
71 See Blanchot, *WD*, 134 (203–4).
72 Blanchot, "The Gravity of the Project," *PW*, 61.
73 Blanchot, "The Gravity of the Project," *PW*, 64.
74 See Blanchot, *UC*, 29–31 (52–4).
75 See Blanchot, "I Think It Suits a Writer Better. . .," *PW*, 173. Also see, *LVK*, 122.
76 For a discussion of this appeal and Blanchot's part in it, see Hill, "'Not in Our Name': Blanchot, Politics, the Neuter," *Paragraph* 30, no. 3 (2007): 141–59.
77 On the two languages in general, see Blanchot, *WD*, 20 (38), *IC*, 48 (68–9), and Blanchot's letter to Bataille of January 24, 1962, in Georges Bataille, *Choix de lettres, 1917–1962*, ed. Michel Surya (Paris: Gallimard, 1997), 595–6. On the differences between *le politique* and *la politique*, see Philippe Lacoue-Labarthe and Jean-Luc Nancy, *Retreating the Political*, ed. Simon Sparks (London: Routledge, 1997).
78 Derrida, *Politics of Friendship*, trans. George Collins (London: Verso, 1997), 47–8.
79 Blanchot, *UC*, 30 (53). Also see his remarks on communication in *SL*, ch. 6. Yet see Derrida, *Of Grammatology*, corrected ed., trans. Gayatri Chakravorty Spivak (Baltimore, MD: Johns Hopkins University Press, 1997), 5.
80 See Lacoue-Labarthe, *Heidegger, Art and Politics*, trans. Chris Turner (Oxford: Basil Blackwell, 1990), ch. 1. Yet toward the end of *The Order of Things* Michel Foucault writes in bold terms about the change at hand, and credits Blanchot, among others, as an index of its coming. See his *The Order of Things: An Archeology of the Human Sciences*, no trans. given (New York: Vintage Books, 1970), ch. 10, esp. 384.

81 See, for example, Jean-Luc Nancy, *The Inoperative Community*, and Derrida, *Politics of Friendship*.
82 Levinas quotes this letter, not giving Blanchot's name but giving sufficient clues to identify him as its author, in "Judaism and Revolution," *NTR*, 116. Also see Blanchot, "Do Not Forget," *PW*, 124–9.
83 Blanchot, "Intellectuals Under Scrutiny," 223 (*IQ*, 55).
84 Quoted by Lévy, *Adventures on the Freedom Road*, 318. Also see Blanchot's "What is closest to me. ...," *PW*, 170.

Part 3

On Narrative

7

The Neutral Reduction

Thomas L'Obscur

When Blanchot entitled his first novel *Thomas l'Obscur* (1941) he immediately released it into what would become an increasingly complex network of literary, philosophical, and religious associations, not all of which would help elucidate it. Some of these associations are borne out in the text itself, which plainly deals in some way or other with the figure of a twin or double, and thus places the book in a series of nineteenth- and twentieth-century narratives to do with the *Doppelgänger* or double, the twin, and the *alter ego*, and raises all sorts of issues, directly philosophical or at least of clear interest to philosophers, about human being. Other of these associations can tease the reader with dubious significance for reading the 1941 *roman* or, indeed, the *récit* that it became in 1950.[1] For *Thomas l'Obscur* is itself a double or twin, existing in two authorized versions, each of which calls forth interpretations based on what is in it and what its title merely attracts. So, for example, one may ask if one is right on opening *Thomas l'Obscur*, in either version, to recall the Pre-Socratic thinker, Heraclitus "the Obscure," on whom Blanchot was to write about much later in *L'Entretien infini* (1969)?[2] If so, how should he be recalled? What would be the proper "quantity of connection" to seek between his thought and Blanchot's or Blanchot's narrator?[3] Would it be enough of a connection to place the novel under the sign of "philosophy and literature" and perhaps even to make it an example of what is commonly called, though usually in no more than an impressionistic way, a "philosophical novel?"

Heidegger, a privileged thinker for Blanchot since the late 1920s, tells us that Heraclitus was called "the Obscure" [ὁ Σκοτεινός], "even when his writings were preserved intact," although now we can read him only in fragments.[4] "Because we can scarcely surmise what the well-spring is that gives the writing of Heraclitus its unity, and because we find this source so difficult to think we are justified in calling this thinker 'the Obscure'" (102–3). Here obscurity is understood by way of difficulty, not simply a hard problem to solve but something that resists thought itself, thought taken in Heidegger's sense of *Denken*, reflective meditation, which is contrasted to calculative thinking. "Even the inherent meaning of what this epithet ['the Obscure'] says to us remains obscure," Heidegger adds (103). We cannot delimit why and how Heraclitus was regarded as obscure, we are told; and one index of that inability is that, as Heidegger says, the Greek thinker is also, and perhaps more fundamentally, "the

Lucid," for he "tells of the lighting whose shining he attempts to call forth into the language of thinking" (103). Heidegger was always attracted to the metaphor of light, as in his early re-conception of phenomenology as letting "that which shows itself be seen from itself in the very way in which it shows itself from itself."[5] He includes Heraclitus in his itinerary, however, only when he begins to understand the event as the lighting of the world.[6] The ancient Greek is held to think "questioningly into the lighting" (123), much as Heidegger does himself in the years after making the *Kehre*.

As absorbing as Heidegger's elucidation of Heraclitus is, it does nothing to clear a path for understanding *Thomas l'Obscur*, at least not as regards Blanchot's original intention with the title. For the German thinker first lectured on the ancient Greek in the summer semester of 1943 in the course *Der Anfang des abendländischen Denkens (Heraklit)*, two years after *Thomas l'Obscur* had been published and over a decade after the writing of it had commenced. Perhaps Heidegger influenced Blanchot's explicit reflections on the obscure in *L'Entretien infini* (1969), though one should be reticent in making such claims about a thinker whose intellectual vanishing points were established early in his writing life.[7] At any rate, his own sense of the word "*l'Obscur*" was well and truly in place long before then, and if it was shaded by the epithet associated with Heraclitus it was from the angle of Blanchot's own reading of the Greek.[8] Yet Blanchot had no need to look as far away as Heraclitus to ponder the obscure. He had Mallarmé close to hand, whose work impinged heavily on him as a novelist and critic, and whose unique writing he affirmed in several early reviews, most particularly in "La poésie de Mallarmé est-elle obscure?," published on February 24, 1942, only months after *Thomas l'Obscur*.[9] In that column Blanchot reviews Charles Mauron's *Mallarmé l'obscur* (1941), an attempt to explain the poems line by line, and finds it sadly inadequate to the poems themselves. True poetry, such as Mallarmé's, is not an object, he says, but a power of vision that gives "the reader the feeling of himself being explained and contemplated."[10] Poetry is a matter of counter-intentionality, then, and counter-intentionality will figure significantly in much of his own writing in narrative prose, including *Thomas l'Obscur* where it is associated with obscurity. More generally, we should not assimilate too readily what Mauron means by *l'obscur* in *Mallarmé l'obscur* with what Blanchot means by the same word in *Thomas l'Obscur*. For one thing, Mauron assumes that Mallarmé's poems can be made clear by paraphrase, and that seems not to be the case with the obscure Thomas.

If little of Heraclitus, and nothing of Heidegger's Heraclitus, satisfies our desire to link him to the character of Thomas in Blanchot's *roman* and *récit*, we are not thereby left completely adrift in attempting to situate the work in history. We are equally likely to recall Thomas Hardy's last novel, *Jude the Obscure* (1895), and here we do indeed have characters, the motif of doubling, and another sense of "obscure" in play.[11] *Thomas l'Obscur* can be read as the mortally truncated love story of Thomas and Anne, while *Jude the Obscure* insists on being approached as the cross-fated love story of Jude and Sue. Hardy's narrator tells us of Sue's "double nature," and Jude and Sue almost get married at St. Thomas's, but the threads that join the two novels are few, far between, and very slight.[12] The narrator sees Sue as "double" only because she eludes traditional categories of female character and appropriate behavior; the word carries no special philosophical weight. Jude and Sue are "poor obscure people"

(248), obscurity here meaning that they are indistinctly seen, if seen at all, by those who matter in society, especially those in the university colleges of Christminster, Hardy's imaginary Oxford. In particular, the rigid class system of England has kept Jude, for all his innate talent and ambition, academically undistinguished, and made him forever unknown to literary fame, a "mute inglorious Milton," as Thomas Gray put it so poignantly.[13]

Blanchot's Thomas may not stand out in his society, but *Thomas l'Obscur* is not a novel of social criticism as *Jude the Obscure* is. And if Jude and Sue are "shadowed by death" (327), it is not in the same ways that Thomas and Anne are. Only one event in Hardy's novel is remotely akin to anything in Blanchot's narrative. It is the graveyard scene following the devastating discovery of the deaths of their children in their temporary lodgings in Christminster. "A man with a shovel in his hands was attempting to earth in the common grave of the three children, but his arm was held back by an expostulating woman who stood in the half-filled hole. It was Sue. . ." (329). Yet when we place this scene against its supposed counterpart in *Thomas l'Obscur* we find little basis for comparison. "As soon as the grave was finished, when Thomas threw himself into it with a huge stone tied around his neck, he crashed into a body a thousand times harder than the soil, the very body of the gravedigger who had already entered the grave to dig it."[14] Thomas finds himself already in the very grave he has dug for himself. As the narrator goes on to say, Thomas "was really dead and at the same time rejected from the reality of death" [*était réellement mort et en même temps repoussé de la réalité de la mort*] (36; 77–8; 40). And this statement, unlike the narrator's harrowing image of a mother's grief in *Jude the Obscure*, involves philosophy from the very beginning, and not only because of the adverb "*réellement*" and the noun "*réalité*." It makes a bold claim about the relations of life and death that invites dialectical inspection.

If the title of Blanchot's novel does not indicate a vantage point from which to approach the narrative, perhaps the motif of the double or twin will aid us. Nineteenth-century literature, especially fiction, brooded on the figure of the double. Alfred de Musset's poem "La nuit de décembre" (1835) turns and turns again on the appearance of "Une pauvre enfent vêtu de noir, / Qui me ressemblait comme un frère," who is finally revealed to be Solitude.[15] Musset's double is benign; not so with others later in the century, beginning with the one described in Edgar Allan Poe's tale "William Wilson" (1840), in which the main character encounters another man exactly like him. "Not a thread in all his raiment—not a line in all the marked and singular lineaments of his face which was not, even in the most absolute identity, *mine own!*"[16] This double of the narrator shadows him for years until, right at the end, the narrator kills him. "I could have fancied that I myself was speaking," the narrator says, when he hears his double's last words (356). "*You have conquered, and I yield,*" the double says, "*Yet, henceforward art thou also dead—dead to the World, to Heaven and to Hope! In me didst thou exist—and, in my death, see by this image, which is thine own, how utterly thou has murdered thyself*" (357). This is the closest that the literary tradition of the double comes to the strange experience explored in *Thomas l'Obscur*, although there are indeed two William Wilsons, not an otherness in the one William Wilson, and Poe's story participates more fully in the genre of the grotesque than Blanchot's, and Blanchot's narrative is more philosophical than psychological in its ambitions.

A similar intensity of psychological focus that is found in Poe's tale marks Dostoevsky's *The Double*, itself published in two forms, that of 1846 and 1866. Yakov Petrovich Golyadkin goes home one night and at last fully sees a figure that has been brushing past him in recent times. Sitting on his bed in an overcoat and hat was "none other than himself, Mr. Golyadkin, himself, another Mr. Golyadkin, but exactly like him, in a word, what is called his double in every respect. . ."[17] One of the characters in the story, Anton Antonovich, says, "let me tell you something: the very same thing happened to her aunt on my mother's side. Before she died she also saw her double. . ." (68). The link of doubleness and death is marked again. It will be found also, though in a quite different way, in Robert Louis Stevenson's *The Strange Case of Dr. Jekyll and Mr. Hyde* (1886), in which a drug enables the amiable Dr. Henry Jekyll to become his sinister counterpart, the violent Mr. Edward Hyde. At first the character is able to pass back and forth between the two personalities, but in time he cannot control the changes, which require more and more of the potion in order for it to work effectively. Eventually, he runs out of the brew, and cannot change back from being Edward Hyde. The novel ends with Hyde facing the choice of killing himself or being executed for his crimes. In Stevenson's story, the figure of the double is less a matter of animating the uncanny than of a dramatic presentation of the psychiatric idea of "disassociation" or "split personality," the dark side of the Jekyll having been hiding in him and only needing a stimulus to emerge.

Between the two versions of Dostoevesky's *The Double*, Gérard de Nerval wrote *Aurélia* (1854), a signal narrative for Blanchot, one that also evokes a *Doppelgänger* and ponders the same premonition of death.[18] Here, though, the double is not asserted to be flesh and blood but is the product of an overheated imagination.

> By a strange effect of vibration it felt as though [*il me semblait*] his voice was echoing in my own chest, and that my soul was, so to speak, assuming a dual existence—distinctly divided between vision and reality. For a second I thought of making an effort to turn towards the person in question; then I shivered as I remembered a well-known German superstition which says that everyone has a *double* and that when you see him death is close at hand.[19]

Equally far from the naturalism of Poe and Stevenson, however stretched, is Guy de Maupassant's story "Lui?" (1883). Here the imagined double is directly called a phantom. The narrator comes home to find him in his chair: "I could see him perfectly clearly: his right arm was hanging down, and his legs were crossed; his head, leaning back on the chair, a little to the left, gave an unmistakable impression of a man asleep."[20] An apparently external phantom, however, enters the narrator's mind, dividing him from himself. "He won't show himself again—that's all over. But he is there all the same—in my thoughts. Even though he remains invisible, that does not prevent him from being there . . ." (142).

Of course, a double could be present while also remaining invisible, and this is exactly what happens in Joseph Conrad's story of an *alter ego*, "The Secret Sharer" (1912). A young, inexperienced captain, his boat anchored at the head of the Gulf of Siam, allows an escaped sailor from another vessel to climb aboard his ship and hide in his cabin. The captain must whisper to him in order to avoid detection. "He was not a bit like me, really; yet, as we stood leaning over my bed-place, whispering side by side, with our dark heads together and our backs to the door, anybody bold enough to open it stealthily would have been treated to the uncanny sight of a double captain busy talking in whispers with his other self."[21] No one has parsed this odd situation better than Walter J. Ong: "The stranger-double is somehow there in the captain's own cabin because the captain himself feels a stranger on his own ship, and this because he is a stranger to himself in his own soul."[22] Ong extends his psychological sense of what is at issue in Conrad's tale in an ontological direction. The captain's entertaining of his double "reveals a rift, a limitation inside our own beings, but a rift which opens its own way to salvation—for it is a rift which comes from our bearing vicariously within ourselves the other with whom we must commune, and who must commune with us, too, and thereby compensate for the rift, the limitation, in our persons" (53).

In passing from psychology to ontology we are getting closer to what is at issue in *Thomas l'Obscur*, although we are not quite there yet. Ong, a Jesuit priest, moves very quickly from talk of human being to talk of salvation. And we may recall that the doubling in human being that he has in mind has a long history in philosophy and the church. In theology there are several versions, all drawing to a greater or lesser degree on the Platonic dualism of body and soul. They are not always driven by an appeal to different substances or properties, however. In an influential formulation, St. Augustine distinguishes between "two kinds of life," one regulated by need and the other oriented to delight.[23] In this life we are perpetually caught in a tension between them, much as we might long for a life composed only of pure delight. A more striking version of doubling in theological anthropology goes back at least as far as Origen's commentary on the Song of Songs, written *circa* 240, and Origen ingeniously credits it with an even earlier starting point. He claims that Moses in Genesis records, "the making of two men, the first *in the image and likeness of God*, and the second *formed of the slime of the earth*."[24] St. Paul is interpreting these passages of Genesis, Origen thinks, when he writes, "but though our outward man perish, yet the inward *man* is renewed day by day" (2 Cor. 4:16), and Moses "sees Paul, who understood what Moses wrote much better than we do" (25). For Origen, following Paul, "there are in fact two men in every single man" (25), and we may hope for salvation when we turn from the corruptible man formed of slime to the incorruptible man who is made in the image of God. This means, of course, that we can overcome the doubleness of our mortal being precisely by salvation. Or, to look at the statement from behind, a view to which Blanchot would be far more sympathetic, there can be no salvation because we cannot overcome our doubleness.

Some of Blanchot's readers have found this a hard lesson to learn and have sought to find a parallel in a noncanonical religious text despite the lack of empirical influence from the one to the other. "For there is nothing obscure [or hidden or secret] that will not become shown forth": so reads a passage from one of the Oxyrhynchus Greek fragments discovered in 1897 and 1903, that were later found to belong to the Gospel of Thomas, which, for all its departures from what was to become orthodoxy, remains a discourse of salvation.[25] The linking of obscurity and the name Thomas has encouraged some of Blanchot's readers to find a hidden path that runs from the lost gospel to the novel. "*Thomas the Obscure* has long seemed to us," George Quasha and Charles Stein write, "to echo in some impossible way *The Gospel of Thomas*."²⁶ It could not be a possible echo, unless Blanchot had read the Oxyrthynchus fragments or *The Acts of Thomas*, which was found in Syriac and published in 1871. The Gospel of Thomas was discovered intact at Nag Hammadi only in 1945, along with *The Book of Thomas the Contender*, four years after the publication of *Thomas l'Obscur*. In the Gospel, the Book, and the Acts, "Thomas" is Judas Thomas, the twin of Jesus. Indeed, the "Sinai text" of *The Acts of Thomas*, dated to the fourth or fifth century, speaks solely of Judas, and only the later Syriac text, dated to 936, uses Thomas as a proper name.²⁷ Over the years the ordinary Hebrew word for twin, *te'om* [Aramaic *t'oma*, Arabic *tau'am*], has become a proper name, "Thomas."²⁸ And sometimes, as in the Gospel of John, the Greek word for twin, Δίδυμος [Didymus], has also been mistaken for a proper name. Consider what the disciple says when Jesus proposes to go to Bethany, regarded as a dangerous journey because the Jews had recently tried to stone Jesus: "Then said Thomas, which is called Didymus, unto his fellow disciples, Let us also go, that we may die with him" (John 11: 16).²⁹

There is no authentic echo of the Gospel of Thomas in *Thomas l'Obscur*, partly for chronological reasons and partly because the novel rejects the vision of human being appearing properly and fully under the sign of light. Yet Thomas asks in his gospel, "On the day that you were one, you made two. And when you are two, what will you do?" (Thomas, 11), and, as we shall see, this is precisely the situation in which Thomas finds himself at the start of *Thomas l'Obscur* and a question that the reader asks of him. Parallels between texts can always be found if one looks hard enough. The obscurity of the Gospel of Thomas can be overcome by referring to Hellenistic myths of *exitus-reditus*, however, which have no purchase on *Thomas l'Obscur*. It takes more than a name and the word "*l'Obscur*" to be of help in interpreting the work, but the distance to which Blanchot's readers will go in order to find a "reading head" for *Thomas l'Obscur* is a powerful indication of the work's mystery or secret, to use two quite different words that were close to Blanchot at the time of writing the novel.³⁰

*

In order to bypass misleading associations prompted by the title of the *roman* and *récit* and to avoid a temptation, perhaps by succumbing to it for a moment, let us look ahead from 1941 and 1950 to glimpse how Blanchot himself responded to the obscurity of *Thomas l'Obscur* after he had written all of his narratives, save *L'Instant de ma mort* (1994). In the first of his full-length fragmentary works, *Le Pas au-delà* (1973), he returned obliquely to his first novel, and asked a question that had perplexed him for decades. "From where does it come, this power of uprooting, of destruction or change, in the first words written facing the sky, in the solitude of the sky, words by themselves without prospect or pretense: 'it—the sea' ['*il—la mer*']?"³¹ As any reader of Blanchot will quickly recognize, what is summoned here is the opening sentence of *Thomas l'Obscur*: "Thomas sat down and looked at the sea" [*Thomas s'assit et regarda la mer*] (7, 23, 9), a sentence that was there from the very beginning (*TS*, 11). Also evoked, if more discreetly, is a duality that runs throughout Blanchot's writing, in narrative and criticism. There is negativity, "this power of uprooting, of destruction or change," particularly as construed by Hegel ("the labor of the negative").[32] And there is also what Blanchot will come to call the Neutral or the Outside, the *il* or it, which is a main concern of *Le Pas au-delà*. Without trying to explain the Outside in any detail right now, let us remain with Blanchot's words, and say with him that it "attracts us, were we allowed, having disappeared from ourselves, to write within the secret of ancient fear" (1).

This Outside is not something wholly exterior to *Thomas l'Obscur*, a philosophical concept developed after writing both versions of the narrative that could explain both after the fact, and perhaps turn the *roman* and *récit* into allegories of Blanchot's metaphysical stance as developed in *L'Espace littéraire* (1955) and *L'Entretien infini* (1969). It is already indicated, but not named, in the difficult liminal text set in italics that marks the transformation of the *roman* into the *récit*, a paragraph the second sentence of which condenses much of Blanchot's "philosophy of literature" into a few words. Both of his narratives are the same, he says, "if one is right in making no distinction between the figure and that which is, or believes itself to be, its center, whenever the complete figure itself expresses no more than the search [*la recherche*] for an imaginary center."[33] Each version of *Thomas l'Obscur* is a means, not an end, it would seem: a quest, two among "an infinity of possible variants," for a point that does not exist before the quest begins and that attains reality only in the movement of the narrative toward it. It is in writing that we are drawn to this elusive point, this Outside, where we lose any sense that we may have of being unified over time or even at an instant: an encounter with death, though not one's empirical demise. Blanchot addresses himself as well as his reader: "Do not hope, if there lies your hope—and one must suspect it—to unify your existence, to introduce into it, in the past, some coherence by way of the writing that disunifies" (2; 8). One cannot place two pieces of writing, *Thomas l'Obscur* and *Le Pas au-delà*, beside one another and discern a continuity that gives substantial content to an "I" that signs itself "Maurice Blanchot" and in doing so makes an ontological as well as a legal claim. And that is because writing, in and of itself, disperses unity, including the presumed unity of the author (determined by way of consciousness, soul, spirit, or whatever). This death by writing is one variant of "the ancient fear."

Indeed, what Blanchot holds to be happening to himself in the writing of *Thomas l'Obscur* applies to everyone, writer or not, he says in a fragment later in *Le Pas au-delà*:

> If it is true that there is (in the Chinese language) a written character that means both "man" and "two," it is easy to recognize in man he who is always himself and the other, the happy duality of dialogue and the possibility of communication. But it is less easy, more important perhaps, to think "man," that is to say, also "two," as separation that lacks unity, the leap from 0 to duality, the I thus giving itself as the forbidden, the between-the-two (39; 57).

Blanchot is thinking of the character *ren*, which, as an ideograph, means more than two things. It is usually translated as "benevolence," but along the lines that Blanchot suggests it means both "man" and "human belonging."[34] Doubles and doubling clearly make up a thread that runs throughout Blanchot's writing, and not just in his early novels *Thomas l'Obscur* and *Aminadab* (1942). In the *roman* and *récit*, however, there is reason to think that Thomas becomes two, while in *Le Pas au-delà* and other more philosophical works it seems that Blanchot holds that human beings are always and already divided. Despite this difference, the coherence that Blanchot is unwilling to find in the sequence of his writings in case it misleadingly indicates a unity of self, one that he rigorously doubts at all points, is surely there, if not at the level of substance, then at the levels of theme, style of questioning, and idiom. But that is not to say that he is affirming the same thing in 1941 and 1950 as he is in 1973. Coherence is a weaker state than identity, self-identity, or unity. And of course, it would have been possible for Blanchot to argue for the coherence of a life's work without also arguing for personal self-identity or unity.[35]

Blanchot's own reflection on the change of *Thomas l'Obscur* from *roman* to *récit* has raised several intriguing philosophical questions, mostly in metaphysics though also bearing on the philosophy of literature. One is the status of the point that is projected by the writing of a narrative (or perhaps any text). On the one hand, it is not claimed to be real, in the sense of existing irrespective of human consciousness; while, on the other hand, it serves to disperse any presumed unity in a person, and therefore has real effects. Blanchot seems to be committed to a form of dualism, more likely one of properties than substances, since the Outside (or, as he sometimes calls it, the imaginary) does not seem to be anything like a substance and yet bespeaks more than would be involved in claiming that language requires two sorts of predicates when offering a full description of the world. And he appears to maintain that there is an interaction between these properties, for the Outside has definite effects in the world: it disperses what might have been taken as unified, and the person concerned experiences this loss of personal unity. Also in question, then, is the nature of experience: for given there is no unity of consciousness for Blanchot, whether transcendental or substantive, who or what is the subject of the experience? Indeed, since Blanchot thinks of experience, especially the experience of writing, as a brushing against death, the complete loss of selfhood, can we speak properly of it as "experience" in the first place? More generally, how does the distinction between life and death, as Blanchot draws it, fit with "human being?" Plainly, none of these questions can be answered in a few words here and now, but they will continue to press on us as we read *Thomas l'Obscur*, as will further questions soon to emerge.

*

In both versions, *Thomas l'Obscur* begins by drawing attention to a permeable line between reality and appearance, self and other, whether by way of Thomas's "conviction" [*certitude*] (7; 24; 10) or his "fantasy" [*rêverie*] (14; 33; 17). The surface of the sea into which he goes swimming "was lost in a glow which seemed the only truly real thing [*la seule chose vraiment réelle*]" (7; 24; 9), and Thomas, who gets into trouble while in the water, which he is convinced does not exist, "sought to free himself from the insipid flood which was invading him [*l'envahissait*]" (7; 25; 10), experienced an "intoxication of leaving himself, of slipping into the void [*glisser dans le vide*]" (8; 27; 11) and, even more strangely, felt that he was "dispersing himself [*se disperser*] in the *thought* of water" (8; 27; 11; my emphasis).

Later, back on land, and walking though a small wood, he has what at first seems to be an odd fantasy that picks up on the blurring of external reality and thought: "outside himself there was something identical to his own thought which his glance or his hand could touch" (14; 32; 17). In his disordered state, Thomas finds himself repulsed by the correspondence theory of truth, in particular the version of it affirmed by St. Thomas Aquinas: *veritas est adequatio rei et intellectus*, that is, truth is "the conformity of thing and intellect."[36] Then the narrator goes a step further. "Soon the night seemed to him gloomier and more terrible than any night, as if it had in fact issued from a wound of thought which had ceased to think, of thought taken ironically as object by something other than thought" (14; 33; 17). Here, Thomas passes from an epistemological fantasy to an ontological one. He momentarily becomes a subjective idealist of a peculiar kind, taking external reality as a product of his past thought; but he is a frustrated idealist in that this reality is interpreted, against his understanding of it, to exist without reference to his subjectivity. Rational thought slowly begins to re-order what was a fantasy world, restoring its ontological integrity, and then, "His solitude no longer seemed so complete, and he even had the feeling that something real had knocked against him and was trying to slip inside [*se glisser en lui*]" (15; 33; 18). We pass back from ontology to epistemology. The exterior world, now firmly registering itself as abiding outside his consciousness and existing independently of it, is giving itself to him as so many items of knowledge. Yet his experience of it remains vivid: "from all evidence a foreign body [*un corps étranger*] had lodged itself in his pupil and was attempting to go further" (7; 34; 18). It is not just a mite of dust in his eye but the entire scene before him. To which he adds, in what will become a significant speculation after the death of Anne, "Perhaps a man slipped in [*se glisser-t-il*] by the same opening" (15; 34; 18).

Interlaced with these observations, we find the narrator's reflections on changes of perception and being perceived that are distinct from his fantasy. In the night, his eye does not merely modify itself to accommodate the darkness; it changes in a qualitative way. "Not only did this eye which saw nothing apprehend something, it apprehended the cause of its vision. It saw as object that which prevented it from seeing. Its own glance entered into it as an image, just when this glance seemed the death of all image" (15; 33; 17–18). Thomas can see the night, and in a moment of auto-affection can see himself seeing the very darkness of the night. And when Thomas reads in his room, in a passage that indicates how you and I should be reading the *roman* or *récit* that we have opened, we find a scene in which the reader's intentionality is matched, in an edgy way, by the counter-intentionality of language itself. "He was reading. He was reading with unsurpassable meticulousness and attention," we are told, and then there comes one of the scenes of metamorphoses into monstrosity that will come to punctuate the narrative: "In relation to every symbol, he was in the position of the male praying mantis about to be devoured by the female" (25; 44; 27). Thomas "perceived all the strangeness there was in being observed by a word as if by a living being, and not simply by one word, but by all the words that were in that word, by all those that went with it and in turn contained other words, like a procession of angels opening out into the infinite to the very eye of the absolute" (25; 44; 28). Soon he finds himself being explored by "obscure words [*des paroles obscures*], disembodied souls and angels of words" (26; 45; 29).³⁷ And then his struggle with words is heightened and strangely rendered concrete: "He was locked in combat with something inaccessible, foreign, something of which he could say: That doesn't exist. . . and which nonetheless filled him with terror as he sensed it wandering about in the region of his solitude" (27; 46; 30).

Thomas encounters a limit-phenomenon, which shows itself only at an extremity of consciousness; it impinges on Thomas in space but exists "outside time" (27; 47; 31). He senses that it is replaced by another phenomenon, also given at the limit, which has a distinct way of not being present. Doubtless the writing of any literature performs a reduction, a conversion of the gaze from that of the natural attitude to another that answers more fully to experience.³⁸ And certainly Blanchot (or one of his *alter egos*) came to think that it precipitated an endless reduction that is not quite the same as Husserl's εποχή or any of his modes of reduction.³⁹ Here, though, Thomas has made an apparently ordinary phenomenological reduction. Always, the reduction involves a shift from asking "What?" to asking "How?" although usually it takes place within the field of present being (with at least one profile of the phenomenon being present). But here Thomas passes to the question "How?" in an attempt to register the precise shading in which the phenomenon is absent from him. "It was a modulation of that which did not exist, a different mode of being absent, another void in which he was coming to life" (27; 46; 30). Is this an experience of a change from blank nonexistence to the eerie sifting of being and nonbeing that is the Outside? There is insufficient evidence to say for sure. There follows a struggle between a "sort of Thomas" (27; 47; 32) who leaves him to fight the threatening phenomenon, and who finds himself "bitten or struck. . . by what seemed to him to be a word, but resembled rather a giant rat, an all-powerful beast with piercing eyes and pure teeth" (28; 47-8; 32).⁴⁰ The border between language and nonlinguistic reality is once again deemed to be equivocal. More disturbing still, the limit between life and death is revealed not to be absolute.

In a passage we have already touched on when considering possible parallels between *Thomas l'Obscur* and *Jude the Obscure* we find a knot in the thread we have been following:

> This grave which was exactly his size, his shape, his thickness, was like his own corpse, and every time he tried to bury himself in it, he was like a ridiculous dead person trying to bury his body in his body. There was, then, henceforth, in all the sepulchers where he might have been able to take his place, in all the feelings which are also tombs for the dead, in this annihilation through which he was dying without permitting himself to be thought dead, there was another dead person who was there first, and who, identical with himself, drove the ambiguity of Thomas's life and death to the extreme limit. (35-36; 76-77; 38-39)

To make plain what is happening, and perhaps to link it to the literary tradition of the *Doppelgänger* already noted, the narrator points to "a double [*un sosie*] wrapped in bands, its senses sealed with the seven seals, its spirit absent" that occupies Thomas's place, "this double" [*ce sosie*] being "the unique one with which no compromise was possible, since it was the same as himself" (36; 77; 39). As the biblical allusion to Rev. 5: 1 ("And I saw in the right hand of him that sat on the throne a book written within and on the backside, sealed with seven seals") makes clear, this double is completely sealed, unable to be opened except by the very God who has no place in the world of the *roman* and the *récit*. This Thomas, the double of the living Thomas, to use a description that will become dubious, is utterly obscure, and he is obscure because he is already dead, and dead without hope of resurrection whether before the last day or on it. And so the living Thomas knows himself, in an intolerable paradox, "to be dead, absent, completely absent from his death" (36; 77; 40). "He was really dead and at the same time rejected from the reality of death" (36; 77–8; 40).

It should be noted that the claim that one is already dead while apparently alive is a very common one. Christians believe that when one is baptized one is buried with Christ. ("Know ye not, that so many of us as were baptized into Jesus Christ were baptized into his death?" says St. Paul in Rom. 6: 3.) But plainly this Christian sense of being dead while still being alive can be put to one side. Blanchot is elaborating a quite different concept. Thomas is pictured as one of the walking dead, an image that is at once gothic yet quite unlike anything one might find in a story by Horace Walpole, Mary Shelley, Bram Stoker, or Matthew Lewis. He appears "at the narrow gate of his sepulcher, not risen [*non pas ressuscité*] but dead, and with the certainty of being snatched at once from death and from life" (37; 79; 42).[41] At first he is called a "mummy [*momie*]," then Blanchot returns to a biblical image that he adapts in his own way: "He walked, the only true Lazarus, whose very death was raised [*la mort même était ressuscitée*]" (38; 79; 42; trans. slightly modified). It will be noted that Blanchot, quite properly, prefers the verb *ressusciter* to the noun *la résurrection* for the raising of the biblical Lazarus of Bethany (John 11: 1–46). In La Bible de Jérusalem Jesus and Martha use the word "*la résurrection*," twice, the second time while naming the general resurrection, "*la résurrection, au dernier jour*" (John 11: 24) and the first when Jesus declares, in one of his powerful "I am" statements, "I am the resurrection" [*Moi, je suis la résurrection*] (John 11:25). Yet when Jesus says to Martha, "Thy brother shall rise again" [*Ton frère ressuscitera*] he means he will be revived now, today, and not only at the resurrection at the last day, which is a qualitatively different sort of event in which mortal bodies will be definitively transformed into immortal bodies.[42]

It is because Jesus *is* the resurrection, divinely powerful and commanding, and Martha believes him to be so, that he can revive Lazarus now, though his friend remains mortal, with death to come again. (*The Golden Legend* has him becoming the first bishop of Kittim and remaining so for thirty years before he dies; another legend has him becoming bishop of Marseille and eventually being buried in Vézelay.[43]) Thus John 11: 44: "Le mort sortit, les pieds et les mains liés de bandelettes, et son visage était enveloppé d'un suaire. Jésus leur dit: 'Déliez-le et laissez-le aller.'" There is no talk of a transformed body here, such as one finds in John 20: 26 when Jesus enters the upper chamber even though the doors are shut and talks with Thomas who does not believe that Jesus has risen from the dead. It is worth noting that in the biblical narrative it is the same disciple, Thomas, who announces to the other followers of Jesus that, dangerous as it is (because of the attempt to stone Jesus reported in John 10:31), they should all follow Jesus to Bethany. In the fourth gospel Thomas silently observes the raising of Lazarus to new life while later doubting that Jesus has been resurrected; in the *roman* and *récit*, it is Thomas's *death* that is raised. Parallels between the Gospel of John and *Thomas l'Obscur* are at best sharply ironic.[44] The same is true of the synoptic gospels, as Blanchot's treatment of the daughter of Jairus makes plain (89; 289; 100).

That passage introduces the narrator's reflections on Anne's corpse. "She had stopped at the point where she resembled only herself [*elle ne ressemblait qu'à elle-même*], and where her face, having only Anne's expression, was disturbing to look at" (89; 289; 100). The peculiar expression "she resembled only herself" is important in the philosophical economy of the *roman* and the *récit*. It is this self-resemblance that generates a peculiar effect. "At the moment everything was being destroyed she had created that which was most difficult: she had not drawn something out of nothing (a meaningless act), but given to nothing, in its form of nothing, the form of something. The act of not seeing had now its integral eye" (90; 291; 102). In dying Anne has become her own image; for a while, she is both herself and her image. A fissure in being has been discerned that allows us to glimpse, as it were, the Outside. Blanchot will return to this in "Two Versions of the Imaginary" (1951), one of his most concise and philosophically powerful reflections on the relations of being and the neutral.[45] Ironically enough, his friend Levinas will adapt the insight as the *point d'appui* of his remarkable critique of art, "La réalité et son ombre" (1948). "Reality would not be only what it is, what it is disclosed to be in truth, but would be also its double [*son double*], its shadow, its image."[46]

I pass from Anne's death over the preceding love story of Thomas and Anne, in which Anne herself is revealed as not quite coinciding with herself and as "already dead" (82; 283, 91), to the crucial depicting of Thomas that will unravel what it means for Thomas's death to have been raised. In doing so, I bypass not only memorable chapters of great human passion but also the narrative's intense reworking of a mythological rather than philosophical scene—the story of the death of Eurydice—and the difficult question of the relation, or perhaps non-relation, of the mythological and the philosophical in both the *roman* and the *récit*. Proclus declared, "All theology among the Greeks is sprung from the mystical doctrine of Orpheus," the word "theology" meaning here partly wisdom literature deriving from the Orphics and partly what the word "metaphysics" covers in its sense of dealing with the highest ground.[47] And Francis Bacon took the story of Orpheus to be "a picture of universal philosophy," the word "philosophy" being broader in scope then than it is now.[48] But in *Thomas l'Obscur* at least, philosophy arranges itself in tension with the narrative of Orpheus's descent to the underworld and his ascent from it. Several philosophers are evoked in the narrative, especially in the *roman* (Socrates, Pascal, Descartes, Spinoza), although none is more important than Descartes. The central dispute in the *roman* and the *récit* is not between Orpheus and the King of the Dead but between Thomas and Descartes. Before we get to that passage, though, we need to listen to Thomas speaking after Anne's death.

Before this moment, the narrator has spoken of Thomas being already dead. Now Thomas himself speaks himself of being dead, of subsisting in "the paradox and the impossibility of death" (92; 295; 104). Death, for him, is not "a slight accident" that touches the end of his life, as it is for other people, but "an anthropometric index," for, as he says, "I was real only under the name of death" (92; 296; 105). Here, unlike earlier and later in the *roman* and *récit*, Thomas speaks of his condition as singular, not general, doubtless because it turns entirely on his experience of being dead while apparently still alive.[49] This conception of death requires us to distinguish an anterior death from an empirical death. Thomas knows that he will die one day but takes himself to have already suffered an anterior death, a death that has been "raised" from the grave, and when death finally comes to him it will be "the death of death" (91; 293; 103). At the back of this notion is Hegel's conception of the ego as "the power of the negative."[50] After the death of Anne, Thomas enjoys a deep "serenity" that "made of every instant of [his] life the instant in which [he] was going to leave life" (92; 294; 103-4). Absent from Anne and his love of her, Thomas not only flees the horizon of the world but also flees from his flight; he experiences a "supreme moment of calm" (103; 309; 121). If life is the power of the negative—change, destruction, uprooting—then the refusal to exercise that power, the lapse into radical passivity, is death in life. The "I" remains abstract, does not fulfill any possibilities; it becomes a "perfect nothingness [*néant*]" (96; 301; 110). Without Anne, Thomas has passed from "you [*toi*]-consciousness (at once existence and life) to you [*toi*]-unconsciousness (at once reality and death)" (98; 303; 114). He is "infinitely more dead than dead" (104; 310; 122), even though alive, because he feels himself to be without relation, without possibilities that can be realized, and without any opposition to overcome. In Hegel's terms, he is universal, without any contradiction between himself and his genus, so that, with his death, "the species died each time, completely" (93; 297; 106).[51]

Thomas l'Obscur is not concerned simply to chart the experience of non-experience of a man who is dead to life and, it seems, dead in life; it converges on the non-relation of twins, one of whom is dead in life while the other is the "obscure Thomas." The narrative approaches its climax with the "dead" Thomas, "the same as a living person but without life," wondering how to reach the obscure Thomas, "the same as a dead person but without death," who has somehow slipped into him:

> Death was a crude metamorphosis beside the indiscernible nullity which I nevertheless coupled with the name [*nom*] Thomas. Was it then a fantasy, this enigma, the creation of a word [*un mot*] maliciously formed to destroy all words? But if I advanced within myself, hurrying laboriously toward my precise noon, I yet experienced as a tragic certainty, at the center of the living Thomas, the inaccessible proximity of that Thomas which was nothingness [*ce Thomas néant*], and the more the shadow of my thought shrunk, the more I conceived of myself in this faultless clarity as the possible, the willing host of this obscure Thomas [*cet obscur Thomas*]. (97-98; 303; 112-13)[52]

"Thomas" slides from a proper name to a common noun meaning "twin," and the double in this word endangers the operations of language. (Exactly how it does will become apparent only in Blanchot's essays, as we shall see.) The living-dead Thomas is the host of the obscure Thomas: the inaccessible one depends on the living-dead one. One of the twins is "perfect nothingness," an abyss, while the other is neither nothingness nor being but what Blanchot will come to call the neutral.[53] He is the one who belongs, as it were, to the Outside. "I found myself," the living-dead Thomas says, "with two faces, glued one to the other. I was in constant contact with two shores. With one hand showing that I was indeed there, with the other—what am I saying?—without the other, with this body which, imposed on my real body, depended entirely on a negation of the body, I entered into absolute dispute with myself" (96-97; 301; 111).[54]

This dispute suddenly takes the form of rethinking a canonical moment in modern philosophy, Descartes's "*Je pense donc je suis*" in the *Discourse on Method* (1633), later recast in Latin as *ego cogito, ego sum* in his *Principles of Philosophy* (1644). "It was then," Thomas says, "that, deep within a cave, the madness of the taciturn thinker appeared before me and unintelligible words rung in my ears while I wrote on the wall these sweet words: 'I think, therefore I am not' [*Je pense, donc je ne suis pas*]" (99; 304; 114).[55] Is this Plato's cave, or is the cave a figure for Thomas's skull? Either way, there is a sudden illumination. For on saying these words Thomas has a vision of a great lens that captures the rays of the sun and, redirecting them outward, burns out whatever it aims at. "I think, it said, I am subject and object of an all-powerful radiation; a sun using all its energy to make itself night, as well as to make itself sun" (99; 304; 115).[56] This visionary lens is the Hegelian ego, a pure negativity that expends itself in action in order to make history. The firm establishment of an ego, an "I," Thomas tells us, entails the destruction of that ego or "I" and, with it, all solid ground for thought. Far from seeking epistemological security, Thomas's "goal of [his] understanding" becomes the obscure Thomas, "A sort of being composed of all that which is excluded from being" (105; 311; 124). And, as happened earlier in the *roman* and *récit*, Thomas feels the dark gaze of this obscure Thomas: "it is him who understands me [*qui me comprend*]" (105; 312; 124; trans. slightly modified).

It was Descartes who, in the discovery of the *cogitatio*, first performed the phenomenological reduction, as Husserl acknowledged. "It is a most noteworthy fact that the fundamental consideration that inaugurates the entire course of the development of modern philosophy was nothing other than the staging of a phenomenological reduction."[57] Much modern European philosophy, from Descartes to Marion, was to brood on the *cogitatio*, and phenomenology was to elaborate a highly influential and flexible extension of it: the idea that the *cogito* is not isolated and pure but actually involved with the world. The converted gaze that could be brought about by performing the reduction presented us with a world of things that was meaningful for us because we were involved from the beginning in constituting its meaning. Consciousness is shown to have been always in an intentional relationship with the things of the world. Or, if it must be put more directly, human being is, from the first, being in relation.

With this in mind, let us continue to read Thomas's reflections on the obscure Thomas, a non-relation between the twins that is occluded in the English translation:

> Invisible and outside of being, it perceives me [*me perçoit*] and sustains me in being. Itself, I perceive it [*Lui-même. . . je le discerne*], an unjustifiable chimera if I were not there, I perceive it [*je le discerne*], not in the vision I have of it [*j'ai de lui*], but in the vision and the knowledge it has of me [*il a de moi*]. I am seen. Beneath this glance [*ce regard*], I commit myself to a passivity which, rather than

diminishing me, makes me real. I seek neither to distinguish it [*à le distinguer*], nor to attain it [*à l'atteindre*], nor to suppose it [*à le supposer*]. Perfectly negligent, by my distraction I retain for it [*je lui garde*] the quality of inaccessibility which is appropriate to it [*qui lui convient*]. My senses, my imagination, my spirit, all are dead on the side on which it looks at me [*où il me regarde*]... I am seen. (105; 312; 124-25)[58]

If the reduction gives us a richer sense of our relationship with things, including other people (though only as phenomena), showing that we are intimately involved in the production of their meaning for us, then can we speak coherently of a reduction here? We can—in terms of counter-intentionality. Yet caution is needed, for this is not a description of what it is like to be reduced, to become a phenomenon for someone else. Not at all: the neutral reduction, as I shall call it, shows that the relationship that the obscure Thomas has with his twin brother falls outside relationship, at least of the kinds that classical phenomenology countenances. It leads him to the abyss. The obscure Thomas is always and already involved with his twin though in a manner that is not described for us. The living-dead Thomas cannot find his double in an intentional horizon and therefore cannot exfoliate the concrete meaning of the other from whom he is divided. To be sure, the obscure Thomas can be indicated in his obscurity: his phenomenality can be felt but he cannot be brought into the light of intelligibility. He cannot become a phenomenon and must remain haunting the Thomas whose aching, relentless voice we hear as we read the narrative. The obscure Thomas remains in what the narrator calls, in an expression to which Blanchot was to return many times, investing it with increased significance, "*une autre nuit*" (105; 311; 124), the space where being passes into image and back again without end and without point.

Descartes and Thomas remain phased counterparts in both the *roman* and the *récit*. In a sense, they too form a double.[59] The one inaugurates modern philosophy; the other, by way of his twin, either challenges the scope of that philosophy or extends it in a new direction, one that includes the discussion of what passes under being—the neutral, the Outside—as well as being itself. The one insists on epistemic certainty; the other prizes being convinced, which may take place in a reverie instead of a state of cold, analytic reason. The one adduces a firm ground; the other opens a space of "error," eternal wandering between being and the Outside.[60] Whatever else he does in this narrative, Blanchot challenges the much-prized "unity of reason" in the history of philosophy. There is no way in which Thomas and his twin can be brought together in anything that could plausibly be called a unity. "There are three errors to be avoided in the sciences," St. Bonaventure wrote, by way of allergic reaction to the radical Aristotelianism that he believed to have beset and endangered the University of Paris, "One of these is against the cause of being, another is against the ground of the understanding, and the third is against the order of living."[61] *Thomas l'Obscur* may not be guilty of radical Aristotelianism but it nonetheless wanders in all three "errors."

*

Many things remain to be discussed and evaluated: Blanchot's philosophy of the subject, his philosophy of experience, and his philosophy of death, and in what ways these philosophical questions appear in the *roman* and the *récit*, and make it, in one sense or another, what used to be called a "philosophical novel." In conclusion, though, I restrict myself to one point that has been raised: as we have heard, the narrator speaks of the noun "Thomas" as "the creation of a word [*un mot*] maliciously formed to destroy all words" (97; 303; 112).[62] Presumably, he has in mind the early statement that one of the twins who comprise "Thomas" is an abyss, as already noted. It is addressed in different terms in the essays, indirectly at first in *Comment la littérature est-elle possible?* (1942) and finally quite directly in "La littérature et le droit à la mort" (1947–8). At the very end of that long and powerful probing of the relations between writing and death, Blanchot once again attends to the figure of the double. This time, though, it is not a character in a novel but a strange power that abides at the heart of language:

> Now nothing can prevent this power—at the very moment it is trying to understand things and, in language, to specify words—nothing can prevent it from continuing to assert itself as continually differing possibility [*une possibilité toujours autre*], and nothing can stop it from perpetuating an irreducible *double meaning* [*un double sens irréducible*], a choice whose terms are covered over with an ambiguity that makes them identical to one another even as it makes them opposite.[63]

The double, here, is language as negativity and language as neutral. If we think of language solely by way of its daily work in the world, its ability to construct meaning, then that very conception of language will be undermined by its ghostly, abyssal double, the neutral.

Without death, Blanchot says (following Hegel, especially Kojève's Hegel), there could be no meaning; and this is because meaning relies on the possibility of separating essence from its empirical shell. Language is the form of the "essential content" of what is expressed, Hegel argues in the *Phenomenology of Mind*. When an ego expresses itself in language and is understood by others, "its existence is itself dying away."[64] Kojève puts this more dramatically in a well-known passage about a dog and the concept of a dog: "if the dog were not *mortal*—that is, essentially *finite* or limited with respect to its duration—one could not *detach* the Concept from it—that is, cause the Meaning (Essence) that is embodied in the *real* dog to pass into the *non*living word."[65] And yet death is not always an end; sometimes it is encountered passively as an endless dying, and then the clarity of death, of negativity, of the concept, is lost, and we have only the neutral vaguely pressing on us. Then the author's consciousness is raised, like Lazarus, before or after his or her actual demise by the mere act of reading. Blanchot describes this neutral existence several pages before he reaches his conclusion in "La littérature et le droit à la mort":

> The writer senses that he is in the grasp of an impersonal power that does not let him either live or die: the irresponsibility he cannot surmount becomes the expression of that death without death which awaits him at the edge of nothingness; literary immortality is the very movement by which the nausea of a survival which is not

a survival, a death which does not end anything, insinuates itself into a world, a world sapped by crude existence (340; 327).

In writing, then, we find ourselves both forming meaning and condemning ourselves to a meaningless, neutral existence in the reader's consciousness. One odd thing about this perception is that what most other writers in all periods of history have prized above all other things, being in a position to make Shakespeare's boast in Sonnet 18 about having written "eternal lines," is recast by Blanchot as something horrific. For him, it has the sort of terror found in certain stories of Poe but raised to philosophical dignity. To want literary fame, for Blanchot, amounts to having a desire for a ghostly half-existence to be feared and unable to be eliminated even if one turns out, in the end, to have been a very minor writer. Even more peculiar, perhaps, is that this shudder before literary immortality is not a rhetorical flourish in a single essay that could be taken as a defense mechanism against literary failure. It is a position that Blanchot explores relentlessly in later essays and fragmentary writings.[66] And yet the Neutral is said in many ways: it involves more than the survival of endlessly dying authorial consciousness; it also directs us to a doubling in being itself, as we have seen with the death of Anne and as is taken up, and directed to a different end, in Levinas's philosophy of art. But what is philosophy was once narrative. In 1941 *Thomas l'Obscur* marked a particularly powerful literary presentation of this fissure in human being, one that Blanchot would reinforce in the 1950 redaction of the *roman* into the *récit* and would continue to explore until his last published words.

Notes

1 The 1941 *roman* was not reissued after the appearance of the 1950 *récit* until 2005, two years after Blanchot's death in 2003. It was never disowned, however, and it returned in an eerie manner, quoted without explanation on the back of the *récit* in Gallimard's "L'Imaginaire" edition of 1992. An early draft of the *roman*, dating from 1931-37, has been discovered, edited, and very recently published. See Blanchot, *Thomas le Solitaire*, ed. Leslie Hill et Philippe Lynes (Paris: Kimé, 2022). The relations between the three published narratives in the *Thomas* series will take a considerable time to establish, and I shall make only limited references to *TS* in this chapter: my references to it will appear mainly in the notes.
2 See Blanchot, "Heraclitus," *IC*, 85–92 (119–31). The piece first appeared in *Nouvelle Revue Française*, 85 (1960), 93–106, and was reprinted in *EI*, 119–31. Blanchot alludes to Heralcitus in a short piece on Gaston Bachelard, "Le Feu, l'eau et les rêves" (1942), now collected in *CL*, 244. Robert Lamberton raised the possibility of a connection between Blanchot and Heraclitus in his "*Thomas* and the Possibility of Translation," added to the English translation of the *récit* version of *Thomas l'Obscur*. See *TO*, 19–24.
3 I take the expression "quantity of connection" from Jacques Derrida. See his *The Archeology of the Frivolous: Reading Condillac*, trans. John P. Leavey, Jr. (Pittsburgh, PA: Duquesne University Press, 1980), 72.

4   Heidegger, "Aletheia (Heralcitus, Fragment B 16)," *Early Greek Thinking: The Dawn of Western Philosophy*, trans. David Farrell Krell and Frank A. Capuzzi (San Francisco, CA: Harper and Row, 1975), 102. Blanchot started to read *Sein und Zeit* in 1927 or 1928, an event that was, he said decades later, "a true intellectual shock." See his "Thinking the Apocalypse," *PW*, 123. Yet also see Blanchot's dismissal of Heidegger in his review of Denis de Rougemont's *Penser avec les mains*, *L'Insurgé* 3 (27 janvier 1937): 5.
5   Heidegger, *Being and Time*, 58.
6   Heidegger, *The Essence of Human Freedom: An Introduction to Modern Philosophy*, trans. Ted Sadler (London: Continuum, 2002), §11, and "Aletheia," 118. In modern German, *die Lichtung* is a clearing in a forest; however, Heidegger reties the word to its original association with light, *Licht*.
7   Levinas figures the intellectual relationship between Heidegger and Blanchot by way of convergence, not influence. See his "The Poet's Vision," *PN*, 129.
8   See Blanchot's "Comment découvrir l'obscur?," the second part of a long essay nominally concerned with Yves Bonnefoy, that appeared in *Nouvelle Revue Française* 83 (1959), two numbers of the journal before the publication of "Héraclite." It was reproduced in *EI*, 57–69. It is easy to imagine the Blanchot of *Thomas l'Obscur* resonating with Heraclitus's remarks, "Only the living may be dead" (from Fragment 78) and "I am as I am not" (from Fragment 81). See Heraclitus, *Fragments*, trans. Brooks Haxton, foreword James Hillman (New York: Viking, 2001), 49, 51.
9   Blanchot's review appeared in *Journal des débats* (24 février 1942): 3, and was reprinted in *FP(F)*, 126–31. As with all the reviews that, revised or not, appeared in *FP(F)*, the piece is not reprinted in *CL*. A translation, "Is Mallarmé's Poetry Obscure?" may be found in *FP*, 107–11.
10 Blanchot, "Is Mallarmé's Poetry Obscure?" 111. Blanchot's fear of paraphrasing poetry was life long. See his note of regret that he may have been guilty of turning poems of Louis-René des Forêts into a "prose approximation" in "Rough Draft of a Regret," *VE*, 10 (*VA*, 17).
11 Also see Thomas Hardy, "He Follows Himself," in *The Complete Poetical Works of Thomas Hardy*, ed. Samuel Hynes, 3 vols. (Oxford: Clarendon Press, 1984), vol. 2, 422–3.
12 Hardy, *Jude the Obscure*, ed., intro. and notes Patricia Ingham (Oxford: Oxford University Press, 2002), 200. Also see 221 and 327. That Hardy chooses to name the imaginary church "St. Thomas" perhaps indicates that Jude and Sue would never have become truly one in marriage.
13 Thomas Gray, "Elegy Written in a Country Church-Yard," in *Thomas Gray and William Collins, Poetical Works*, ed. Roger Lonsdale (Oxford: Oxford University Press, 1977), 36.
14 Blanchot, *TO*, 35, 76, 38. Throughout, I shall cite this English translation of the *récit* first, followed by the relevant page of the French *roman*, followed by the relevant page of the French *récit*. Lamberton draws attention to the scene in Hardy's novel in "*Thomas* and the Possibility of Translation," 123. I do not know whether Blanchot ever read *Jude the Obscure*. He makes no mention of Hardy in his early reviews gathered in *CL* or *FP*. Firmin Roz translated Hardy's novel into French as *Jude l'obscur* (Paris: Ollendorff, 1901).
15 See Alfred de Musset, *Oeuvres complètes*, ed. Philippe van Tieghem (Paris: Éditions du Seuil, 1963), 153–5.
16 Edgar Allan Poe, "William Wilson," *Poetry and Tales* (New York: The Library of America, 1984), 356.

17 Fyodor Dostoevsky, *The Double: Two Versions*, trans. Evelyn Harden (Ann Arbor: Ardis, 1985), 57.
18 See, for example, Blanchot, "Un essai sur Gérard de Nerval," *Journal des débats* (22 juin 1939): 2, and Blanchot's review of Albert Béguin's *Gérard de Nerval* in *L'Insurgé*, 33, 25 août, 1937, 4. The Nerval who wrote under his portrait *"Je suis l'autre"* would clearly be a sympathetic figure for the Blanchot of *Thomas l'Obscur*.
19 Gérard de Nerval, "Aurélia," *Selected Writings*, trans. and intro. Geoffrey Wagner (Ann Arbor: The University of Michigan Press, 1957), 121–2.
20 Guy de Maupassant, "He?" *The Dark Side: Tales of Terror and the Supernatural*, foreword Ramsey Campbell, intro. Arnold Kellet (New York: Carroll and Graf, 1989), 139.
21 Joseph Conrad, *The Secret Sharer*, ed. Daniel R. Schwarz (Boston: Bedford Books, 1997), 34.
22 Walter J. Ong, "Voice as Summons for Belief: Literature, Faith, and the Divided Self," in *The Barbarian Within and Other Fugitive Essays and Studies* (New York: Macmillan, 1962), 52.
23 See St. Augustine, Sermon 255, *Sermons*, part 3/7: *On the Liturgical Seasons* (230–272B), trans. and notes Edmund Hill, ed. John E. Rotelle, The Works of Saint Augustine (New Rochelle, NY: New City Press, 1993), 161, and Sermon 302, *Sermons*, part 3/8: *On the Saints* (273–305A), trans. and notes Edmund Hill, ed. John E. Rotelle, The Works of Saint Augustine (Hyde Park, NY: New City Press, 1994), 300. Whether knowingly or not, Blanchot inherits from Augustine in his understanding of different attitudes to communism. See Blanchot, "On One Approach to Communism," *F*, 95–6 (112).
24 Origen, *The Song of Songs: Commentary and Homilies*, trans. and ed., R. P. Lawson, Ancient Christian Writers (New York: The Newman Press, 1956), 25. Origen has in mind Gen. 1: 26 and 2: 7.
25 The Gospel According to Thomas, 5 (my additions in square brackets), *The Gnostic Scriptures*, trans., intro. and annotations Bentley Layton (London: SCM Press, 1987), 381.
26 George Quasha and Charles Stein, "Afterword: Publishing Blanchot in America," *SHBR*, 523.
27 See A. F. J. Klijn, ed., *The Acts of Thomas: Introduction, Text, and Commentary*, 2nd rev. ed. (Leiden: Boston, 2005), 1–4.
28 Nancy muddies the waters when he implies that "Thomas" comes from the Greek "thauma," meaning "wonder." See his "The Name God in Blanchot," in *Dis-Enclosure: The Deconstruction of Christianity*, trans. Bettina Bergo et al. (New York: Fordham University Press, 2008), 87. However, Isidore of Seville, *Etymologiae* (*c.* 600–*c.* 625) proposes that the name means "abyss" and is followed by Jacobus de Voragino, *The Golden Legend or Lives of the Saints Englished* by William Caxton, ed. F. S. Ellis, 7 vols., vol. 2 (London: Dent, 1900), 138. Thomas Blount in his *Glossographia* (1656) writes of the name as follows: "Thomas (Hebr.) signifies twin, or, as some will have it, bottomless deep," thereby indicating modern skepticism about "abyss" as the etymological meaning of the name. Presumably, the second meaning came about by creatively relating *te'om*, the Hebrew word for twin, to *tehom*, the Hebrew word for abyss in Gen. 1: 2. Segond and the Bible de Jérusalem both translate *tehom* by "abîme." Blanchot may well have come across the meaning in the Scriptures, in Isidore or Voragino and been intrigued by what he found there.
29 Derrida entertains the possibility of reading *Thomas l'Obscur* "as an abyssal, meditative fictive recollection of [the] evangelical episode," namely the scene of *noli*

ne tangere. See Derrida, *On Touching—Jean-Luc Nancy*, trans. Christine Irizarry (Stanford, CA: Stanford University Press, 2005), 335 n. 23. Also see n. 27 above.

30 I take the expression "reading head" from Derrida, "Living On: Borderlines," *Parages*, 133.
31 Blanchot, *SNB*, 1 (8). There is a thread in *Thomas l'Obscur* that is sewn into the latter text: "I am truly in the beyond, if the beyond is that which admits of no beyond [*pas d'au-delà*]" (104–5; 311; 123).
32 Hegel, *The Phenomenology of Mind*, trans. and intro. J. B. Baillie, intro. George Lichtheim (New York: Harper and Row, 1967), 81.
33 Blanchot formulates the same idea as a general account of narrative in "Encountering the Imaginary," *BC*, 7 (15). The passage was originally published as "Le chant des sirènes," *Nouvelle Nouvelle Revue Française* 19 (juin 1954): 104.
34 My thanks to Gloria Davies for explaining the Chinese character *ren* to me.
35 Blanchot speaks of unity rather than identity or self-identity. It is important to note, though, that unity and identity (or self-identity) are not the same, especially when talking of personhood. See, for example, Lynne Rudder Baker, *The Metaphysics of Everyday Life: An Essay in Practical Reason* (Cambridge: Cambridge University Press, 2007), ch. 4.
36 Aquinas, *Truth*, vol. 1, q. 1 art. 1, *responsio*.
37 The expression "*des paroles obscures*" is added in the *récit* version of the narrative.
38 See on this point the very interesting letter that Edmund Husserl wrote to Hugo von Hofmannsthal on January 12, 1907, *Briefwechsel*, 10 vols, vol. 7: *Wissenschaftlerkorrespondenz*, ed. Elisabeth Schuhmann and Karl Schuhmann (Boston: Kluwer, 1994), 135.
39 See Blanchot, "René Char and the Thought of the Neutral," *IC*, 304 (448). The views presented about the reduction are given by one person in a conversation and are not specifically endorsed by Blanchot. Also see Blanchot's assessment of the value of phenomenology in "Atheism and Writing: Humanism and the Cry," *IC*, 250–2 (374–6). For Husserl's theory of reduction, see his *First Philosophy: Lectures 1923/24 and Related Texts from the Manuscripts (1920–1925)*, Husserliana 14, trans. Sebastian Luft and Thane M. Naberhaus (Dordrecht: Springer, 2019), Part 2. Finally, see Alain David, "La réduction," *Magazine littéraire*, 424 (octobre, 2003), 64–6, and my "Une réduction infinie," *Cahiers de l'Herne*, 2014, Blanchot special issue, ed. Dominique Rabaté and Éric Hoppenot, 323–8.
40 On the fantasy of the rat in *TO (1)*, see Jacques Lacan, "De la realization du fantasme," *Magazine littéraire*, 424 (2003), 46–7. Lacan's text was delivered at his seminar on June 27, 1962.
41 In the *roman* the sentence reads "qu'il était arraché en même temps à la vie et à la mort" (79) while in the *récit* the sentence reads "d'être arraché en même temps à la mort et à la vie" (42).
42 The point is likely to be appreciated only by those well versed in Christian theology of the resurrection. Even in French ecclesiastical language *ressusciter* is sometimes used as a verbal form when one is needed to substitute for the noun *la résurrection*. But this usage can lead to theological confusion. Nancy, for one, misses the point of the distinction in his essay "Blanchot's resurrection" [*Résurrection de Blanchot*], *Dis-Enclosure*, 89–97. Unfortunately, he is encouraged to make the mistake by, among other sources, the Bible de Jérusalem, which has the heading, before John 11, "Résurrection de Lazare."
43 See Jacobus de Voragino, *The Golden Legend*, 23.
44 The same is true of Blanchot's use of Lazarus in "Literature and the Right to Death." See his *WF*, 327 (316).

45 See Blanchot, *SL*, 258 (347).
46 Levinas, "Reality and its Shadow," *CPP*, 6.
47 Proclus, *The Platonic Theology*, trans. Thomas Taylor, pref. R. Baine Harris, 6 vols. (Kew Gardens, NY: Selene Books, 1986), vol. 1, 6, p. 13. Also see Aristotle, *Metaphysics*, 1026a.
48 Francis Bacon, "Orpheus, or Philosophy," *The Wisdom of the Ancients and Miscellaneous Essays* (New York: Walter J. Black, Inc., 1932), 250. It should be noted that in the *Symposium*, 179d, Plato allows Orpheus to be characterized by Phaedrus as a weak creature, something of a coward for not dying for his wife. In classical philosophy, then, he is not a figure of philosophical dignity.
49 The later episode I have in mind is when Thomas sits beside a girl on a bench and says, "I was her tragic double" (100; 306; 117), an insight that seems to be shared by the girl.
50 Hegel, *The Phenomenology of Mind*, 94.
51 See Hegel, *Philosophy of Mind: Being Part Three of the "Encyclopedia of the Philosophical Sciences" (1830)*, trans. William Wallace and A. V. Miller, foreword J. N. Findlay (Oxford: Clarendon Press, 1971), 11.
52 In the *roman* Blanchot writes "*ce Thomas-néant*," a stronger formulation than "*ce Thomas néant*" in the *récit*. The original expression is found in *TS*, 246. Also, see "Thomas" regarded as a word rather than as a name in 116, 322, 135. The *roman* has "le mot de Thomas," while the *récit* has "le mot vide de Thomas." The English translation has "Thomas's empty word," which misses some of what Blanchot actually writes.
53 Early in the *roman* and *récit*, Thomas is referred to as "the sort of abyss which was himself" (15; 34; 19). For "Thomas" as "abyss," see n. 28 above.
54 In *Thomas le Solitaire* we read, "Je recevais de ce double, en réalité mon essence première, confiné au néant, ma figure et ma nécessité," 245.
55 James H. Nichols, *TS*, 247.
56 See *TS*, 247.
57 See Husserl, *The Basic Problems of Phenomenology: From the Lectures*, trans. Ingo Farin and James G. Hart (Dordrecht: Springer, 2006), §16. Husserl observes with dismay that Descartes relinquished the reduction on discovering it.
58 See *TS*, 255.
59 See Mark C. Taylor, *Altarity* (Chicago, IL: The University of Chicago Press, 1987), 222.
60 Blanchot explores this idea in *SL*, 237–8 (318–21).
61 St. Bonaventure, *Collations on the Seven Gifts of the Holy Spirit*, intro., trans. Zachary Hayes, notes Robert J. Karris, Works of St. Bonaventure, 14 (St. Bonaventure, NY: Franciscan Institute Publications, 2008), 176.
62 See *TS*, 246.
63 Blanchot, "Literature and the Right to Death," 343–4 (330–1).
64 Hegel, *Phenomenology of Mind*, 530.
65 Alexandre Kojève, *Introduction to the Reading of Hegel: Lectures on the "Phenomenology of Spirit,"* ed. Raymond Queneau, ed. Allan Bloom, trans. James H. Nichols (Ithaca, NY: Cornell University Press, 1969), 141. I discuss this issue with slightly different emphases in my *The Dark Gaze*, ch. 4.
66 See, for example, *IC*, 48 (68–9), *SNB*, 75 (105), and *WD*, 20, 37 (37, 64).

8

"Lès-Poésie?"

Levinas reads *La Folie du jour*

Blanchot's short narrative "Un récit"—or "Un récit?": the difference has attracted considerable comment—first appeared in the short-lived Parisian review *Empédocle* in May 1949, and was reissued by Fata Morgana under the definitive title *La Folie du jour* in 1973.[1] Only as a little book, published in the wake of May 1968 and at a highpoint of Blanchot's intellectual standing in France, did it begin to attract attention beyond avant-garde literary circles.[2] One significant instance of this new awareness and esteem is Levinas's "Exercises sur 'La Folie du jour.' Approche de Blanchot," which was published in the February 1975 number of *Change* and became the final of four texts devoted to his old friend gathered in *Sur Maurice Blanchot* (1975).[3] That Levinas admired Blanchot's narrative works, especially the first edition of *Thomas l'Obscur* (1941), is amply testified, not least of all by the wartime notes written in captivity in which he planned to launch a career as a novelist.[4] And that, after the war, he distanced himself from most art, including a great deal of literature, is also evident from even the most cursory reading of "La réalité et son ombre" (1948). "Art," he writes in that fierce essay, is "essentially disengaged"; it "constitutes, in a world of initiative and responsibility, a dimension of evasion" and, worse, "There is something wicked and egoist and cowardly in artistic enjoyment."[5]

Yet Blanchot largely evades his friend's strictures because his work disrupts any authorial pretension to classical literary mastery and *le beau style*. There is a world, Levinas tells us in 1971, in which "no human suffering keeps from being in order [*n'empêche de s'ordonner*]," and yet in the same breath he recognizes that Blanchot "reminds that world that its totality is not total—that the coherent discourse it vaunts does not catch up with another discourse which it fails to silence." In the five brief sentences that follow he nicely captures much of what Blanchot wishes to tell us. "That other discourse is troubled by an uninterrupted noise. A difference does not let the world sleep, and troubles the order in which being and non-being are ordered in a dialectic. This Neuter is not a someone, nor even a something. It is but an *excluded middle* that, properly speaking, is not even [*n'est même pas*]. Yet there is more transcendence than any world-behind-the-worlds ever gave a glimpse of."[6] Presumably religious transcendence merely ends in a higher state of immanence, and this is not so with the Neuter. And presumably the Neuter must be taken in an anti-realist sense.

Earlier, in "Le regard du poète" (1956), a long review of *L'Espace littéraire* (1955), Levinas was more nuanced in his estimation of his friend's achievement. He drew attention, amid much insight and much praise, to a blind spot in Blanchot's gaze. The stricture is less to do with him as a reader of Mallarmé and Kafka, Hölderlin and Rilke, than as a diagnostician of the figure of the modern writer, in particular the ground—which for Levinas is at best a playground—for his or her authenticity. "If the authenticity Blanchot speaks of is to mean anything other than a consciousness of the lack of seriousness of edification," Levinas pointedly says, "anything other than derision—the authenticity of art must herald an order of justice, the slave morality that is absent from the Heideggerian city."[7] Presumably, Blanchot's narrative writing up to that time, from *Thomas l'Obscur* (1941) to *Celui qui ne m'accompaignait pas* (1953), including "Un récit" (1948), announces, directly or indirectly, positively or negatively, "an order of justice." The same cannot be said for all of his critical writing, it seems.

What upsets Levinas when reading *L'Espace littéraire*? He seizes upon a footnote toward the end of the book where Blanchot specifies the artist's mission. An artist should "call us obstinately back to error, to turn us toward that space where everything we propose, everything we have acquired, everything we are, all that opens upon the earth and in the sky, returns to insignificance, and where what approaches is the nonserious and the nontrue, as if perhaps thence sprang the source of all authenticity."[8] "Error" here is written in full awareness of its root in Latin, *errare*, "to wander, to go astray." The art we need today, art that is nourished by Lautréamont and Sade, as well as the authors already mentioned, enables us to move away from a world fixed by God or the gods, from traditional norms of literature, even from "being" as rigorously determined by philosophers such as Hegel and, above all, Heidegger. Blanchot's dark phenomenology of art seems to be couched in terms ("earth," "sky") that Heidegger had made familiar in "Das Ding" (1950).[9] Yet it also contests those very terms, for it consists in indicating something other than the truth of being, as Heidegger would have it, namely, that mysterious excluded middle Blanchot calls the "Neutral" or the "Outside." It would be better to say, then, that Blanchot offers a counterpart to phenomenology, for the Outside only ever approaches and never appears as such.

There are at least two reasons why Levinas might take umbrage with his friend. In the first place, he might well hear, a little too quickly, Heidegger's word *Eigentlichkeit* whispered behind Blanchot's *authenticité*.[10] Blanchot does not use the word to translate Heidegger's German in *Sein und Zeit* (1927), for he does not look to that which is true (or genuine) or to the true state of being but rather to that which escapes both "truth" and "being." Yet also he does not distance himself sufficiently for Levinas from the Heidegger who thinks that *Dasein* is in each case mine, and for whom *Mitdasein* and *Miteindersein* are derivative of *Dasein*.[11] The truth that the other person's face silently commands "Do not kill me!," along with the moral seriousness of this command, is not acknowledged. In the second place, Levinas, as an advocate of ethics as first philosophy, recoils from Nietzsche's view, adapted by Blanchot, that with the abolition of the "real world" the "apparent world" also crumbles.[12] Henceforth, for Blanchot, to live authentically in accord with an uncompromising nihilism one must look to the nonserious and the nontrue, which derive from the approach of the Outside. This is not an affirmation of the frivolous but rather the view of thoroughly demystified existence that one finds elsewhere affirmed as "the ultimate insignificance of lightness" [*l'ultime insignifiance de la légèreté*], and that troubles the self-ordering of the Heideggerian city.¹³

Reflecting on Levinas's sharp reaction to Blanchot's note, we begin to see that the philosopher does not grasp all the aspects of the notion of the Outside that he acclaims. He affirms its status as an excluded middle, a third that frustrates any dialectical or fusional drive to totality yet fails to appreciate how strongly it conflicts with his own views. For Blanchot, the Outside can be discerned in various ways: in ordinary suffering, when time seems to stall; amid the everyday; and in intransitive—for him, literary—writing; yet also in the ceaseless oscillation of being and nonbeing, which happens when something becomes an image of itself. For him, this awareness of the relation between being and nonbeing signals the approach of the non-world of image, a neutral state that can only fascinate us and, in doing so, bind us to itself. Yet it cannot concern us; it does not offer itself to us by way of experience, only as something impossible to bring into that realm, and therefore comes to be dubbed "the impossible."¹⁴ Levinas had already rejected that specter in no uncertain terms in "La réalité et son ombre" where he recognizes that it precedes the workaday world of initiative and action, and thereby has the ability to mire characters in a temporal "meanwhile" and to hold readers immobile before it.¹⁵ In some respects, it resembles what he calls the *il y a* at about the same period, the inability to cancel being, for even when something is absent, even permanently absent, one nonetheless intuits the presence of that absence.¹⁶ For Levinas, one escapes the *il y a* by responding to another person, and yet it seems that for Blanchot that avenue is not available. Certainly, Levinas comes in "Exercises" to affirm what he calls the "extra-vagant" (170) dimension of narrative, and his hyphen recalls the Latin patrimony of the French—*extra* ("outside") and *vagari* ("wander")—yet he does so without fully endorsing, perhaps without fully realizing, what motivates Blanchot's affirmation of radical error in literature.

Of course, Levinas is quite right to say in "Le regard du poète" that the Blanchot of *L'Espace littéraire* abstains "from ethical preoccupations, at least in explicit form" (137).¹⁷ When Blanchot turns to consider ethics more directly it will be in terms of an adjustment of the program of *Totalité et infini* (1961) by way of the Outside. He will not accept that the asymmetry of the other person with respect to me is properly basic.¹⁸ One important step on the path to this discussion will be the writing of "Comment découvrir l'obscur?" (1959), in which Blanchot will indicate a peculiar phenomenology of this Outside, of something quite other than light and being, and this will enable him to chart a different course from the one that Levinas undertakes in his insistence that ethics, as first philosophy, revolves around the other person as enigma, rather than as phenomenon.¹⁹ When the other person speaks to me I hear the irreducible strangeness of the Outside, and that strangeness orients me to think of community rather than any individual.

Yet in 1975 Levinas finds an ethical moment, a call for justice, in *La Folie du jour*, and makes it the thesis of his reflections on the *récit*. His main idea is, as he says, that even though texts are always open to various interpretations, "the irreducible (inspired) exoticism of poetry refers back to [*en appelle à*] a saying *properly so-called*, a saying that thematizes, even if it may be obliged to unsay itself in order to avoid disfiguring the secret it exposes" (157). Actually, he goes further than this claim in his fourth exercise, finding in the *récit* "a way out" of the endless suffering of the human condition, co-ordinate with interiority. This interiority is one with "the *closure of being*" (158), the Western obsession with being which runs from Parmenides to Heidegger and which he had identified as early as *De l'évasion* (1935). This exit is found, he says, by developing a "relation to the other" (165). Is his reading of the *récit* justified?

*

When we see that Levinas entitles his commentary "Exercises" we might, at a pinch, think of Epictetus's two-stage model of philosophical education. First, we master theory and then, through spiritual exercises, seek to apply it to our own lives.[20] And we might entertain the idea that he is led to title his piece in this manner because of a supposed Stoic element in *La Folie du jour*. For we are told, almost at the very start, "this life gives me the greatest pleasure. And what about death? When I die (perhaps any minute now), I will feel immense pleasure.... I experience boundless pleasure in living, and I will take boundless satisfaction in dying" [*cette vie me fait le plaisir le plus grand. Alors, la mort? Quand je mourrai (peut-être tout à l'heure), je connaîtrai un plaisir immense. . .j'éprouve à vivre un plaisir sans limites et j'aurai à mourir une satisfaction sans limites*].[21] Yet Stoic pedagogy also rings very faintly in the idea of a schoolboy's exercise: Levinas, remember, was director of the École Normale Israélite Orientale (ENIO) from 1945 to 1961. ("Exercises" would be an unorthodox example of pedagogy, however, written, as it is, in jagged French and moving in a halting manner, at once overly compressed and sometimes unclear in its passage from sentence to sentence.) Also, while Blanchot's narrator claims to be indifferent to the accidents of life and death, his tranquility does not seem to have been brought about by adherence to virtue for its own sake and one does not look even to Seneca for finding satisfaction in death; at the most one's demise brings release from desire and pain.[22] And yet perhaps an echo of Stoicism is not a mere distraction, at least with regards to Levinas, as we shall see.

Appropriately enough, Levinas begins by commenting on the title of the *récit*: "Madness of today, but madness of the day also in the sense that, in it, day is madly desired, and in the sense that day—clarity and measure—goes mad there, and, hence, especially, in the sense that the madness of day is contrasted with the madness or panic of night" (158). Perhaps it needs to be brought out a little more strongly that the expression "*folie du jour*" also names the madness or extravagance of light, especially of daylight. Exactly what "*folie*" means for Levinas, and for Blanchot, for there is no reason to think that they agree at all points, is left unmarked; but let us remain with "*jour*" for the moment. To which day or days does it refer? Not to France after the Occupation, Levinas says, but rather it "seems to bear a greater resemblance to 1968" (159), a claim to which he returns ("inanity and madness, twenty years later" (169)) but which is left to dangle, even while we recall the remark about "the lack of seriousness of edification." Levinas continues: "These pages do not even reflect what was going on in 1948 on the level of the history of ideas.... *The Madness of the Day* might therefore be said to be free from any temporal limitations" (159).

If *La Folie du jour* does not take on one or another of the primary philosophical colors of post-Liberation Paris—neither that of Camus, Marcel, and Sartre, nor that of Raymond Aron—it is of a piece with Blanchot's own itinerary. "Un récit" was composed amid dense reflection on Lautréamont, Sade, and Hölderlin, texts in which the question of madness is seldom absent, even when not explicitly posed.[23] One might look, for instance, to the very end of "L'Expérience de Lautréamont" (1948), parts of which appeared over the same few months that saw the publication of "Un récit." Blanchot concludes his long essay by comparing Hölderlin and Lautréamont. The German poet, he thinks, was "truly and absolutely united with the light to which he had the strength to sacrifice all his forces and that, in return, brought him this unique glory of a child's reasoning wherein all the splendor of impersonal clarity shines forth."[24] The French poet, however, "was unable to disappear within madness, being born of madness." He too had the "force of light within him" which was "an unlimited aspiration, which the extreme moment designates the sole, ideal and real point at which, ceasing being himself, he can become, outside of himself, completely himself, in the end coming forever into the world at the ultimate moment that makes him disappear from it" (163–4; 187–8).

Connections between light and madness are at the very heart of *La Folie du jour*, but we would do well to approach them with caution. We first hear of madness when the narrator recalls having lost people he has loved, presumably in the recent war: "I went mad when that blow struck me, because it is hell" [*Je suis devenu fou quand ce coup m'a frappé, car c'est un enfer*] (6; 20). Indeed, the war is characterized directly thereafter as "the madness of the world" [*la folie du monde*] (6; 20). Note, though, that the extreme moment of that violence, when the narrator is almost executed, is precisely the point when he stops "being insane" [*être insensé*] (or "foolish," "senseless"...) (6; 20).[25] He appears to be on an even keel when later "a lunatic" [*un fou*] (8; 22) stabs him in the hand and, still later, again for no apparent reason, another person crushes glass in his eyes. After that second event he becomes convinced "that [he] is 'face to face' with the madness of the day" [*je fus convaincu que je voyais face à face la folie du jour*] (11; 25). This is no sudden vision but rather a making evident of the truth of a situation, regardless of whether the judgment is made correctly or incorrectly. When recovering from his injury in half-light, the narrator longs for daylight, which would be perfectly normal: "and if seeing would infect me with madness, I madly wanted that madness" [*et si voir c'était la contagion de la folie, je désirais follement cette folie*] (12; 25).

This is an extreme desire, to be sure, yet I draw attention to the "*et si*"; the narrator has not lost his power of reason or perhaps the power to feign reason. Finally, after he agrees to be locked up, one of the doctors sees another inmate, an old man with a white beard, jumping on his shoulders and hears the narrator say, impatiently, "Who are you, Tolstoy?" [*Tu es donc Tolstoi?*] (16; 29), which makes the doctor think (according to the narrator) that he is "truly crazy" [*bien fou*] (16; 29). But we are not invited to trust the doctor's supposed judgment. Nor are we to credit a literary intelligence to him. Presumably, he does not know Tolstoy's *On Insanity* (1910) to which the narrator most likely alludes. We read there something that he might well recall: "Recently I happened to visit two large establishments for the mentally deranged, and the impression I received was that I saw establishments built by mentally deranged people suffering from one common epidemic form of lunacy, for patients suffering from different forms of lunacy which do not resemble the common epidemic form."[26] A distaste for the medical profession continues right to the end of the *récit*. When it is almost over "a specialist in mental illness" [*un spécialiste des maladies mentales*] (18; 31) interrogates the narrator, we have no particular ground to think that the specialist is called for.

One should take care before saying that the narrator is clinically mad, and should consider his black humor, which tends to deflate situations: for example, *le sang dégoutait sur mon unique costume* ["the blood was dripping on my only suit"] (22; 8), he says in response to having his hand cut with a knife, and *C'étaient de joyeux moments* ["Those were happy times"] (29; 16), which he remarks by way of concluding the episode when he was being beaten by inmates in the hospital. Also, one should be circumspect in categorically denying that the narrator is a little touched; the mad can sometimes appear quite reasonable if one accepts the confines of their disorder, and this man experiences delirium when seeing a perfectly ordinary occurrence: the conjunction of a woman with a pram and a man entering a building. He interprets this apparently banal event eschatologically. "Here it comes, I said to myself, the end is coming: something is happening, the end is beginning" [*Voici qu'elle arrive, me disais-je, la fin vient, quelque chose arrive, la fin commence*] (10; 24). I shall return to it later. Equally eccentric is his reaction to facing the end: "I was seized by joy" [*J'étais saisi par la joie*] (10; 24). And yet we have been prepared for this sort of response from the opening paragraph: "I will take boundless satisfaction in dying" [*j'aurai à mourir une satisfaction sans limites*] (5; 19).

Is there evidence other than the direct allusions to *folie* in the *récit* that should be considered before concluding? There is: the second figure of the law as recounted in the latter part of the story. We hear that the narrator was "attracted to the law" [*la loi m'attirait*] (9), perhaps as a profession, or perhaps he found her charming. (We know already that he prizes women, "beautiful creatures" [*belles créatures*] (7; 21), for their equal acceptance of life and death.) In any case, it is abnormal for someone to call to the law, "Come here; let me see you face to face" [*Approche, que je te voie face à face*] (9; 22). Only Moses, who receives the Law from the Most High and talks with him "face to face" and "mouth to mouth," comes to mind (Exod. 33: 11, Num. 12: 8). The law, in *La Folie du jour*, would be a figure of what Levinas comes to call *autrui*, someone accorded, on phenomenological grounds, a moral height above whoever is addressing her, but of course she does not respond, for which the narrator is thankful. (A little later we hear of the narrator seeing the madness of the day "face to face" (11; 22), but it cannot be *autrui*, no more than the law, despite its height, for neither is human.) The narrator declines engaging with the law by not suing the man who crushed glass in his eyes and disapproves of a doctor who litigates a patient who has fooled him by taking a drug without telling him. In addition, he dislikes thinking of his various talents as judges "ready to condemn" him [*prêts à me condamner*] (14; 27), and, from the beginning, observes the power of the medical profession, which imposes its own protocols on him regardless of the pain it causes him. Yet the most disturbing evocation of the law comes when the doctors who act as kings are interrogating him. "Behind their backs I saw the silhouette of the law. Not the law everyone knows, which is severe and hardly very agreeable: this law was different" [*Derrière leur dos, j'apercevais la silhouette de la loi.*

Non pas la loi que l'on connaît, qui est rigoureuse et peu agréable: celle-ci était autre] (14; 28). His former attraction to the law, the first law, must have faded.

How is this second law different? Because the narrator seems "to terrify her" (15; 29); she is "perpetually on her knees" before him (15; 29), as though he is now *auturi*. At times their relationship has the character of *une folie*, a fling. "Once she had made me touch her knee—a strange feeling. I had said as much to her: 'I am not the kind of man who is satisfied with a knee!' Her answer: 'That would be disgusting!'" [*Elle m'avait une fois fait toucher son genou: une bizarre impression. Je le lui avais déclaré: Je ne suis pas homme à me contenter d'un genou. Sa réponse: Ce serait dégoûtant!*] (16–17; 30). Without doubt, the first sight of the law has a romantic element to it. The narrator sees her in silhouette—a black and featureless shadow—as if in a scene in a *film noir* of the period, and if we take the narrator, being neither learned nor ignorant, as fulfilling Diotima's requirement for being a lover, we should not be surprised at this turn of events.[27] Of course, an unusual light would be needed to produce a silhouette of the law, something that contrasts sharply with its exteriority. Call it the light of consciousness. There is some textual support for the claim, since the law takes the narrator's gaze to be "a bolt of lightning" [*la foudre*] (15, 28), recognizing, perhaps, what Derrida was to remark years later with respect to Levinas, that phenomenology relies on "the violence of light."[28]

If we closely follow what the law says to the narrator, we find that she sets him above authority, that she praises him outrageously, that she commends justice to him, that the two of them are forever bound together, and that she is intent upon his glory. I take it that the silhouette of the law, which is all that the narrator sees, is a figure for writing, which, for Blanchot, contests all rules, plays games—"*ce jeu insensé d'écrire*," as Mallarmé says, and as Blanchot likes to quote—, creates an author only to let him or her fade the moment one stops writing, remains forever bound to the person who writes, converges with left-wing demands for justice, and that forever is capable of resurrecting his or her consciousness, whether the author be alive or dead, in a ghostly half-life.[29] Writing is the silhouette of the Outside, which our mundane laws seek to contain and which nonetheless irrupts through them and imposes its own law on us in various ways.

*

Madness, for Blanchot, is therefore several things at once: insanity, experience of the measureless light of divine inspiration, whether as a return to childhood or as an extravagant struggle to overcome constraints, and erotic adventure. It is also the "absence of work," not simple laziness but *désœuvrement*, in which a text or a person resonates with the Outside in its approach and becomes disengaged from any dialectic. In that absence of work, we are told by Blanchot in 1960, "discourse ceases, so that, outside speech, outside language, the movement of writing may come, under the attraction of the outside."[30] This is madness in the sense of being unhinged from an established order.

Levinas is attentive solely to the last of these senses of "madness," which he regards as a symptom of the "*closure of being*," a "hellish unfreedom" (159), a suffocation in selfhood that "lurks at the very heart of the joys, the day, and the unshakable happiness described in the opening lines of our text" (160). He approaches this madness under the sign of weariness:

> Weariness [*la fatigue*] keeps recurring in the text; the void fills itself with itself, repose doesn't settle down. Weariness [*Lassitude*]—precisely. There is no progressive dialectic, in which the moments of the story spring up in their newness, before contracting their freshness by all they conserve. The circular return of the Identical does not even follow a long-term cycle. It is a twirling on the spot: happiness is obsessed in its very permanence, the outbreak of madness sinks back into madness, into oppression, into an unbreathable interiority without exterior. Is madness a way out, or is the way out madness? (161-62)

Levinas's concern with the "presence of the present" being "immobilized" (159) is familiar to readers of "La réalité et son ombre" (1948); it is at the hub of his criticism of art. And the inability of someone to break free from the fatigue associated with the *il y a* is of course a dominant theme of *De l'existence à l'existant* (1947). If *La Folie du jour* does not, for Levinas, "reflect what was going on in 1948" (159), it seems to resonate with precisely what *he* was thinking and writing at that time. He does not seem to recognize this as a "temporal limitation" of the story, however.

In the late 1940s Levinas recognized that the only way of escaping the stultifying oppression of the *il y a* is to leave the suffocating solitude of the self and move toward the Good, which can occur only when one salutes another person and recognizes and values his or her irreducible otherness. Madness is not the way out of banal existence, as it was for Artaud and van Gogh, and before them the Breton of *Nadja* (1928), let alone for proponents of Dionysian excess such as Bataille; rather, a rethinking of philosophy so that ethics, not metaphysics, is first philosophy will indicate that exit, and this turning upside down of the intellectual world doubtless seemed to some of his contemporaries to be nothing short of madness. In order to assimilate *La Folie du jour* to his own thought, Levinas must find a "way out" that is delineated in the story. The fourth exercise does precisely that. "Relation to the other—a last way out. From one end to the other of the story, this relation is present" (165). He points to the narrator's experience of the loss of loved ones, which causes him such pain, but gravitates on one brief scene, which I have already mentioned. "The little scene in which, in front of the courtyard door, a man steps back to let a baby carriage through, is the event of an advent—that is, the moment when something abnormal ensues: one person withdraws before the other, one *is* for the other. Whence the narrator's lightheartedness, which seems to lift him above being" (165-6). Let us look more closely at this scene.

The narrator certainly sees the man think twice and step aside so that a woman can enter a door with a pram. Notice, though, that the narrator does not do anything except observe, and while this small, ordinary event has extraordinary significance for him—it "excited me to the point of delirium" [*me souleva jusqu'au délire*] (10; 24)—exactly what it means is quite beyond him. We might say that the man who steps aside is merely displaying good manners and that there is no moral dimension to his act. Yet Levinas does not draw a strict distinction between manners and morals. Following him, we might agree that the man is "for the other," and we might think of this by way of *la transascendance*, but we have no reason to say the same of the narrator.[31] He merely enters the courtyard after the woman has disappeared, takes in how very cold it is, and lingers there "in the joy and perfection of this happiness" [*la joie et la perfection de ce bonheur*] (10; 24). Far from seeing moral action as an exit from his situation, the narrator remains pleasurably within himself. What strikes him is not the goodness of the event he has witnessed but its *reality*, and that the day "having stumbled against a real event, would begin hurrying to its end" [*ayant buté sur un événement vrai, allait se hâter vers sa fin*] (10; 24). In case we overlook the statement, the narrator underlines it in the very next paragraph, "All that was real; take note" [*Tout cela était réel, notez-le*] (11; 24). Reality, for the narrator, would seem to be purely sensory. The only thing he dislikes about the prospect of dying is that "Suffering dulls the senses [or 'stupifies']" [*Souffrir est abrutissant*] (6; 19). He says, "I see the world— what extraordinary happiness! I see this day, and outside it there is nothing" [*je vois le monde, bonheur extraordinaire. Je le vois, ce jour hors duquel il n'est rein*] (6; 20); in other words, all that there is in the day is sensory: no past, no future, and surely no transcendent realm. What disturbs him most of all about the medical experiment of covering him with mud is that "My sense of touch was floating six feet away from me" [*Mon tact errait à deux mètres*] (7; 21). Immediately before the scene of the woman with a pram, "the gloomy spirit of reading" [*sombre esprit de la lecture*] (9; 23) insults him, and being at a low point, he could not even have answered the question "Who was I?" [*Qui étais-je?*] (10; 23). (Of course, it can be a hard question to answer even if one is at a high point in life.[32]) So when he sees the woman, the pram, and the man, when he feels the cold in the courtyard, he is impressed by the sensuous reality of these things; they have a solidity that the realm of spirit does not have. Time seems to click into gear once more; if it has stalled with the encounters with the lunatic and the spirit of reading, and with a loss of selfhood, it now picks up speed and finds a direction.

I return to Levinas's remarks on weariness as a dominant motif in *La Folie du jour*, at least until the narrator sees the woman with a pram. Now the narrator does not speak of fatigue; on the contrary, his testimony is given with noticeable vigor, returning time and again to declarations given in the first person ("I am not learned; I am not ignorant" [*Je ne suis ni savant ni ignorant*] (5; 19), "I have wandered" [*J'ai erré*] (5; 19), "I have loved people" [*J'ai aimé des êtres*] (6; 20), "I am not timid" [*Je ne suis pas craintif*] (8; 22), "I must admit I have read many books" [*Je dois l'avourer, j'ai lu beaucoup de livres*] (9; 22) and so on) or posing questions in order not to answer them ("Is my life better than other people's lives?" [*Mon existence est-elle meilleure que celle de tous?*] (6; 20), "Can I describe my trials?" [*Puis-je décrire mes épreuves?*] (7; 21) "Am I an egoist?" [*Suis-je égoïste?*] (8; 21)). Almost frenetic, the testimony lurches from one statement or evocation to another, sometimes so briefly as to perplex the reader as to its significance for the narrator or the story he is telling. The episode of the woman with a pram is exemplary here; and yet the narrative runs on, past this episode, as though seeking a *dénouement*. Throughout, the narrator appears to be distanced from the very events he undergoes. It is less a matter of alienation from the world than something stranger: a sense of not having any agency, of being thrown from one event to another, which results in the staccato narrative. It is this relentless self-interrupting of the narrative by the narrator himself that becomes the true "subject" of *La Folie du jour*, a technique that Blanchot probably learned from Kafka.[33] It reaches its apotheosis when, at the end, the narrator begins to retell his story. There is a disjunction between events we presume to have occurred (but which are perhaps taking place only in the story) and the significance of them for those who know who they are and who embody institutional power. For the narrator, some of those events, the ones that most interest the medical world, may have been lived through but not at the center of his consciousness. They fall outside the bounds of his story.

We only apparently reach a point when the plot becomes unlaced, which is when the narrator has glass crushed into his eyes, for we are never told who injures him or why. The shards of glass seem to intensify the daylight, making it as though immediate and without measure, and when it is removed he must rest with a film under his eyelids for seven days—the biblical number of fullness, and especially of the seven seals in Revelation—which becomes for him "the spark of a single moment" [*la vivacité d'un seul instant*] (11; 25).[34] Notice that the narrator takes himself to be called "to account" [*comptes*] in that week, yet his judges, the seven days, perhaps a metaphor for the seven angels of Revelation, who act as one, light itself, are mad and without any restraint. We think once more of Lautréamont and Hölderlin. On waking in hospital, the very idea of engaging with a lesser law—that of suing for special or general damages—strikes him as risible; and in his convalescence, when he must wear dark glasses, he finds that he would experience again the fire of the seven days, the transcendent luster of the seven angels, if only he could see properly. In seeing that the days or angels are without ground, the narrator is unmoored from the usual anchors, ropes, and cables, undergoes *désœuvrement*, and so disorientation becomes his task.

It seems then that the Outside is acknowledged in two distinct ways in *La Folie du jour*. One recognizes its approach in the distance between the "I" and the apparently random events that occur to him, which becomes a distance within himself, dividing him from himself. The narrator does not experience this disunion by way of fatigue, however, although such a thing is possible. In a later *récit* attuned to weariness a speaker ironically observes, perhaps to himself, that he is too fatigued to affirm that weariness can prompt a reduction to the non-world of the Outside. He simply overhears, as it were, a voice whispering that it is so, a voice that is close to the Outside:

Do you really believe you can approach the neutral through weariness, and through the neutral of weariness, better hear what occurs when to speak is not to see? I do not believe it, in fact; I do not affirm it either. I am too weary for that. Only, someone says this close to me, someone I do not know; I let them talk, it is an inconsequential murmur.

[Crois-tu vraiment que tu puisses t'approcher du neutre par la fatigue et, par le neutre de la fatigue, mieux entendre ce qu'il arrive, quand parler, ce n'est pas voir? Je ne le crois pas, en effet; je ne l'affirme pas non plus; je suis trop fatigué pour cela; quelqu'un, seulement, le dit près de moi, que je ne connais pas; je le laisse dire, c'est un murmure qui me tire pas à conséquence.][35]

Yet if the Outside is indicated in a passive non-relation to oneself, it also presents a counterpart to itself in sheer intensity, in being "face to face" with a mad light: the Most High is revealed to be crazy, like the doctors as Tolstoy sees them, and in any case hiding us from the Outside as it truly gives itself, as an extreme limit-phenomenon.[36] Even here, in this false encounter with the Outside, the narrator bespeaks a distance from himself: "At times I said to myself, 'This is death. In spite of everything, it's really worth it, it's impressive'" [*Parfois, je me disais: 'C'est la mort; malgré tout, cela en vaut la peine, c'est impressionnant*] (11; 25).

*

Levinas writes on *La Folie du jour* in 1975. Some years before then Blanchot had devoted several dialogues to his friend's mature thought in *Totalité et infini* (1961). One of the voices in "Tenir parole" (1962) ponders the relation between "myself" and *autrui*. Of this relationship, one voice says, "Emmanuel Levinas would say that it is of an ethical nature, but I find in this word only secondary meanings. That *autrui* should be above me, that his speech should be a speech of height, of eminence—these metaphors appease, by putting it into perspective, a difference so radical that it escapes any determination other than itself."[37] The primary meaning of the encounter with another person is given in speech when it is figured as primary, not derived from sight. Another dialogue, "L'Indestrucible" (1962), augmented in *L'Entretien infini* (1969), argues that I and another person subsist in a "third relation," neither given by way of dialectic nor by way of absorption by the other person. This third relation holds the two parties together and apart in the activity of speech; it is, as he says, "the very extent of the Outside."[38] He goes on to erode Levinas's claim that the ethical height of another person is a given, insisting that the other person and I abide in a relation of double dissymmetry, one that does not flatten the ethical sphere into a plane, and rephrasing the object under scrutiny from *autrui* to the community.[39] In short, Blanchot is clear that there is no exit from the Outside, and that it is only by way of the Outside that one can properly encounter another person: we may speak of justice but only if we do so in the awareness that it derives from a more fundamental situation than ethics ever countenances. For what is crucial is not meeting the other person as a stranger but regarding him "*as a man in his strangeness—that which escapes all identification.*"[40]

To be sure, Blanchot's understanding of the Outside develops over the years from 1948 to 1969, in part through the intellectual rapport he has with Levinas's philosophy. Yet it does not change in major ways. The conversations about Levinas's magnum opus at the start of *L'Entretien infini* can be read as an oblique response to his reservations about *L'Espace littéraire*. Yet in "Exercises sur 'La Folie du jour'" Levinas makes no reference to this response and writes as though Blanchot were following the philosophical position outlined in *De Existence à la existent*. Levinas wonders if he might be accused on "*lès-poésie*" in his reading of *La Folie du jour*, because he plans to consider only a few passages of it and respond to their texture.[41] But the charge would be more surely justified on the ground that Levinas does not acknowledge the story's affirmation of the inescapability of the Outside. In the end, Levinas does not read *La Folie du jour*; he applies his own philosophy to it, seeing there by way of several spiritual exercises a story written by a version of himself, perhaps the novelist he never became, and not the story written by his friend Blanchot.

Notes

1. In particular, see Jacques Derrida, "Title to be Specified," trans. Tom Conley, in *Parages*, ed. John P. Leavey (Stanford, CA: Stanford University Press, 2011), 214–15.
2. One index of the esteem in which Blanchot was held at this period is the special issue of *Critique* 229 (juin 1966) which was consecrated to his work.
3. See Levinas, "Exercises on 'The Madness of the Day,'" *On Maurice Blanchot*, bound with *PN*, 156–70. In the original journal publication Levinas notes that he has received a book by Daniel Wilhem, *Maurice Blanchot, la voix narrative* (Paris: Union Général d'Éditions, 1974), of which he has not been able to take account; the note is dropped in *SMB*. Perhaps Blanchot alludes to the same book in "Après coup." See *AC*, 92.
4. See Levinas, *Oeuvres*, 3 vols. series discontinued, vol. 1: *Carnets de captivité et autre inédits*, ed. Rodolphe Calin et al. (Paris: Grasset, 2009), 98.
5. Levinas, "Reality and its Shadow," *CPP*, 12.
6. Levinas, "A Conversation with André Dalmas," *PN*, 154–5.
7. Levinas, "The Poet's Vision," *PN*, 137.
8. Blanchot, *SL*, 247 n. 8 (332 n. 1).
9. See Heidegger, "The Thing," in *Poetry, Language, Thought*, trans. and intro. Albert Hofstadter (New York: Harper and Row, 1971), 171. Levinas is of course aware of this aspect of Blanchot's thought. See "The Poet's Vision," *PN*, 137.
10. See Heidegger, *Being and Time*, 167.
11. See Heidegger, *Being and Time*, 68.
12. See Friedrich Nietzsche, "How the 'Real World' at last Became a Myth," *Twilight of the Idols*, bound with *The Anti-Christ*, trans, intro. and commentary R. J. Hollingdale (Harmondsworth: Penguin, 1968), 41.
13. Blanchot, *OWM*, 43 (83).
14. See, for example, Blanchot, *IC*, 45–8 (64–8).
15. See Levinas, "Reality and Its Shadow," 8–11.
16. See Levinas, *EE*, ch. 4.
17. Blanchot's post-war left-wing political commitments are evident, though, in at least one text that precedes the publication of this book. See Blanchot, "Dionys Mascolo: Le Communisme," *La Nouvelle Revue française*, 12, décembre 1953, 1096–99, reprinted as "Sur une approche du communism," *A*, 109–14. An English translation, "On One Approach to Communism," appears in *F*, 93–7.
18. See Blanchot, "Tenir parole," *La Nouvelle Nouvelle française*, 110, février 1962, 290–8, and "L'Interruption," *La Nouvelle Nouvelle française* 137 (mai 1964): 869–81. The first "dialogue" and part of the second were republished in *EI*, 84–93, 106–12. English translations may be found in "Keeping to Words" and "Interruption (as on a Riemann surface)," *IC*, 59–65, 75–9.
19. See Blanchot, "Comment découvrir l'obscur," *La Nouvelle Revue française* 83 (1959): 867–79, reprinted in *EI*, 57–69, and, in English, "How to Discover the Obscure?," *IC*, 40–8. Also see Levinas, "Phenomenon and Enigma," *CPP*, 61–74.
20. See Epectetus, *Dissertationes*, 1. 26. 3. Also see Musonius, *Dissertationum a Lucio Digestarum Reliquiæ*, 6.

21 Blanchot, *MD*, 5 (9).
22 Blanchot distances himself from Stoicism in *SL*, 101 (125). Also see Seneca, *Epistulæ Morales ad Lucilium*, 12.4.
23 For the importance of Hölderlin to Blanchot's *récit*, especially the essay "La Parole 'Sacrée' de Hölderlin" (1946), see Leslie Hill, *Blanchot: Extreme Contemporary*, 95–102.
24 Blanchot, *LS*, 163. Also see Blanchot, "La Folie par excellence," *Critique*, 45, février 1951, 99–118, which may be found in English translation as "Madness *par excellence*," *BR*, 110–28. The motif of the burning light may also be found in Blanchot's reflections on Georges Bataille's *L'Expérience intérieur*. See *FP*, 37 (47).
25 Blanchot testifies to the attempted execution in his *IM*.
26 Leo Tolstoy, *On Insanity*, trans. Ludvig Perno (London: C. W. Daniel, 1936), 31.
27 See Plato, *Symposium*, 204a. On this motif, see Sarah Kofman, *Comment s'en sortir?* (Paris: Galilée, 1983), 97–8.
28 See Derrida, "Violence and Metaphysics: An Essay on the Thought of Emmanuel Levinas," *Writing and Difference*, trans. and intro. Alan Bass (London: Routledge and Kegan Paul, 1978), 84–92.
29 Stéphane Mallarmé, "Villiers de l'Isle-Adam," *Oeuvres complètes*, 2 vols., Bibliothèque de la Pléiade, ed. Bertrand Marchal (Paris: Gallimard, 2003), vol. 2, 23. Also see the conclusion of Blanchot's "Dionys Mascolo: *Le Communisme*."
30 Blanchot, "La Marche de l'écrivisse," *La Nouvelle Revue française*, 91, mai 1960, 937, which was reprinted as "Parler, ce n'est pas voir," in *EI*, 35–45. In English, "Speaking is not Seeing," *IC*, 25–32.
31 The word "transascendance" was coined by Jean Wahl and taken up by Levinas. See Wahl, *Human Existence and Transcendence*, 28. See Levinas, *TI*, 35 n. 2.
32 See, for quite different examples, Blaise Pascal, *Pensées*, ed. and trans. Roger Ariew (Indianapolis: Hackett Pub. Co., 2005), S567/L688, and André Breton, *Nadja* (1928; rpt. Paris: Gallimard, 1945), 7.
33 See Blanchot, "The Narrative Voice (the 'he,' the neutral)," *IC*, 384 (563). On the nature of the *récit*, see Blanchot, "The Song of the Sirens," *BC*, 6 (13).
34 It is worth noting that for Levinas an immediate contact with the sacred, without the mediation of reason, would be an instance of *la folie*. See Levinas, "To Love the Torah More than God," *DF*, 144.
35 Blanchot, *IC*, xx–xxi (xxii).
36 Cf. Hölderlin, "Das Höchste," in Hamburger, trans., *Friedrich Hölderlin*, 638.
37 Blanchot, "Keeping to Words," *IC*, 63 (89–90).
38 Blanchot, "The Relation of the Third Kind: *Man without Horizon*," *IC*, 69 (98).
39 Blanchot, "The Relation of the Third Kind," 70–1 (100–1). The difficulty of thinking community is explored by Blanchot in *UC*, 12 (25–6).
40 Blanchot, "The Relation of the Third Kind," 74 (105).
41 Levinas, "Exercises on 'The Madness of the Day,'" 157.

9

Ethics of the Image[1]

In March 1956 there appeared in *Monde Nouveau* a relatively short piece by Levinas entitled "Maurice Blanchot et le regard du poète."[2] It is an extended review of *L'Espace littéraire*, published by Gallimard the previous summer, which is also spiked with a polemic against Heidegger. Levinas observes that Blanchot is close to the Heidegger of *Vorträge und Aufsätze* (1954), almost to the point of immediate intellectual intuition, and is just as quick to register the distance between the two on a decisive issue.[3] On Blanchot's account of literature we are led away from the world of dwelling and rootedness that Heidegger affirms in his meditations on art. Here as elsewhere, Levinas is profoundly disturbed by Heidegger's slighting of ethics, especially value ethics, and, in turning to show that his friend finds a way beyond the primacy of *Sein*, he observes parenthetically that Blanchot "also abstains from ethical preoccupations, at least in explicit form."[4] A little later he remarks, more pointedly, that Blanchot's concern with "authenticity" must one day "herald an order of justice" if it is to be more than "a consciousness of the lack of seriousness of edification, anything other than derision."[5] Clearly, Levinas is uneasy at the proximity of his friend to the Heidegger of *Sein und Zeit* (1927) and beyond, having managed to free himself from "the climate of that philosophy," starting in "De l'évasion" (1935) and then more completely in *De l'existence à l'existant* (1947).[6] The invitation is for Blanchot to render his ethics explicit, and the review hints at how this can be done. Other essays by Levinas, later collected in *Sur Maurice Blanchot* (1975), return to the prediction or hope registered in the review that someone will express "the latent meaning" of his friend's novels and *récits*, and there is no doubt when reading his reflections on *L'Attente l'oubli* (1962) and *La Folie du jour* (1973) that for Levinas their manifest meaning is ethical, at least in part.[7]

Levinas hints at how Blanchot might pass from an implicit to an explicit ethics by considering the status of the image in his work. In clarifying what is at issue he bypasses the Sartre of *L'Imaginaire* (1940) and *Qu'est-ce que la littérature?* (1947). Blanchot, we are told, finds the idea of *l'art engagé* "inconsistent for the simple reason that the effect of art in history is quite negligible."[8] Left unconsidered is Sartre's view that consciousness works in irreducible perceptual and imaginative modes. Instead, we hear that for Blanchot, "the image precedes perception" and constitutes a "transcendent vision" (130; 13). No mention is made of an image requiring an intentional consciousness, or of a link between imagination and freedom.[9] Nothing is said about the epistemological status of an image, and certainly nothing about an image offering "a degraded knowledge" [*savoir dégradé*].[10] Overlooking Sartre and disagreeing with him are not wholly unexpected with Levinas, especially at this stage of his writing life. His intellectual path had started to unfurl before and during the Second World War and his reading of the philosopher's works published in those years had been late and cursory.[11] Yet Levinas would have read Blanchot's reflections on Jean Pouillon's *Temps et roman* (1946) in *Les Temps modernes*. There Blanchot draws close to Sartre as regards "bad faith," while articulating his view that in a novel no real object or even an image abides behind words but only an empty set of relations and intentions.[12] Perhaps along with Sartre's own *Qu'est-ce que la littérature?*, serialized in *Les Temps modernes* (1947), these reflections stimulated Levinas to compose "La réalité et son ombre" (1948).

At any rate, in Levinas's affirmation of the other person and his lack of close attention to Sartre we might see, with all the clarity of hindsight, an early sign of the shift, as Raymond Aron phrased it, from an ethics of conviction to an ethics of responsibility.[13] From Sartre's side, we recall the editorial "correction" of "La réalité et son ombre" (1948) that prefaced its publication in *Les Temps modernes*.[14] The enigma is that, in the review of *L'Espace littéraire*, Levinas associates the image with an implicit ethics in Blanchot whereas, in "La réalité et son ombre," he disassociates the two in a sharp way. There, as is well known, ethics begins by criticizing the image. In the commentary on *L'Espace littéraire*, though, the possibility is raised that the image can have ethical significance if it is only treated in the proper manner.

*

Levinas fastens onto the final footnote in *L'Espace littéraire*, just before the book frays into four appendices. "And is the nontrue [*non-vrai*] an essential form of authenticity?" Blanchot asks. He remarks that the more "the world is affirmed as the future and the broad daylight of truth, where everything will have value, bear meaning, where the whole will be achieved under the mastery of man and for his use," the more "art must descend toward that point where nothing has meaning yet."[15] The artist and the poet are called to turn us toward "what approaches," namely "the nonserious and the nontrue [*le non-sérieux et le non-vrai*], as if perhaps thence sprang the source of all authenticity" (247 n. 8; 332 n. 1). The word that irritates Levinas is not *non-vrai*, which in fact motivates his own guiding question with respect to art in "La réalité et son ombre": "what is the *non-truth* [non-vérité] of being?"[16] There is no insistence that ethics should have an essential tie with truth: the important moral category of truth-telling falls to one side for him. The category at issue is meaning, and ethics seeks to be meaningful in a way other than that traditionally given by presence or representation. Indeed, since no ethics for Levinas can be supported by a theory of disclosure, coherence, or correspondence, it cannot be grounded in a prior theory of truth. He is bothered, rather, by the word *non-sérieux*, which elicits the charge of "derision" [*raillerie*], and by the word *authenticité*, which translates Heidegger's *eigentlich* in *Sein und Zeit* § 9. "As modes of Being, authenticity and inauthenticity... are both grounded in the fact that any Dasein whatsoever is characterized by mineness [*Jemeinigkeit*]."[17]

Much later, in *L'Écriture du désastre* (1980), Blanchot will reflect, "If there is, among all words, one that is inauthentic, then surely it is the word 'authentic.'"[18] Even as early as *L'Espace littéraire*, though, it can be seen that the expression "the source of all authenticity" [*la source de toute authenticité*] is alien to Heideggerian *eigentlich*. In writing, we are told there, the artist becomes attuned to the approach of *le Dehors* or the Outside, the bottomless fund of empty images outside the dialectic and its driving negativity. One's secure relation with death as a passage from being to nonbeing (or a higher state of being) is interrupted, and one is exposed to the other side of mortality, the endlessness of dying, by way of fascination and *désœuvrement*. Authenticity, then, would have nothing to do with "mineness"; it would signal an encounter with an otherness so radical that it would entail a loss of the power to say "I" and mark the apogee of experience, even at the risk of it being, in the suspension of all historical negativity, non-experience. None of this is *non-sérieux* in the sense of mocking matters of moral gravity, yet it indicates another world than that characterized either by "edification" or by "the seriousness, the suffering, the patience, and the labor of the negative."[19] It is a non-world beneath the one constructed by dialectic.

Experience, for the Blanchot of *L'Espace littéraire*, is undertaken in an exemplary way through art. "Writing changes us," he says.[20] At the same time, art maintains itself in a final, tenuous rapport with the sacred no longer understood as a consequence of the divine life but as the neutral Outside. Attenuated as this interpretation of the sacred is, it nonetheless remains close to a poetic thought of the departed gods and distant from the everyday demands of ethics. If "an order of justice" is implicit in "the source of all authenticity," and if this source is being perpetuating itself as nothingness, it is hard to see where justice might be concealed. Levinas found his way to ethics though a meditation on art in *De l'existence à l'existant*. He discovered there the heaviness of the *il y a*, noted the emergence of consciousness, and then discovered the intrigue of ethics in the advent of *autrui* and, in particular, the recognition that my relationship with the other person is asymmetrical in favor of him or her. "Interpersonal space is initially [*initialement*] asymmetrical," he says.[21] The adverb is important, for even though I will eventually recognize myself as one other among many others it is essential, Levinas thinks, for me to admit that ethical asymmetry precedes all claims to distributive justice. To pass from an ontology of the same to the otherness of the Outside, from dwelling to wandering, from possibility to impossibility, as Blanchot does, is admirable, Levinas thinks. "Does Blanchot not attribute to art the function of uprooting the Heideggerian universe? Does not the poet, before the 'eternal streaming of the outside,' hear the voices that call away from the Heideggerian world?"[22] Yes indeed, and yes, the (Blanchotian) poet does. But to avoid evil—given in the figure of Amalek who attacks the Jews as they leave Egypt—the experience at issue must be of another human being, not of the approach of the Outside.[23] A stress on wandering should not exclude welcoming the other person.[24] The question is whether Blanchot can uncover justice in the interruption of the world by empty images that cannot be experienced in any usual meaning of the word.

At no time does Levinas suggest that Blanchot follow the path that he has already chosen for himself and accordingly give up his preoccupation with the neutral Outside, abandon his "transcendent vision," in order to secure a site for ethics.[25] To be sure, Levinas rejects the neutrality of Heideggerian being, that "neuter which illuminates and commands thought, and renders intelligible [*commande la pensée et rend intelligible*]."²⁶ Blanchot agrees, finding this neuter "a little shameful," and in his turn Levinas commends his friend's criticism that has, he says, "contributed to bring out" the "impersonal neutrality" of "Heideggerian being."²⁷ What Blanchot will come to call the neuter (or even the Neuter) is not *Sein*, although he evokes the poles of being and nonbeing when construing the Outside as "being ceaselessly perpetuating itself as nothingness."²⁸ Nor does Blanchot merely accept his friend's endorsement of ethics over and against fundamental ontology. One of the speakers in the dialogue "Connaissance de l'inconnu" (1961) doubts the aptness of the word "ethics" in their conversation because it fails to identify with all due rigor "the impossible relation that is revealed in the revelation of *autrui*," namely what will be called "the third relation." And in "Tenir parole" (1962) one of the friends admits that he hears "only secondary meanings" in the word.²⁹ "Ethics" strikes Blanchot as a dangerous word because, as Heidegger argues in his "Letter on 'Humanism'" (1948), it derives from metaphysics, and Blanchot's thought, as condensed in *L'Entretien infini*, is an attempt to rethink everything without reference to truth, unity, and the subject.³⁰ An adjusted or reinvented vocabulary is required if the insights of *Totalité et infini* (1961) are to be mobilized in all their force.

*

L'Espace littéraire begins and ends with a consideration of the image. In a note to the final sentence of the opening meditation, "La solitude essentielle," several matters are raised about the connection between language and image that recall "La littérature et le droit à la mort" (1947–8), and that cast doubt on the received assumption that perception precedes imagination. "Perhaps, before going further, one ought to ask: what is the image?"³¹ After making that suggestion, Blanchot directs us to one of the appendices, "Les deux versions de l'imaginaire."³² The intricate arguments and readings of *L'Espace littéraire* are needed, it seems, for an answer to be given to this beguilingly simple question. And although an answer is given there, the inquiry does not lose its pertinence but guides Blanchot in later work.³³

In his review of *L'Espace littéraire* Levinas does not comment on "Les deux versions de l'imaginaire," even though his approach to Blanchot is largely predicated on his friend's account of the image. Perhaps it might be expected. Just as the two men are close in their elaborations of the *il y a* and *le Dehors*, while developing them in quite different ways, so too they agree in their phenomenology of the image while putting it to distinct ends. Consider Levinas in "La réalité et son ombre." He argues there against the dogma that art grasps the truth of reality. Art certainly disengages itself from the world but does not rise above it toward the eternal; on the contrary, it establishes itself by way of a rapport with what is "beneath" the world, by way of what Jean Wahl calls "transdescendence."³⁴ The claim puts Levinas at odds with Sartre's phenomenology of the image and with any phenomenology that situates itself, as it must, in the sphere of light.³⁵ Sartre's doctrine of images "insists on their transparency" with respect to "the world it represents" but fails to determine the function of the image, specifically its ability to produce the unreal.³⁶ Sartre posits an *analogon*, a vehicle from the actual to the imaginary—the paint on a canvas, the performance of a symphony by a certain orchestra—of the image, while insisting that our appreciation of art is confined to the image. Uninterested in the concrete execution of an artwork, Levinas has no such middle term: "the thing is itself and is its image," he says, and dubs "this relationship between the thing and its image ... resemblance." (6; 133). A phenomenology prepared to depart from the philosophy of light would be constrained to admit that in the image being "*resembles* itself" and in doing so "doubles itself and immobilizes" (10; 140).

Both these words, "doubles" and "immobilizes," are salient. In art the image serves to replace being and it remains entirely passive. Art does not give us in the image a luminous instant miraculously captured by an artist who translates it from time into space and holds it high above the everyday. Not at all: the image has a quite different ontology and temporality. It obscures reality and abides in a time beneath time. We can discern this strangeness in being aware that no subject of a portrait, no character in a narrative and no speaker in a poem can ever complete the action at issue and is condemned, as it were, to exist in a perpetual "meanwhile," to live "a lifeless life" (9; 139).[37] (It is at heart the same sort of iconoclasm that animated the Byzantine Emperor Leo III (726–30) in his rejection of holy images.[38]) The phenomenology of the event that Levinas proposes here turns on the pre-human rather than the human. It is not a question of an artist having a double consciousness in which an imaginative mode is more highly developed than a perceptual mode. Instead, the claim that no phenomenon can give itself without also giving its image implies that there is a "fissure in being" which is "the work of being itself."[39] The artist brings certain qualities to this attunement with being, yet the attunement itself has nothing extraordinary about it. Needless to say, "image," for Levinas, is used more generally than any Anglo-American literary historian would allow.[40] His concern is with ontology, not rhetoric, and ultimately with the ethical consequences of the ontological fissure he identifies. Art is not concerned with "the thing," but with "its image." As he puts it in a fine, biting sentence, "So art drops the prey for the shadow."[41]

Art, for Levinas, ultimately turns on a relation within being, not between beings. This ontological fissure removes art from *Sein*, but not sufficiently far to prevent our silent fascination with the work of being and, before long, an indifference to the suffering of other beings. Art also produces the unreal, a situation to which Sartre has been far more attentive than Heidegger. Positing the unreal is not so much an index of our freedom, however, as of art's ability to distract us even more from our responsibility for other people. It is as though attention to the image can lead us away from the world of "mineness," only to keep us entranced by idols, within sight of our captivity and subject to an Amalek who has become subtler over the years. Now he does not have to attack us as we leave our captivity because he has already corrupted us. We are given over to artistic pleasure and have become, as he says in Hobbesian tones, "wicked and egoist and cowardly" (12; 146). Given the iconoclastic thrust of the criticism, one might think that Levinas would launch a theological criticism of the image. Not so. Only a philosophical critique of the image, one that motivates a passage from passivity to action, can save us from this threat. Such would be the impetus to ethics, although it would be naïve to assume that this requires us to set ethics against art. The very nature of modern literature, as Levinas concedes in the final paragraph of "La réalité et son ombre," is to have introduced a critical attitude to "artistic idolatry" to the artwork (13; 148).[42]

If we read that final paragraph and give due weight to it, we will surely think of the Jena Romantics and the notion of the "literary absolute."[43] We will recall Flaubert and Mallarmé, Pound and Eliot, and Celan and Stevens, as writers who, in exemplary ways, follow them in having critical reflection incorporated in the literary work. Levinas reminds us that this critical attitude to literature goes back to Dostoyevsky and Goethe, Molière and Shakespeare. As soon as the modern notion of "literature" comes into play—and, in Shakespeare's case, long before—the writers who matter most to us demonstrate a critical experience of it in one or more ways.[44] *The Lyrical Ballads* (1798) marks a deliberate rethinking of received notions of "literature" as well as "poetry," and the same can be said, if sufficient respect is shown for the particular case, of *Ulysses* (1922) and *Finnegans Wake* (1939). In a later reflection on Blanchot, "La Servante et son maître" (1966), Levinas admits that all poetry and narrative, from Homer to Proust, introduces "a meaning into Being" and brings about a "move from Same to the Other, from *I* to the other person."[45] And so a question arises. Would it be true that the only writers who fall prey to Levinas's strictures in "La réalité et son ombre" are those who write with little or no critical attitude toward conceiving their writing as art? If so, these writers would fall outside the canon of Western literature. It is easy to see why Levinas, who fears losing moral focus by being caught up in rhythm, would be upset by the pulsing beat of Swinburne's chorus to "Atlanta in Calydon" ("Before the beginning of years / There came to the making of man . . . "), by the lulling music of Tennyson's "Idylls of the King," or by a recitation of Longfellow's "Hiawatha" (to choose only examples in English), but hard to understand why literature needs a stringent philosophical critique from the perspective of ethics. A fine awareness of moral issues and how they are treated in novels and poems and plays is part and parcel of making judgments about literary texts. No one can properly read Jane Austen, George Eliot, or Henry James without that sort of awareness being a part of the reading experience.

We need to distinguish two threads that run through Levinas's thoughts on art. First, in the language of *Autrement qu'être* (1974), which is already beginning to be heard in "La Servante et son maître," we could say that the art that matters to us unsays itself and consequently does not slide unchecked into the said. For Levinas, "the word poetry . . . means the rupture of the immanence to which language is condemned, imprisoning itself. I do not think this rupture is a purely esthetic event . . . Inseparable from the verb, it ['poetry'] overflows with prophetic meaning" (185 n. 4, 79 n. 3). (He is thinking of the Hebrew word *nabi*, meaning "prophet." Words bubble up in the prophet, much as they do in the poet who, after all, also can be a straight talker in a world of moral compromise and dirty hands.) And, in the same piece, we hear a strange echo of an important line in "La réalité et son ombre"—"Saying lets go of what it grasps"—that draws renewed attention to the final paragraph of the earlier essay (146; 38). Art as saying has the ability to unsay itself, to interrupt its movement toward self-enclosure. The ethical force of poetry, its ability to suspend the *conatus essendi*, should not be diminished. It should certainly not be assimilated to any formalist categories, whether of literary criticism or "experimental writing," and by the same token it should not thereby exclude formal concerns. Yet the former is precisely what one sees when following the other thread that runs through Levinas's meditations on art. There "interruption" or, as it becomes in a late, important interview, "obliteration," is assimilated without critical reserve to the themes of fragmentation and incompletion prized by the *avant garde*.

In that interview Levinas condemns in passing Leonardo da Vinci's "La Gioconda" ("Mona Lisa") because of "its perfection in a world of suffering and evil."[46] Even were one sure whether Levinas has in mind da Vinci's delicate idealization of his subject, his mastery of visual illusion, his blending of a face and body with a landscape relaxing into fantasy, his ability to capture an "inner life" in his subject's placid hands, or his minute, crisscrossed brushwork, "perfection" would not be a useful term of criticism. I detect here the overweening ambition of ethics, the subsumption of all that is nonethical to ethics, that comes upon Levinas in the years leading up to and away from *Totalité et infini*, and also his distaste, which I share, for casting art as religion. (I think of Hegel evoking da Vinci's figures that "do not lack the sublimity which reverence for the dignity and truth of religion demands."[47]) The beauty of Mona Lisa's face does not remove her admirer from the world to indulge endlessly in idle joys of aesthetic contemplation, however. It holds us for a short while only, and then we return to the world, refreshed, with renewed wonder at life, knowing that something of la Gioconda's mystery passes through everyone we meet. There is a moral force in this experience, for when we encounter people mired in misery, we know ourselves to be obliged to help them precisely because of his mystery (*imago dei*, "being," "spirit," "life," "mortality" . . .). One does not have to wait for the painting itself to show signs of being obliterated by time for this to happen.[48] Art leads us away from being preoccupied with our being in the world, as Levinas admits, and if it does so at the risk of momentary silence and a lack of immediate attention to other people, it does so no more than reading or writing "first philosophy." *Totalité et infini* is, Derrida says, a work of art.[49] He is correct not because Levinas's prose is beautiful or because the book exhibits an especially pleasing structure but because in one important sense the book works in the manner of art rather than philosophy. *Totalité et infini* does not persuade a reader by the generality of a coercive argument but by provoking a singular change of life in much the same way as a work of art does.[50] "Du mußt dein Leben ändern" ["You must change your life"] as Rilke memorably says in response to an archaic torso of Apollo.

Whatever problems "perfection" poses for ethics are also to be found in art that courts imperfection. "Il y avait qu'il fallait détruire et détruire et détuire, / Il y a que le salut n'est qu'à ce prix" [*One had to destroy and destroy and destroy / There was salvation only at this price*] writes Yves Bonnefoy in "L'Imperfection est la cime," perhaps recalling his early years with the surrealists.[51] His work over many years testifies to the value for him of negativity in the 1940s for the writing of lyric poetry. Yet this negativity is historically conditioned and also meets its limit in history. The *avant garde* can have as uncritical an attitude toward art as any "new formalist" or "mainstream" artist. To break form, affirm parabasis, allow language to speak: these things modify magic and halt intoxicating rhythms, to be sure, but none of them is by itself a reliable index of artistic or ethical value. These gestures have become so thoroughly institutionalized, their variations so predictable, and their advocates so incapable of distinguishing adventure from nostalgia, that they now largely characterize art without displaying a critical edge in doing so. They are the "literary absolute" not because they incorporate criticism but because they are self-enclosed, fascinated by their own presumed literariness. The ethical critique that can value Blanchot and Leiris, Atlan and Sosno, can also expose the aridity of belated *avant garde* groups that attracted attention some decades ago such as the practitioners of language poetry and the members of the Cambridge school of poetry.

*

We might say, smiling a little, that Levinas's phenomenology of the image is itself and its image. According to that bon mot, we would find the image of Levinas's phenomenology of the image in Blanchot's "Les deux versions de l'imaginaire" and, since it is placed closer to art than to ethics, we might be tempted to say that art drops Levinas for Blanchot. But perhaps we should not yield so readily to temptation and should consider saying something quite different, that ethics has a choice upon whom to seize: Levinas or Blanchot.

Usually, Blanchot admits, we think of imagination following perception. Yet the distance between object and image is, he argues, not between the two but within the former. "The thing was there; we grasped it in the vital movement of a comprehensive action—and lo, having become image, instantly it has become that which no one can grasp, the unreal, the impossible."[52] His example is "the mourned deceased" who "begins to *resemble himself*" (257; 346). He had already used it the year before "Les deux versions de l'imaginaire" appeared, in "Le Musée, l'art et le temps" (1950), and his presentation is a little clearer there than in the later essay:

> Resemblance is not a means of imitating life but of making it inaccessible, of establishing it in a double that is permanent and escapes from life. Living figures, men, are without resemblance. One must wait for the cadaverous appearance, the idealization by death and the eternalization of the end for a being to take on the great beauty that is its own resemblance, the truth of itself in a reflection. A portrait—one came to perceive this little by little—does not resemble because it makes itself similar to a face; rather, the resemblance only begins and only exists with the portrait and in it alone.[53]

I pause to note that this is not quite what Levinas says in his account of the image. The philosopher stresses that resemblance occurs as part of "the work of being," whereas the novelist indicates that it happens by dint of the artwork. Yet if Blanchot's language—"resemblance," "inaccessible"—recalls Levinas to any extent, the example of the corpse brings Heidegger to mind, and first of all his discussion of the "deceased" in *Sein und Zeit* ¶ 47. For Blanchot, the dead one is "at first extremely close to the condition of a thing," which is a little more chilling than Heidegger's reflection that the dead body, "which is just-present-at-hand-and-no-more is 'more' than a *lifeless* material Thing."[54] For Heidegger, there is an interval of solicitude before the dear departed becomes *vorhanden* that slips past Blanchot. We remain with the dead one, the German says, while the Frenchman, looking from another angle, observes that the corpse remains with us. It obtrudes upon the scene not only in being apparent in a world that is no longer seamless but also in dissolving the world as such. Like a damaged tool, the dead person becomes an "image" of himself (258; 347). This image cannot be grasped, and it attunes us to the imaginary.

It seems as though Blanchot were composing "Les deux versions de l'imaginaire" with *Sein und Zeit* ¶ 16, the analysis of equipment that has become unusable, before him. And it might be thought that he also has *Kant und das Problem der Metaphysik* (1929) open to § 20, the discussion of image, and schema in Kant.[55] Now Kant, at least in the 1781 edition of the first *Kritik*, figures human beings as essentially imaginative creatures. The imagination [*Einbildungskraft*] produces *schemata*, rules for the spontaneous creation of images, and so mediates the generality of the understanding and the particularity of intuitions. Kant chooses examples from mathematics and the animal world.[56] Curiously, Heidegger seizes upon the corpse in order to clarify the distinction between image and schema. A copy, he says, "can only directly copy the likeness and thus reveal the 'image' (the immediate look) of the deceased himself."[57] He passes from photograph to death mask to face: "the photograph, however, can also show how something like a death mask appears in general . . . the death mask can show in general how something like the face of a dead human being appears. But an individual corpse can also show this." (64). What interests Heidegger is how something appears "in general" (64), how schema and image relate to one another or, if you like, how the One shines through the Many.

Throughout the *Kantbuch* Heidegger is concerned to show that the imagination is the root of sensibility and understanding and, in particular, that it is indeed a *Kraft*, a power, an interpretation of "I" along the lines of "I can." The imagination is transcendental partly because it is the condition of possibility for the unity of intuition and apperception and partly because it establishes transcendence, which for Heidegger is our ability to engage with the world and which presumes a fusion of knower and known. Now Blanchot differs from Kant, and especially Heidegger's Kant, in all these emphases and their consequences. He has no interest in finding an affinity between *Bilden* and *Bauen*, and his concern is with fragmentation and not mediation. If he insists on a "prior transcendence" of the image, it is not to indicate an identity between knower and known but to signal that the image derives from a structure of resemblance that precedes the alternation of being and nonbeing. For Blanchot, the corpse reveals that, with the final exhaustion of negativity, the image of the dead one opens onto the imaginary or Outside, and that the "I" is unmade according to its image.

> No matter how calmly the corpse has been laid out upon its bed for final viewing, it is also everywhere in the room, all over the house. At every instant it can be elsewhere than where it is. It is where we are apart from it, where there is nothing; it is an invading presence, an obscure and vain abundance . . . . We do not cohabit with the dead for fear of seeing *here* collapse into the unfathomable *nowhere*.[58]

Blanchot had considered the situation earlier, using the same vocabulary of resemblance, in his first novel, *Thomas l'Obscur* (1941), some seven years before Levinas ventured his analysis in "La réalité et son ombre." As we have seen in Chapter 7, the novel, and the later *récit* that bears the same title, are obsessively concerned with the doubling of the clear and the obscure in the very person of Thomas. Here is Thomas meditating on the relation of identity and difference when viewing Anne's corpse:

> She was not sleeping. She was not changed, either. She had stopped at the point where she resembled only herself [*au point où elle ne ressemblait qu'à elle-même*], and where her face, having only Anne's expression, was disturbing to look at. . . . I took her hand. I placed my lips on her forehead. I treated her as if she were alive and, because she was unique among the dead in still having a face and a hand, my gestures did not seem insane. Did she appear alive, then? Alas, all that prevented her from being distinguished from a real person was that which verified her annihilation. She was entirely within herself . . . in death, abounding in life. She seemed more weighty, more in control of herself. No Anne was lacking in the corpse of Anne.[59]

"She had stopped at the point where she resembled only herself": should we therefore say that Levinas's phenomenology of the image is the double of Blanchot's?

Perhaps so; but, as with the provenance of the *il y a*, it hardly matters who came up with the idea. Neither Levinas nor Blanchot shows the slightest concern to claim originality here. Of more significance is what happens to Anne. Before long she enables Thomas to pass from image to the imaginary, from the world of meaning to the approach of the Outside:

> At the moment everything was being destroyed she had created that which was most difficult: she had not drawn something out of nothing (a meaningless act), but given to nothing, in its form of nothing, the form of something. The act of not seeing had now its integral eye . . . . The silence, the real silence, the one which is not composed of silenced words, of possible words, had a complete vocal system with lips, cords, palate, without which the mute are only false mutes.[60]

Image precedes perception, as Levinas said of Blanchot, but not without mimicking the means of perception.

Levinas and Blanchot share the same account of the image while taking it in quite different directions. Where the one finds resemblance at work in being, the other detects it in the artwork. And where the philosopher identifies ethics as a way of overcoming the *il y a*, the writer figures the approach of the Outside as essential to literature. To pass from image to the imaginary is to be fascinated, caught in a dark gaze that freezes the observer. Without this interruption, no work can claim to be literature; yet unless one breaks free of the gaze, no work can be completed. Such is the beginning of an oscillation connoted by the word "image" that Blanchot will assimilate in later writing to the doctrine of eternal return.

*

Levinas thinks that the image can lead us from *inter-esse* to *dis-inter-esse*; it has an ethical function, albeit a preliminary one that is fraught with the danger of lapsing into silence. In *La Folie du jour*, for instance, the ethical function is plain: "the *other* of the Image and the Letter rend the *same* of the Said, according to a modality of awakening and sobering up."[61] For Blanchot, however, it is not the image that is essential to "ethics" but rather the "split in being," the flow of empty images that constitutes the Outside and that opens up the relation that I can have with the other person. We can speak of "ethics" here, but not as value theory or even first philosophy. It would be the word we use to describe "the impossible relation that is revealed in the revelation of *autrui*." That insight comes, as we have seen, from "Connaissance de l'inconnu," the first of Blanchot's three dialogues on and around *Totalité et infini*, the book that, more than any other, prompted Blanchot to make his ethics explicit and, in doing so, to adjust the meaning of "ethics" as proposed by his friend.

We can overhear this adjustment being made in the third of the dialogues, "Le rapport du troisième genre (homme sans horizon)." One of the speakers ventures that we affirm an "I without a self" that moves between "no one and someone."[62] The response that is called forth has been brewing for some time:

> Perhaps, also, it is time to withdraw this term *autrui*, while retaining what it has to say to us: that the Other [*l'Autre*] is always what calls upon "man" (even if only to put him between parentheses or between quotation marks), not the other [*autre*] as God or other [*autre*] as nature but, as "man," more Other than all that is other [*plus Autre que tout ce qu'il y a d'autre*] (72; 102).

Can one withdraw *autrui*, the central word of Levinas's ethics as first philosophy, without dismantling his entire program of reforming philosophy as ontology? It seems so to the first speaker, whom I quote at length:

> Therefore, and before we delete it, let us keep in mind that *autrui* is a name that is essentially neutral and that, far from relieving us of all responsibility of attending to the neutral, it reminds us that we must, in the presence of the other [*l'Autre*] who comes to us as *Autrui*, respond to the depth of strangeness, of inertia, or irregularity and idleness [*désœuvrement*] to which we open when we seek to receive the speech of the Outside. . . . All the mystery of the neutral passes, perhaps, by way of the other [*autrui*], and sends us back to him; passes, that is to say, through this experience of language in which the relation of the third kind, a non-unitary relation, escapes the question of being as it does that of the whole, leaving us exposed to "the most profound question," that questioning of the detour through which the neutral—which is never the impersonal—comes into question. (72; 102).

Autrui indicates something more fundamental than it can name: a neutral mode of relation, which exceeds the duality of human being and God or human being and nature. Levinas calls this "a relation without relation," meaning that the rapport with the other person occurs but does so without presuming equality between the parties.[63]

The ethics implied by Levinas is insufficient, Blanchot suggests, precisely because of the seriousness that his friend attaches to *Autrui* and to the asymmetrical relation that he says I have with him or her, if I can say even that much about this stranger to being. "*Autrui*" partly conceals what it seeks to reveal in that it appears to be a self that speaks from above me, to belong to an order of being—the divine, the natural—rather than to mark an interruption of being. Similarly, "asymmetry" blocks what tries to manifest itself because it is set against symmetry and reciprocity. The alternative beyond Levinasian asymmetry or "relation without relation" is double dissymmetry in which each party relates to the other asymmetrically, each recognizing the ethical transcendence of the other without any ground, natural or divine, able to justify the apposition. This is the "third relation." Blanchot indicates that it is based neither on a dialectic in which the other is subsumed by the same nor on an immediacy in which the self is fused with the other. It is a plural and mobile way of being together that is set in motion not by *being* or *a being* but by an *interruption of being*.

This interruption of being needs to be examined. We are used to Levinas talking of the face in these terms, including the thought of the face performing an ἐποχή of phenomenology, and even with him finally acknowledging that art can supply a face.[64] Yet Blanchot speaks otherwise. He tells us that this interruption occurs when there is no intermediary between two human beings, only "the exigency that is speech."[65] Another person, as *autrui*, does not present himself or herself in the field of my vision but outside all visible horizons, in speech, which Blanchot quickly assimilates to the Outside because speech maintains us in a mobile and doubly transcendent relationship that resists unification. "In speech, it is the outside that speaks in giving rise to speech, and permitting me to speak," he says, while making it clear that the relation in question is not between two identifiable agents (55; 79). When the other person speaks, he or she is "no one," meaning, first of all, no one in particular, and similarly there is nothing at all special about me when I respond. In *L'Écriture du désastre*, where the Outside has been refigured as disaster, the matter is cast as advice, "let the disaster speak in you."[66] My encounter with the other person is characterized by an antecedent responsibility for him or her that does not turn on any gifts that I might have or even on my singularity as an individual. *L'Écriture du désastre* again: "The responsibility with which I am charged is not mine, and because of it I am no longer myself [*je ne suis plus moi*]."[67] The "no longer" is perhaps misleading, for the "I" appears only in the accusative, as a "me," and only (but always) before another. It has never enjoyed the privilege of the *cogito*.[68]

In any human encounter we are faced with a dire alternative, "to speak or to kill."[69] It might seem, then, that Blanchot seeks to render his ethics explicit by way of speech, not the image. Yet a closer look reveals that the distinction is delusive. In "Parler, ce n'est pas voir," the first dialogue in *L'Entretien infini*, one of the conversation partners seizes upon the nature of the image. Like the author of "Les deux versions de l'imaginaire," he tells us that the image is "not the object's double [*le double de l'objet*], but the initial division [*le dédoublement initial*] that then permits the thing to be figured" and goes on to make a bolder claim, that "still further back than this doubling it is a folding, a turn of the turning [*le ploiement, le tour du tournant*], the 'version' that is always in the process of inverting itself and that in itself bears the back and forth of a divergence [*divergence*]" (30; 42). What specificity does this turning have? We are told immediately. "The speech of which we are trying to speak is a return to this first turning" (72; 102). *Autrui*, we learn in "Tenir parole," is "A presence diverted [*détournée*] from any present" indeed "infinitely diverted [*détourné*]," not a being but a neutral speech at the origin of the image (59, 85; 62, 89).

"Ethics," for Blanchot, does not begin in a passage from being to beings, as it does for Levinas, but in the recognition that the other person's speech is a neutral interruption of being. It precedes perception and begins not with the image but with what enables images. With its faint sense of "altruism" and the lingering suspicion that asymmetry is supported by undisclosed theological assumptions, "*autrui*" must be replaced by another word, "*communauté*," which Blanchot will shade with the adjective "*inavouable*" to suggest that the plural and mobile way of being with others cannot form a matrix of power and hence possibility (70, 56, 71; 99, 80, 101). A Blanchotian ethics would situate itself beyond social contract and individual decision, moral law and virtue, as well as desire, and would seek to respond to the human relation regarded as outside all possibility ("I can," "I must," "I want," and so on). Like Levinas, Blanchot argues that the other person is inaccessible to me and that I am obligated to him or her by a relation that is anterior to any actual encounter we might have. For Blanchot, this is a relation that can never be satisfied because it responds to a voice that bespeaks an interruption of being, and not a being. I am called radically into question not by another being but by a neutral relation that holds us together, side by side rather than joining us together, and that exposes us to the endlessness of dying.[70] It is here that Levinas and his friend part company. The scare quotes around "ethics," for Blanchot, indicate that it cannot find meaning in presence or representation, and Levinas would of course agree. For Blanchot, ethics cannot even find an alternate meaning, what Levinas calls (with a backward glance to Husserl) "an ethical *Sinngebung*," because it finally escapes any and all meaning.[71]

This is not to say that the human relation is meaningless, only that the primal turning that is at the heart of speech cannot be locked into Husserl's order of meaning. The circulation from meaning to lack of meaning, from image to imaginary, cannot be halted. In "ethics," as in love, one accedes to an "overbidding, an outrage of life that cannot be contained within life."[72] It is explosive communication, a moment of madness in ethics as it is conventionally understood, that can be affirmed but not sustained. "Ethics" is not simply a part of life, then, but is what Blanchot calls "counter-living."[73] It cannot be distinguished strictly from politics, just as it cannot help us to clarify differences between friendship, love, and community. "We have two lives that we must try to live together, although they are irreconcilable," he says.[74] "One life is tied to the future of 'communication,' when the relations between men will no longer, stealthily or violently, make things out of them."[75] Such is everyday life, in which one struggles for justice, seeks to understand and to be understood. Yet there is a counter-life that must also be acknowledged, and here the quotation marks around the word "communication" have been removed, making it into a limit-experience. In this other life one "greets communication outside the world, immediately, but on condition that this communication be a disruption of the 'immediate,' an opening, a wrenching violence, a fire that burns without pause" (96; 113). It is here that "*Man can become the impossible friend of man, his relation to the latter being precisely with the impossible*" (95–6; 112).[76]

Counter-living, or "ethics," if you will, irrupts in friendship, love, and community as they are usually understood, even though it does not last. And so, in a sense, Blanchot never attains the "order of justice" that Levinas calls for because his "ethics" cannot settle into any order, even that proposed by Levinas, and indeed upsets all order. In the words of *L'Écriture du désastre*, "Responsibility . . . withdraws me from my order—perhaps from all orders and from order itself."[77] Nonetheless, Blanchot is explicit that "ethics" begins in the passage of the image to the imaginary, the very opening of the neutral or the Outside. Perhaps Levinas sensed exactly the same thing when reading *L'Espace littéraire*.

Notes

1. Kevin Hart, "Ethics of the Image," *Levinas Studies* 1 (2005): 119–38. https://doi.org/10.5840/levinas200519.
2. Levinas, "Maurice Blanchot et le regard du poète," *Monde Nouveau* 11, no. 96 (1956, mars): 6–19.
3. See Levinas, "The Poet's Vision," *PN*, 129 (*SMB*, 12). Levinas returns to this thought in "Exercises on 'The Madness of the Day,'" also in *PN*, 159 (*SMB*, 59).
4. Heidegger objects to "value philosophy" partly because it divides philosophy into sub-disciplines, a methodological gesture that skews the exigencies of thought and partly because it relies on truth considered as propositions, not as disclosure. See *Being and Time*, ¶ 44 (c). Also see his strictures on "ethics" in "Letter on 'Humanism,'" *Pathmarks*, 268–71. Levinas, "The Poet's Vision," *PN*, 137 (*SMB*, 23).
5. Levinas, *PN*, 137 (*SMB*, 24). Also see the discussion in the previous chapter.
6. Levinas, *EE*, 19 (19).
7. See, for example, Levinas, *PN*, 133 (*SMB*, 17), 148, 155, 166 (*SMB*, 40, 52, 68). But also note the reservation in *PN*, 184 n. 4 (*SMB*, 78 n. 3).
8. Levinas, *PN*, 129 (*SMB*, 12).
9. Levinas would have been aware of Husserl's early phenomenology of the image and Sartre's reliance on it. See Husserl, *Logical Investigations*, trans. J. N. Findlay, 2 vols. (London: Routledge and Kegan Paul, 1970), vol. 2, 593–6.
10. See Sartre, *The Imaginary: A Phenomenological Psychology of the Imagination*, trans. Jonathan Weber (London: Routledge, 2004), 60.
11. See Jill Robbins, ed., *IRB*, 43.
12. See Blanchot, "Le roman, œuvre de mauvaise foi," *Les Temps modernes*, no. 19 (avril 1947), *CC*, 106–7. The text originally appeared in *Les Temps modernes*, no. 19 (avril 1947), 1304–17, and recapitulates some of the arguments that would appear in *PF*.
13. See François Dosse, *History of Structuralism*, 2 vols., trans. Deborah Glassman (Minneapolis: University of Minnesota Press, 1997), vol. 2, 283. Blanchot makes the acute observation many years after that there is a strange convergence of Sartre and Levinas with respect to ethics. See *WD*, 22 (41).
14. "T.M." (actually, Maurice Merleau-Ponty) notes in the italicized preface to the essay in *Les Temps modernes* that Sartre's ideas have only been partly considered by Levinas, that in *L'Imaginaire* Sartre had already expressed unease with the image, and that Sartre was far more optimistic about literature and its social possibilities than Levinas. See Levinas, "La réalité et son ombre," *Les Temps modernes* 38 (1948): 769–70.
15. Blanchot, *SL*, 247 n. 8 (332 n. 1).
16. Lévinas, "Reality and Its Shadow," 3 (*IH*, 126).

17 Heidegger, *Being and Time*, 68. See Levinas's comments on *Eigenlichkeit* in "The Other, Utopia, and Justice," *EN*, 225–6 (256).
18 Blanchot, *WD*, 60 (98).
19 G. W. F. Hegel, *The Phenomenology of Mind*, trans. J. B. Baillie (New York: Harper and Row, 1967), 81.
20 Blanchot, *SL*, 89 (108). In "The Two Versions of the Imaginary" Blanchot proposes the remarkable idea of living "an event as an image," 261 (352). Earlier, in *LS*, Blanchot had ventured an original view of authorial experience: "Between his work and his lucidity, he establishes an impulse to compose and to develop, mutually, an extremely difficult task, important and complex, a task that we call *experience* . . . ," *LS*, 77 (90).
21 See Levinas, *EE*, 95 (163).
22 Levinas, "The Poet's Vision," *PN*, 139 (*SMB*, 25–6).
23 See Levinas's discussion of Amalek in "For a Place in the Bible," *ITN*, 18–19 (*HN*, 27–8). Blanchot also talks about Amalek in "L'Écriture consacrée au silence," *Instants* 1 (1989): 239–41.
24 It should be noted that Levinas develops an account of dwelling in *TI*, 2 D. This theme is explored by Jacques Derrida in "A Word of Welcome," *Adieu to Emmanuel Levinas*, trans. Pascale-Anne Brault and Michael Naas (Stanford: Stanford University Press, 1999).
25 See for instance Levinas, *Ein*, 50–1 (40). Levinas observes at. 49 (40), that Blanchot "does not speak of the 'there is'" but he does not notice how *il y a* runs through the very work he has in mind, *ED*, or recall a passage such as the following from "Le Dernier mot" (1935-6), "It was only after I had walked some distance that they began to howl again: trembling, muffled howls, which at that hour of the day resounded like the echo of the words *there is*" [*hurlements tremblants étouffés, qui, à cette heure du jour, retentissaient comme l'écho du mot* il y a], *VC*, 45 (*RE*, 117–18).
26 Levinas, "Philosophy and the Idea of Infinity," *CPP*, 51 (*DEHH*, 169).
27 Blanchot, "L'Étrange et l'étranger," *La Nouvelle Revue Française* 70 (1958), 681 n. 1. Levinas, *TI (F)*, 298 (*TI*, 332).
28 Blanchot, *SL*, 243 (326). He speaks of the impossible in these terms. See his *IC*, 47 (66). The word "neuter" is set in both lower case and upper case in *SNB*, 72–6 (101–7). Also see Levinas, "A Conversation with André Dalmas," *PN*, 153; *SMB*, 49.
29 Blanchot, *IC*, 55, 63 (78, 89).
30 See Blanchot, *IC*, xii (vii). Blanchot would be dubious about restoring "ethics" (or "ontology") in the sense of pondering "the abode of the human being," Heidegger, "Letter on 'Humanism,'" 271.
31 Blanchot, *SL*, 34 n. 3 (32 n. 1).
32 Blanchot had published "Les deux versions de l'imaginaire" several years before it was collected in *EL* in *Cahiers de la Pléiade*, 12 (1951), 115–25.
33 See Blanchot, "Vast as the Night," *IC*, 318–25 (465–77). Also see *WD*, 126 (193).
34 See Wahl, *Human Existence and Transcendence*, 28.
35 See Levinas, *EE*, 85 (145).
36 Levinas, "Reality and its Shadow," 5 (*EHH*, 132).
37 Also see Blanchot's remarks about Balzac's characters in "Le roman, œuvre de mauvaise foi," 112.
38 See my essay, "The Profound *Reserve*," in *After Blanchot: Literature, Criticism, Philosophy*, ed. Leslie Hill, Brian Nelson and Dimitris Vardoulakis (Newark, DE: University of Delaware Press, 2005), 40–5.
39 Levinas, "Reality and its Shadow," 8 (*IH*, 137 and 138).

40 See, for example, Paul de Man, "Intentional Structure of the Romantic Image," *The Rhetoric of Romanticism* (New York: Columbia University Press, 1984), 1–17.
41 Levinas, "Reality and its Shadow," 12 (*IH*, 145).
42 On iconoclasm and anti-iconoclasm in Levinas and Blanchot, see my essay "The Profound *Reserve*," 35–57.
43 See Lacoue-Labarthe and Nancy, *The Literary Absolute*.
44 See Derek Attridge, "'This Strange Institution Called Literature': An Interview with Jacques Derrida," *Acts of Literature*, ed. Derek Attridge (London: Routledge, 1992), 41.
45 Levinas, "The Servant and Her Master," *PN*, 147 (*SMB*, 39).
46 Levinas, *O*, 22.
47 Hegel, *Aesthetics: Lectures on Fine Art*, 2 vols., trans. T. M. Knox (Oxford: Clarendon Press, 1974), vol. 2, 880.
48 See Levinas, *O*, 30–2.
49 See Derrida, "Violence and Metaphysics," *Writing and Difference*, trans. Alan Bass (London: Routledge and Kegan Paul, 1978), 312 n. 7.
50 Yet see Blanchot's remarks on Levinas's prose in "Knowledge of the Unknown," *IC*, 52 (75).
51 Yves Bonnefoy, *Poèmes* (Paris: Mercure de France, 1978), 117.
52 Blanchot, *SL*, 255 (343).
53 Blanchot, "The Museum, Art, and Time," *F*, 32 (42–3).
54 Blanchot, *SL*, 257 (345) and Heidegger, *Being and Time*, 282.
55 Nancy draws attention to this passage and its relevance for Blanchot's discussion of the image in his *Au fond des images* (Paris: Galilée, 2003), 168 n. 1. Also see on this topic Georges Didi-Huberman, "De ressemblance à ressemblance," in *Maurice Blanchot: Récits Critiques*, ed. Christophe Bident and Pierre Vilar (Tours: Éditions Farrago / Éditions Léo Scheer, 2003), 162–7. Heidegger's earlier discussion of the image (1924–5), in his commentary on Plato's *Sophist* 232b–236c should be noted. See Heidegger, *Plato's Sophist*, trans. Richard Rojcewicz and André Schuwer (Bloomington, IN: Indiana University Press, 1997), § 58 c.
56 See Kant, *Critique of Pure Reason*, trans. Norman Kemp Smith (London: Macmillan, 1933), A 141.
57 Heidegger, *Kant and the Problem of Metaphysics*, 4th ed., enlarged, trans. Richard Taft (Bloomington, IN: Indiana University Press, 1990), 63–4.
58 Blanchot, *SL*, 259 (349).
59 Blanchot, *TO (1)*, 207. The passage appears, shortened as indicated by the ellipses, in the version of the novel that Blanchot published as a *récit* at 100. I have followed the translation by David Lamberton, *TO*, 89–90, and made silent changes when needed.
60 Blanchot, *TO*, 90 (*TO* 1, 208; *TO* 2, 102).
61 Levinas, *PN*, 158 (*SMB*, 58).
62 Blanchot, *IC*, 71 (102).
63 Levinas, *TI*, 80 (*TI(F)*, 79).
64 See, for example, Levinas, *EN(F)*, 232 (262), and *O*, 20.
65 Blanchot, *IC*, 68 (97).
66 Blanchot, *WD*, 4 (12).
67 Blanchot, *WD*, 13 (28). Also see 18 and 64 (35 and 105). Blanchot writes here with *AE* in mind.
68 On this topic, see my book *The Dark Gaze*, ch. 4.
69 Blanchot, *IC*, 62 (88).
70 See Blanchot, *UC*, 41 (69).

71 Levinas, "The Ruin of Representation," *DEH*, 121 (*DEHH*, 135). Blanchot seems to credit Levinas with this view when he reflects on "responsibility": "We ought to try to understand the word has it has been opened up and renewed by Levinas so that it has come to signify (beyond the realm of meaning [*sens*]) the responsibility of an other philosophy," *WD*, 25 (45).
72 Blanchot, *UC*, 41 (69).
73 Blanchot, *WD*, 26 (47). Blanchot notes the temptation of ethics "with its conciliating function (justice and responsibility)" and also its inevitable madness, *WD*, 27 (48). On the topic of counter-life, see my essay "The Counter-Spiritual Life," *The Power of Contestation*, 156–77.
74 Blanchot, "On one Approach to Communism," *F*, 95 (112).
75 Blanchot, *F*, 96 (112–13).
76 See Blanchot's note to this passage on p. 296 (112), and my discussion of it in *The Dark Gaze*, 205–6.
77 Blanchot, *WD*, 25 (45–6).

Part 4

On Being Jewish

10

The Third Relation

"I consider as an axiom this identical proposition, which receives two meanings only through a change in accent; namely, that what is not truly *a* being is not truly a *being*."[1] Thus Leibniz to Arnaud on April 30, 1687. He underlines the point in the following sentence, bringing all the authority of the history of philosophy to bear on his cause: "It has *always* been thought that one and being are reciprocal terms" (191; my emphasis). He is surely right to speak with such firmness. Indeed, he is doing little more than repeating Plotinus when the sage declares in *Ennead* 6.9, "It is by the one that all beings are beings . . . For what could anything be if it was not one?"[2] Those are the words with which Plotinus begins one of his most influential tractates, and in doing so he is citing a commonplace drawn from Aristotle's *Metaphysics*: "in a sense unity means the same as being," the Philosopher says, supporting the claim in three ways:

> (a) from the fact that it has a meaning corresponding to each of the categories, and is contained in none of them—e.g., it is contained neither in substance nor in quality, but is related to them exactly as being is; (b) from the fact that in "one man" nothing more is predicated than in "man" (just as Being too does not exist apart from some thing or quality or quantity); and (c) because "to be one" is "to be a particular thing."[3]

We are not talking, then, of numerical unity, which may be found in the category of quantity, but of transcendental unity, which is convertible with being. In the neighborhood of this general claim, we might recall Plato telling us in book seven of *The Republic* that, "the study of unity will be one of the studies that guide and convert the soul to the contemplation of true being."[4]

Despite the ample confirmation that Leibniz could gain from the tradition for his axiom, support that passes from Aristotle to St. Thomas Aquinas's commentary on *De Anima* and beyond, there is another sense of unity in play.[5] Plotinus may have started the ninth tractate of book six by alluding to Aristotle on transcendental unity as convertible with being but, as his phrasing suggests ("the one"), he goes on to make a different point, that the One, the absolutely original, transcends being. He points to "this marvel of the One, which is not existent, so that 'one' may not here also have to be predicated of something else."[6] This conclusion sends us back to Plato's *Parmenides*, where the imposing Eleatic tells us in his first hypothesis that "the one has no share in being at all."[7] Clearly, even once we put aside numerical unity, there are two remaining senses of "one" at issue in Greek philosophy; and Proclus, in his commentary on the

Parmenides, distinguishes them plainly as that which transcends being and that which is co-ordinate with it.[8] We may say that the philosophy that answers to ancient Greek thought tends to agree with Aristotle or with Plotinus or that it interlaces the two in various ways. The same holds true of Christian theology in its conceptions of God as "beyond being," as Pseudo-Dionysius the Areopagite has it, and as his own act of being, as Aquinas proposes.[9] The two strands were often developed separately in Christianity, although Aquinas was to tie them neatly together. The divine essence is pure subsistent *esse*, which is really distinct from *ens* (an individual, which has its *esse* only as a divine gift) and is therefore beyond being (*ens*) while also, equally clearly, being itself. Jean-Luc Marion will venture to say that Aquinas's God, understood as his own act of being, is precisely "God without being."[10]

Blanchot comes most sharply into focus for us when we see him contesting the issues that have just been raised: the reciprocity of being and unity, and the primacy of the One beyond being. This engagement can rightly be said to last all his writing life, from the figure of the double Thomas in *Thomas l'Obscur* (1941) to the celebration of the fragmentary in *L'Écriture du désastre* (1980). To see Blanchot in this way is not simply to claim him for philosophy and to evaluate him solely in its terms. Rather, the point of proceeding in this way is to establish the stance Blanchot adopts with respect to some philosophical issues, a stance that informs all that he writes. There is good reason to select *L'Entretien infini* (1969) as a moment of maximum intensity in this struggle with philosophy, and within that text to focus on the conversations between two unnamed speakers, who are perhaps the weary men of the untitled series of fragments that prefaces the book, two tired souls who sit around a table as if to leave room for another person who might "*consider himself their true interlocutor, the one for whom they would speak if they addressed themselves to him.*"[11] These meandering conversations occur in the first section of the book, "la parole plurielle: *parole d'écriture*," and mostly turn around Levinas's *Totalité et infini* (1961), albeit sometimes at a distance. Of these conversations it is the one entitled "Le rapport du troisième genre (homme sans horizon)" that speaks the most boldly against the unity of being.

I would like to establish as plainly as possible what Blanchot means by "le rapport du troisième genre," and raise some questions with respect to it. I wish to consider what he takes to follow from his position (if the word be allowed in a context that affirms plurality and mobility) and something that he does not develop from it. Throughout, it must be kept in mind that although Blanchot joins issue with philosophical questions, he does not do so in the genre of the article or the treatise. At the same time, *L'Entretien infini* is not simply a collection of occasional pieces; its various parts have been revised with care, its philosophical vocabulary adjusted in the interests of coherence and precision, and the different texts, in their disparate genres, integrated into a whole. One of the ironies of the work is that, committed as it is to the questioning of unity and set against the very idea of the "beautiful Work" (262; 391), it is nicely fashioned into an ensemble. To read *L'Entretien infini* well one must find the right level from which to question it, and that process of orienting ourselves requires us to take seriously Blanchot's reflections on the nature of questioning with which the work begins.

*

Although the form of philosophical research changes over the centuries, philosophers do not usually reflect for long on the literary and pedagogic forms in which they conduct their investigations. Nonetheless, Blanchot suggests, critical reflection on the ways in which research is pursued will lead us to an essential possibility of research in our time, indeed, to a link between this essence and our epoch. In its highest period, that of German idealism, philosophy is brought almost completely under the cover of the University. The sage dresses as a professor; the disciple becomes a student; philosophy is structured into courses of lectures where it is characterized by the communication of a given content in an approved style, which is to be mastered and reproduced with only a small range of individual variation tolerated. Paul Valéry once observed that, in the age of *les philosophes*, "the public was created by an easy style," and it may be added that, in the age of Kant and Hegel, a philosophical audience was deformed by rebarbative styles.[12] Yet many analytic philosophers who summarily reject German idealism and all that follows from it as lacking the clarity and rigor to which they aspire can hardly be said to have mastered and perpetuated an easy style. Few of them write with the lucidity and grace of G. E. Moore or J. L. Austin. Doubtless, Husserl is right when he says that, "clarity does not exclude a certain horizon [*Hof*: 'halo'] of indeterminacy," yet the attempt to exclude that horizon by deflecting issues about the world to pre-packaged philosophical questions, frequently removes us far from good prose.[13] Analytic philosophers like Rudolf Carnap and Wilfred Sellars tend not to *write* so much as to *write up*, and they do so with their guild in mind, not the creation of a broad public in need of enlightenment, or—in many cases—even a public at all.

Blanchot invites us to step back and survey the history of human thought from an unexpected angle. If we do, he promises, we will see two dominant ways of engaging in speculation and critique. One of these is oriented toward continuity, he thinks, and the discourse of the *universitas* is its highest point; the other is drawn toward discontinuity, it is a dis-cursus, a broken course that prefers the fragment and the essay to the dissertation and the article. Among those thinkers who walk this other path, Blanchot tells us, are Lao Tzu and Confucius in China, Heraclitus and even Plato's Socrates in Greece, and more recently individuals such as Pascal and Nietzsche, right up to Char and Bataille.[14] The list can easily be extended to include Kierkegaard and Wittgenstein, not to mention the Heidegger of the *Beiträge* (1936-8) and *Besinnung* (1938-9). Perhaps Blanchot would be less than happy if he were prodded to extend his list in the direction that the name of Pascal suggests. For his list could well include the Desert Fathers and Mothers whose sayings are preserved in the *Apophthegmata Patrum et Matrum*, the Evagrius Ponticus who wrote the chapters on prayer, the Eckhart of the homilies, the St. John of the Cross of the poems, and many others.

Whether Blanchot has sound reasons for not multiplying names in this field of writing is something to consider in a moment. Beforehand, it should be stressed that he does not simply oppose the continuous with the discontinuous. When it becomes excessive, the continuous can also be disruptive, and he cites Lautréamont, Proust, Breton, and Joyce as examples of a scandalous continuity, an attempt to "say everything" [*tout dire*] and trouble comprehension in doing so.[15] Doubtless the twentieth century does not have a privilege in this respect: think of Samuel Richardson's *Clarissa* (1741) and the Marquis de Sade's *Justine* (1791), for example. Also, one might propose another list that includes excessive commentaries such as Origen's, St. Bernard's and John of Ford's on the Song of Songs, and exorbitant works like Aquinas's *Summa theologiæ* and Karl Barth's *Church Dogmatics*, themselves vast fragments. Blanchot will tell us that the *Summa* is more a style of answering than questioning (3; 1). The point is not well made; Aquinas's questions spawn other questions, and only the fact that the *Summa* is for advanced students stops them from ramifying endlessly; it is often far from evident what Aquinas's answers will be, and some of them surprised his contemporaries. Yet even if we were to agree with him, we still might not think that the same can rightly be said of Barth's remarkable work, though for different reasons.

To attend to the "broken course" of research is to be confronted by what Blanchot calls "interrelational space" (5; 4), that of master and student. The master "represents a region of space and time that is absolutely other" (5; 5), meaning that his or her questioning comes not from an acquired body of positive knowledge but from what remains unknown and therefore strange. Teaching introduces for student and master alike "a *relation of infinity* between all things, and above all in the very speech that assumes this relation" (6; 5). Note that this relation is opened by the master's speech, not by the master as such, and as soon as the master intrudes on the scene of teaching through charisma, erudition, or prestige—in a word, by mastery—the relation closes. Presumably, from Blanchot's viewpoint, the medieval *Questiones disputatæ* would not supply good examples of this pedagogical space because each occasion is an opportunity for the master to show his mastery, if not in public debate, then in written response to debate. The infinite relation between master and student would be infinite not because it is interminable, as in Hegel's "bad infinity," or because it contains the infinite curled up within the finite, as in Hegel's "good infinity," but because it is marked by a radical discontinuity between finite terms.[16] And so the infinite relation is "the very *interruption* of relations" (6; 5). What is opened in the dissymmetric rapport between master and student, in the speech of genuine questioning, is the possibility of the "incommensurable" becoming a "measure" (6; 5), Blanchot tells us. It is hard to make decent sense of the thought, which seems nonsensical on a first reading, and its meaning will become apparent only later, in the context of ethics.

*

This speech of questioning is "always already written," Blanchot insists, by which he means that it does not derive from the idealist assumption that speech is tied to self-identity but rather contests it and, in doing so, affirms itself as "an anonymous, distracted, deferred, and dispersed way of being in relation" (xii; vii). This amounts to what he calls "first writing," something very close to *la différance*, although Blanchot wishes to keep in play speech as well as writing—hence the expression *parole d'écriture*—in order to maintain a proximity with Jewish thought.[17] At any rate, this way of being in relation "challenges the notion of being as continuity or as a unity or gathering of beings" (10; 11). The questioning that leads us to discern this infinite relation is what Blanchot calls "the most profound question," that of the neutral, which he takes to precede inquiry into being and unity. It is a question that is usually hidden by historically dominant forms of thought—Christian theology, in the main, and also Hegelian dialectic—but that starts to be posed at the change of epoch. So radical is the question that it tends to be diverted to the more usual concerns of an age. For instance, in the patristic and early medieval periods of Christianity the question of the neutral becomes confused with the question of God. The neutral relation is misidentified as the relation with the deity beyond being. And in *Sein und Zeit* (1927) the question of the neutral is mistaken for the *Seinsfrage*. Heidegger fails to distinguish cleanly between being and the neutral Outside and ends up with a neutral conception of being and not the neutral that precedes being. Now, though, in our change of epoch—*L'Entretien infini* is published, remember, in 1969, the year after *les événements de mai*—the question of the neutral is beginning to be posed more clearly, by Derrida (in the non-thought of *la différance*), by Deleuze (in a new understanding of Nietzsche's eternal return), by Levinas (in the response to *autrui*), and by several others, not the least of whom is Blanchot himself. On reading *L'Entretien infini* one cannot help but sense that Blanchot appears as the master and we readers are his students, and that he teaches us in plural speech, always and already written—published in journals then carefully (if not always fully) revised—in texts that are "nearly anonymous" (435; 637), and consequently without any need for us to see him face to face.

The nature of philosophical thinking, approached by way of teaching, can point us to the relation of the third kind. Yet the question needs to be posed with the rigor that is proper to it. The relation is "of the third kind," Blanchot thinks, because it falls outside the two usual ways of depicting a rapport. The first of these is unity achieved by dialectic, as one finds preeminently in Hegel, in which continuity is maintained by dint of *Aufhebung*. And the second is union that is attained immediately by being absorbed by the absolutely Other [*l'absolument Autre*] (66; 94), whether it be being or the One that, like Plotinus, he holds to be transcendentally prior to being.[18] It will quickly be seen that the second relation is also Hegelian insofar as it is the simple immediacy that Hegel rejects. Hegel associates this simple immediacy with feeling, not understanding, and quickly identifies the *unio mystica* with it.[19] In evoking the ecstasy of dissolution, Blanchot seems to follow Hegel in this identification, though not necessarily in identifying mystical experience and *Gefühl*, while also entertaining several other candidates for inclusion in the second relation: Bataille's notion of "the rapture of communication" (68; 96), the unity of affection promised by the *tutoiement* (77; 108), and perhaps the fascist idea of the people's sudden fusion with the State, all of which serve to eliminate distance between two or more people.

No close reading of the writings of the great Christian mystics will yield anything like simple immediacy, and historical reflection on mystical theology will conclude that, in the Latin West at least, there was little or no talk of union of being with God until the twelfth century, despite the various formulations of the *scala paradisi*. Even in the East, St. Gregory of Nyssa's remark in his commentary on the Song of Songs is characteristic: "According to the true words of the Lord (Matt. 5: 8), the pure in heart will see God. They will receive as much as their minds can comprehend. However, the unbounded, incomprehensible divinity remains beyond all understanding."[20] No union of minds is possible because we will pass into God eternally without comprehending him: such is Gregory's teaching of ἐπέκτασις. St. Bernard of Clairvaux urged the union of wills between humans and God, *unitas spiritus*, not the unity of substance. And St.

Bonaventure argued that while we can be one in affection with God our being remains distinct from his: the finite is not simply collapsed into the infinite. Therefore, in standard Christian teachings, East and West, there is no "fusion" (66; 95) of the soul with God.[21] A better example of the second relation is what Bataille calls "communication," the anguished contact made with "what we can't reach without dissolving ourselves, what's slavishly called God."[22] Union is said to happen immediately in inner experience. And so it is an atheistic modification of mysticism that allows us better to understand the second relation. Here "methods of immediation" (66; 95)—drinking alcohol, smoking, looking at photographs of a man being tortured, and techniques of yoga, all of which Bataille used at one time or another in his quest for inner experience—are in evidence, unlike in friendship, romantic love, and the ecstatic relation of people with the State in fascist politics.[23]

In general, the relations that Blanchot specifies are of two kinds, those that exhibit equivalence, and those that do not. Are there other relations of equivalence that Blanchot does not mention? There are; and he freely admits that he does not mention all of them, and that those he details are chosen "more or less arbitrarily" (66; 94), and only because they pertain to human beings. In principle, symmetrical relations $((\forall a)(\forall b), aRb \longrightarrow bRa)$ could be considered, although Blanchot would doubtless object that they reduce the otherness of the other person, and the same objection would hold with respect to transitive relations $((\forall a)(\forall b)(\forall c) (aRb \ \& \ bRc) \longrightarrow aRc))$. Set theory is evidently of limited use here, although it is not unreasonable to appeal to it since, as we shall see, Blanchot himself gestures to differential geometry in his presentation of the third relation. Putting such considerations aside for the moment, it needs to be said that it is odd that Blanchot makes no mention of analogical relations between people, or between human beings and God, since, on both sides of the channel, it is a widely accepted part of the discussion of the problem of other minds and central to debate in the philosophy of religion.[24] Analogy need not reduce the other to the same in all respects. It certainly does not do so in the analogy between human beings and God: as Aquinas points out, our knowledge of God's being goes by way of "knowing *what it is not*."[25] Nor does Husserl think that the other person is simply a modification of myself; he or she will be "an appresented Ego" but will nonetheless remain "an *other* Ego" whose alterity is retained and respected.[26] More generally, and in terms that Husserl does not use, the other person's uniqueness is not compromised by the claim that he or she is relatively singular (i.e., the singularity in question is relative to the category of being human, as well as to Aristotle's ten categories). And without a notion of relative singularity the concept of another human being would be unintelligible. At any rate, Blanchot does not multiply versions of the relation of the first kind, and we have no choice it seems but to turn directly to his formulation of the relation of the third kind.

And yet there is reason to pause, for both before and after "Le rapport du troisième genre" Blanchot speaks of two relations, not three. In a review of Dionys Mascolo's *Le Communisme: révolution et communication ou la dialectique des valeurs et des besoins* (1953) he tells of there being "two lives that we must try to live together, though they are irreconcilable."[27] (We are bound to recall *Thomas l'Obscur*.) In one life we limit ourselves "to the form of the simplest needs" and all values are converted into needs. "This means that in collective relations we should have no other existence but the one that makes possible the movement by which the man of need is brought to power."[28] Another life

> is the life of relations that are called private: here, we have no need to wait nor are we able to wait. Here, it would seem that out of desire, passion, the exaltation of extreme states, and also through speech, *man can become the impossible friend of man, his relation to the latter being precisely with the impossible*: sufficiency is shattered, communication is no longer that of separated beings who promise each other a recognition in the infinitely distant future of a world without separation (95–6; 112).

Whether Blanchot was aware of it or not, his distinction recalls a well-known contrast drawn by St. Augustine in a sermon delivered in 418, most likely in Carthage. "There are two kinds of life; one involved with delight, the other with need. The one involved with need is toilsome, the one involved with delight is delicious."[29] That Blanchot puts the distinction to a new use is evident, and that St. Augustine will return in Blanchot's work is perhaps expected.

Later, in 1971, Blanchot will revise this formulation of the two lives, expressing doubt over the distinction between collective and private relations, and saying, "In both cases, is it not a question of relations that could not be those of a subject to an object, nor even of a subject to a subject, but relations in which the relationship of the one to the other affirms itself as infinite or discontinuous?" (296 n. 3; 112 n. 1). Here, it seems, the original distinction gives way to the third relation, although the second term of the original distinction seems more like the third relation than the first does. Nor is this the only departure from the program of "Le rapport du troisième genre." In *Le Pas au-delà* (1973) we are told that, "it is easy to recognize in man he who is always himself and the other, the happy duality of dialogue and the possibility of communication."[30] And in *L'Écriture du désastre* (1980) we are reminded that, "there must always be at least two languages, or two requirements: one dialectical, the other not; one where negativity is the task, the other where the neutral remains apart, cut off both from being and from not-being."[31] In both later texts the second relation has dropped out entirely. Perhaps Blanchot decided that "communication" does not result in unity after all.

At any rate, the governing intention of the third and final formulation in "Le rapport du troisième genre" is "to try to think the Other, try to speak in referring to the Other without reference to the One and without reference to the Same" (67; 95). No attempt is made to disguise the radical nature of the claim: the two partners in dialogue realize that they are "going to become guilty of a parricide—one in regard to which Plato's would be an act of pious filiation" (67; 95). The allusion is to *Sophist* 241d where the Eleatic Stranger asks Theatetus not to think that he is turning into "a sort of parricide" by contending forcibly "that after a fashion not-being is and on the other hand in a sense being is not."[32] Given Blanchot's admiration for Levinas, it is no surprise to learn that Blanchot's reference also goes by way of *Totalité et infini*, where it is declared, "Being is produced as multiple and as split into same and other; this is its ultimate structure. It is society, and hence it is time. We thus leave the philosophy of Parmenidean being."[33] For Blanchot and Levinas alike, the parricide is not just of Father Parmenides but of all philosophers of the One, and of unity and being, beginning with one of the most recent, Husserl, the father of phenomenology, in whose language Blanchot casts the assault, perhaps because in his mind it has made the assault possible in the first place.[34]

*

Two related claims are urged. First, the other human being is to be thought without reference to any horizon, whether it is that of the One, Being, or "the unity of being" (67; 95). And second, the other person is not to be constituted within my horizon or even within a horizon that he or she projects. "The Other: not only does he not fall within my horizon, he is himself without horizon" (69; 98). It will quickly be seen that the first claim is the more extreme and the less plausible. There may be reasons why we should not construe the other person wholly in terms of being but rather as an interruption of being, although the notion needs to be clarified and the reasons examined. Yet it is far more difficult to accept as even minimally intelligible the proposition that the other person is not answerable to unity in any way. Even if we were to agree that the other person does not have a unity of substance there would still be a reason to retain unity as a horizon, as the condition of possibility for him or her to appear in the first place and for us to be able to recognize him or her.

Consider the two parts of the second claim. The first is that the other person does not fall within my horizon. Now other people, like everything else in the world, can and do appear within my intentional horizon, and when they appear they are phenomena. The objection to this state of affairs is not descriptive but normative, namely, Levinas's insistence that the irreducibility of the other person to a phenomenon ought to be required as a fundamental presupposition of ethics. In order to give philosophical weight to this normative judgment Levinas has recourse to Descartes's argument in the third of the *Meditations on First Philosophy* that infinity precedes the finite in consciousness.[35] Moved by "metaphysical desire" we are fundamentally oriented toward the other person: such is *Totalité et infini* when stripped down to its most basic structure. Several years later, Levinas will propose that we have a non-intentional psyche behind consciousness, and that this psyche guarantees that the call of the other person will be heard, despite the power of intentionality to determine the meaning of things in the world. Such is the structural change made in *Autrement qu'être* (1978), in part as a reply to the criticisms of *Totalité et infini* ventured by Blanchot and Derrida, and in part as a positive response to the material phenomenology of Michel Henry.[36]

The second part of the second claim is that the other person does not have a horizon. When Husserl talks in the first volume of *Ideas* of the fringe, limit, or horizon, *der Horizont*, he has in mind a "*horizon of indeterminate actuality, a horizon of which I am dimly conscious*," and is thinking primarily of visual perception.[37] As he goes on to say,

> a mental process which has become an Object of an Ego-regard, which therefore has the mode of being made an object of regard, has its horizon of unregarded mental processes; a mental process seized upon in a mode of 'attention' and possibly in unceasing clarity, has a horizon of inattention in the background with relative differences of clarity and obscurity as well as salientness and lack of salientness (§ 83).

Here, horizon and phenomenality are co-ordinate notions for Husserl, "horizon" being for him the limit of perception, and "phenomenality" no more than the ability of an object to manifest itself in one or more regions of being. According to Husserl, we apprehend an object in "the *stream of mental processes as a unity*" (§ 83). Things are different with Heidegger, for whom phenomenality is the beingness of being, understood as the right and power of something to show itself from itself in its proper mode of presentation.[38] "Horizon," in *Sein und Zeit*, denotes the temporality of being, while in Heidegger's lectures on Nietzsche it specifies the range of possibilities open to human beings by way of their given perspectives.[39] It is with the disputation of all these things in mind that Blanchot, in "Parler, ce n'est pas voir," proposes to prize speech over sight, because, as he says, "It is still true that sight holds us within the limits of a horizon" (28; 40).[40]

One may well pause to wonder whether the change of one theoretical sense over another is sufficient to call unity into question.[41] After all, why should hearing a sentence differ, in terms of apprehending a unity, from seeing a person? If the point of prizing hearing over seeing is to put pressure on unity, one would have to do more than elevate a unity of stages over a unity of parts. But this is the wrong way to approach the issue. Blanchot's point, I take it, is that the other person has no unity in an ethical rather than a metaphysical sense: I am obliged to help the other person not because of anything that makes him or her one and the same—*a* being or a *being*—but simply because I am called upon to help. Just as it does not matter whether the other person is Edward who is thirty-nine and lives in special accommodation in south-east Washington, DC, or Julie who is sixty-seven and sleeps on the streets of Philadelphia, so too it does not matter who is being called upon to help. I am not hailed because I am Kevin Hart, the one and the only, but because I am the first person on the scene when help is needed. In being called upon by the other person, who impinges on me without a horizon of unity because the call is ethical, my sense of personal uniqueness is lost in the interest—or, better, disinterest—of ethics. The encounter with the other person can be said to be marked by strangeness precisely because it is not a meeting between two identifiable individuals, each secure in their sense of unique selfhood. Blanchot will say that the meeting is impersonal, and he is right insofar as it does not matter ethically if it is me or someone else who helps the other person; and yet it must be said that as soon as I begin to do something the encounter is personal. In *L'Écriture du désastre* Blanchot will point out that the other person and I each lends ourselves to unity, to the extent that each of us gives the impression of being singular and irreplaceable (13; 28).[42] This is what he calls a "'false' unity" (2; 8); it is called into play only in order to help us indirectly challenge the rule of unity and the One, which is done in the human relation rather than in elaborating an alternative to metaphysics. Yet "'false' unity" or even unity has a way of reasserting itself.

*

"Man without horizon" would be given to me only in speech, Blanchot thinks, and this speech would interrupt the continuity and unity of my being. If one hears these words in context, one will think of Derrida, and rightly so. One recalls his early stress on the priority of *archi-écriture* with respect to *écriture*.[43] But if one hears them obliquely, at the very edge of their context, one could be forgiven for thinking it is Blanchot, not Marion, who is seeking to turn Husserl away from the object as phenomenon, and to deflect Heidegger away from being as the true concern of phenomenology, in order to make them recognize the priority of givenness. One might think it is Blanchot, not Marion, who seeks to erase the horizon from phenomenology because the horizon modifies what gives itself.[44] Yet one will also tell oneself that the givenness that Blanchot prizes is not that of saturated phenomena, at least not in the terms that Marion uses to describe them, but that of the neutral that impinges on one in and through the other person.[45] Of course, Marion does not have the unity of being his primary target. And yet unity is rendered questionable in saturated phenomena in which, for example, an event is not limited to "an instant, a place, or an empirical individual, but overflows these singularities and . . . covers a physical space such that no gaze encompasses it with one sweep."[46]

Nor does Marion doubt the reality of God, although he does not conceive the deity within the horizon of being understood as *ens* or finite being. His concern is to query the priority of being with respect to what Husserl calls "the givenness of a reduced phenomenon" [*die Gegebenheit eines reduzierten Phänomens*].[47] Similarly, it may be said that Marion affirms the visual in a way that Blanchot does not: interested in icons as they both are, they nonetheless diverge in that the one is taken with the divine gaze and the other with a dark gaze.[48] Furthermore, unlike Blanchot, Marion sometimes talks of multiplying horizons, not erasing them. For all that, one should be readily and fully forgiven for hearing the words "man without horizon" as though they directed us to what gives itself. For both Blanchot and Marion attend to what is exceptional with respect to the history of metaphysics: the one to what he calls the neutral, the other to what he calls saturated phenomena. And in responding to what gives itself each writer finds that he has to revise the philosophy of the subject that he has inherited from Descartes. Blanchot finds that the "I" is gently turned aside into a "one" or a "no one," and Marion discovers that the subject receives himself only from what is given to him, changing his status from subject to *l'adonné*.

What comes to us in the experience of language, according to Blanchot, is mystery. We should not let "mystery" make us think of the ineffability of the divine but let it evoke something between two words as Heidegger uses them, *Unheimlichkeit* and *Geheimnis*, the former meaning a feeling of the uncanny and the latter suggesting an openness to the mystery of being. This mystery or strangeness is not experienced in the sense of *Erlebnis* because it is not a phenomenon but is encountered in the mode of non-experience. Blanchot tells us that non-experience shares the same defining trait as experience, and in the pursuit of his own conclusions Marion will add that what gives itself comes to us in the mode of counter-experience.[49] One's attempts to process the excess of intuition over intentionality into firm experience and then hard knowledge are disappointed not only in extraordinary moments (e.g., encountering the risen Christ) but also in the banal moments of everyday life.[50]

For Blanchot, the strangeness that conducts the advent of the other person is, we might say, a phenomenality without phenomenon. The other person does not dazzle me, as an idol would, although his or her coming is unforeseeable, does not depend on a horizon, and cannot be borne. In *Au Moment voulu* (1951) the neutral approaches the narrator when he bumps into a wall and feels,

> une violence horrible, une abomination, d'autant plus intolérable qu'elle semblait m'atteindre à travers une couche fabuleuse de durée qui brûlait tout entière en moi, immense et unique douleur, comme si je n'avais pas été touché à ce moment, mais il y a siècles et depuis des siècles, et ce qu'elle avait de révolu, de tout à fait mort, pouvait bien la rendre plus facile mais aussi plus difficile à supporter, en faisant d'elle une persévérance absolument froide, impersonnelle, qu n'arrêtait ni la vie, ni la fin de la vie.

> [a horrible violence, an atrocity, all the more intolerable because it seemed to come to me across a fantastic layer of time, burning in its entirety inside me, an immense and unique pain, as though I had not been touched at this moment but centuries ago and for centuries past, and the quality it had of being sometimes finished, something completely dead, could certainly make it easier to bear but also harder, by turning it into a perseverance that was absolutely cold, impersonal, that would not be stopped either by life or by the end of life.] [51]

And in *Celui qui ne m'accompaignait pas* (1953) the neutral leaks through a chance word:

> quelque chose de tout autre, à travers cette parole, s'était fait jour, avait cherché une issue, quelque chose de plus ancien, d'effroyablement ancien, qui avait peut-être même lieu en tout temps, et en tout temps j'étais cloué sur place.

> [something quite different had come to light through this remark, had sought a way out, something older, dreadfully old, which had perhaps taken place at all times, and at all times I was tied to the spot].[52]

In both cases, we passively witness the eternal return of what was at best a limit-phenomenon, and yet it has a powerful and terrible phenomenality.

Unlike Marion, Blanchot rarely talks about the phenomenological reduction, and when he does it is with a twist. Consider the following fragment from *Le Pas au-delà*: "The certainty that in writing he was putting between parentheses precisely this certainty, including the certainty of himself as the subject of writing, led him slowly, though right away, into an empty space ..."[53] At other times, he summons the reduction in a way that is not all that far from Marion's "third reduction." For Marion, the third reduction, in which phenomena are led back to the givenness that precedes their showing, is precipitated by deep boredom, *Langeweile*. Marion's reduction takes its cue from Heidegger's *Gestimmtheit* or attunement and his coinage *Befindlichkeit*, the state of finding oneself in a situation and in the mood appropriate to it. Deep boredom, for Marion as for Heidegger, sharply reveals to me that I am in the world because all my usual concerns and comforts no longer have the power to distract me from my existential situation. For Heidegger, *Langeweile* attunes me to being, while for Marion, it exposes me to the call of givenness that is otherwise blocked by the call of being.⁵⁴ Now Blanchot, like Heidegger, turns away from any methodological reflections on the reduction; yet he too appeals indirectly to it.⁵⁵ The *Befindlichkeit* in question is the state of suffering, fatigue, or affliction when there is no relief in sight. "What has happened?" he asks. "Suffering has simply lost its hold on time, and has made us lose time." We are led elsewhere, "delivered over to another time—to time as other, as absence and neutrality; precisely to a time that can no longer redeem us, that constitutes no recourse. A time without event, without project, without possibility" (44; 63). Reflecting on what has occurred, Blanchot says, "it is not beyond the trial of experience, but rather that trial from which we can no longer escape. An experience that one will represent to oneself as being strange and even as the experience of strangeness [*l'expérience de l'étrangeté*]" (45; 63). Suffering is not *Erlebnis*, nor is it a non-experience in the sense that we are not exposed to peril; on the contrary, it contains the defining trait of experience, namely that very exposure to danger.

The phenomenality involved in this experience of strangeness does not come from any transcendence, whether in the religious or phenomenological sense of the word. Levinas will use Wahl's neologism "transascendance" to denote the peculiar nature of the height of *autrui*, an elevation that calls forth in me metaphysical desire for the other person, a desire without concupiscence, and Blanchot will quietly take over its sense before adapting it.⁵⁶ Yet Wahl's companion word "transdescendance" is also appropriate to Blanchot. When placed in the neighborhood of his thought, it indicates that which comes from beneath phenomena, as it were, from a stagnant realm of image that cannot be shaken from phenomena, and that breaks into the world of sense and meaning through the attunement of suffering, fatigue, or affliction, disorienting us, and in doing so demoting the "I" from its status as a constituting subject to a bare witness of what is occurring.⁵⁷ If we find Marion and Blanchot talking in almost the same words here, it is because each, in his own way, has stretched phenomenality beyond what Husserl and Heidegger have made of it. It is a power of manifestation that precedes showing, exceeds objects and even being, and belongs properly to givenness, although Blanchot and Marion differ in their thinking of what is given. The more phenomenality is stretched, whether from object to what gives or from the object to what approaches from the Outside, the more pressure is put on unity. Looking at Blanchot and Marion from a distance, we find them standing with their backs to one another, the one thinking the third relation and the other the third reduction, the one attending to a realm of phenomena richer than usual, and the other preoccupied by a ghostly realm that is infinitely poorer than phenomena, the one embracing the Catholic faith and the other endorsing an implacable atheism.

Readers of Marion's *Étant donné* (1997) will note that from time to time he has recourse to a strange syntax, "X without X," and that this phrasing occurs when he is confronted by the phenomenality of givenness that is in excess of that of poor phenomena such as numbers as well as of common phenomena such as pens and pencils. He will speak of "the present without presence" [*la présent sans la présence*] (79; 115), "gift without giver" [*un don sans donateur*] (100; 144) and "origin without origin" [*origine sans origine*] (174; 245). In the same way but inversely, because he is responding to a poverty that empties us of the power to say "I," Blanchot conceives of the man without horizon as "a being without being, a presence without a present [*être sans être et présence sans présent*]"(69; 98). It is this peculiar syntax, long familiar to readers of Blanchot, which comes to the fore in the discussion of the third relation. I take it that it is Blanchot himself who appears at the end of the discussion as the "*true interlocutor*" of the weary conversationalists and that he is the one who calls the relation "the neutral relation" or "the relation without relation [*le rapport sans rapport*]" (73; 104). Wherever it appears, this peculiar syntax calls for clarification, and a part of that clarification is the indication of heritage.

*

Anyone who points us to *Totalité et infini* as a source for the expression will surely have good reason to do so. Listen to Levinas: "For the relation between the being here below and the transcendent being that results in no community of concept or totality—a relation without relation [*relation sans relation*]—we reserve the term religion."[58] Note that for Levinas there is no continuous or immediate rapport between human beings and God, not the slightest trace of mysticism. We are in relation with God only indirectly, and that happens when we respond here and now to the call of the widow, the stranger, or the orphan. Here, then, the "*X* without *X*" syntax indicates a deflection from divine transcendence and secures the ethical primacy of what Levinas prescriptively calls "religion." Yet it is possible for exactly the same syntax to embrace transcendence instead of recoiling from it, and that has been its traditional function in Christianity. Severus, bishop of Milev, told St. Augustine in Letter 109 that we are to love God in a special way: *modus sine modo* was his phrase, for which he may well have been indebted to Augustine in the first place.[59] We should love God in a measure without measure, he says, a scale without scale, a way without a way: in a word, we should love God without limit.

As already noted in the introduction, Augustine had already used a similar phrasing in his *The Literal Meaning of Genesis* when he praised God as "Measure without measure . . . Number without number . . . Weight without weight" [*mensura sine mensura . . . numerus sine numero . . . pondus sine pondere*], the *X* without *X* syntax serving as a figure of transcendence and ineffability.[60] Yet when Severus uses the same syntax it is not to evoke transcendence but to characterize how we love God. Accordingly, depending on the context, the "*X* without *X*" syntax can be put to quite different ends. It can indicate that God, as absolutely singular being, falls outside the ten categories, and therefore cannot be measured with respect to them. In this way it is a metaphor of transcendence. Also, though, it can indicate a mustering of all one's powers, animated by a renovated *imago dei*, to love without limit, and here it is appropriate for a creature that is subject to the categories. In the latter sense, the syntax informs the traditional answer of how we are to love God, as distinct from what God has created. St. Bernard of Clairvaux, for one, declares at the beginning of his *De diligendo deo* that we are to love God *modus sine modo*.[61] Yet St. Bonaventure in his *De Mysterio Trinitatis* also uses the same expression to mean the unlimited nature of the divine immensity.[62] Aquinas uses the expression in his commentary on Peter Lombard's *Sententiæ*, and, more interestingly, in the *Summa theologiæ* by way of glossing St. Bernard's use of *modus sine modo*. On Aquinas's reading, the point of the syntax is to say, "the more we love, the better we love."⁶³ No measure is appropriate to love given that the end in view is God. The thought of loving God *modus sine modo* amounts to the First Great Commandment (Matt. 32: 37–8).

I do not know how finely Blanchot was aware of the theological history of the "*X* without *X*" syntax, or if he reinvented the syntax in the 1940s, although when he talks of the human relation as "another modality (without a mode)" [*une autre modalité (sans mode)*] (77; 108) the echo of Severus, Bernard, and Bonaventure seems too strong to discount. It is evident that Blanchot keeps both of the expression's possible senses in play while nonetheless directing them to human rather than divine ends. On the one hand, the Outside escapes the categories not because it is divine but because it exhibits transdescendance. Here the second *X* evacuates the first *X* of whatever intuition to which it lays claim, and the syntax performs the act of writing *sous rature*. On the other hand, my relation with another person, not God, is not one to which I can prescribe a limit in advance; it is excessive. *Autrui* speaks to me from a height of transascendance, as Levinas says, even though Blanchot insists that this speech comes to me through an experience of strangeness, of the other being without horizon and the "I" denuded of uniqueness. Whatever theological heritage there is in Blanchot's talk of the relation without relation passes, however, through Heidegger as well as Levinas, as should already be evident in the style and tone of the conversation that Blanchot hosts, recalling, as it does, "A Dialogue on Language" and talk of "staying on the path . . . unswerving, yet erring."⁶⁴ In his lecture "Hölderlin's Earth and Heaven" (1959), Heidegger listens with care to a fragment by the poet, sometimes called ". . . Der Vatikan. . .," especially the lines "really / whole relation, including the center" [*wirklich / Ganzem Verhältnis, samt der Mitt*], which he interprets by referring to Hölderlin's essay "On Religion" (1797?).⁶⁵ There, earth and heaven, and the connection between them, form the "more tender infinite relation."⁶⁶

"Infinite," here, as Heidegger says, recalls the "speculative dialectic of Schelling and Hegel," and then he adds,

> In-finite means that the ends and the sides, the regions of the relation, do not stand by themselves cut off and one-sidedly; rather, freed of one-sidedness and finitude, they belong *in*-finitely to one another in the relation which "thoroughly" holds them together from its center. The center, so called because it centers, that is, mediates, is neither earth nor heaven, God nor man. The in-infinity that is to be thought here is abysmally different from that which is merely without end, which, because of its uniformity, allows no growth. On the other hand, the "more tender relation" of earth and heaven, God and man, can become more in-finite. For what is not one-sided can come more purely to light from the intimacy in which the named four are bound to each other. (188)

We see here the transformation of the infinite relation into the *Geviert* or Fourfold. Several pages later, Heidegger takes the transformation as given: "What comes is the whole in-finite relation in which, along with god and mankind, earth and heaven belong" (200). So the infinite relation becomes a metaphor of what Heidegger had already explored in "The Thing" (1950); it exemplifies the step back from a metaphysical to a post-metaphysical thinking, from representing things as *res* to contemplating them as a gathering of earth and heaven, gods and mortals. Yet where Heidegger wishes to replace the unity of self-identity with gathering, Blanchot proposes to go in another direction, that of ethics, and, in time, leave unity altogether behind.[67] Oddly enough, for someone who has closely followed Heidegger's path of thought, he draws on modern science as well as modern art for support.

Schönberg, Worringer, and Klee all contest the unity of the artwork, Blanchot notes in "Ars Nova" (1963), and then reminds us that science teaches that the universe is curved, perhaps not with a positive curvature, which would give it the form of a sphere, but with a negative curvature, yielding "a Universe escaping every optical exigency and also escaping considerations of the whole—essentially non-finite, disunited, discontinuous" (350; 514). Faced with this surprising reality, one that jolts us just as much if not more than when our ancestors were shaken by the Copernican revolution, human beings would have to take "the measure of an exteriority that is not divine, of a space entirely in question, and even excluding the possibility of an answer" (350; 514). We would be confronted with a measure without measure, exactly as was adumbrated in the discussion of master and student, an Outside in which "unity" (and hence "universe") makes no sense. Blanchot departs from Heidegger in naturalizing the third relation. At the same time, he does not affirm a change from *res* to relations but rather to the *interruption* of relations. The two differences are bound together in his formulation of the third relation, in the moment when the master appears at the table, having been listening to the two voices, and surprises us in his confession of lack of mastery. He is "*neither close to the one, nor close to the other; being, nevertheless, one of them and being the other only insofar as I am not me*" (72; 103). His pedagogy has consisted only in interrupting himself to the extent that he is a "self." Nonetheless, like a good teacher, he steps back from all the positions that have been raised and summarizes what has been most instructive.

Four points are made, and I would like to look closely at the third, in which the naturalization of the third relation continues. The process will continue further, for, following a hint from Valéry, Blanchot develops an even more suggestive mathematical analogy for written speech in the following conversation, "L'interruption: *Comme sur une surface de Riemann*." Blanchot recapitulates as follows:

> *The neutral relation, a relation without relation, can be indicated in yet another manner: the relation of the one to the other is doubly dissymmetrical.* We have recognized this several times. We know—at least we sense—that the absence between the one and the other is such that the relations, if they could be unfolded, would be those of a non-isomorphic field in which point A would be distant from point B by a distance other than point B's distance from point A; a distance excluding reciprocity and presenting a curvature whose irregularity extends to the point of discontinuity. (73; 104)

With the word "discontinuity" we are directed to an endnote that helps us to interpret the passage by way of ethics and not, as we might have expected, to a discussion of fields without relation-preserving isomorphisms. The mathematical metaphor, it seems, is drawn from Levinas who uses it in *Totalité et infini* in a deformalized manner to indicate that intersubjective space is curved upward toward the other person. The claim is not merely a consequence of there being different points of view, Levinas warns, but of "the surplus of truth over being" (291; 324). That is, the elevation of the other person with respect to me cannot be mapped onto my elevation with respect to him or her. This original "'curvature of space,'" Levinas says, "is, perhaps, the very presence of God."[68]

Blanchot will reject the asymmetry at issue here because of this reference to the presence of the divine. The oddity of a curvature being a mode of presence will perhaps make us think that the divine presence occurs as a mode without a mode, leaving only a trace. Such would be Levinas's point, albeit expressed here with reference to St. Augustine and the tradition that comes from him. For his part, Blanchot insists that the human relation is "devoid of religion" and tolerates no mention of the gods (59; 84), let alone God; and his reason would presumably be because the human relation occurs in an ethical space where all unity has been compromised. Yet if one believes in God, this reason will hardly dissuade one from continuing in that belief. It is perfectly consistent to maintain that God exists and that the call of the other person undoes my claim to uniqueness. To which one may add the important point that it is only the initial call for help that evacuates me of my sense of being a singular being. For the one who gives help concretely in the world is someone with a history and a social identity, as is the one who receives that help. If this criticism pushes Blanchot toward a more reasonable position than he seems to allow, it will also be noticed that in dismissing asymmetry he makes Levinas's ethics appear more reasonable. For the most common stumbling block encountered when reading *Totalité et infini* is the heavy stress that ethics is unilateral and not contractual, singular and not universal: we cannot expect the other person to act with regard to us as we do toward him or her. Accordingly, Blanchot speaks of a double dissymmetry in which each person is the other of the other, neither claiming to exist independently of the other or the relation between them. The dissymmetry does not flatten out ethical space; on the contrary, it introduces another non-isomorphic relation, for now my elevation with respect to the other person cannot be mapped onto his or her relation with me, while his or her elevation with respect to me still cannot be mapped onto my relation with him or her. By the same token, Blanchot does not propose that in some cases one dissymmetry goes higher or lower than the other; it is the human, he thinks, that prompts talk of dissymmetry, not cultural distinctions adopted by men and women.

In dismissing Levinas's sense of asymmetry Blanchot also breaks with a well-known Christian account of it, and in seeing what he rejects, whether knowingly or not, we can also begin to place his project in perspective. Aquinas argues that the relations between God and Creation are not at all the same as those between creation and God. Our relations with God are real, *relatio realis*, as we saw in Chapter 2; we depend ontologically on him. Yet God's relations with us are merely relative, *relatio rationis tantum*; his being does not depend on us.[69] The divine love for created beings is wholly free and without self-interest, for God gains no perfections by either the act of creation or the sustaining of creation. On this understanding of creation, we can distinguish between God and the universe: notions of same and other play roles within the universe, but God, who transcends the universe, cannot be figured as "other" in the sense in which everything that is not me is other. Not at all: God would be other than us in a sense that is beyond Aristotle's and Kant's categories of relation.[70] As glimpsed earlier, the divine alterity converges with God's absolute singularity. We cannot know God because God is pure subsistent *esse*, not *ens*, and we have no thoroughgoing idea what this *esse* is.[71] While it would be inaccurate to say that *esse* is an interruption of being since *esse* precedes and preserves *ens*, it would be true to say that it is discontinuous with it. It is not the same sort of discontinuity that Blanchot proposes, however: for Aquinas it is a break between *esse* and *ens*, while for Blanchot it is a rupture between being and ethics. Nonetheless, the thought allows us to keep the two thinkers together for a moment.

Blanchot's claim is that God—presumably, he means the concept of God—derives from the One. Yet there is reason for anyone who follows Aquinas to doubt that this is so. For we cannot predicate unity of God in the same way that we can predicate it of anything in the universe. As pure subsistent *esse*, and therefore absolutely singular, God's unity is unlike any other unity in creation. We have no metaphysical entitlement to say that God is both one and triune—that judgment relies entirely on revelation—but we have no metaphysical barrier that forbids us to predicate both unity and multiplicity of God. The revelation of divine trinity should not surprise us if we accept Aquinas's metaphysics of God's being. When we look at Blanchot's case against unity, we see that it consists of an initial ethical interruption of ontology: I and the other person both lose our sense of unity, and yet we regain it to some extent in the very exercise of morality, in my giving help to the other person. In the loss of that sense of unity, I may experience (without *Erlebnis*) the approach of the Outside; and yet that nonevent has no power to make me doubt the reality of God whose being precedes the formation of ethical space. Indeed, I may well say that my relations with God are double, being concerned with daily actions of goodness and moments of adoration that break with the practice and limits of everyday life. No doubt of it, my relation with God will differ from my relation with another person. Even if the other person is the Most High, as Blanchot would say, he or she is not the absolutely singular God. In each case, however, the encounter will initially strip me of my uniqueness. Blanchot will cite the call to ethical action; and the Christian will speak, instead, of stripping himself of the old man in Adam in order to put on the new man in Christ. For Blanchot, although he does not draw attention to it, my uniqueness will return to me in ordinary commerce with the other person; and for the Christian, God will be in relation with *me*, a unique historical individual in need of salvation.

Does the double dissymmetry of the third relation point toward a nontheological future, as Blanchot thinks it does? In their different ways Levinas and Marion have helped us to see that it does not do so by itself. One would already have to be an atheist, on other grounds, to take the third relation as consistent with a nontheological world. If one believes in God, then the third relation appears only as a displaced Christian idea that we are to love God *modus sine modo*, with all our hearts and minds, not in the relation between a human being and God but solely in the relation between two human beings. The Christian who reads Blanchot has a disconcerting, double experience. At first one encounters an atheist of high moral stature, an example of *homo humanus* at his most impressive, and then one finds in his discourse the terms of the religious tradition that he contests and finds oneself being taught obliquely what one learned elsewhere, and what Blanchot most certainly does not want to teach.

Notes

1. Gottlieb Leibniz, *Discourse on Metaphysics, Correspondence with Arnauld, Monadology*, intro. Paul Janet (La Salle: Open Court Publishing, 1973), 191.
2. Plotinus, *Enneads*, 7 vols., trans. A. H. Armstrong, Loeb Classical Library (Cambridge, MA: Harvard University Press, 1988), vol. 7, 6. 9. 1.
3. Aristotle, *Metaphysics*, trans. Hugh Tredennick and G. Cyril Armstrong, Loeb Classical Library, 2 vols. (Cambridge, MA: Harvard University Press, 1935), vol. 2, 10. 2. 1054a 9–18.
4. Plato, *The Republic*, Plato 6, trans. Paul Shorey, Loeb Classical Library (Cambridge, MA: Harvard University Press, 1935), 525a.
5. Aquinas notes, "for unity follows being" in his *Commentary on Aristotle's "De Anima."* trans. Knelm Forster and Silvester Humphries, intro. Ralph McInerny (Notre Dame: Dumb Ox Books, 1994), vol. 2, 1. 234.
6. Plotinus, *Ennead* 6. 9. 5. 31–3.
7. Plato, *Cratylus, Parmenides, Greater Hippias, Lesser Hippias*, Plato 4, rev. ed., trans. H. N. Fowler, Loeb Classical Library (Cambridge, MA: Harvard University Press, 1939), *Parmenides*, 141e. Of course, the statement is contradicted in the second hypothesis.
8. See *Proclus' Commentary on Plato's "Parmenides,"* trans. Glenn R. Morrow and John M. Dillon, trans. and notes John M. Dillon (Princeton, NJ: Princeton University Press, 1987), 581. Alain Badiou will later multiply senses of "one." See his *Being and Event*, trans. Oliver Feltham (London: Continuum, 2005), 89.
9. See Pseudo-Dionysius Areopagite, *The Divine Names*, 4. 3. 697 a, 18. 716 a, 19. 716 c-d, in *The Divine Names and Mystical Theology*, trans. and intro. John D. Jones (Milwaukee: Marquette University Press, 1980), and St. Thomas Aquinas, *Truth*, 3 vols., vol. 3, q. 21 art. 5, reply.
10. See Marion, "St. Thomas Aquinas and Ontotheology," in *Mystics: Aporia and Presence*, ed. Michael A. Kessler and Christian Sheppard (Chicago, IL: Chicago University Press, 2003), 38–75.
11. Blanchot, *IC*, xiv (x).
12. Valéry, "Voltaire," in *Masters and Friends*, trans. Martin Turnell, intro. Joseph Frank, The Collected Works of Paul Valéry, vol. 9, 143.
13. Husserl, *Ideas for a Pure Phenomenology and a Phenomenological Philosophy*, 1: *General Introduction to Pure Phenomenology*, trans. Daniel O. Dahlstrom (Indianapolis: Hackett Publishing Co., 2014), § 84. I owe the word "deflect" in this context to Stanley Cavell.
14. Blanchot, *IC*, 6–7 (6).
15. See Blanchot, *IC*, 9 (9–10). He speaks of "saying everything" in various places. See, for example, *BC*, 45, 63, 122, 205 (64, 89, 166–7, 279).
16. See Hegel, *Lectures on the Philosophy of Religion*, ed. Peter Hodgson, 3 vols., vol. 2: *Determinate Religion*, trans. R. F. Brown, et al. (Berkeley, CA: University of California Press, 1987), 258.
17. See my discussion of first and second writing in *The Dark Gaze*, 177. Plainly, Blanchot must overcome a very strong emphasis in Judaism on unity, as is evident in the Shema. Yet he argues for dialogue rather than monotheism as Judaism's gift to the West. See *IC*, 127 (187).
18. See Blanchot, *IC*, 433 (635).
19. See Hegel, *Lectures on the Philosophy of Religion*, vol. 1, 444–5.

20 St. Gregory of Nyssa, *Commentary on the Song of Songs*, trans. and intro. Casimir McCambley (Brookline, MA: Hellenic College Press, 1987), 161.
21 See Bernard McGinn, "Love, Knowledge, and Mystical Union in Western Christianity: Twelfth to Sixteenth Century," *Church History* 56, no. 1 (1987): 7–24. I am indebted to McGinn's article. Blanchot talks of "mystical fusion" in *WD*, 24 (44).
22 Bataille, *Guilty*, trans. Bruce Boone, intro. Denis Hollier (Venice, CA: The Lapis Press, 1988), 139 (*Oeuvre complètes*, vol. 5, 388). Bataille's sneering adverb ("slavishly") is unfortunate. Earlier, Blanchot endorsed Bataille's limit-experience without qualification. See his essay "Inner Experience," in *PF*, 37–41 (47–52).
23 See, for example, Bataille, *Inner Experience*, trans. and intro. Leslie Anne Boldt (Albany: State University of New York Press, 1988), 15 (*OC*, 5, 28). Yet it should be added that Bataille's raptures were sometimes spontaneous. See *Inner Experience*, 34 (*OC*, 5, 46).
24 Yet, at the time when Blanchot was writing the pieces that compose *EI*, analogical explanations in the problem of other minds were in low repute, mainly owing to Wittgenstein's response to the problem in his *Philosophical Investigations* (1953).
25 See Aquinas, *Summa contra Gentiles*, 5 vols., trans., intro. and notes, Anton C. Pegis (1955 rpt; Notre Dame: Notre Dame University Press, 1975), vol. 1. 14. 2.
26 Husserl, *Cartesian Meditations: An Introduction to Phenomenology*, trans. Dorion Cairns (The Hague: Martinus Nijhoff, 1977), 116. The point is made by Derrida in his "Violence and Metaphysics," *Writing and Difference*, 123 (180–1). Yet see Husserl, *First Philosophy*, 619 n. 2.
27 Blanchot's review appeared in *Nouvelle Nouvelle Revue Française*, 12 (1953), and was reprinted in *AM*, 109–14.
28 Blanchot, "On One Approach to Communism," *F*, 95 (112).
29 St. Augustine, Sermon 255, *Sermons*, vol. 3: 6, *Sermons on the Liturgical Seasons* (230–272B), trans. and notes Edmund Hill, ed. John E. Rotelle, The Works of Saint Augustine (New Rochelle, NY: New City Press, 1993), 161. Also see in the same series Sermon 229E, *Sermons*, part 3: 6, *Sermons on the Liturgical Seasons* (184–229Z), 280.
30 Blanchot, *SNB*, 39 (57).
31 Blanchot, *WD*, 20 (38).
32 Plato, *Theaetetus, Sophist*, Plato 7, trans. Harold North Fowler, Loeb Classical Library (Cambridge, MA: Harvard University Press, 1928), 241d.
33 Levinas, *TI*, 269 (301–2).
34 See Blanchot, *IC*, 250–1 (374–5). It is worth reminding ourselves at this point what Heidegger observes about the Parmenidean One: "We know that this unity is never empty indifference; it is not sameness in the sense of mere equivalence. Unity is the belonging-together of antagonisms. This is original oneness," *An Introduction to Metaphysics*, trans. Ralph Manheim (New York: Anchor Books, 1961), 117.
35 See Levinas, *TI*, 48–50 (40–2). Descartes's notion of infinity here might well be recognized as agnostic. See, for example, Maurice Blondel, "Le christianisme de Descartes," *Revue de Métaphysique et de Morale*, 4 (1896), 551–67.
36 See Blanchot's dialogues in part one of *IC*, Derrida, "Violence and Metaphysics" in *Writing and Difference*, and Michel Henry, *The Essence of Manifestation*, trans. Girard Etzkorn (The Hague: Martinus Nijhoff, 1973).
37 Husserl, *Ideas*, 1 § 27.
38 See Heidegger, *Being and Time*, 58.
39 See Heidegger, *Being and Time*, 38, 1, 488, *Nietzsche*, 4 vols., vol. 3: *The Will to Power as Knowledge and as Metaphysics*, trans. Joan Stambaugh, David Farrell Krell,

Frank A. Capuzzi, ed. David Farrell Krell (San Francisco: Harper and Row, 1987), 148.
40 On this theme, see Blanchot's letter to Derrida quoted by Bident in his *La vie versée dans les récits*, 184–5.
41 On hearing and sight as the two theoretical senses, see Hegel, *Aesthetics*, vol. 1, 38.
42 On this claim, see Levinas, "Philosophy and Transcendence," *AT*, 5 (29).
43 See in particular Derrida's discussion of *archi-écriture* in *Of Grammatology*, 60 (88). Derrida himself criticizes "the unity of the sense of being" on page 22 (36).
44 See Marion's comment on Levinas's reaction to his idea that phenomenology should suspend the horizon in *God, the Gift, and Postmodernism*. ed. John D. Caputo and Michael J. Scanlon (Bloomington, IN: Indiana University Press, 1999), 66.
45 See Jean-Luc Marion, *Being Given*, § 21.
46 Marion, *Being Given*, 228 (318).
47 See Husserl, *The Idea of Phenomenology*, trans. William P. Alston and George Nakhnikian, intro. George Nakhnikian (The Hague: Martinus Nijoff, 1973), 40. I have followed Marion's rendering of the German, as translated by Jeffrey L. Kosky, in *Being Given*, 15 (25).
48 See Blanchot, "The Museum, Art, and Time," *F*, 23 (33). Also see my essay "The Profound *Reserve*," 35–57.
49 See Blanchot, *WD*, 50–1 (85), and Marion, *Being Given*, 215–16 (300–1).
50 See Marion, "The Banality of Saturation," trans. Jeffrey L. Kosky, *Counter-Experiences: Reading Jean-Luc Marion*, ed. Kevin Hart (Notre Dame: Notre Dame University Press, 2007), 383–418.
51 Blanchot, *WTC*, 4 (13–14).
52 Blanchot, *OWM*, 24 (47–8).
53 Blanchot, *SNB*, 2 (9).
54 See Heidegger, *Hölderlins Hymn "Germanien" und "Der Rhein,"* ed. S. Ziegler, *Gesamtausgabe* 39 (Frankfort: Klostermann, 1980), 121ff, and Marion, *Reduction and Givenness: Investigations of Husserl, Heidegger, and Phenomenology*, trans. Thomas A. Carlson (Evanston, IL: Northwestern University Press, 1998), 186–92 (280–9).
55 See Heidegger, *The Basic Problems of Phenomenology*, trans., intro. and lexicon by Albert Hofstadter (Bloomington, IN: Indiana University Press, 1988), 21.
56 See Wahl, *Human Existence and Transcendence*, 28.
57 See Blanchot, *SL*, 243 (326).
58 Levinas, *TI*, 80 (79). Of course, Blanchot was using the same syntax in the 1940s: he did not learn it from Levinas' book.
59 Augustine, *Letters 100–155*, The Works of Saint Augustine, section 2/2, trans. and notes Roland Teske, ed. Boniface Ramsey (Hyde Park, NY: New City Press, 2003), 84.
60 Augustine, *The Literal Meaning of Genesis*, 2 vols., trans. John Hammond Taylor (New York: Paulist Press, 1982), vol. 1, 3. 8.
61 St. Bernard of Clairvaux, *On Loving God* (Kalamazoo, MI: Cistercian Publications, 1995), 1.1. Bernard McGinn observes that Meister Eckhart quotes Bernard's expression five times. See McGinn, "St. Bernard and Meister Eckhart," *Cîteaux, commemtarii cistercienses* 31 (1980): 378 and n. 24.
62 St. Bonaventure, *Disputed Questions on the Mystery of the Trinity*, trans. and intro. Zachery Hayes, Works of St. Bonaventure (St. Bonaventure, NY: The Franciscan Institute, 2000), vol. 3, 4. 1, reply 1. Bonaventure acknowledges Augustine's early "The Nature of the Good" where the expression does not appear although the concept does.
63 See Aquinas, *Summa theologiæ*, 2a2æ, q. 27, art. 6.

64 See Heidegger, "A Dialogue on Language," in *On the Way to Language*, trans. Peter D. Hertz (New York: Harper and Row, 1971), and "Epilogue" (to "The Thing"), *Poetry, Language, Thought*, trans. Albert Hofstadter (New York: Harper and Row, 1971), 186.
65 Hamburger translates the lines as follows, "True to / Total Proportions, Including the Centre," *Friedrich Hölderlin*, 613. Also see Hölderlin, "On Religion," *Essays and Letters on Theory*, 92.
66 Heidegger, "Hölderlin's Earth and Heaven," *Elucidations of Hölderlin's Poetry*, 188.
67 See Blanchot, *IC*, 67 (95).
68 Levinas, *TI*, 291 (324). In Blanchot's and Levinas's use of mathematical metaphors one might see a foreshadowing of Badiou's discussion of the "multiple without-One" and his use of mathematics. See his *Being and Event*, trans. Oliver Feltham (London: Continuum, 2006), *passim*.
69 See Aquinas, *Summa theologiæ*, 1a, q. 13 art. 7, c; 1a, q. 28, art. 1, ad 3; 1a, q. 45 art. 3, *On the Power of God*, trans. Lawrence Shapcote (1932; rpt. Eugene, OR: Wipf and Stock, 2004), 1, q. iii, iii, and *Truth*, vol. 1, q. 4 art. 5, reply.
70 See Robert Sokolowski, *The God of Faith and Reason: Foundations of Christian Theology* (Washington, DC: Catholic University of America Press, 1982), ch. 2 and 3. Also see David Burrell, *Faith and Freedom: An Interfaith Perspective* (Oxford: Basil Blackwell, 2004), ch. 1 and 14.
71 Yet see Aquinas, *An Exposition of the "On the Hebdomads" of Boethius*, intro. and trans. Janice L. Schultz and Edward A. Synan (Washington, DC: The Catholic University of America Press, 2001), 55. There Aquinas sees that in God "To Be and What It Is" do not differ.

11

From *The Star* to *The Disaster*

Almost sixty years separate the publication of Franz Rosenzweig's *Der Stern der Erlösung* (1921) and Blanchot's *L'Écriture du désastre* (1980). It is difficult to say if these two books should be seen as utterly distinct, the atheist having laid aside as completely hopeless the intense spiritual hope of the observant Jew, or if they are fundamentally in accord, the Frenchman confirming and extending, though in a new direction, the crucial intuitions of the German. It is hard to specify the relation that would encompass the two, in part because each is a work that remains solitary, largely outside the hubbub of philosophical and theological discussion, and Blanchot does not refer to Rosenzweig in *L'Écriture du désastre* and only in passing elsewhere.[1] Yet it is enticing to think that Blanchot's idea of the "relation without relation," worked out in dialogue with Levinas, may help us to think these two books together without thereby making them into a false unity.[2] Could it be that they abide, like two separated voices, in a relation that is marked by a violent interruption—the Shoah—that nonetheless keeps them together? Also, though, it is possible that there is another, more mediated, relation in play. It is intriguing to think that Levinas himself is the one who keeps these two works in relation for us, the one opening the space in which *Totalité et infini* (1961) could be written, and the latter responding in part to that work and its profound companion, *Autrement qu'être* (1974).[3] In thinking of *Der Stern der Erlösung* and *L'Écriture du désastre* with the Shoah and Levinas between them, we might better understand the change in thinking that was glimpsed last century in these two works, a change that Rosenzweig dubbed "the new thinking" and that Blanchot called simply "thought."[4]

If the two books are joined, it is mostly along a common, hyperbolic line of criticism. For both Rosenzweig and Blanchot question one of the most deep-seated assumptions of philosophy, that there is a unity of thought.[5] Let us begin with Rosenzweig. Right at the beginning of *Der Stern der Erlösung*, we are reminded that, "It is the unity of thinking that enforces its right by asserting the totality of the world against the multiplicity of knowledge. The unity of the logos founds the unity of the world as a totality" (18). Accordingly, "he who questions the totality of being, as is the case here, refutes the unity of thinking. He who does this throws the gauntlet to the whole venerable brotherhood of philosophy from Ionia to Jena" (18). Later, he declares with equal confidence, "We have broken the All to pieces, and now each piece is an All unto itself" (34) and resigns himself to the "imperfect work of our knowledge" (34). Exactly what this fragmentation means for us is spelled out much later: "The mythical God, the plastic world, tragic man—we are holding the pieces in our hands. We have really shattered the All" (93). Idealist philosophy from Parmenides to Hegel has come to an end, it seems, and Rosenzweig does not hesitate to call it pagan philosophy, since it affirms immanence over transcendence.[6] His philosophy (and he insists that it is a philosophy, not a theology) is one of transcendence.[7] It involves an ascent, sure, though no θέωσις, and is principally a philosophy of God's free descent into the world, one broad enough to include the Shekinah and the Incarnation. From the beginning of its second part, once the logic of the "system" has been expounded, it is a positive philosophy, in Schelling's sense of the expression, a philosophy in touch with the here and now.[8]

Idealism serves as a figure of philosophy as such for Rosenzweig, and once it has been overcome there opens the possibility of thinking anew, and one project of this new thinking is reconceiving the nature of unity. The world is not constituted by thought, as traditional idealism has claimed; it is not monological, formed from within by the logos, but is more than logical, or—as Rosenzweig has it—metalogical; it includes the logos yet precedes it and cannot be encompassed by it. In terms of method, also, philosophy can no longer be monological but must become dialogical; the philosopher must turn from producing the great System in the solitude of his study or before the podium in a lecture theater and be transformed into a *Sprachdenker*, a speech-thinker, someone in whom philosophy emerges out of conversation with others. The new thinking begins with the recognition that lived existence, communal as well as individual, is prior to essence. Yet this new beginning is itself prompted by something given in experience, namely the fear of death. Only by rejecting the assurances that philosophy gives us that death is really a shelter from life can we begin to think freshly, both about the world and our actions in it. Just as the world is metalogical so too men and women are metaethical, beings who practice ethics rather than draw their humanity solely from it.[9]

The cosmos, as conceived by the Greeks, is "*securus adversus deos*" (22), insulated from the gods, and this is not because the Greeks turned away from their divinities but because Olympus was always a world unto itself, without any need to refer to the villages and fields below. For all the Greeks' talk of the gods, and for all the West's long absorption with classical mythology, the Greeks in fact developed "a world without gods" (42), even when their deities were taken to rule the whole world. The Greeks lived without hope or fear of Apollo and Zeus establishing concrete relationships with mortals. (The rapes of Europa, Leda, Persephone, and others would be no more than gossip on this view.) Similarly, medieval Christian theology has also been set against God to the extent that it has construed God as existing *a se*, eternal, immutable, omniscient, omnipotent, and not needing to form any relations with human beings.[10] He already enjoyed all possible perfections before Creation. No matter when and where it takes place, thinking is safe from the disturbance of the divine whenever it believes that it can explain the whole from within its limits, which it does by diminishing relations between God and human beings. So, for the Greeks, the gods are simply the highest beings of the cosmos. For Islam, God is unconditioned and perfect, utterly apart from the world. And for those medieval Christians whose theology depends on Plato and Aristotle (presumably without the adjustments made by Aquinas), God is the highest ground of being.[11] The old thinking regards creation as a rift between God and human beings, while the new thinking will figure it by way of a relation between world and creator.

Rosenzweig introduces this thought somewhat abstractly. First, he states his general position with respect to the idealist strain in philosophy: "So thinking, moreover, which is itself the unity of its own internal multiplicity, establishes the unity of being, and certainly, it is not in the degree where it is a unity, but a multiplicity" (19). Rather than entertain a world that is nothing other than mere multiplicity, however, he looks elsewhere for unity: "But now, the unity of thinking insofar as it directly concerns thinking alone and not being, falls outside of the cosmos of being = thinking. This cosmos itself, insofar as it is the overlapping of two multiplicities, now has its unity entirely beyond itself" (19). Rosenzweig breaks with Schelling, then, for whom (at least in the Stuttgart seminars of 1810) "cosmos" is co-ordinate with "system."[12] The unity beyond the cosmos that Rosenzweig discerns as the basis for his system—the "new thinking"—can be presented only by way of paradox. As we are told in the *Urzelle*, "This something attached to reason beyond (said *logically*: 'beyond') reason is a unity, which is *not* the unity of two: not to be formulated as equation, rather unity *aside* from duality, the equals sign in both equations, but, with respect to the difference of its application there."[13] We should not identify the divine *Urgrund* or dark abyss from which God creates himself with the God who freely enters into a relationship with us.

As can be seen from this allusion to Schelling's later philosophy of religion, Rosenzweig does not escape German idealism (as Heidegger hoped to do) so much as modify it; and he does so by pitting it against itself and drawing from time to time on other of its critics, especially Kierkegaard and Nietzsche. One piece of idealism he takes is Kant's doctrine of the noumenal world. It is there, beyond the cosmos, where God abides, although we can approach Him through prayer and not merely through moral action. Schelling of course would not subscribe to the idea of the noumenal world, Kant being for him the clergyman of *Clara* (1810?) who denies any relation between this world and the next. Yet Rosenzweig picks and chooses among idealist systems, taking only what is needed for the new thinking. Another, more important piece for him is Schelling's notion of the *Urgrund*. Rosenzweig allows these thoughts to point him outside the absolute idealism of Hegel, that increasingly determinate process of thinking about thinking.[14] Unity will come, he says, only from outside the cosmos. And when we pass "Towards the 'outside,'" Rosenzweig says, "the world is thus deprived of that truth" that has sustained the idealist strain of philosophy in all its variations over the centuries (21).

That Rosenzweig borrows from Kant and Schelling does not commit him to either philosophy in its broad lines or in all the details that gather around a motif. For one thing, he rejects the philosophy of time as Kant develops it in the Transcendental Aesthetic of the *Kritik der reinen Vernunft* (1787). No longer is time conceived as a pure form that is given *a priori*.[15] Instead, time is deformalized, and for Rosenzweig the *a priori* horizon is to be replaced by one that is informed by Schelling's notion of the three ages in his *Die Weltalter* (1811–15) and by the experience of the Jews. In his great fragment on the three ages, Schelling tells us very little about the second of his three ages, the present, and—assuming that we reject *Clara* as the start of the third book—nothing at all about the future. Yet he tells us a great deal about the first, a past that was never present, an "eternal past" that belongs to God before creation.[16] Excited by this idea, Rosenzweig interprets it in the direction of Lurianic Kabbalah. The *Urgrund*, pure self-identity, an essence that does not yet exist, posits itself as both an object and a subject, and thereby comes into being. That much is Schelling. The view that God comes into existence by way of withdrawing from his essence so that he can freely relate to us in history is Rosenzweig's Kabbalistic reading of Schelling, an interpretation that grounds the philosophy of transcendence that he develops.[17]

Time, for Schelling and for his Jewish admirer, is not successive, reaching a concrete determination of *Geist*, so much as overlapping: we live in the three ages of the world in different ways although at one and the same time. *Die Weltalter* begins by declaring, "The past is known, the present is discerned, the future is intimated."[18] For Rosenzweig, the past is Creation, the present is Revelation, and the future is Redemption. As we have seen, metalogic changed the nature of *ontologica specialis* as inherited from Christian Wolff's *Vernünftige Gedanken von Gott, der Welt under der Seele der Menschen, auch alle Dingen überhaupt* (1719) so that God, Man, and World no longer comprise a whole ordered from within by thought but a system of relations instead. Now, with the deformalization of time, we have another triangle, one formed by the apexes of Creation, Revelation, and Redemption, and it intersects with the first. And so the Star of David appears, newly charged with philosophical dignity, and since all six categories are common to the two religions, it encompasses Christianity as well as Judaism. Rosenzweig calls it "the Star of Redemption."

*

It seems, then, as though Rosenzweig challenges the unity of thought in philosophy only to recast it at the level of theology. This is the conclusion that will be reached if one quickly reads *Der Stern*, for all its criticisms of Hegel, as a deeply Hegelian work, as though the first two parts of the book, "The Elements" and "The Path," are sublated in the third part, "The Configuration."[19] Even so, "theology" would not be quite the right word here, if only because the Hegelian *Aufhebung* retains the content of theology while changing its form into philosophy. Also, while Rosenzweig plainly draws from Hegel, he does so, as we have seen, while also adapting from others and using what he takes to contest the dialectic and its drive toward totality. The unity that is conferred from the viewpoint of theology comes from beyond the cosmos and is beyond the range of the dialectic: Rosenzweig's God is not intelligible as *Geist*. Besides, whatever unity Rosenzweig affirms in the third book of *Der Stern der Erlösung* is one that takes account of human being as already doubled and of redemption itself as divided. We are doubled, he thinks, insofar as only a human being is a self ("B = B," as his logic has it) capable of experiencing revelation, and therefore able to say "I"; and yet, "All relation finds its foothold only between third persons; the system is the world in the form of the third person."[20]

More complicated is the division in redemption itself, which is required for Judaism and Christianity both to be true. One difficulty that stems from the rejection of thought is that it is not clear on what basis either Judaism or Christianity can maintain its integrity as a religion. How can the God beyond the cosmos, beyond totality, confer unity on either Judaism or Christianity? Let us limit ourselves simply to the Christian religion, and to one of the main challenges it has faced in maintaining doctrinal coherence. Rosenzweig approaches the question historically, in a quasi-Hegelian dialectical narrative, by considering how Christianity overcomes the challenge of having a divided essence, of its truth being distributed between faith and reason. The problem does not emerge with St. Augustine, he thinks, because Christianity was able to convert pagan philosophers with its discourse of love. Against pagan philosophy, however, love was impotent. With the Emperor Justinian's closure of Plato's Academy in Athens in 529, and a more general suppression of paganism, φιλοσοφία became "an opponent as intangible as a phantom and yet very colorfully visible and hung as it were like a painting on the wall, against which the power of action—and here, the power of love—was inadequate to win the victory" (298).

It is an elegant conceit, and Rosenzweig allows it to develop fully: "Before the picture on the wall, medieval Scholasticism had put up a curtain that it could open and close; for it was only a curtain before that most dreadful thought—precisely in the Christian sense most doubtful, because it was a hindrance to the mission—of a twofold truth, a truth of reason opposite the truth of faith" (298). The allusion is to the specter of *duplex veritate*, double truth, the modern name of a philosophical stance that was popularized by Ernst Renan in his *Averroès et l'averroïsme* (1867). Whether it was distinctly held or not, the philosophical view precipitated a crisis in the church. The earliest and most dramatic instance of it is the condemnation by Étienne Tempier, bishop of Paris, in 1277 of some Masters in the lower faculty of the University of Paris. The bishop objected to those radical Aristotelians who said that certain things are "true according to philosophy, yet not according to the Catholic faith, as if these were two contrary truths" (*vera secundum philosophiam, sed non secundum fidem catholicam, quasi sint duae contrariae veritates*).[21] Two Masters, Siger of Brabant and Boethius of Dacia, were named, although no attempt was made to distinguish what they actually taught from what their enemies said they taught.[22]

Moving quickly and lightly over his material, Rosenzweig suggests that the church "seemed again to disintegrate [*zersetzen*] for these three centuries, in fact four centuries, counting the aftermath" (299). "Disintegrate" is far too strong a word, and Rosenzweig completely ignores the synthesis of *fides et ratio* provided by Aquinas that was to sustain the Catholic Church through the centuries. It might be noted also that Rosenzweig bypasses without comment Aquinas's teaching that the divine *esse* could abide with all possible perfections without the cosmos; one does not need to appeal to Schelling's dark abyss when one has Aquinas's doctrine of God. That said, Rosenzweig is entirely correct to point out that the specter of *duplex veritate* reappeared in the sixteenth century. In the eighth session of the Fifth Lateran Council on March 11, 1513, Leo X addressed all philosophers, admonishing them that they were not to teach that the rational soul is mortal "at least according to philosophy (*secundum saltem philosophiam verum*)," for theology teaches that it is immortal. "And since truth cannot contradict truth (*Cumque verum vero minime contradicat*)," Leo says, "we define that every statement contrary to the enlightened truth of the faith is totally false and we strictly forbid teaching otherwise to be permitted."[23] Leo did not name Pietro Pompanazzi in his decree but an interpretation of the philosopher's teaching that the immortality of the soul was certain for faith but not for reason was undoubtedly in the minds of his advisers.[24] Pompanazzi's book, *Tractatus de immortalitate animæ*, was not published until 1516, and when it appeared Leo obliged the philosopher to retract his teaching.

For Rosenzweig, the upshot of the Fifth Lateran Council was the overcoming of "the evil thought of twofold truth" (299), by faith, and this led directly to the upsurge of Protestantism and the irruption of another problem there. Again, Rosenzweig draws from Schelling (though surely with a bow to Joachim of Fiore as well), this time to give himself the three ages of Christendom: the Petrine (or Catholic) age, beginning with the Edict of Milan in 313; the Pauline (or Protestant) age, beginning with Luther's posting of the ninety-five theses to the door at the Wittenberg Castle Church in 1517; and the Johannine age, which has been developing since 1800, the symbolic year that for Rosenzweig marks the fulfillment of German idealism and the beginning of *Weltanschauungsphilosophie*.[25] With the final banishing of the *duplex veritate*, we see the passage from the Petrine to the Pauline Church. "Faith had quite simply forgotten the body in the spirit. The world had slipped away from it," we are told. "Of course, it had gotten rid of the doctrine of twofold truth. But in return, it dealt in a twofold reality, that is to say of the purely inner reality of faith and the purely outer reality of an increasingly worldly world; the greater the tension between the two, the better this Protestantism felt" (299–300). This is the world first of Luther and then, over a century later, of Kant's attempt to limit reason in order to supply a place for moral faith.[26]

When fully elaborated, German idealism was to reject this exclusive attention Christianity gives to faith, whether it be Luther's *fiducia* or Kant's moral faith. (Rosenzweig is presumably thinking of Hegel's acidic remark in 1802 that, with Kant, Jacobi, and Fichte, "Philosophy has made itself the handmaid of a faith once more.")[27] And, with this rejection, Christianity was to take another turn, this time toward what Rosenzweig calls the "Christianity of the future" (300) or the "Johannine completion" (302). It is worth noting that Rosenzweig does not take into consideration Hegel's criticism of the very idea of a noumenon, whether the deity or something else beyond the cosmos: it is unintelligible to us, and therefore beyond both reason and faith.[28] Suffice it to say that Christian faith, bearing witness to Christ, is "faith in the way" (363), and is able to unite "those who bear witness into a union in the world" (363) by way of the invisible church. "And so faith establishes union of individuals as individuals for a mutual task, a union is rightly called *Ekklesia*" (364). It is a distinctly Protestant understanding of "church." Protestant also is the way in which God confers unity on the church, namely by "the illumination of prayer" (414) and the "yearly cycle" of liturgical prayer (414). No reference is made to the life of sacraments.

And so the Hegelian story of the overcoming of *duplex veritate* comes to an end, and in doing so it leaves us with Christianity—and Protestantism, first of all—as the religion of "the eternal way in the world" (363), a way that is given *sub specie aeternitatis*, caught between an absolute past and an absolute future. "Both, beginning and end, are for him at every moment equally near, because both are in that which is eternal; and only for this reason does he know himself at each moment to be [the] central point" (360). Judaism survives as the other true monotheism and is by contrast with Christianity the religion "of the eternal life of the people" (363). Islam, the third

Abrahamic religion, drops out of consideration without a satisfactory reason for its disappearance. Both Judaism and Christianity are held to be true, and since no attempt is made to reconcile their conflicting truth claims the unity of thought has been undone. Each religion gains its unity not from participating in a frozen eternity but by being in a free relation with the living God. The primal elements of God, World, and Man are not fused from within by thought but are brought into a relationship with one another by way of Creation, Revelation, and Redemption. The pattern that Rosenzweig calls "the Star of Redemption" is a "new unity" (273) and a "new totality" (273), a gathering that is given in lived and therefore shifting relationships, not guaranteed by an appeal to a timeless whole.[29]

Drafted on postcards during the First World War, *Der Stern der Erlösung* was composed during one of Europe's greatest catastrophes, and begins, as we have seen, with a meditation on the fear of death. Yet Rosenzweig's voice speaks to us from before 1933, in a world innocent of the disaster that is the Shoah, a disaster for the Jews yet also for Christians—and all the more so if it is not experienced as a wound that goes to the heart of Christian theology and Christian practice. Levinas was surely right to say that the German guards in the camps knew their catechism.[30] No such innocence exists in Blanchot's *L'Écriture du désastre*, and it cuts to a level beneath confession, eschewing any hope in keeping Judaism and Christianity in the one configuration. It is a book of experience, of what "experience" of the disaster might be: first of all, experience par excellence, exposure to peril, yet also, since it is not a lived event, non-experience, an attunement to the Outside that is suffered in a state of radical passivity in which one loses the power to say "I."[31] When Levinas reflects on the book, he underlines his friend's concern with "an event which is neither being nor nothingness" which Blanchot calls "disaster" and which "signifies neither death nor an accident, but as a piece of being which would be detached from its fixity of being, from its reference to a star, from all cosmological existence, a *dis-aster*."[32] For Levinas, the disaster is a version of the *il y a*, the grim persistence of being even in the absence of being, and certainly Blanchot meditates on the *il y a* at important moments of the book.[33] Levinas makes no mention, however, of his friend's engagement with the ethical concerns developed in *Totalité et infini* and *Autrement qu'être*. Nor does he note that *L'Écriture du désastre* broods on the Shoah, interlacing it with Blanchot's signature themes, which Levinas identifies obliquely, of dying, writing, and the approach of the Outside.

*

If we read *L'Écriture du désastre* with *Der Stern der Erlösung* as a lens, we will quickly identify several motifs that come sharply into focus. First of all, we will note the attack on the unity of thought, the fear of "false" unity (2; 8), the affirmation of an irreducible doubling of the subject (an "I" and a "he" or "it" [*il*]), and, as we shall see, a new version of the *duplex veritate*. Like Rosenzweig, Blanchot is not simply arguing against Hegel; he incorporates him into his vision, though all the time denying his System any hope of sublating his fragmentary nonsystem. Second, we will observe that Blanchot rejects the comforting notion of the cosmos. "Would the cosmic be a little heaven in which to survive, or with which to die universally, in stoic serenity? A 'whole' which shelters us, even as we dissolve therein, and which would be natural repose—as if there were a nature outside of concepts and names?" (75; 121). He affirms the Outside, the non-place where image reigns, in which possibility finds no traction, and which eternally returns in writing and in the recognition of the human relation. Attuned to the Outside, "I" am divided, lose all my possibilities, and experience time differently, as though it were a stagnant pool rather than a stream. Such is the disaster. Yet Blanchot differs sharply from Rosenzweig in rejecting the possibility that one can find God beyond the cosmos or that the Outside is divine. That transcendence occurs, he concedes, though he says that its success occurs "only in a negative form" (91; 143), namely what Wahl calls "transdescendance," which for Blanchot is the Outside or the Neutral.[34] An implacable atheist, Blanchot denies "the idea of salvation, of redemption" (13; 27), suspecting that such ideas breed fear, and suspecting also that atheism, unless conceptually clarified by way of the Outside, is merely "a privileged way of talking about God" (92; 145).

Third, it is apparent just on opening *L'Écriture du désastre* that it is a fragmentary work, having learned if not from 1800 then without fail from 1798, the first year of the *Athenaeum* (1798–1800) and the affirmation of the fragment. The possibility for thought opened in 1798, Blanchot thinks, is not the production of masterly aphorisms of the sort that Friedrich Schlegel dreamed in Fragment 206 ("A fragment, like a miniature work of art, has to be entirely isolated from the surrounding world and be complete in itself like a porcupine") or that Rosenzweig imagined ("and now each piece is an All unto itself").[35] It is something far more daring. Blanchot specifies what is at issue in Schlegel's fragment on fragments in three statements, each of which is phrased negatively, for Schlegel seeks to lead the fragment back toward the aphorism. This failure of nerve comes down to,

(1) considering the fragment as a text that is concentrated, having its center in itself rather than in the field that *other* fragments constitute along with it; (2) neglecting the interval (wait or pause) that separates the fragments and makes of this separation the rhythmic principle of the work at the structural level; (3) forgetting that this manner of writing tends not to make a view of the whole more difficult or the relations of unity more lax, but rather makes possible new relations that except themselves from unity, just as they exceed the whole.[36]

In terms of form, at least, what will constitute "thought" for Blanchot is precisely the putting into play of these three statements in an affirmative manner.

When that play, "this mad game of writing" [*ce jeu insensé d'écrire*] as Mallarmé called it, begins, we will gradually pass from the fragment to the fragmentary, from Schlegel to Nietzsche, from internal relations, characteristic of idealism, to "the third relation" in which neither dialectic nor fusion has a role to play.[37] We will slowly change how we read and write and, therefore, how we think. If we read the "Note" that introduces *L'Entretien infini*, we hear a voice that speaks in the tone of someone announcing a new age of the world. Once it has emerged from idealism and oriented itself toward "the aleatory force of absence," writing will "devote itself solely to itself as something that remains without identity"; it will open up new possibilities, new ways of being in relation that do not derive from essences.[38] Like Rosenzweig, totality will be rethought by way of relation; unlike him, however, there will be no "new totality," only the "relation without relation." And finally, like Rosenzweig, Blanchot will affirm the eternal past, not, however, as Creation but as the immemorial past as Levinas understands the expression: the groundless ground of ethics.

In *L'Écriture du désastre* this affirmation of the fragmentary becomes the counterpart of the grand systems of German philosophy of which *Der Stern der Erlösung* was perhaps the last as well as being one of the first works to make out what may be beyond systems. *L'Écriture du désastre* will not form a star of redemption but will talk about living in a world without a star to guide us and without redemption. He will name "the four winds of spirit's absence," an atheistic equivalent of the four horsemen of the Apocalypse in Rev. 6: 1–8, traditionally known as Pestilence, War, Famine, and Death, and renamed by Blanchot:

> These names, areas of dislocation, the four winds of spirit's absence, breath from nowhere—the names of thought, when it lets itself come undone and, by writing, fragment. Outside. Neutral. Disaster. Return. Surely these names form no system. In their abruptness, like proper names designating no one, they slide outside all possible meaning without this slide's meaning anything—it leaves only a sliding half-gleam that clarifies nothing, not even the outside, whose frontier is nowhere indicated. (57-58; 95)

No fifth horseman, the Messiah, will come, according to Blanchot, for the Messiah is already here and will "come" only when we listen to him. "Anyone might be the Messiah—must be he, is not he" (142; 215). We are not to speak of the Messiah "in Hegelian language" (142; 215), presumably the language that construes Judaism as the religion of sublimity, because his coming announces not the end of history but a time that is "more future ... than any prophesy could ever foretell" (142; 215).[39]

Could Blanchot be alluding to Rosenzweig, among others? It is doubtful, if only because Rosenzweig speaks rather differently about the Messiah than Hegel does. "Opposite Israel," he says, "the eternally beloved of God, the eternally faithful one and eternally complete one, there stands the one who eternally comes, eternally waits, eternally wanders, eternally thrives, the Messiah" (326). And later he evokes the idea of the "remnant" of Israel who will welcome the Blessed One. "If the Messiah comes 'today,' the remnant is ready to receive him" (427). There is no doubt that Rosenzweig awaits the Messiah. Not so Blanchot. For him, the coming of the Messiah is a way of evoking an absolute future, the time of the eternal return of the Outside, which only ever approaches and never installs itself in a present moment. Accordingly, Blanchot can elsewhere say that "prophetic speech is that speech in which the bare relation with the Outside could be expressed, with a desolate force, when there are not yet any possible relations, primal powerlessness, wretchedness of hunger and cold, which is the principle of the Covenant, that is to say, of an exchange of speech from which the surprising justice of reciprocity emerges."[40]

*

Prophetic or Messianic speech therefore expresses the disaster, not redemption, and we better understand what "disaster" means, what the approach of the neutral Outside "means," when we reflect on the Shoah. The defining characteristic of Auschwitz, Blanchot suggests, is "senselessness," not horror (83; 132), that is, living without being able to project a horizon from one's *ego cogito*, living in the complete absence of possibility understood as "I can." In the camps people were subject to a time that was an endless, gray present, without past or future: a stagnant pool. Stripped of the power to say "I," they found themselves in another way of being, one that surprisingly breaks with totality. It is marked by what Blanchot calls the "relation without relation," a rapport between two people that holds them together and apart, without one person having dialectical mastery over the other or fusing immediately with him or her in the elation of romantic love. Unable to speak, and least of all to speak in the language of their guards—to "play their game," as we say—they were nonetheless able to hold in reserve a "true *speech*" [*vraie* parole] of justice that could not be given voice in the camps.[41] It was this speech that could finally be spoken by the survivors, and that he calls Messianic because it bears testimony to the relation through which we identify the other person as irreducibly human, without the mediation of religion, myth, ideology, value, sentiment, or power. "The thought of the disaster," he writes, forms a silence in which "the other who, keeping still, announces himself" (12-13; 27). Thought, then, requires us to recognize that anyone *might* be the Messiah, the one who heralds the realm of justice, and *should* be the Messiah. Although Antelme does not use this language and respects the difference between the death camps and the labor camps, Blanchot points to his friend's *L'Espèce humaine* (1957) as exemplary of the thought of the disaster.[42]

The disaster makes us pass from expecting the Messiah to each of us accepting the role of being a messiah. This thought also finds support in Blanchot's reading of Levinas. What Blanchot chiefly takes from his friend is summed up in one, strong sentence in *L'Écriture du désastre*: "The responsibility with which I am charged is not mine, and because of it I am no longer myself" (13; 28). I am not responsible for the other person in the sense that I ever agreed to look after him or her, or that I concurred with a bill of human rights, composed in a past present, that constrains me to help him or her, or that I anticipate a just State in a future present that can come into being if and only if I and others work for social justice. Instead, the responsibility for the other person that I assume comes to me from a past that was never present and never will be. One might say it is Schelling's "eternal past," and in a sense it is, although for Levinas God deflects direct approaches into an ethical relation with the orphan, the widow, and the stranger. God "comes to mind" only in moral action and does not appear as Creator or directly as Lord.[43]

"Creation" is not a word that Blanchot rejects, although he uses it in an unusual way, as when, writing of reading, he evokes somewhat dramatically "the experience of creation ... the torments of the infinite."[44] In his reflections on Levinas, however, we may say that he speaks of creation without ever quite using the word, as though the concept hovers over the page, quietly whispering "creation" in order to denote not the origin of the cosmos so much as the birth of responsibility in me. It is certainly not the creation of my soul or my "true self." On the contrary, the other person does not call on me, a singular, indispensable individual, and in doing so confirm my uniqueness. Instead, I am merely "the first come or the least of men; by no means the unique being I would like to be" (18; 35). If I am to be a messiah, it is not because of any special commission I have been given by God or any particular quality that I may have that makes me more fit for the task than the next person. Any truly responsible person would be a messiah, and the unspoken challenge that Blanchot puts before us is that perhaps we are still waiting for a messiah to come.

In the Preface to *Totalité et infini* Levinas says, "We were impressed by the opposition to the idea of totality in Franz Rosenzweig's *Stern der Erlösung*, a work too often present in this book to be cited."[45] To the extent that Blanchot engages Levinas—that is, often and intensely—*Der Stern der Erlösung* remains darkly in the background of his reflections, shaping them without drawing attention to itself or when and how it does its work. Perhaps Rosenzweig's voice can be indistinctly heard from time to time, as part of a chorus, in Blanchot's polemic against unity and the One. Yet there is at least one moment when Blanchot is closer to Rosenzweig than Levinas is, and that is on the issue of the unity of truth. In *Totalité et infini* Levinas skirts the old problem of *duplex veritate* when he argues that justice precedes truth. "The transitivity of teaching, and not the interiority of reminiscence, manifests being; the locus of truth is society. The *moral* relation with the Master who judges me subtends the freedom of my adherence to the true."[46] There is no gulf between the truths of reason and the truths of faith at issue here. Rather, truth is considered only as a figure of freedom—the freedom of the intellect to comprehend phenomena and render them intelligible—and Levinas's claim is only that, because the other person resists being regarded as a phenomenon, my freedom is posterior to my responsibility and is limited by it. Blanchot does not contest this position. However, he proposes something that comes to seem very close to *duplex veritate*, not a division between faith and reason but between two relations that are irreducible to one another, each of which claims to be true.

In his poem "With happiness stretchd across the hills" (1802) William Blake says, "a double vision is always with me."[47] Blanchot quotes the line (slightly mistranslated) in French in a short, early piece on Blake: "*Il y a en moi une double vision*."[48] One might well say of Blanchot that he has a "doubled vision" in him. In *L'Entretien infini* he maintains that we are bound by a double relation, that is, "*naming* the possible, *responding* to the impossible" (48; 69). Nothing fundamentally changes in *L'Écriture du désastre*: "there must always be at least two languages, or two requirements: one dialectical, the other not; one where negativity is the task, the other where the neutral remains apart, cut off both from being and from not-being. In the same way each of us ought both to be a free and speaking subject, and to disappear as passive, patient" (20; 38). The first language is Hegelian and dialectical; the second is neutral and non-dialectical; and neither can gain traction with respect to the other. Nor can we distribute these languages neatly into the realms of the public and the private.[49] Each speaks its own truth, which cannot be reduced to the other and cannot be reconciled in a higher truth. The two are related only in terms of the infinite relation or "relation without relation," and no "new unity" can ever hold them together otherwise. Blanchot's universe, "a term henceforth deceptive" as he admits, is "non-finite, disunited, discontinuous" and there is nothing beyond it, no divinity and not even the Outside, capable of conferring a "new unity."[50] Thought must slowly re-imagine itself in this non-world.

One main difference between "the new thinking" and "thought" is that the former rejects the philosopher's God in order to welcome the biblical God while the latter rejects both. "If, I say, the old [thinking] addressed the problem whether God is transcendent or immanent, then the new [thinking] attempts to show how and when He turns from the distant into the near God, and again from the near into the distant."[51] Thus Rosenzweig; and as Ellen T. Charry, one of his most acute readers, points out, the upshot of the new thinking is to pass from resolving, as Hegel did, the "contradiction between an infinite and eternal God and a finite and temporal world" to thinking "the disjunction" being "within God himself. The paradox of eternality and temporality in God is thus the same as that which relates God and the world or the world and humanity."[52] If we are still to talk of God as one, as the Shema tells us to do ("Hear, O Israel: The LORD our God is one LORD," Deut. 6: 4), then this is a divine unity that lives with, rather than surpasses, difference.[53] Again, I quote Charry, "Reality is not a totality or a unity as 'philosophy from Ionia to Jena' had it, but a dualistic unity which is neither fully separated nor fully unified" (106). Blanchot may well appreciate that the "new thinking" draws close to the relation without relation, and hence "thought," but will doubtless reply that his atheism is based on a rejection of unity, and that for him unity is conceptually prior to the Judeo-Christian conception of God.[54] To which one can imagine Rosenzweig responding that, in positing Unity above God, and fighting against it, Blanchot appears to be struggling more directly against Gnosticism than against either Judaism or Christianity. The "new thinking" and "thought" are close when arguing against an idealism they consign to the past and, when arguing for a future, less distant from one another than is sometimes supposed except, of course, in the matter of religious hope.

Notes

1 See Blanchot, "Being Jewish," IC, 124, 128 (181, 188). Because of the paucity of reference to Rosenzweig by Blanchot, Hoppenot has little to say about Rosenzweig in his *Maurice Blanchot et la tradition juive*.
2 See Blanchot, "The Relation of the Third Kind (Man Without Horizon)," in IC, 66–74 (94–105). Blanchot evokes the temptation of "'false' unity" in WD, 2 (8).
3 See Levinas, TI, 28. ED grew out of some earlier fragments by Blanchot, "Discours sur la patience (*en marge des livres d'Emmanuel Levinas*)," *Le Nouveau Commerce* 30–1 (1975): 19–44.
4 See Franz Rosenzweig, "The New Thinking" (1925), in *Philosophical and Theological Writings*, trans. and ed. Paul W. Franks and Michael L. Morgan (Indianapolis, IN: Hackett Publishing Co., 2000), 109–39, and Blanchot, WD, 1 (7). Rosenzweig conceived "the new thinking" as an enterprise that involved other thinkers, including Eugen Rosenstock-Huessey, Martin Buber, and Ferdinand Ebner.
5 Also see Rosenzweig, "The New Thinking," 134–5. For a fuller account of the unity of thought, see Chapter 10, "The Third Relation."
6 See Rosenzweig, "'Urzelle' to the *Star of Redemption*" (1917), *Philosophical and Theological Writings*, 50, 69.

7 See Rosenzweig, "The New Thinking," 110.
8 See, for example, Schelling, *On the History of Modern Philosophy*, trans. and intro. Andrew Bowie (Cambridge: Cambridge University Press, 1994), 133.
9 For Rosenzweig's discussion of the metalogical and the metaethical, see *The Star of Redemption*, trans. Barbara E. Galli (Madison, WI: University of Wisconsin Press, 2005), 19–21, 16–17.
10 Rosenzweig moves very quickly over complex material. His remarks on Arabic scholasticism are perhaps more to the point than his allusions to Christian scholasticism. See *The Star of Redemption*, 124–7. Certainly, Rosenzweig allows that God may love Creation, even though He does not depend ontologically on it. See *The Star of Redemption*, 176–8. For Aquinas's views on the relations between God and Creation, see *Summa theologiæ*, 1a, q. 13 art. 7, c; 1a, q. 28, art. 1, ad 3; 1a q. 45 art. 3, *On the Power of God,* trans. Lawrence Shapcote (1932; rpt. Eugene, OR: Wipf and Stock, 2004), 1, q. iii, iii, and *Truth*, vol. 1, q. 4 art. 5, *responsio*.
11 On this theme, see Robert Sokolowski, *The God of Faith and Reason*, ch. 2–4.
12 Schelling, "Stuttgart Seminars," in *Idealism and the Endgame of Theory: Three Essays*, trans. and ed. Thomas Pfau (Albany, NY: State University of New York Press, 1994), 197.
13 Rosenzweig, "'Urzelle' to the *Star of Redemption*," 56.
14 Rosenzweig's insistence that the divine nature is not a "dark ground" or anything else that can be named with Eckhart's, Böhme's, or Schelling's words indicates his transformation of a concept, not an avoidance of naming his source for it. See *The Star of Redemption*, 34. Also see the comment on Schelling in "'Urzelle' to the *Star of Redemption*," 56.
15 See Kant, *Critique of Pure Reason*, Transcendental Aesthetic, § 4.
16 See Schelling, *The Ages of the World*, trans. and intro. Jason M. Wirth (Albany, NY: State University of New York Press, 2000), 39. The discussion of the present is confined to the 1815 lecture *Über die Gottheiten von Samothrake*.
17 Stéphane Mosès offers an admirable discussion of Rosenzweig's debt to Schelling in his *System and Revelation: The Philosophy of Franz Rosenzweig*, foreword Emmanuel Levinas, trans. Catherine Tihanyi (Detroit, MI: Wayne State University Press, 1992), 39–45. It should be noted that in *Of Human Freedom* (1809) Schelling takes a dim view of the divine withdrawal. See his *Of Human Freedom*, trans. James Gutmann (Chicago, IL: Open Court Publishing Co., 1936), 11, 28–9.
18 Schelling, *The Ages of the World*, xxxv. Also see pp. 76, 80.
19 See, for example, Else-Rahel Freund, *Franz Rosenzweig's Philosophy of Existence: An Analysis of 'The Star of Redemption'*, trans. Stephen L. Weinstein and Robert Israel, ed. Paul R. Mendes-Flohr (The Hague: Martinus Nijhoff, 1979), 5.
20 Rosenzweig, "'Urzelle' to the *Star of Redemption*," 60. For the interpretation of "B = B," see *The Star of Redemption*, 78.
21 *Chartularium Universitatis Parisiensis*, 1, 543, no. 473.
22 See Roland Hissette, *Enquête sur les 219 articles condemné à Paris le 7 mars 1277*, Philosophes médiévaux, 22 (Paris: Publications Universitaires, 1977). Fernand Van Steenberghen points out that Boethius of Dacia states "(*philosophorum*) *sententia in nullo contradicit sententiae christianae fidei nisi apud non intelligentes*" and "*Ideo nulla est contradictio inter fidem et Philosophum*," *Thomas Aquinas and Radical Aristotelianism* (Washington, DC: The Catholic University of America Press, 1980), 97.
23 Leo X, "*Damnatur omnis assertio contraria veritati christianæ fidei illuminatæ*," in *Decrees of the Ecumenical Councils*, ed. Normal P. Tanner, 2 vols. (London: Sheed and Ward, 1990), vol. 1, 605.

24 The view that Pomponazzi held a doctrine of double truth was propagated by Ernest Renan in the third edition of his *Averroès et l'averroïsme: essai historique* (Paris: Calmann-Lévy, 1867). Martin L. Pine launches a defense of Pomponazzi, arguing that he did not hold a theory of double truth, in his *Pietro Pomponazzi: Radical Philosopher of the Renaissance* (Padova: Editrice Antenore, 1986).

25 See *The Star of Redemption*, 114. The best account of the three ages, and in particular what 1800 means for Rosenzweig, is offered by Franks and Morgan in their edition of Rosenzweig's *Philosophical and Theological Writings*, 27–43. I am indebted to their discussion.

26 It is doubtful, however, that the *duplex veritate* was banished in this period. One of its strongest statements is given by Luther in his "The Disputation Concerning the Passage: 'The Word Became Flesh' (John 1: 14)" (1539), trans. Martin E. Lehmann, *Luther's Works*, 55 vols., vol. 38, *Word and Sacrament*, vol. 4, ed. Martin E. Lehmann, gen. ed. Helmut T. Lehmann (Philadelphia: Fortress Press, 1971). See especially the second thesis: "In theology it is true that the Word was made flesh; in philosophy the statement is simply impossible and absurd," 239.

27 Hegel, *Faith and Knowledge*, trans. and ed. Walter Cerf and H. S. Harris (Albany, NY: State University of New York Press, 1977), 56.

28 See William Wallace, trans., *Hegel's Logic: Being Part One of the "Encyclopaedia of the Philosophical Sciences" (1830)*, foreword J. N. Findlay (Oxford: Clarendon Press, 1975), §§ 44, 45.

29 Peter Eli Gordon proposes the suggestive expression "temporal holism" for the "new totality" that Rosenzweig has in mind. See his *Rosenzweig and Heidegger: Between Judaism and German Philosophy* (Los Angeles, CA: University of California Press, 2003), 203.

30 See Levinas, "Interview with François Poiré," *IRB*, 40–1.

31 For examples of the approach of the Outside, see Blanchot, *WTC*, 4 (13–14), and *OWM*, 24 (47–8).

32 Levinas, *EeI*, 50.

33 See Blanchot, *WD*, 65, 116 (108, 178). I leave aside the important and delicate question as to the relations between the *il y a* and the Outside. Suffice it to say that for Levinas the *il y a* can be overcome, and this event is needed for ethics to begin while for Blanchot the human relation subsists in and through the approach of the Outside.

34 See Wahl, *Human Existence and Transcendence*, 28.

35 Friedrich Schlegel, *Philosophical Fragments*, trans. Peter Firchow, foreword Rodolphe Gasché (Minneapolis, MN: University of Minnesota Press, 1991), 45. Blanchot quotes this fragment in "The Athenaeum," *IC*, 359 (527).

36 Blanchot, "The Athenaeum," 359 (527).

37 Blanchot quotes Mallarmé's expression as an epigraph to *IC* as well as in the first numbered paragraph in "The Absence of the Book," *IC*, 422 (620).

38 Blanchot, "Note," *IC*, xii (vii).

39 Hegel says nothing about the Jewish conception of the Messiah in his Berlin lectures on the philosophy of religion. See, however, his remarks on the Messiah as a concept formed by way of political expectations in his early essay "The Positivity of the Christian Religion," *Early Theological Writings*, trans. T. M. Knox, intro. and fragments trans. Richard Kroner (Philadelphia, PA: University of Pennsylvania Press, 1971), 158–9.

40 Blanchot, "Prophetic Speech," *BC*, 80 (111). Blanchot adds a little later, "speech prophesies when it refers to a time of interruption, that *other* time that is always

present in all time and in which people, stripped of their power and separated from the possible (the widow and the orphan), exist with each other in the bare relationship in which they had been in the desert and which is the desert itself—bare relationship, but not unmediated, for it is always given in a prior speech," 81.
41 Blanchot, "Humankind," *IC*, 134 (197).
42 See Robert Antelme, *The Human Race*, trans. Jeffrey Haight and Annie Mahler (Malboro, VT: The Malboro Press, 1992), 5.
43 See the essays in Levinas's collection *GCM*.
44 Blanchot, "Reading," *SL*, 196 (259).
45 Levinas, *TI*, 28.
46 Levinas, *TI*, 101.
47 David V. Erdman, ed., *The Complete Poetry and Prose of William Blake*, new and rev. ed., commentary by Harold Bloom (Los Angeles, CA: University of California Press, 1982), 721.
48 Blanchot, "The Marriage of Heaven and Hell," *FP*, 29 (38).
49 See Blanchot, "On One Approach to Communism," *F*, 296 n. 3 (112 n.).
50 Blanchot, "Ars Nova," *IC*, 350 (514).
51 Rosenzweig, "The New Thinking," 122.
52 Ellen T. Charry, *Franz Rosenzweig and the Freedom of God* (Bristol, IN: Wyndam Hall Press, 1987), 106.
53 Charry points out with good reason that "although [Rosenzweig] did not exempt God from his metalogical principle, neither did he draw all the conclusions about God that were implied by his presuppositions," and she suggests that drawing his conclusions would distance him from orthodoxy. See her *Franz Rosenzweig and the Freedom of God*, 107.
54 See Blanchot, "The Absence of the Book," *IC*, 433 (635).

12

"The *Absolute* Event of History"

The Shoah and the Outside

We often think of *L'Écriture du désastre* (1980) as being Blanchot's reflections on two things above all, the utter horror of the Shoah and the anguish produced by the approach of the Outside, both of which he calls disaster; and when we read the work with that assumption in mind we find ourselves unsettled by the question how the two things hang together, if indeed they do.[1] That Anglophones are encouraged to read *L'Écriture du désastre* in just that way is evident: in English the title of the translation reads *The Writing of* the *Disaster* [my emphasis], and even before we open the text we are invited to think of HaShoah above all. For the 1986 cloth edition has a cover image of what seems to be a disfigured scroll, while the 1995 paperback edition reproduces on its cover a fragment of the Torah that had been used as a backdrop for Nazi executions of Jews in Pultusk, Poland; it is preserved now in the Holocaust Memorial Museum in Washington, DC.[2] In French the title has been pointed in exactly the same direction though in another way entirely, by Claude Lanzmann's widely discussed documentary film *Shoah* (1985), the script of which the filmmaker calls "writing of disaster."[3] And perhaps Blanchot's reference to the film a year after it was shown has helped to secure for some of his more devoted readers the Shoah as the primary reference of his work.[4]

There is of course good reason to object, right at the start, that Blanchot uses the word "*désastre*" many times before he does so in *L'Écriture du désastre*. Like many French men and women, he refers to the defeat of France in June 1940 as "*le désastre,*" and that was before the Shoah occurred.[5] And one might point out that only a few of the 403 fragmentary passages in the text address the Shoah in any way at all.[6] As we read *L'Écriture du désastre* we find ourselves faced with elliptic ponderings about desire and disaster (each word derives from Latin, the one from *de* + *sidus* and the other from *dis* + *astro,* so both allude to stars); we encounter thoughts about moral responsibility for the other person (especially as investigated by Levinas), about the immemorial loss of selfhood (in particular with respect to Donald Winnicott and Serge Leclaire); we are asked to read two "primal scenes" of apprehending the Outside drawing close, one apparently autobiographical (Blanchot as a child), and one about the poet as an anti-Narcissus; and we are incidentally invited to reflect about atheism, *Ereignis*, forgiveness, the gift, Jena Romanticism, Jewish Messianism, and other topics. *L'Écriture du désastre* is an archipelago of remarks, injunctions, broodings, anecdotes, somber lyrical riffs, and questions, and the Shoah is perhaps not even at what we might be tempted to call its center. A better candidate for that position, if one really wants to read the text against its grain, would be the prose poem "(Une scène primitive?)" in which Blanchot appears as a child receiving a joyful revelation that there is no God, no overarching meaning to reality.[7] Yet even if the Shoah is not the animating concern of the text, the very fact that it is one of the topics leagued with the thought of the Outside rouses us to query the link purportedly between them.

Is there a connection between the Shoah as a disaster and the disaster that Blanchot associates early and late with writing? Blanchot himself gives us reason to doubt it, since he says, early in the gathering of fragments, "I will not say that the disaster [*le désastre*] is absolute; on the contrary, it disorients the absolute."[8] And then, much later, we read, "*The holocaust, the* absolute *event of history—which is a date in history—that utterburn* [cette toute-brûlure] *where all history took fire . . . ."*[9] At first it is puzzling to hear tell of any historical event as "absolute," since we would generally regard all events as unavoidably conditioned by the temporal processes that envelop them. No event fully absolves itself from time and place; historians trace the causes and the effects of even the Shoah. Hegel's God is the *absolute Idee*, being in and for itself, and his incarnation could be construed as an absolute event in world history (although Hegel does not write in just those terms). Yet Blanchot is thinking the absolute otherwise, not as historically unconditioned but as an event that stands apart from all others in Western history, including many others that should still appall us—the Armenian massacres, the Gulag, the "ethnic cleansing" of the Bosnian War, and the Russian invasion of Ukraine, to name only a few in modern times—or that share certain traits with the Shoah; and this claim of being set apart from all other events is presumably justified by the Nazi quest to murder all Jews, regardless of the cultural, religious, intellectual, moral, political, or physical determinants that distinguish us one from another, by the efficiency of the modern bureaucratic machine that killed without passion, and also by dint of their view that "the final solution" would benefit the world.[10]

Two issues come quickly to the fore. The first concerns whether the Shoah can properly be called "absolute" in the sense of unrepeatable and what can follow from this sort of claim. Presumably, if the Shoah is held to be unique in history it must be in a sense that is qualitatively distinct from that of other historical events, which are themselves distinctive even if similar to many other events, and I have already given three criteria that justify such a claim. To maintain that the Shoah is absolutely individual, whether by way of Nazi intention or by way the emerging function of the extermination camps, is to distinguish it from all other atrocities, although one cannot with any confidence extend the claim to the future. We have no idea what sort of dire events may come later this century or in another century. There may be genocide that is even more cruelly and more efficiently achieved, whether directed at the Jews or other people. There is always the possibility that the Shoah may have to yield its status as being absolutely unique to being relatively unique, which of course is not to diminish its horror one jot. Related to this first concern is the consequence of speaking of the Shoah in ways that separate it qualitatively from all other monstrosities. For it can always be appealed to in a rhetorical manner to distract attention from other instances of human wickedness, including those that were contemporaneous with it (e.g., the barbarities of the Russians as they moved toward the Eastern Front), and it can be used to support aggressive policies, such as those affecting the Palestinians, for instance.

The second issue is internal to Blanchot's thought. We may wonder if the advent of the Outside can indeed disorient something incommensurable with other historical events, something that interrupts them and cannot be measured by them, no matter how abhorrent they have been. At the same time, even if we know *L'Espace littéraire* (1955) and the other writings where Blanchot broods on the approach of the Outside, we shall surely wonder how this disaster can be figured in the context of history, and in the history of the Shoah in particular, and, if it can, what its pertinence there might be. We are likely to think first of the Outside as it almost touches and certainly disconcerts the writer, if only because that scene is so starkly lit in Blanchot's earlier works. In writing—intransitive writing, as he emphasizes—one passes from an "I" to a "he" or a "she" or an "it" [*il*]; one becomes other than what one presumes to be oneself. Of course, one's empirical ego remains, as does the constituting ego, which generates what Husserl would call a phenomenological onlooker.[11] Unlike Husserl, though, Blanchot insists that this observer does not perceive the being of phenomena but their loss of being. For when writing one brushes against a non-world of image. We remember that signal and terrifying essay "La littérature et le droit à la mort" (1949) and the counterintuitive sense of literature that is given there, of something that seems interior to the writer being in fact "the outside" [*le dehors*].

In a thoroughly Nietzschean manner Blanchot often thinks of art by way of the artist, not the work, and he does so when pondering the Outside. Disaster is evoked primarily with respect to writing, and it involves anguish for the author, while, in a phased counterpart, reading involves the communication of contact with the origin, the loss of reality as it passes into image, and calls forth a "light, innocent yes" from the reader, an affirmation of the neutral.[12] Yet one hardly thinks of Blanchot, like Nietzsche, regarding art as a value for life. Art is an "experience through which the consciousness discovers its being in its inability to lose consciousness, in the movement whereby, as it disappears, as it tears itself away from the meticulousness of an I." This fraught consciousness, he goes on to say, "is re-created beyond consciousness as an impersonal spontaneity, the desperate eagerness of a haggard knowledge which knows nothing, which no-one knows, and which ignorance always discovers behind itself as its own shadow changed into a gaze."[13] Art compromises the nothingness of death, then; it grants the artist a ghastly quasi-resurrection on either side of the grave, a nonlife of consciousness without selfhood, each time it is viewed or read. Several years after "La littérature et le droit à la mort," in *L'Espace littéraire*, Blanchot speaks in words that make the Outside seem even less attractive. Art, he says there, indicates "the menacing proximity of a vague and vacant outside, a neutral existence, nil and limitless; art points into a sordid absence, a suffocating condensation where being ceaselessly perpetuates itself as nothingness."[14] Given that, why write?

One answer is because literature, and art generally, puts us directly in touch with what is the case; we may avoid the complicated detour of philosophy. Art does not bring us to the "true world" or even the "apparent world" but, as Nietzsche saw, to the space we can enter when we twist free of the distinction.[15] For Blanchot, art conducts us to image, and image evacuates being as such yet without leaving a simple void that at a pinch could be regarded as at least pure. Image, note, not image*s*: as noted in Chapter 3, Blanchot does not prize the coruscating visual figure, such as one finds so memorably in poems by Eliot, Pound, and Williams, but insists on writing leading the author into a state of image understood as a circular passage from being to nothingness and from nothingness back to being. And here we begin to see what it could mean to say that the writer is only *approached* by the Outside, since all that he or she experiences is a movement from reality to non-reality, one that can always be cut short by a sudden return to reality. In truth, it is the author who almost touches the Outside by writing; and it cannot appear as phenomenon because strictly it is without being. Also, it must be pointed out that the author elicits experience of the Outside by the act of writing (or even, Blanchot suggests, in the wake of writing).[16] Yet because one cannot master this experience—because, for Blanchot, image does not supply the traction one needs for experience—it has the phenomenological sense of coming over the writer, like a mood. It is as though works of literature were icons of the Outside, and the writers, aberrant icon makers, were fascinated by the dark gaze that comes from the Outside even as they attend to the job in hand, writing a poem or a story.

If this sense of losing the possibility of mastery in the act of writing is honestly acknowledged, Blanchot thinks, the work before one cannot be fashioned into a whole. Fragmentary texts or those that spill over into endless discourse are therefore to be regarded as testimonies to the artist's struggle with disaster. By the time of *L'Entretien infini* (1969) he speaks, as we have already noticed once or twice in this book, of writing that devotes itself "solely to itself as something that remains without identity, and little by little brings forth possibilities that are entirely other: an anonymous, distracted, deferred, and dispersed way of being in relation," which is precisely what he calls the Outside.[17] Blanchot commends those writers—Artaud, Char, Kafka, and Sade, among others—who variously allow themselves to yield to the Outside as it impinges on them and produce works that upset the canons of literary mastery and the pleasures of *le beau style* whether by seeking to say everything (Sade and Proust, for instance) or by trying to write in a fragmentary way (e.g., Joubert and Char). Inevitably, we wonder about those writers—Homer and Vergil, Shakespeare and Racine, Richardson and Goethe, among so many others—whose works seem not to fit into Blanchot's canon. Did they never accede to the Outside? Or, if they did, did they refuse to take it with all due seriousness?

I leave these questions to echo without answers, for two reasons. In the first place, Blanchot's heavy emphasis on the author, not the work, makes it impossible to give satisfactory answers: we would need to know about the author's experience when composing, which is generally hidden from us. And in the second place, the criterion of surrendering to the Outside seems to be very flexible. One could say, for instance, that Lawrence Sterne's *Tristram Shandy* (1759-67) is, if only in its relentless digressions, repetitions, and amplifications, like Sade's *Juliette* (1797-1801). As such, it exceeds most social and cultural norms in its desire to say everything, not often by way of scandalously revealing what Christian morality condemns but by writing intransitively and thereby secreting things that are usually directed to an end, subordinated to it, and even hidden in deference to it. Appeals to the Outside cannot be used as a means of doing literary criticism, especially practical criticism; for, as noted in the very first chapter, *L'Espace littéraire* is anterior to all critique and exegesis; it is reflection on the act of writing, its relation with the origin of art, not evaluation of particular pieces of writing.[18] Nonetheless, we are likely to remain puzzled by the status of Blanchot's canon within the canon (or perhaps canon apart from the canon).

The Outside is not always so inscrutable. At first glance, it may well seem that Blanchot's view of it changes quite significantly from 1955 to 1969. In the later period it is associated not with "a sordid absence" that invisibly preys upon the writer who becomes in our eyes almost heroic in his or her endurance of it but rather with a new way of being human, indeed, with a utopian vision of society as beyond any party politics. The appearance is deceptive, since Blanchot had regarded communism as "an affirmation that is entirely *other*" long before *les événements de mai* 1968, indeed as early as 1955 when he had also perceived its convergence with the experience of the artist.[19] The potential political dimension of the Outside is underlined in "L'homme de la rue" (1962) where we are told that the person on the street is always on the verge of becoming "political man."[20] No doubt the person on the street can always spontaneously join *une manifestation*, but public demonstrations are only a small part of political life. One can become politicized by reading a newspaper or by listening to the radio at home. Nonetheless, the claim makes one think about the possible range and nature of the Outside, and the thought shall remain with us. Yet while a canon of writers and a form of politics can be commended as more preferable than others, one could not do the same for any historical event, let alone those that are dire, the Shoah above all. It seems to be one thing, then, to mark an unexpected convergence between art and a political program, especially one seen through utopian lenses, and quite another to discern a conjunction between the Shoah and the Outside.

*

As we have already seen, in *L'Écriture du désastre* Blanchot uses the word "holocaust," which is problematic because of its suggestion that the attempted annihilation of the Jews was a sacrifice.[21] The Hebrew השואה, "catastrophe" or "calamity," has a stronger claim to denote the event. The first recorded use of it in English, according to the OED, is 1967, and it appears to have been used all that often in French only after Lanzmann's film. As a common noun it is a biblical word—see, for instance, Zeph. 1: 15—though nowadays in modern Hebrew, when the singular form *HaShoah* is used, it names the Nazi attempt to annihilate Jewry in Europe.[22] Hebrew-speaking Jews have used the word as early as the German invasion of Poland, years before the discovery of the extermination camps.[23] One might well translate השואה by "*désastre*," as Lanzmann suggests, yet Blanchot figures the meaning of the latter word by way of a creative etymology: he does not follow the usual semantic path, regarding a disaster as something ill-fated because of the unfavorable position of a planet but takes another path and thinks of it as the state of "being separated from the star," a "break with every form of totality," and the condition of having to wander without a fixed point of orientation.[24] These senses of the word seem more adequate to the uprising in Paris of 1968 than to what was suffered at Auschwitz and the other death camps. We may also ponder whether Blanchot's endless meditation on death and dying is appropriate to what we know of the camps. For Auschwitz names murder, rather than death, evokes terror and dehumanizing treatment of men, women, and children rather than "the ease of dying."[25]

In searching for a plausible connection between the Shoah and the Outside we note that Blanchot proposes a duality of an unusual sort, one that involves the phenomenal, on the one hand, and something neutral that purportedly precedes it, on the other. The duality is given as an injunction we have heard in earlier chapters: "there must always [*il faut toujours*] be at least two languages, or two requirements: one dialectical, the other not; one apart, cut off both from being and from not-being."[26] Dedicated readers of Blanchot will recall a similar dictum in *L'Entretien infini*, one phrased by way of continuous action: naming the possible and responding to the impossible.[27] Exactly what motivates and justifies the necessity of these charges to us is unclear, as is their status. Are they regulative norms, moral commands, political precepts, or pragmatic ways of coping with reality? Are they beliefs of some sort?

When we read *L'Écriture du désastre* a little more closely we may not find definite answers to these questions, although we may well become clearer about the aim and scope of the duality. We realize that it turns on a distinction between experience and non-experience, event and nonevent, and we understand that no straight line divides the two, for non-experience shares a decisive trait with experience, what we might call intransitive endurance. We see that the duality involves a contrast between work and absence of work, the freedom of a subject to think and act and the passivity of a prisoner (in a concentration camp) or a hostage (in a moral situation as Levinas sees it).[28] And we also understand that the distinction places an entire philosophical thematic —perhaps even "philosophy" itself—on one side and something else on the other with no possibility of reconciling or overcoming the two. One language is "dialectical," presumably Hegelian or Marxist but maybe also Socratic and Medieval (as part of the trivium), and the other language is neutral, given neither to dialectic nor to fusion, and is cued to the Outside.

In reflecting on this distinction, we may well question whether we can rightly separate experience and non-experience so simply in reference to the "I." There are large-scale events that exceed the possibility of being grasped by any individual or even a group or a generation, and the same might be said of micro-events. Social history does not seem to be wholly written with Blanchot's sense of experience in play.[29] And there are passive syntheses that structure personal experiences of which we are quite unaware unless we engage in a genetic phenomenological investigation, which is rare in the extreme. The reservation is important, for it is entirely possible for the distinction Blanchot draws to foreclose on appropriate distinctions essential for understanding how inmates acted and reacted in the camps. It allows for those inmates to be conceived entirely as victims and not to have the slightest agency when testimony and history speak otherwise. The Fortunoff Video Archive provides oral historical evidence (with all the problems of fallible memory involved) of individual Jews who were determined to defy the Nazis as long as their strength allowed them to do anything.[30] And we somberly remember the *Sonderkommando* revolt of October 1944.

Another reflection on the distinction leads us to quite other areas. We would be wrongheaded to characterize the second language Blanchot identifies as antiphilosophical and mistaken even to regard it as simply nonphilosophical (e.g., as "literary" or "testimonial,"). For while Western thought has never quite been able to name the Outside and has never fully been able to come to terms with its neutrality, it has nonetheless almost touched on it from time to time. Apophatic theology with its characteristic syntax of neither-nor has been in the service of approaching an ineffable deity when, according to Blanchot, it should have been used to identify the Outside.[31] Heraclitus and Nietzsche, to name two important figures in Blanchot's philosophical canon, have sometimes broached the Outside in their thinking. So too has Levinas; and we must remember that Blanchot's fragmentary text has a genesis in a reading of *Autrement qu'être* (1974).[32] The other person is radically outside me, beyond the net of my intentional rapport with the world. He or she is indeed an enigma, not a phenomenon. Yet it is Nietzsche's thought of the eternal return that generates a main problematic of Blanchot's extended work. (Strictly speaking, we should say this work elaborates eternal return without the thought of the will to power or, rather, with a certain understanding of passivity.[33]) How can the Outside return if it is not a phenomenon in the first place? How can we ever discover the Outside if it does not manifest itself in the order of phenomena? Is it always thought and therefore, as Kant tells us, not phenomenal?

*

We have already heard part of an answer to the second question in thinking about the artist's relation with image. Yet Blanchot approaches it from another perspective in *L'Entretien infini*, in a long meditation on poetry and the sacred, elicited by a reading of Yves Bonnefoy's *L'Improbable* (1959). One prompt to becoming aware of the Outside, Blanchot thinks, is our consciousness of internal time. We would be drawn into "an entirely other experience," he writes, "if it happened that this experience were that of a time out of synchrony and as though deprived of the dimension of passing beyond, henceforth neither passing nor ever having had to pass."[34] This experience is not difficult to find, he tells us, for it may be discerned "in the most common suffering, and first of all in physical suffering." (So, for Blanchot thought, even agonizing thought, cannot be strictly identical with disaster.) He is not considering the case of undergoing sharp or even blunt pain, for then, hard though it may be, one knows that the misery will end, even if that end is death. Instead, he has in mind suffering without any end: no point and no terminus.

What happens in this state?

> Suffering has simply lost its hold on time, and has made us lose time. Would we then be freed in this state from any temporal perspective and redeemed, saved from time as it passes? Not at all: we are delivered over to another time—to time as other, as absence and neutrality; precisely to a time that can no longer redeem us, that constitutes no recourse. A time without event, without project, without possibility; not that pure immobile instant, the spark of the mystics, but an unstable perpetuity in which we are arrested and incapable of permanence, a time neither abiding nor granting the simplicity of a dwelling place.[35]

Suffering leads us not above phenomena but, as it were, beneath them. It leads us out of the illusions of a permanent supersensible world that we can touch in contemplative prayer, and away too from the pagan consolation of living in a given place with long-inherited pieties to cherish and practice.[36]

This train of thought allows me to turn briefly to a question raised a little earlier, whether belief is involved in any way in affirming the Outside. Blanchot is eager to reassure us that disaster cannot be figured in the register of belief or faith; if anything, he writes, it is commensurate with "*a sort of disinterest*" because the approach of the Outside deflects the "I" toward the third person.[37] Yet we may well pause before accepting his view, in part because the Outside does not seem to be anything one could establish as true by sound and valid arguments and in part because we do not find it affirmed in common or even uncommon human experience in any clear or definite manner. Could Blanchot's thought of the Outside be a belief in a nonreligious sense, an attitude adopted to what is taken to be the case? Nietzsche figures belief as "a considering-something-true."[38] For Heidegger, Nietzsche's thought of the eternal return is a belief in just this sense; it determines "*how* the world essentially *is*," namely perpetual becoming: the eternal return is "the Being that determines all beings."[39] In the same way, one might suggest that for Blanchot the approach of the Outside, disaster, which itself is said to recur eternally, is how things are, with the caveat that it is not the Being of beings or even what he will come to prefer to call *Seyn*, a non-metaphysical understanding of Being.[40] Indeed, at several points in *L'Écriture du désastre* Blanchot proposes that disaster is thought (apparently using the "is" of identity), and if so this would be why it could return without ever being a phenomenon. For, as we say, thoughts return to us.

When Blanchot writes of suffering he does so in a Heideggerian manner, one that breathes the air of the German thinker's first seminars in which there was talk, partly directed against Husserl, of a reduction from beings to being.[41] Suffering prompts reduction of an unusual kind, Blanchot thinks, not from the natural attitude to the transcendental attitude, as for Husserl, but from the world of meaning and work to the non-world of the Outside and idling there. We pass from one understanding of "experience" to another, from that which we can master by the activity of an "I," whether empirical or transcendental, to that which imperils us by dispossessing us of such mastery.[42] One of the burdens of *L'Écriture du désastre* is that the Outside never quite becomes an event or an experience, and so it is strictly immemorial. It is not that one enjoys substantial selfhood and then, by dint of an accident, loses it; one has never had it in the first place. In being led back to the Outside through the experience of suffering one realizes that the "I" has never been established, certainly not in the way that Descartes thought possible. One is a subject, if one is, legally and politically but not metaphysically. "In a sense," Blanchot writes, "the 'I' cannot be lost, because it does not belong to itself. It only is, therefore, not its own, and therefore as always already lost" and, later we find the lapidary paradox, "'I' die before being born."[43] So the approach of the Outside is a disaster, but not one in a series of empirical events, catastrophic or tragic, that could be detailed over the course of a life.[44] Instead, it is an unmooring from any sure thing that had it actually existed would have served to guide us or insulate us: God, the One, the Self, Truth, and so on.

In Blanchot's discussion of Bonnefoy it is "the most common suffering" that attunes us to the Outside: not anything sharp but "a phantom of suffering," a dulling of the "I."[45] Yet it must be said in all simplicity that the suffering endured in the camps was uncommon in the extreme, all the more so as concentration camps became extermination camps. Once again it must be asked what link, if any, there is between the Shoah and the approach of the Outside. I think the question can be answered in two ways, one from a great distance and another from up very close to his texts. In the first place, one might say that, for Blanchot, what led to the possibility of the Shoah was not the pervasive nihilism in Europe between the wars but rather a lack of thought about what had long been happening in Europe, beginning with Hegel but not confined to him or to philosophy: a sense that the West had consummated its own end, and that the consequences of this exhaustion needed to be thought through so that the end did not repeat itself ever more violently in history.[46] Only if one writes in a certain way—the fragmentary—can what he calls the "absolute event of history" be deflected from happening again in another form.[47] By promoting "an anonymous, distracted, deferred, and dispersed way of being in relation," such writing will eventually shift all that we have valued in the West—God, Self, Truth, and so on—and enable us to move to a "communism beyond communism," beyond the violence of the 1917 Revolution which was itself a consequence of failing to think the end of the West.[48]

We have a moral responsibility to make that shift precisely because of the Shoah. As Blanchot says, in an undated letter to Bernard-Henri Lévi (but addressing the dead of Auschwitz), that I have quoted before, "You who are now dead, you who died for us and often because of us (because of our shortcomings) [*O morts, morts pour nous et souvent par nous (par notre défaut)*] you must not be allowed to die a second time, and silence must not mean that you sink into oblivion."[49] In pausing after reading these moving words, we need to reflect on the motif of sacrifice—*morts pour nous*—which is one with the very word "Holocaust" and which Blanchot nowhere examines. At the same time, we should ponder the motif of a second death, as happens to Eurydice when Orpheus descends to the underworld in order to reclaim her, which is so common in Blanchot's writing. The dead of Auschwitz cannot return to the world, and we cannot speak properly of what horrors they suffered, but our silence must not be the silence of forgetting. Eurydice died a second time by too direct a look of her husband. Blanchot's gaze at those who were in Auschwitz will be indirect in order to respect the brute fact of their deaths.

In the second place, an answer comes into focus for us when we recognize that in *L'Écriture du désastre* Blanchot does not attend principally to the actual murder of Jews and others at Treblinka, Belzec, Sobibor, Chelmo, and Auschwitz itself. His concern, rather, is with the affliction of the prisoners, and the fragments in question see into that dark world through what a historian would regard as a narrow aperture. For Blanchot relies very heavily on the French translation of Hermann Langbein's documentary study of life and death in the camps, *Menschen in Auschwitz* (1972).[50] More than Langbein's book, however, it is Antelme's testimony to life in concentration camps, *L'Espèce humaine* (1957), which guides Blanchot in his remarks on the Shoah and the Outside.[51] Antelme was a political *déporté* and his was not a Jewish experience of the camps—there were no gas chambers at Buchenwald or Gandersheim—and this is important, as we shall see. We need to remember that in French commentary on the Second World War the word *déporté* can well elide crucial differences between political prisoners and the Jews.[52] Antelme's book is nonetheless a searing account of the hunger, fear, powerlessness, degrading labor, sickness, mistreatment, and lack of hope that pervaded all the camps. Different groups populated Auschwitz-Birkenau, and the camp's function changed from its establishment in May 1940 to the first gassings of Jews with Zyklon B in September 1941 to the beginning of the systematic gassings of Jews in June 1942. At first inmates were neglected on purpose and worked until they dropped, then forced labor started, and finally Jews were mostly murdered on arrival. Only 10–15 percent of each later shipment of Jews were allowed to work, some in the gas chambers, and these people usually survived a short time at best.

We need also to remember two things. First, many Gentiles were also subject to mass murder in the camps: the first such event at Auschwitz was of mental patients, none of whom was Jewish.[53] And, second, as already noted, there were heroic acts of individual and group resistance in the death camps, and even a few successful escapes: passivity was not the entire story.[54] Those things said, Blanchot's dialogue on this piercing testimony gives us a clue as to why, in his mind, the Shoah and the Outside must be thought together.

*

The participants in the eponymous dialogue "L'Espèce humaine" allow themselves to be guided by the question "Who is *Autrui*?," which, Blanchot quickly says, he associates with Antelme's book. At first the affiliation is surprising, to say the least, since most readers would tend to regard it as pre-eminently Levinas's question, and Levinas has been a tonic presence in *L'Entretien infini* long before Blanchot turns to Antelme. Indeed, Blanchot raises that exact question in one of several dialogues consecrated to *Totalité et infini* (1961). Those dialogues are at once admiring and critical, and it is especially important to see how they serve to refigure the status of the other person with respect to me as Levinas specifies it. For Levinas, the relation between Self and Other is asymmetrical in favor of the other person who speaks to me from on high in the mode of command. "The Other is not the incarnation of God," he writes, "but precisely by his face, in which he is disincarnate, is the manifestation of the height in which God is revealed."[55] And it must be noted right away that the deity Levinas has in mind here is conceived by way of goodness, not being; the ontological or metaphysical nature of God is bracketed.

Early on, one of the participants in Blanchot's dialogue "Connaissance de l'inconnu" observes, "Let us leave aside God [*Laissons Dieu de côté*]—the name is too imposing."[56] Yet later in the same dialogue the deity returns when one of the participants recalls Levinas saying, "All true discourse . . . is a discourse with God, not a conversation held between equals," which is explicated as follows: "This speech of eminence, which speaks to me from very far away, from very high above (or very far below), is the speech of someone who does not speak with me on an equal footing and such that it is not possible for me to address myself to *autrui* as though he were another Myself" (56). The participant goes on to worry whether this speech could be no more than "tranquil humanist and Socratic speech," and has reservations about the French philosopher's reliance on oral communication. Is it no more than what Socrates prizes in *Phaedrus* 274b–277a, the passage where he condemns writing? Does it not have the irruptive force that Blanchot ascribes to "plural speech?"

A later dialogue, one more distantly tuned to Levinas' *Totalité et infini*, "Le rapport du troisième genre," returns to consider the way in which *autrui* impinges on me. "True strangeness, if it comes to me from man, comes to me from this Other that man would be."[57] Later, one of the participants clarifies this strangeness: "An experience in which the Other, *the Outside itself* [le Dehors même], exceeding any positive or any negative term, is the 'presence' that does not refer back to the One, and the exigency of a relation of discontinuity where unity is not implied" [my emphasis] (71). By this stage Blanchot has pushed Levinas's sense of the other person quite beyond his friend's chosen bounds. This happens in two stages or perhaps three if one considers that Blanchot and Levinas begin from different points. For Levinas figures the ethical relation in general whereas Blanchot treats it as arising from "being Jewish" and that situation—for Blanchot a moral state—being generalized over time.[58] First, Blanchot revises the asymmetry between the other person and myself on which Levinas insists. For I am the other of the other person, he counters, thereby stepping away from the intimate phenomenological theater to adopt a third-person perspective. Yet this is not a dialectical move that flattens moral height and that re-establishes as it were a Euclidean plane as the ground of moral life, a ground on which ethics presumes a *habitus* for virtue deep inside the self or a moral or political contract forged in an historical present whether past, present, or to come. In preference, we should speak of a "double dissymmetry," he writes,

> a double discontinuity, as though the empty space between the one and the other were not homogenous but polarized: as though this space constituted a non-isomorphic field bearing a double distortion, at once infinitely negative and infinitely positive, and such that one should call it neutral if it is well understood that the neutral does not annul, does not neutralize this double-signed infinity, but bears it in the way of an enigma.[59]

Of course, in revising asymmetry to double dissymmetry Blanchot is able to remove God from the scene of ethics, at least the God who comes to mind for Levinas.

The second stage of recasting Levinasian ethics consists of rethinking the scope of the *il y a*, "this impersonal, anonymous, yet inextinguishable 'consummation' of being, which murmurs in the depths of nothingness itself."[60] As Blanchot acknowledges, the *il y a* is close to the Outside, even to the point of being a synonym for it at times.[61] Yet for Levinas the *il y a* needs to be overcome for moral life to commence. As he says, "Consciousness is a rupture of the anonymous vigilance of the *there is*; it is already hypostasis; it refers to a situation where an existent is put in touch with its existing."[62] Not so for Blanchot, since, as we have seen, it is precisely this "anonymous vigilance" that detaches consciousness from selfhood; and ethics for him turns on the approach of the Outside in the very speech of the other person. With each new person's speech it comes, and this is in large part what justifies the language of return. More, since the Outside hollows out the interiority that has marked individuality, at least in modern times, the ethics of the moral agent is itself of secondary value. "If the question 'Who is *autrui*?' has no direct meaning, it is because it must be replaced by another: 'What of the human "community," when it must respond to this relation of strangeness between man and man—a relation without common measure, an exorbitant relation—that the experience of language leads one to sense?'"[63]

*

What might seem to be a digression concerning Blanchot's reworking of ethics according to Levinas is in fact merely an attempt to identify a connection between the Outside and the Shoah as economically as possible. For while Blanchot is almost exclusively an essayist in his critical work two of his books are very carefully revised to make arguments over varied and undulating territory. *L'Espace littéraire* is one and *L'Entretien infini* is another. In the latter work Blanchot carefully prepares what to his mind is the proper configuration of the Outside and community in his engagement with *Totalité et infini* in part one, "La parole plurielle," and then draws on it in "L'Indestructible" in part two, "L'Expérience-Limite." It is there that the question "Who is '*Autrui*'?" is detached from Levinas and re-assigned to Antelme in the context of dying and death in the camps. The axial claim in that essay is announced at the end of the opening paragraph: "In affliction we approach the limit where, deprived of the power to say 'I,' deprived also of the world, we would be nothing other than the Other that we are not."[64] It will be noted right away that Blanchot now specifies the Outside differently. Rather than speaking of a passage from *je* to *il*, and the otherness of the *il*, he directly evokes a movement from *je* to *Autre*.[65]

We need to remember that "L'Espèce humaine" is a dialogue, not an essay, and so we must be circumspect about assigning particular remarks to the Blanchot who signs the whole. Yet the thesis that Antelme and those with him in Buchenwald and Gandersheim lost the power to say "I" and in effect assumed the role of the other person, the one from whom the strangeness of the Outside comes, is accepted by both participants. Those who are reduced to eating scraps in order to survive nonetheless retain an ego, one speaker admits, yet we are told that it is "*an egoism without ego*," an attachment to life that has become impersonal and "in some sense neutral."[66] The other speaker then insists that this bare existence intent only on survival does not amount to any form of personal sovereignty. "When, therefore, my relation with myself makes me the absolutely Other [*l'Autre*] whose presence puts the power of the Powerful radically into question, this movement still signifies only the failure of power—not 'my' victory, still less 'my' salvation."[67] Only in this state of passivity, this situation in which one's "I" has become a "he" or a "she" or even an "it," can one "receive the unknown and the foreign, receive them in the justice of a true *speech*."[68] It is this speech that comes from the Outside, and in saying so the speaker utters a belief in precisely the sense that Nietzsche specifies.

Yet Blanchot realizes that even in somewhere as horrid as Buchenwald or Gandersheim elements of society can re-establish themselves:

> Among those who were deported [*les déportés*] there were doubtless relations that allowed them to reestablish an appearance of society, that therefore allowed each

one the occasion to feel himself or herself momentarily a self vis-à-vis someone in particular, or even to maintain a semblance of force in confronting those who were the Powerful (if only because the political struggle continued in the rest of the world and was preparing a new day). Had it been otherwise, everything would have immediately given way to a death without end. But what in this situation remains essential, its truth, is the following: the camp confined no more than a bondless entanglement of Others [*hommes Autres*], a magma of the other [*autrui*] face to face with the force of a Self that kills, and that represents nothing but the untiring power to kill. (134; 198)

Perhaps too little is said here, for we know that in both sorts of camps hierarchies were quickly formed, even if they varied with the shifting populations of the camps: Germans and Austrian criminals were at the top, Jews and Gypsies were far beneath, and the *Muselmänner* drifted along at the very bottom. And perhaps too much is also said, for we know that those interred in the camps did not tend to group together as one against the SS but that some prisoners had no choice but to cooperate with the SS in order to survive, that certain prisoners, those considered "Aryan," were rewarded with "bonus slips" (which could be cashed in at the Auschwitz brothel), and that there was much interracial and international conflict and even expressions of hatred among inmates.[69] And we should be wary about thinking of the SS as a lump, for there are occasional differences that need to be granted, for example, between those in the Political Department and some of those who served as sentries. The situation in even the extermination camps was not simply that of prisoners against the SS; the field of social tensions, even social violence, was far more complex.

We should test Blanchot's reading of Antelme against what Antelme himself writes in *L'Espèce humaine*. Here is one passage early on in the work about being summoned to a role call at Gandersheim:

A *Lagerschutz* calls out the names, butchering them. In among them, amidst Polish and Russian names, is my name. Laughter when my name is called, and I reply "Present." It sounded outlandish in my ear; but I'd recognized it. And so for one brief instant I had been directly designated here, I and no other had been addressed, I had been specially solicited—I, myself, irreplaceable! [*on m'a sollicité spécialement, moi, irremplaçable!*] And there I was. Someone had turned up to say yes to this sound, which was at least as much my name as I was myself, in this place. And you had to say yes in order to return into the night, into the stone that bore the nameless face. Had I said nothing, they would have hunted for me. . . . Then, having found me, the SS would have worked me over so as to make it clear to me that here being me really meant being me, and so as I'd have the logic of it good and straight in my head: that, around here, I was damned well I, and that this nothing that bore the name that had been read out was damned well me [*que moi c'était bien moi et que c'était bien moi ce rien qui portait ce nom qu'on avait lu*].[70]

Antelme's experience is of having lost power associated with selfhood and individuality and then, tragi-comically, having to claim it in a place where it can play no positive role. Yet, in his mind at least, the SS wishes not simply to extinguish his sense of self but to insist on it, so that it is regarded as a burden to him. Doubtless one aspect of their cruelty is in letting that sense of singularity fade only to retrieve it as something undesirable in any case. Later, at Ganderscheim, the sense of losing one's individuality intensifies as its loss is projected into the future:

> We are being transformed. Our faces and bodies are going downhill, there's no more telling the handsome from the ugly. In three months' time we'll be more different still, we'll be even less distinguishable from one another. Yet each of us will continue, in a vague way, to maintain the idea of his own singularity.[71]

This is not quite "the impossible experience of being for himself or herself the 'other' [*autrui*]" that Blanchot evokes, for the experience seems to be of both the impossible and the possible.[72] People barely survive in the camp, to be sure, but each person tries to grasp hold of his or her singularity right to the end. One can look also to Primo Levi's eloquent testimony about the same thing for support.[73]

For the sake of argument, let us assume that Blanchot is largely right, that those in the concentration camps existed more or less as is evoked in the dialogue, and perhaps we might also grant him that this extreme situation illuminates something essential about the human condition, that it enables us to understand better what is at issue when "two individuals approach one another."[74] Even if we were to accept all this, however, we would surely still admit two pressing distinctions. The first is between quotidian life and life in the camps. For the person on the street, the man or woman in the midst of everyday life, one has already passed from the first to the third person, as Blanchot sees things. "Day-to-day indifference is situation on a level at which the question of value is not posed," he says, and immediately evokes the Outside. "There is [*il y a*] the everyday (without subject, without object), and while there is, the everyday 'he' does not have to be of account; if value nonetheless claims to step in, then 'he' [or 'it,' *il*] is worth 'nothing' and 'nothing' is worth anything through contact with him."[75] Yet even if everyday life is neutral, in Blanchot's sense, it is qualitatively distinct from the supposed neutrality of life in a concentration camp. Second, it is equally important to separate the two sorts of camps. Auschwitz is a difficult case because of its growing complexity and changing functions over the years of the war; it started as a concentration camp and then became an extermination camp; it was very large, not one camp but three interrelated institutions, and the main one, which had the steadiest population, had 18,437 prisoners at the start of 1944 and 14,386 by the middle of the same year; and when the Russians came in January 1945 they liberated some 60,000 men, women, and children.[76]

Given the size of Auschwitz 1, it was possible for many there to experience the repetitive, dehumanizing existence that Antelme describes so memorably, to pass, if you like, from experience, normal or abnormal, to another experience, even if we demur at Blanchot's desire to call it "entirely other." Yet it must be stated clearly that as the war developed the Jews who arrived at Auschwitz, sometimes after long train rides in appalling conditions, were quickly selected for the gas chambers. Counting only French Jews who were sent to Auschwitz between mid-1942 and mid-1944, about 78.5 percent were chosen for immediate annihilation directly at the ramp where the train stopped.[77] Those who had to strip naked and run to the chambers did not, I dare say, experience themselves as having become other than themselves, except in the sense that they had been dehumanized. Rather, they screamed and clambered over one another, each asserting his or her "I," many banging against the locked door in the thin hope of breaking it down; some fought as best they could at the very entrance to the gas chamber in order to hang on to life—life in the first person—at any cost. It is worth hearing the testimony of Zalman Loewenthal, an inmate whose testimony about Auschwitz was hidden in a jar that he buried near the crematorium. Blanchot quotes some impressive words by him that come after a harrowing account of what life was like in Auschwitz—"The truth as it really exists is immeasurably more tragic and terrible"[78]—but he does not quote these earlier sentences:

> And our intelligence is subconsciously influenced by the wonderful will to live, by the impulse to remain alive; you try to convince yourself, as if you do not care about your own life, but want only the general good, to go through with all of this for this and that cause, for this and that reason; you finds hundreds of excuses, but the truth is that you want to live at any price. You desire to live, because you are alive, because the whole world continues to live, and everything that is pleasant, everything to which you are attached, is first and foremost attached to life itself.[79]

Loewenthal, a Polish Jew, was forced on pain of death to work in the *Sonderkommando*, in the gas chambers at Auschwitz, and one might presume that the weight of his experience of daily horror informs his claim, "you want to live at any price," which means one lives with the desire to say "I."

*

The approach of the Outside, what Blanchot calls "disaster," is presented to us in several registers. In intransitive writing, one passes, we are told, from the first to the third person: I become other than myself, and this would seem to occur by dint of yielding to the non-world of image that is inseparable from art. Blanchot's testimony to this situation is not quite unique, but it seems to be restricted to avant-garde writing of the sort that he admires from the Jena Romantics to Louis-René des Fôrets. One apprehends the Outside, also, it seems, in suffering and in thought, while in everyday life one also yields to life in the third person, although, to be sure, one can snap back into one's "I" at any moment. More than anyone else, it is Foucault who draws on disaster, as Blanchot conceives it, as indicating the erasure of the Classical and Renaissance figures of "man," and perhaps it will be seen as marking the beginning of a new understanding of the human being when the *cogito* and transcendental unity of apperception have long since frayed as viable concepts in a philosophical anthropology.[80] Perhaps too this new understanding of the human comes into focus most clearly in extreme situations, far from the reassurance of humanist social and moral norms, and Antelme's *L'Espèce humaine* is one place where we see the "I" flicker, even if Blanchot perhaps pushes us to think that it goes out when Antelme actually cups his hand around the flame to keep it alight.

Yet the extermination camps of the Shoah are different; they bespeak human wickedness at its most overt and most routinized, they point us to men, women, and children who, in the last years of the war, were mostly murdered upon arrival at a camp and who were not passive souls ranged against killers who clung to selfhood and power. Everyday life for the inmates on the *Sonderkommando* was not the same as quotidian life for those back in Paris; and suffering for those imprisoned in the extermination camps was extreme, not a phantom of suffering. The Shoah calls for a differentiated analysis, and fragmentary writing does not lend itself to such a thing. If there is "writing of disaster" directly to do with the Shoah, it is in those texts known as the "scrolls of Auschwitz," and the testimonies of survivors such as Jean Améry, Primo Levi, Elie Wiesel, and those who appeared in *Shoah*.[81] In these documents one does not find much testimony of neutral existence, either in writing or in a vision of a society to come, but the persistence of the desire to say "I."

It is true that, for Blanchot, the West failed for over a century to think through the consequences of its own end (and he includes his younger self in this criticism), and this thoughtlessness about the loss of the self, the loss of transcendence, and the loss of assured truth, created a void in which the Shoah could occur. The proper response to this thoughtlessness today is the writing of disaster, he contends, for only such disorienting writing can possibly deflect something as absolutely horrid as the Shoah from ever happening again. Perhaps, if writing is stronger than human evil; otherwise, it is no more than an oblique cry of "Never again!" Yet Blanchot's hope is stronger: the slide from God, the One, the Self, Truth, and so on, to a form of selfhood that is not centered on the power to say "I," to a way of being in relation one with another that is "anonymous, distracted, deferred, and dispersed," may well change humankind.[82] Maybe there is no more than an intellectual can do as intellectual. For a reader of *L'Écriture du désastre*, however, one would be well advised not to see there a convergence of the Outside and the Shoah but rather a diagnosis of the intellectual's responsibility to think disaster.

Notes

1 See, for instance, Michael Syrotinski, *Deconstruction and the Postcolonial* (Liverpool: Liverpool University Press, 2007), 117, and Gary D. Mole, *Levinas, Blanchot, Jabès: Figures of Estrangement* (Gainesville, FL: University Press of Florida, 1997), 15. The association of disaster and the Shoah in Blanchot's *ED* is marked in Holocaust Studies. See, for example, Noami Mandel, *Against the Unspeakable: Complicity, the Holocaust, and Slavery in America* (Charlottesville, VA: University of Virginia Press, 2006), 32. Geoffrey Hartman relates Blanchot to the Shoah in several places in two important works. See his *The Longest Shadow: In the Aftermath of the Holocaust* (New York: Palgrave Macmillan, 1996), 2, 10, 96, 162, and esp. 39. Also see Hartman's introduction to his edited collection of essays, *Holocaust Remembrance: The Shapes of Memory* (Oxford: Basil Blackwell, 1994), 5. Finally, see his essay, "Maurice Blanchot: The Spirit of Language after the Holocaust," *The Power of Contestation*, 46–65. A

caveat is entered at 53. It should also be noted that the most detailed reading of *ED* to date is offered by Hill in his *Maurice Blanchot and Fragmentary Writing: A Change of Epoch* (London: Continuum, 2012), ch. 4, and that he draws on Shoah testimony.

2 The cloth edition of the translation does not give a source for the cover image. On inquiring about the image, Nebraska University Press informed me that they have no record of the image and that the cover artist is deceased.

3 Claude Lanzmann, *Shoah: An Oral History of the Holocaust*, pref. Simone de Beauvoir (New York: Pantheon Books, 1985), xii.

4 See Blanchot, "Do Not Forget!," trans. Leslie Hill, *Paragraph* 30, no. 1 (2007): 35.

5 See Blanchot, "Après le désastre," *Journal des débats* (juillet 7, 1940): 1.

6 For example, Blanchot writes, "Kafka's narratives are among the darkest in literature, the most rooted in absolute disaster," *WF*, 10 (18). With regard to the number of fragments on the Shoah, I count no more than seven—see pp. 6, 47, 81, 82, 83, 143 (15, 80, 129–30, 130–1, 216)—although there may be many more that are implicitly about it. I should add that on other occasions when Blanchot evokes the Shoah he does not always use the word "*désastre.*" For example, in "Thinking the Apocalypse" he does not, while in "Do Not Forget" he does. See *PW*, 121, 127. I shall not consider in this chapter what might be regarded as Blanchot's anticipation of the Shoah in "The Idyll" and his reflection on it in "After the Fact." See *VC*, esp. 65–6 (*AC*, 95–6). See on this motif Sarah Kofman, *Smothered Words*, trans. Madeleine Dobie (Evanston, IL: Northwestern University Press, 1998).

7 I offer a detailed reading of this passage in my *The Dark Gaze*, ch. 3.

8 Blanchot, *WD*, 4 (12). Yet see the discussion of the absolute as the unconditioned approach of the Outside in Chapter 1.

9 Blanchot, *WD*, 47 (80). Blanchot quotes himself in "Do Not Forget," *PW*, 128. He refers to the Shoah as "an absolute which interrupted history" in *SNB*, 114 (156), he speaks of it as an "absolute caesura" in "Thinking the Apocalypse," *PW*, 122, and he writes of the Second World War as "an *absolute*" because of the Shoah in "War and Literature," *F*, 109 (128). Also see, in the same stream of thought, Philippe Lacoue-Labarthe's evocation of the Shoah as "pure event," *Heidegger, Art and Politics*, trans. Chris Turner (Oxford: Basil Blackwell, 1990), 45.

10 On the topic of killing without passion, it must be noted that the SS were characteristically normal German men usually with no history of sadism before being assigned work in the camps. That alcohol was used and abused by some of the SS when performing their duty, and that this led to states of passion, must be conceded. See Hermann Langbein, *People in Auschwitz*, trans. Harry Zohn, foreword Henry Friedlander (Chapel Hill, NC: University of North Carolina Press, 2004), 273–301. Hannah Arendt, who also holds that the Shoah is an interruption of history, stresses the role of the passionless bureaucrat in evil in her *Eichmann in Jerusalem: A Report on the Banality of Evil* (New York: Viking Press, 1964). For her comments on the uniqueness of the extermination camps, see her *Essays in Understanding 1930–1954: Formation, Exile, and Totalitarianism*, ed. and intro. Jerome Kohn (New York: Schocken Books, 1994), 109, 199, 243. Finally, it must be noted that gas chambers have been reported to have been used in Croatia and North Korea in modern times.

11 See Husserl, *Cartesian Meditations*, 35. Eugen Fink clarifies the phenomenological onlooker, distinguishing "him" or "her," from the empirical ego and the constituting ego in his *Sixth Cartesian Meditation: The Idea of a Transcendental Theory of Method, with Textual Notations by Edmund Husserl*, trans. and intro. Ronald Bruzina (Bloomington, IN: Indiana University Press, 1995).

12 See Blanchot, *SL*, esp. 196 (258–9). Yet Blanchot says, decades later, "Reading is anguish," because it requires each reader to make a leap. This seems to be a different thing from facing the Outside, however. See *WD*, 10 (23).
13 Blanchot, "Literature and the Right to Death," *WF*, 331–2 (320).
14 Blanchot, *SL*, 242–3 (326).
15 See Nietzsche, "How the 'Real World' at last Became a Myth," *Twilight of the Idols*, in *Twilight of the Idols and the Anti-Christ*, trans. and intro. R. J. Hollingdale (Harmondsworth: Penguin, 1968), 40–1.
16 See Blanchot, *WD*, 7, 11, 12 (17, 24, 27).
17 Blanchot, *IC*, xii (viii).
18 Levinas, "The Poet's Vision," *PN*, 127.
19 See Blanchot, "On One Approach to Communism," *F*, 97 (114).
20 Blanchot, "Everyday Speech," *IC*, 241 (359).
21 Yet the word "holocaust" was itself not used at first in connection with the attempt to exterminate the Jews. See Gerd Korman, "The Holocaust in American Historical Writing," in *Holocaust: Religious and Philosophical Implications*, ed. John K. Roth and Michael Berenbaum (New York: Paragon House, 1989), 45–50.
22 For most Jews, especially those in Israel, HaShoah is remembered each year on Yom HaShoah which, since 1953, occurs on the twenty-seventh of Nisan.
23 Reservations about using the word "Shoah" have been voiced. Dominick LaCapra, for one, notes that "For an American to use the term *Shoah* may have a slightly exoticizing potential," *Writing History, Writing Trauma* (2001; Baltimore, MD: Johns Hopkins University Press, 2014), 160.
24 Blanchot, *WD*, 2, 75 (9, 121). Yet see Blanchot's remarks on etymology, 96, 103–4, 116, 119 (150–1, 160–1, 179, 183–4).
25 See Blanchot, "The Ease of Dying," *F*, 149–68 (172–91). It should be made clear, right at the start, that "Auschwitz" names what became three interconnected camps—Auschwitz 1 (Auschwitz main camp), 2 (Birkenau), and 3 (Monowitz)—and that there were forty-five sub-camps around it. A separate camp for the Roma, the *Zigeunerfamilienlager*, was established at Auschwitz 2.
26 Blanchot, *WD*, 20 (38).
27 See Blanchot, "The Great Refusal," *IC*, 48 (68–9).
28 See Levinas, *OB*, 59.
29 See, for example, Bernard Lepetit, ed., *Les Formes de l'expérience: Une autre histoire sociale* (Paris: Albin Michel, 1995).
30 A signal testimony in the Fortunoff Archive in this spirit is that of Helen K., Tape A-35.
31 See Foucault, "Maurice Blanchot: The Thought from Outside," 16. Also see Foucault's reference to Blanchot, as one of the heralds of the modern *episteme*, in *The Order of Things: An Archeology of the Human Sciences* (New York: Vintage Books, 1994), 384.
32 See Blanchot, "Discourse sur la patience," 19–44.
33 See, among other places, Blanchot, *SNB*, 11–16, 21–23, 29–30, 40–2 (21–7, 33–6, 44–5, 58–61) and *IC*, 272–81, 148–50, 158–9 (408–18, 222–5, 237–9).
34 Blanchot, "The Great Refusal," *IC*, 44 (62).
35 Blanchot, "The Great Refusal," *IC*, 44 (63).
36 See Blanchot, "Being Jewish," *IC*, 125 (183).
37 Blanchot, *WD*, 2 (8).
38 Nietzsche, *The Will to Power*, trans. Walter Kaufmann and R. J. Hollingdale, ed. Walter Kaufmann (New York: Vintage Books, 1968), § 15.

39　Heidegger, *Nietzsche*, vol. 2: *The Eternal Recurrence of the Same*, trans. David Farrell Krell (San Francisco: Harper and Row, 1984), 129.
40　See Blanchot's comments on "being without being" in *IC*, 47 (67).
41　See Heidegger, *The Basic Problems of Phenomenology*, trans. and intro. Albert Hofstadter, rev. ed. (Bloomington, IN: Indiana University Press, 1988), 21. There are clear parallels between what Blanchot says of suffering and what Heidegger says of deep boredom. See Heidegger, *The Fundamental Concepts of Metaphysics: World, Finitude, Solitude*, §§ 29–36.
42　See my essay "Une réduction infini," 323–8.
43　Blanchot, *WD*, 64, 101 (105, 157).
44　See Blanchot, *WD*, 3 (9).
45　Blanchot, *IC*, 45 (63).
46　This view is grounded in Alexandre Kojève, *Introduction à la lecture de Hegel: Leçons sur la "Phénoménologie de l'Esprit" professées de 1933 à 1939*, éd. Raymond Queneau (Paris: Gallimard, 1947). Also see Bataille, *Oeuvres complètes*, 12 vols., vol. 5 (Paris: Gallimard, 1973), 369–71, and Blanchot, *TH*.
47　I am indebted to Michael Holland for clarifying this point for me in email discussion of a draft of this chapter.
48　See Blanchot, *IC*, xii (viii).
49　See Bernard-Henri Lévi, *Adventures on the Freedom Road: The French Intellectuals in the Twentieth Century*, trans. and ed. Richard Veasey (London: The Harvill Press, 1995), 318.
50　See Hermann Langbein, *Menschen in Auschwitz* (Vienna: Europaverlag, 1972). Blanchot most likely read the French abbreviation and translation: *Hommes et femmes à Auschwitz*, trans. Denise Meunier, ed. Jacques Branchu (Paris: Fayard, 1975). I shall continue to cite the English translation, *People in Auschwitz*.
51　Perhaps the guidance goes in both directions; it is worth noting that Blanchot places "Être Juif" directly before his consideration of Antelme in *EI* and that he gives a common title to the two pieces.
52　See LaCapra, *Writing History, Writing Trauma*, 158.
53　See Ber Mark, *The Scrolls of Auschwitz* (Tel Aviv: Am Oved, 1985), 4.
54　See Mark, *The Scrolls of Auschwitz*, passim. It should be added both that some inmates committed suicide and that others sought to survive. With regard to the latter, see Lucy Adlington, *The Dressmakers of Auschwitz: The True Story of the Women who Sewed to Survive* (New York: Harper, 2021).
55　Levinas, *TI*, 79.
56　Blanchot, "Knowledge of the Unknown," *IC*, 50 (71).
57　Blanchot, "The Relation of the Third Kind: *Man without horizon*," *IC*, 69 (98).
58　See Blanchot, "Being Jewish" and "Peace, peace to the far and to the near," trans. Leslie Hill, *Paragraph* 30, no. 3 (2007): 28–33.
59　Blanchot, "The Relation of the Third Kind," *IC*, 71 (101).
60　Levinas, *EE*, 57.
61　One unnamed participant in a fragmentary dialogue observes of "(A Primal Scene?)," "*For my part, I hear the inevitability of* there is [*il y a*], *which being and nothing roll like a great wave, unfurling it and folding it back under, inscribing and effacing it, to the rhythm of the nameless rustling*," *WD*, 116 (178).
62　Levinas, *TaO*, 31. Also see his *EE*, ch. 4.
63　Blanchot, "The Relation of the Third Kind," *IC*, 71 (101).
64　Blanchot, "Humankind," *IC*, 130 (192).

65 On the relation between the *il* and *autre*, see *SNB*, 5, 39 (12, 57–8).
66 Blanchot, "Humankind," *IC*, 133 (196).
67 Blanchot, "Humankind," *IC*, 133 (197). It is worth noting that Husserl notes that one becomes another in long sickness. See his *Ideas Pertaining to a Pure Phenomenology and to a Phenomenological Philosophy*, 2: *Studies in the Phenomenology of Constitution*, trans. Richard Rojcewicz and André Schuwer (Dordrecht: Kluwer Academic Publishers, 1989), 266.
68 Blanchot, "Humankind," *IC*, 134 (197).
69 See Langbein, *People in Auschwitz*, 25, 402–13. Also see Robert Sommer, "Sexual Exploitation of Women in Nazi Concentration Camp Brothels," *Sexual Violence against Women during the Holocaust*, ed. Sonja M. Hedgepeth and Rochelle G. Saidel (Waltham, MA: Brandeis University Press, 2010), 45–60. Finally, see Blanchot's own "The Idyll," 20 *AC*, 33.
70 Antelme, *The Human Race*, 21.
71 Antelme, *The Human Race*, 87.
72 Blanchot, "Humankind," *IC*, 135 (199).
73 See Primo Levi, *If This is a Man* bound with *The Truce*, trans. Stuart Woolf, intro. Paul Bailey (Harmondsworth: Penguin, 1979), esp. ch. 11.
74 Blanchot, "Humankind," *IC*, 135 (200).
75 Blanchot, "Everyday Speech," *IC*, 245 (365).
76 See Langbein, *People in Auschwitz*, 53, 51.
77 See Langbein, *People in Auschwitz*, 58.
78 Zalman Loewenthal, "Writings," *The Scrolls of Auschwitz*, 240.
79 Loewenthal, "Writings," *The Scrolls of Auschwitz*, 221.
80 See Foucault, *The Order of Things*, 387.
81 See Jean Améry, *At the Mind's Limits: Contemplations by a Survivor of Auschwitz on Its Realities*, trans. Sidney Rosenfeld and Stella P. Rosenfeld (Bloomington, IN: Indiana University Press, 1980) and Elie Wiesel, *Night*, trans. Marion Wiesel, new pref. Elie Wisel, foreword Françoise Mauriac (New York: Hill and Wang, 2006).
82 See Blanchot, *IC*, xii (vii).

Afterword

Even an encore comes to an end. I had wanted to prolong it by spending time in the archive now being assembled in the Houghton Library at Harvard and adding what I learned there to this book, but the age of Covid-19 prevented a research visit. We now have *Thomas le Solitaire* (2022), an early version of *Thomas l'Obscur* (1941), and it will take some time for readers to absorb it. There is also an unpublished partial revision of this early work at the Houghton, and perhaps this document will tell us still more about the evolution of *Thomas l'Obscur*. Perhaps other documents in the archive will enable a clearer, fuller, or more nuanced understanding of Blanchot. The fascination that his writings exert is very strong, and perhaps never stronger than in his *récits*. Each time I pick up one of these strange narratives I find myself beset by feelings that are difficult to name, that seem to fall between the usual thoughts and emotions one has, even when reading literature, and yet that resonate with something that is mostly dormant in me until I read one of them. The task of writing on the *récits*, on the (nonreligious) mystery that seems just behind the words, the peculiar temporality they evoke, and the passionate yet elusive situations put before the reader, calls insistently to me each time I read one of them.

It has always been so since I first read the opening page of *L'Arrêt de mort* some months after the afternoon as a young schoolteacher I read part of "La littérature et le droit à la mort." I remember that by the time I completed that first page I was holding onto the arms of the chair on which I was sitting doubtless so that I was at least in contact with something I knew to be solid and real and therefore reassuring. Perhaps nothing much has changed in the forty-three years since I first read Blanchot. The critical writing that I have studied about his work, the conversations that I have had with admirable scholars devoted to this work, and the writing that I have attempted myself, have all illuminated this or that facet of the *œuvre*. I am tempted to whisper, from time to time (and only to myself), that I have come to understand Blanchot; yet as soon as I even come close to risking even a silent utterance like this, I stop myself. For I know that there remains a gulf between my apprehension of his works, especially the *récits*, and my comprehension of them. And I am aware that it would be so even if I devoted all my days to reading him and wrote more books about him.

In this study I have written on just two of the *récits*, and my time with them makes me acutely aware of how they offer readers little traction, that we must come to them wearing our own gloves with grip spots or find them in Blanchot's own critical works. The thought of writing on the *récits* in another manner, one as yet not fully manifest, but which will allow them to speak from the imaginary point they posit and see how they elaborate themselves in terms so compelling yet different from all other writing, is forever appealing and formidably challenging. Right now, it seems impossible. But there is such a thing as a second encore, one granted only to exemplary performances such as Blanchot's that have taken us to new depths and new heights.

Bibliography

Works by Maurice Blanchot in French:

(a) Narratives

Thomas l'Obscur: première version, 1941; Paris: Gallimard, 2005.
Aminadab. Paris: Gallimard, 1942.
L'Arrêt de mort. Paris: Gallimard, 1948.
Le Très-Haut. Paris: Gallimard, 1948.
Thomas l'Obscur: nouvelle version. Paris: Gallimard, 1950.
Celui qui ne m'accompagnait pas. Paris: Gallimard, 1953.
"Après coup" précédé par "Le Ressassement eternal." Paris: Éditions de Minuit, 1983.
L'Instant de ma mort. Paris: Gallimard, 2002.
Thomas le Solitaire. Paris: Kimé, 2022.

(b) Critical Works:

Faux pas. Paris: Gallimard, 1943.
Lautréamont et Sade. Paris: Éditions de Minuit, 1949.
Le Part du feu. Paris: Gallimard, 1949.
L'Espace littéraire. Paris: Gallimard, 1955.
Le Livre à venir. Paris: Gallimard, 1959.
L'Entretien infini. Paris: Gallimard, 1969.
L'Amitié. Paris: Gallimard, 1971.
L'Écriture du désastre. Paris: Gallimard, 1980.
La Communauté inavouable. Paris: Éditions de Minuit, 1983.
Une Voix venue d'ailleurs: Sur les poèmes de Louis-René des Forêts. Dijon: Ulysse Fin de Siècle, 1992.
Les Intellectuels en question: Ébauche d'une réflexion. Paris: Fourbis, 1996.
Pour l'amitié. Paris: Fourbis, 1996.
Chroniques littéraires du "Journal des débats," avril 1941- août 1944. Ed. Christophe Bident. Paris: Gallimard, 2007.
Lettres à Vadim Kozovoï suivi de "La Parole Ascendante." Ed. Denis Aucouturier. Houilles: Éditions Manucius, 2009.
La Condition critique: articles, 1945–1998. Ed. Christophe Bident. Paris: Gallimard, 2010.
Chroniques politiques des années trente. Ed. David Uhrig. Paris: Gallimard, 2017.
Maurice Blanchot et Pierre Madaule. *Correspondance, 1953–2002*. Édition établie, présentée et annotée par Pierre Madaule. Paris: Gallimard, 2012.

Works by Maurice Blanchot in English translation:

(a) Narratives (in order of publication in English):

Thomas the Obscure. Trans. Robert Lamberton. New York: David Lewis, 1973.
Death Sentence. Trans. Lydia Davis. Barrytown, NY: Station Hill Press, 1978.
The Madness of the Day. Trans. Lydia Davis. Barrytown, NY: Station Hill Press, 1981.
Vicious Circles: Two Fictions and "After the Fact." Trans. Paul Auster. Barrytown, NY: Station Hill Press, 1985.
When the Time Comes. Trans. Lydia Davis. Barrytown, NY : Station Hill Press, 1985.
The One Who was Standing Apart from Me. Trans. Lydia Davis. Barrytown, NY: Station Hill Press, 1993.
The Instant of My Death bound with Jacques Derrida, *Demeure: Fiction and Testimony.* Trans. Elizabeth Rottenberg. Stanford, CA: Stanford University Press, 2000.
Aminadab. Trans. Jeff Fort. Lincoln, NE: University of Nebraska Press, 2002.

(b) Critical Works (in order of publication in English):

The Space of Literature. Trans. Ann Smock. Lincoln, NE: University of Nebraska Press, 1982.
The Writing of the Disaster. Trans. Ann Smock. Lincoln, NE: University of Nebraska Press, 1986.
"Our Clandestine Companion." In *Face to Face with Levinas*, ed. Richard A. Cohen, 41–50. Albany, NY: State University of New York Press, 1986.
The Unavowable Community. Trans. Pierre Joris. Barrytown, NY: Station Hill Press, 1988.
The Step Not Beyond. Trans. Lycette Nelson. Albany, NY: State University of New York Press, 1992.
The Infinite Conversation. Trans. and foreword Susan Hanson. Minneapolis, MN: University of Minnesota Press, 1993.
The Work of Fire. Trans. Charlotte Mandell. Stanford, CA: Stanford University Press, 1995.
The Blanchot Reader. Ed. Michael Holland. Oxford: Basil Blackwell, 1995.
Friendship. Trans. Elizabeth Rottenberg. Stanford, CA: Stanford University Press, 1997.
The Station Hill Blanchot Reader: Fiction and Literary Essays. Trans. Lydia Davis et al. Barrytown, NY: Station Hill Press, 1999.
Faux Pas. Trans. Charlotte Mandell. Stanford, CA: Stanford University Press, 2001.
The Book to Come. Trans. Charlotte Mandell. Stanford, CA: Stanford University Press, 2003.
Lautréamont and Sade. Trans. Stuart Kendall and Michele Kendall. Stanford, CA: Stanford University Press, 2004.
A Voice from Elsewhere. Trans. Charlotte Mandell. Albany, NY: State University of New York Press, 2007.
Political Writings, 1953–1993. Trans. and intro. Zakir Paul. Foreword Kevin Hart. New York: Fordham University Press, 2010.
Into Disaster: Chronicles of Intellectual Life, 1941. Trans. Michael Holland. New York: Fordham University Press, 2014.
Desperate Clarity: Chronicles of Intellectual Life, 1942. Trans. Michael Holland. New York: Fordham University Press, 2014.

A World in Ruins: Chronicles of Intellectual Life, 1943. Trans. Michael Holland. New York: Fordham University Press, 2016.
Death Now: Chronicles of Intellectual Life, 1944. Trans. Michael Holland. New York: Fordham University Press, 2019.

Works by Emmanuel Levinas in French (in order of first publication):

De l'existence à l'existant. Seconde édition augmentée. 1947; Paris: J. Vrin, 1993.
Totalité et infini: Essai sur l'extériorité. 1961; La Haye: Martinus Nijhoff, 1971.
Difficile liberté. Troisième édition revue et corrigée. 1963; Paris: Albin Michel, 1976.
En dévouvrant l'existence avec Husserl et Heidegger. 1967; Paris: J. Vrin, 1994.
Autrement qu'être ou au-delà de l'essence. La Haye: Martinus Nijhoff, 1974.
Sur Maurice Blanchot. Montpellier: Fata Morgana, 1975.
De l'oblitération: Entretien avec Françoise Armengaud à propos de l'œuvre de Sosno. Seconde édition. Paris: Éditions de la Différance, 1990.
Entre Nous: Essais sur le penser-à-l'autre. Paris: Grasset, 1991.
De Dieu qui vient à l'idée. Paris: J. Vrin, 1992.
Les Imprévus de l'histoire. Montpellier: Fata Morgana, 1994.
Carnets de captivité et autre inédits. Ed. Rodolphe Calin et al. Paris: Grasset, 2009.

Works by Emmanuel Levinas in English translation (in order of publication in English):

Totality and Infinity: An Essay on Exteriority. Trans. Alphonso Lingis. The Hague: Martinus Nijhoff, 1979.
Otherwise than Being or Beyond Essence. Trans. Alphonso Lingis. The Hague: Martinus Nijhoff, 1981.
Ethics and Infinity: Conversations with Philippe Nemo. Trans. Richard Cohen. Pittsburgh, PA: Duquesne University Press, 1985.
Collected Philosophical Papers. Trans. Alphonso Lingis. Dordrecht: Martinus Nijhoff Publishers, 1987.
Time and the Other. Trans. Richard A. Cohen. Pittsburgh, PA: Duquesne University Press, 1987.
Existence and Existents. Trans. Alphonso Lingis. Corrected ed. Dordrecht: Kluwer, 1988.
Difficult Freedom: Essays on Judaism. Trans. Seán Hand. Baltimore, MD: The Johns Hopkins University Press, 1990.
Nine Talmudic Readings. Trans. Annette Aronowicz. Bloomington, IN: Indiana University Press, 1990.
In the Time of the Nations. Trans. Michael B. Smith. Bloomington, IN: Indiana University Press, 1994.
Proper Names. Trans. Michael B. Smith. Stanford, CA: Stanford University Press, 1996.
Discovering Existence with Husserl. Trans. Richard A. Cohen and Michael B. Smith. Evanston, IL: Northwestern University Press, 1998.

Entre Nous: Thinking-of-the-Other. Trans. Michael B. Smith and Barbara Harshav. New York: Columbia University Press, 1998.
Of God Who Comes to Mind. Trans. Bettina Bergo. Stanford, CA: Stanford University Press, 1998.
Alterity and Transcendence. Trans. Michael B. Smith. London: Athlone, 1999.
Is it Righteous to Be?: Interviews with Emmanuel Levinas. Ed. Jill Robbins. Stanford, CA: Stanford University Press, 2001.

Other Works:

Alazet, Bernard et Christiane Blot-Labarrère, Dir., *Marguerite Duras.* Paris: L'Herne, 2005.
Allemann, Beda. "Le retounement natal dans l'œuvre de Hölderlin." *Recherches et débats du centre catholique des intellectuels français,* 24 (1958): 183–99.
Alphant, Marianne. "Une présence secrète." *Libération,* 28 janvier, 1984, 23.
Antelme, Monique et al. Ed. *Cahiers Maurice Blanchot,* 1–6. Les presses du réel, 2011–19.
Antelme, Robert. *The Human Race.* Trans. Jeffrey Haight and Annie Mahler. Malboro, VT: The Malboro Press, 1992.
Aquinas, Thomas. *Summa theologiæ.* Ed. Thomas Gilby and T. C. O'Brien. 61 vols. London: Eyre and Spottiswoode, 1964–75.
Aquinas, Thomas. *Summa contra Gentiles.* Trans., intro. and notes, Anton C. Pegis. 5 vols. 1955 rpt; Notre Dame, IN: Notre Dame University Press, 1975.
Aquinas, Thomas. *Commentary on Aristotle's "De Anima".* Trans. Knelm Forster and Silvester Humphries. Intro. Ralph McInerny. Notre Dame, IN: Dumb Ox Books, 1994.
Aquinas, Thomas. *Truth.* Trans. Robert W. Mulligan. 3 vols. 1954; Indianapolis, IN: Hackett Pub. Co., 1995.
Aquinas, Thomas. *An Exposition of the "On the Hebdomads" of Boethius.* Intro. and trans. Janice L. Schultz and Edward A. Synan. Washington, DC: The Catholic University of America Press, 2001.
Aquinas, Thomas. *On the Power of God.* trans. Lawrence Shapcote. 1932; rpt. Eugene, OR: Wipf and Stock, 2004.
Améry, Jean. *At the Mind's Limits: Contemplations by a Survivor of Auschwitz on its Realities.* Trans. Sidney Rosenfeld and Stella P. Rosenfeld. Bloomington, IN: Indiana University Press, 1980.
Arendt, Hannah. *Eichmann in Jerusalem: A Report on the Banality of Evil.* New York: Viking Press, 1964.
Areopagite, Pseudo-Dionysius. *The Divine Names and Mystical Theology.* Trans. and intro. John D. Jones. Milwaukee, WI: Marquette University Press, 1980.
Aristotle. *Metaphysics.* Trans. Hugh Tredennick. 2 vols. Loeb Classical Library. Cambridge, MA: Harvard University Press, 1933–35.
Armel, Aliette. "Un itinéraire politique." *Magazine littéraire,* 278, juin 1990, 36–40.
Ashbery, John. *The Double Dream of Spring.* New York: Ecco Press, 1976.
Ashbery, John. *Hotel Lautréamont.* New York: Alfred A. Knopf, 1992.
Athanassakis, Apostolos N. Trans. and intro. *The Homeric Hymns,* 2nd ed. Baltimore, MD: The Johns Hopkins University Press, 2004.
Augustine. *Sermons, Part 3/7: On the Liturgical Seasons (230–272B).* Trans. and notes Edmund Hill. Ed. John E. Rotelle, The Works of Saint Augustine. New Rochelle, NY: New City Press, 1993.

Augustine. *Sermons: On the Saints (273-305A)*. Trans. and notes Edmund Hill. Ed. John E. Rotelle, The Works of Saint Augustine, 3/8. Hyde Park, NY: New City Press, 1994.
Augustine. *On Genesis*. Intro., trans. and notes Edmund Hill. Ed. John E. Rotelle, The Works of Saint Augustine, 1/13. Hyde Park, NY: New City Press, 2002.
Augustine. *Letters 100-155*, The Works of Saint Augustine, 2/2. Trans. and notes Roland Teske. Ed. Boniface Ramsey. Hyde Park, NY: New City Press, 2003.
Bacon, Francis. *The Wisdom of the Ancients and Miscellaneous Essays*. New York: Walter J. Black, Inc., 1932.
Badiou, Alain. *Being and Event*. Trans. Oliver Feltham. London: Continuum, 2006.
Baker, Lynne Rudder. *The Metaphysics of Everyday Life: An Essay in Practical Reason*. Cambridge: Cambridge University Press, 2007.
Balthasar, Hans Urs von. *The Glory of the Lord: A Theological Aesthetics*. 7 vols. Trans. Oliver Davies et al. Edinburgh: T. and T. Clark, 1982-89.
Bataille, Georges. *Oeuvres complètes*. 12 vols. Paris: Gallimard, 1970-88.
Bataille, Georges. *Inner Experience*. Trans. and intro. Leslie Anne Boldt. Albany, NY: State University of New York Press, 1988.
Bataille, Georges. *Guilty*. Trans. Bruce Boone, intro. Denis Hollier. Venice: The Lapis Press, 1988.
Bataille, Georges. *Choix de lettres, 1917-1962*. Ed. Michel Surya. Paris: Gallimard, 1997.
Bentham, Jeremy. *Chrestomathia*. Ed. M. J. Smith and W. H. Burston, The Collected Works of Jeremy Bentham. Gen. ed. J. R. Dinwiddy. 34 vols. to date. 1817; Oxford: Clarendon Press, 1983.
Bergson, Henri. *Time and Free Will: An Essay on the Immediate Data of Consciousness*. Trans. R. L. Pogson. London: Allen and Unwin, 1910.
Bernard of Clairvaux, *On the Song of Songs*, 4 vols., vol. 4: *Sermons 67-86*. Trans. Irene Edmonds, intro. Jean Leclercq. Kalamazoo, MI: Cistercian Publications, 1980.
Bident, Christophe. *Maurice Blanchot: A Critical Biography*. Trans. John McKeane. New York: Fordham University Press, 2019.
Bident, Christophe. *La vie versée dans les récits (vers le nom de Blanchot)*. Genève: Furor, 2021.
Bident, Christophe and Pierre Vilar. Ed. *Maurice Blanchot: Récits Critiques*. Tours: Éditions Farrago / Éditions Léo Scheer, 2003.
Blondel, Maurice. "Le christianisme de Descartes." *Revue de Métaphysique et de Morale*, 4 (1896): 551-67.
Bloom, Harold. *Ringers in the Tower: Studies in Romantic Tradition*. Chicago: University of Chicago Press, 1971.
Bloom, Harold. *The Anxiety of Influence: A Theory of Poetry*. New York: Oxford University Press, 1973.
Bloom, Harold. *Stéphane Mallarmé*. New York: Chelsea House, 1987.
Bloom, Harold. "Introduction." In *Paul Valéry*. Modern Critical Views. New York: Chelsea House Publishers, 1989.
Bloom, Harold. *The Western Canon: The Books and School of the Ages*. New York: Harcourt Brace and Co., 1994.
Bonaventure. *Disputed Questions on the Mystery of the Trinity*. Trans. and intro. Zachery Hayes. Works of St. Bonaventure. St. Bonaventure, NY: The Franciscan Institute, 2000.
Bonaventure. *Collations on the Seven Gifts of the Holy Spirit*. Intro. and Trans. Zachary Hayes. Notes Robert J. Karris. Works of St. Bonaventure, 14. St. Bonaventure, NY: Franciscan Institute Publications, 2008.

Bonnefoy, Yves. *Poèmes*. Paris: Mercure de France, 1978.
Bonnefoy, Yves. *Correspondance*, vol. 1, édition établie, introduite et annotée par Odile Bombarde et Patrick Labarthe. Paris: Les Belles Lettres, 2018.
Broeckx, Edmond. *Le Catharisme: Étude sur les doctrines, la vie religieuse et morale, l'activité littéraire et les vicissitudes de la secte cathare avant la croisade*. Hoogstraten: J. Haseldonckx, 1916.
Burket, Walter. *Greek Religion*. Trans. John Raffin. Oxford: Basil Blackwell, 1985.
Burrell, David. *Faith and Freedom: An Interfaith Perspective*. Oxford: Basil Blackwell, 2004.
Caputo, John D. and Michael Scanlon. Ed. *God, the Gift, and Postmodernism*. Bloomington, IN: Indiana University Press, 1999.
Carr, David. *Phenomenology and the Problem of History*. Evanston, IL: Northwestern University Press, 2009.
Caussade, Jean-Pierre de. *Self-Abandonment to Divine Providence*. Trans. John Beevers. New York: Image, 1993.
Char, René. *Oeuvres complètes*. Intro. Jean Roudaut. Bibliothèque de la Pléiade. Paris: Gallimard, 1995.
Charry, Ellen T. *Franz Rosenzweig and the Freedom of God*. Bristol, IN: Wyndam Hall Press, 1987.
Clark, Timothy, et al. Ed. *Disastrous Blanchot*, special issue of *The Oxford Literary Review*. vol. 22, 2000.
Cohn, Robert Greer. *Toward the Poems of Mallarmé*, expanded ed. Los Angeles, CA: University of California Press, 1980.
Conrad, Joseph. *The Secret Sharer*. Ed. Daniel R. Schwarz. Boston: Bedford Books, 1997.
Constantine, David. *Hölderlin*. Oxford: Clarendon Press, 1988.
Constantine, David. *Hölderlin's Sophocles: Oedipus and Antigone*. Highgreen, Tarset: Bloodaxe Books, 2001.
Crouzet, François. *Contra René Char*. Paris: Les Belles Lettres, 1992.
Cummings, E. E. *Complete Poems*. Ed. George James Firmage. 2 vols. London: Granada, 1981.
David, Alain. "La réduction." *Magazine littéraire*, 424, octobre, 2003, 64–6.
De Man, Paul. *Blindness and Insight: Essays in the Rhetoric of Contemporary Criticism*, 2nd. rev. ed. London: Methuen, 1983.
De Man, Paul. *The Rhetoric of Romanticism*. New York: Columbia University Press, 1984.
Derrida, Jacques. *Writing and Difference*. Trans. and intro. Alan Bass. London: Routledge and Kegan Paul, 1978.
Derrida, Jacques. *The Archeology of the Frivolous: Reading Condillac*. Trans. John P. Leavey, Jr. Pittsburgh, PA: Duquesne University Press, 1980.
Derrida, Jacques. *Acts of Literature*. Ed. Derek Attridge. London: Routledge, 1992.
Derrida, Jacques. *Politics of Friendship*. Trans. George Collins. London: Verso, 1997.
Derrida, Jacques. *Of Grammatology*, corrected ed. Trans. Gayatri Chakravorty Spivak. Baltimore, MD: Johns Hopkins University Press, 1997.
Derrida, Jacques. *Resistances of Psychoanalysis*. Trans. Peggy Kamuf et al. Stanford, CA: Stanford University Press, 1998.
Derrida, Jacques. *Adieu to Emmanuel Levinas*. Trans. Pascale-Anne Brault and Michael Naas. Stanford, CA: Stanford University Press, 1999.
Derrida, Jacques. *On Touching — Jean-Luc Nancy*. Trans. Christine Irizarry. Stanford, CA: Stanford University Press, 2005.
Derrida, Jacques. *Psyche: Inventions of the Other*. Ed. Peggy Kamuf and Elizabeth Rottenberg. 2 vols. Stanford, CA: Stanford University Press, 2007.

Derrida, Jacques. *Parages*. Ed. John P. Leavey. Stanford, CA: Stanford University Press, 2011.
Descartes, René. *The Philosophical Works*. Trans. Elizabeth S. Haldane and G. R. T. Ross. 2 vols. Cambridge: Cambridge University Press, 1972.
Desportes, Bernard. Ed. *Dossier Maurice Blanchot*, special issue of *Ralentir Travaux*, hiver 1997.
Dosse, François. *History of Structuralism*. Trans. Deborah Glassman. 2 vols. Minneapolis, MN: University of Minnesota Press, 1997.
Dostoevsky, Fyodor. *The Double: Two Versions*. Trans. Evelyn Harden. Ann Arbor, MI: Ardis, 1985.
Eliot, T. S. *The Complete Prose of T. S. Eliot: The Critical Edition*. Gen. ed. Ronald Schuchard. 7 vols. London: Faber and Faber / Baltimore, MD: The Johns Hopkins University Press, 2021.
Emerson, Ralph Waldo. *Essays: First Series*. New York: A. L. Burt Co., 1900.
Erdman, David V. Ed. *The Complete Poetry and Prose of William Blake*, new and rev. ed., commentary by Harold Bloom. Los Angeles, CA: University of California Press, 1982.
Fénelon, François. *Oeuvres de Fénelon: Archevêque-duc de Cambrai*, nouvelle éd. revue et corrigée avec soin. 10 vols. Paris: L. Tenré et Boistre fils aîné, 1822.
Fink, Eugen. "Ontological Problems of Community." Trans. Michael R. Heim. In *Contemporary German Philosophy*. 2 vols., vol. 2, 1–19. University Park, PA: The Pennsylvania State University Press, 1983.
Fink, Eugen. *Sixth Cartesian Meditation: The Idea of a Transcendental Theory of Method, with Textual Notations by Edmund Husserl*. Trans. and intro. Ronald Bruzina. Bloomington, IN: Indiana University Press, 1995.
Foucault, Michel. *The Order of Things: An Archeology of the Human Sciences*. No Trans. given. New York: Vintage Books, 1970.
Foucault, Michel. "Maurice Blanchot: The Thought from Outside." In Foucault, *Maurice Blanchot: The Thought from Outside*, bound with Maurice Blanchot, *Michel Foucault as I Imagine Him*. Trans. Respectively by Brian Massumi and Jeffrey Mehlman. New York: Zone Books, 1990.
Fouché, Pascal. *L'Édition française sous l'Occupation, 1940–1944*. 2 vols. Paris: Bibliothèque de Littérature Contemporaine, 1987.
Freund, Else-Rahel. *Franz Rosenzweig's Philosophy of Existence: An Analysis of "The Star of Redemption."* Trans. Stephen L. Weinstein and Robert Israel. Ed. Paul R. Mendes-Flohr. The Hague: Martinus Nijhoff, 1979.
Gill, Carolyn Bailey. *Maurice Blanchot: The Demand of Writing*. London: Routledge, 1996.
Godley, A. D. Trans. *Herodotus*. Loeb Classical Library. 4 vols. Cambridge, MA: Harvard University Press, 1981.
Gosetti-Ferencei, Jennifer Anna. *Heidegger, Hölderlin, and the Subject of Poetic Language: Toward a New Poetics of Dasein*. New York: Fordham University Press, 2004.
Gray, Thomas and William Collins, *Poetical Works*. Ed. Roger Lonsdale. Oxford: Oxford University Press, 1977.
Gregory of Nyssa. *Commentary on the Song of Songs*. Trans. and intro. Casimir McCambley. Brookline, MA: Hellenic College Press, 1987.
Grene, David and Richard Lattimore. Eds. *The Bacchæ*. In *The Complete Greek Tragedies*, 9 vols., *Euripides* 5. Chicago: The University of Chicago Press, 1959.
Hamel, Jean-François. *Nous sommes tous la pègre: Les années 68 de Blanchot*. Paris: Éditions de Minuit, 2018.
Hardy, Thomas. *Jude l'obscur*. Trans. Firmin Roz. Paris: Ollendorff, 1901.

Hardy, Thomas. *The Complete Poetical Works of Thomas Hardy*. Ed. Samuel Hynes. 3 vols. Oxford: Clarendon Press, 1984.

Hart, Kevin. *The Dark Gaze: Maurice Blanchot and the Sacred*. Chicago: University of Chicago Press, 2004.

Hart, Kevin. "Une réduction infinie." *Cahiers de l'Herne*, 2014, Blanchot special issue. Éd. Dominique Rabaté and Éric Hoppenot, 323–8.

Hart, Kevin. Ed. *Counter-Experiences: Reading Jean-Luc Marion*. Notre Dame, IN: Notre Dame University Press, 2007.

Hart, Kevin and Geoffrey Hartman. Ed. *The Power of Contestation: Perspectives on Maurice Blanchot*. Baltimore, MD: The Johns Hopkins University Press, 2004.

Hartman, Geoffrey. *Holocaust Remembrance: The Shapes of Memory*. Oxford: Basil Blackwell, 1994.

Hartman, Geoffrey. *The Longest Shadow: In the Aftermath of the Holocaust*. New York: Palgrave Macmillan, 1996.

Hegel, G. W. F. *The Phenomenology of Mind*. Trans. and intro. J. B. Baillie. Intro. George Lichtheim. New York: Harper and Row, 1967.

Hegel, G. W. F. *Philosophy of Mind: Being Part Three of the "Encyclopedia of the Philosophical Sciences" (1830)*. Trans. William Wallace and A. V. Miller. Foreword J. N. Findlay. Oxford: Clarendon Press, 1971.

Hegel, G. W. F. *Early Theological Writings*. Trans. T. M. Knox. Intro. and fragments trans. Richard Kroner. Philadelphia, PA: University of Pennsylvania Press, 1971.

Hegel, G. W. F. *Aesthetics: Lectures on Fine Art*. Trans. T. M. Knox. 2 vols. Oxford: Clarendon Press, 1974.

Hegel, G. W. F. *Hegel's Logic: Being Part One of the "Encyclopaedia of the Philosophical Sciences" (1830)*. Trans. William Wallace. Foreword J. N. Findlay. Oxford: Clarendon Press, 1975.

Hegel, G. W. F. *Faith and Knowledge*. Trans. and ed. Walter Cerf and H. S. Harris. Albany, NY: State University of New York Press, 1977.

Hegel, G. W. F. *System of Ethical Life (1802/3) and First Philosophy of Spirit (Part III of the System of Speculative Philosophy 1803/4)*. Ed. and trans. H. S. Harris and T. M. Knox. Albany, NY: State University of New York Press, 1979.

Hegel, G. W. F. *Lectures on the Philosophy of Religion*. Ed. Peter Hodgson. Trans. R. F. Brown, et al. Berkeley: University of California Press, 1987.

Heidegger, Martin. "Hölderlin et l'essence de la poésie." Trans. Henry Corbin. *Mésures*, 3 (1937): 120–43.

Heidegger, Martin. *Introduction to Metaphysics*. Trans. Ralph Manheim. New Haven, CT: Yale University Press, 1959.

Heidegger, Martin. *On the Way to Language*. Trans. Peter D. Hertz. New York: Harper and Row, 1971.

Heidegger, Martin. *Being and Time*. Trans. John Macquarrie and Edward Robinson. Oxford: Basil Blackwell, 1973.

Heidegger, Martin. *Poetry, Language, Thought*. Trans. Albert Hofstadter. New York: Harper and Row, 1975.

Heidegger, Martin. *Early Greek Thinking: The Dawn of Western Philosophy*. Trans. David Farrell Krell and Frank A. Capuzzi. San Francisco, CA: Harper and Row, 1975.

Heidegger, Martin. *Hölderlins Hymn "Germanien" und "Der Rhein."* Ed. S. Ziegler. *Gesamtausgabe* 39. Frankfort: Klostermann, 1980.

Heidegger, Martin. *Nietzsche*. Trans. David Farrell Krell et al. 4 vols. San Francisco, CA: Harper and Row, 1981–87.

Heidegger, Martin. *The Basic Problems of Phenomenology*. Trans., intro. and lexicon by Albert Hofstadter. Bloomington, IN: Indiana University Press, 1988.
Heidegger, Martin. *Kant and the Problem of Metaphysics*. 4th ed., enlarged. Trans. Richard Taft. Bloomington, IN: Indiana University Press, 1990.
Heidegger, Martin. *Parmenides*. Trans. Richard Rojcewicz and André Schuwer. Bloomington, IN: Indiana University Press, 1992.
Heidegger, Martin. *The Fundamental Concepts of Metaphysics: World, Finitude, Solitude*. Trans. William McNeill and Nicholas Walker. Bloomington, IN: Indiana University Press, 1995.
Heidegger, Martin. *Hölderlin's Hymn "The Ister."* Trans. William McNeill and Julia Davis. Bloomington, IN: Indiana University Press, 1996.
Heidegger, Martin. *Plato's Sophist*. Trans. Richard Rojcewicz and André Schuwer. Bloomington, IN: Indiana University Press, 1997.
Heidegger, Martin. *Pathmarks*. Ed. William McNeill. Cambridge: Cambridge University Press, 1998.
Heidegger, Martin. *Elucidations of Hölderlin's Poetry*. Trans. Keith Hoeller. New York: Humanities Books, 2000.
Heidegger, Martin. *The Essence of Human Freedom: An Introduction to Modern Philosophy*. Trans. Ted Sadler. London: Continuum, 2002.
Heidegger, Martin. *On the Essence of Language: The Metaphysics of Language and the Essencing of the Word, Concerning Herder's Treatise "On the Origin of Language."* Trans. Wanda Torres Gregory and Yvonne Unna. Albany, NY: State University of New York Press, 2004.
Heidegger, Martin. *Contributions to Philosophy (Of the Event)*. Trans. Richard Rojcewicz and Daniela Vallega-Neu. Bloomington, IN: Indiana University Press, 2012.
Henry, Michel. *The Essence of Manifestation*. Trans. Girard Etzkorn. The Hague: Martinus Nijhoff, 1973.
Heraclitus. *Fragments*. Trans. Brooks Haxton. Foreword James Hillman. New York: Viking, 2001.
Herder, Johann Gottfriend von. *Philosophical Writings*. Trans. and ed. Michael N. Forster. Cambridge: Cambridge University Press, 2002.
Herman, Jean. Trans. *Laure: The Collected Writings*. San Francisco, CA: City Lights Books, 1995.
Hill, Geoffrey. *Collected Poems*. London: Penguin, 1985.
Hill, Leslie. "Blanchot and Mallarmé." *MLN*, 105, no. 5 (1990): 889–913.
Hill, Leslie. *Blanchot: Extreme Contemporary*. London: Routledge, 1997.
Hill, Leslie. "'Not in Our Name': Blanchot, Politics, the Neuter." *Paragraph*, 30, no. 3 (2007): 141–59.
Hill, Leslie. *Nancy, Blanchot: A Serious Controversy*. New York: Rowman and Littlefield, 2018.
Hill, Leslie. *Blanchot politique: Sur une réflexion jamais interrompue*. Genève: Furor, 2020.
Hill, Leslie and Michael Holland. *Blanchot's Epoch*, special issue, *Paragraph* 30, no. 3 (2007).
Hissette, Roland. *Enquête sur les 219 articles condemné à Paris le 7 mars 1277*. Philosophes médiévaux, 22. Paris: Publications Universitaires, 1977.
Hölderlin, Friedrich. *Sämtliche Werke*. Ed. Friedrich Beissner. 15 vols. Stuttgart: W. Kohlhammer Verlag, 1952.
Hölderlin, Friedrich. *Oeuvres*. Trans. Philippe Jaccottet. Paris: Gallimard, 1967.

Hölderlin, Friedrich. *Essays and Letters on Theory*. Ed. Thomas Pfau. Albany, NY: State University of New York Press, 1988.
Hölderlin, Friedrich. *Poems and Fragments*. Trans. Michael Hamburger. London: Anvil Press, 1994.
Hölderlin, Friedrich. *Hyperion or The Hermit in Greece*. Trans. Ross Benjamin. Brooklyn, NY: Archipelago Books, 2008.
Hölderlin, Friedrich. *The Death of Empedocles: A Mourning Play*. Trans. and intro. and notes David Farrell Krell. Albany, NY: State University of New York Press, 2008.
Holland, Michael. "From Crisis to Critique: Mallarmé for Blanchot." In *Meetings with Mallarmé in Contemporary French Culture*, Ed. Michael Temple. Exeter: University of Exeter Press, 1998.
Hopkins, G. M. *Poems*. Ed. W. H. Gardner. 3rd ed. London: Oxford University Press, 1948.
Hoppenot, Éric. *Maurice Blanchot et la tradition juive*. Avant-propos Éric Marty. Paris: Éditions Kimé, 2015.
Hubert, Henri and Marcel Mauss, *Sacrifice: Its Nature and Functions*. Trans. W. D. Halls. Foreword E. E. Evans-Pritchard. Chicago: University of Chicago Press, 1981.
Husserl, Edmund. *Logical Investigations*. Trans. J. N. Findlay. 2 vols. London: Routledge and Kegan Paul, 1970.
Husserl, Edmund. *The Idea of Phenomenology*. Trans. William P. Alston and George Nakhnikian. Intro. George Nakhnikian. The Hague: Martinus Nijoff, 1973.
Husserl, Edmund. *Cartesian Meditations: An Introduction to Phenomenology*. Trans. Dorian Cairns. The Hague: Martinus Nijhoff, 1977.
Husserl, *Ideas Pertaining to a Pure Phenomenology and to a Phenomenological Philosophy, 2: Studies in the Phenomenology of Constitution*. Trans. Richard Rojcewicz and André Schuwer. Dordrecht: Kluwer Academic Publishers, 1989.
Husserl, Edmund. *Briefwechsel*, 10 vols., vol. 7: *Wissenschaftlerkorrespondenz*. Ed. Elisabeth Schuhmann and Karl Schuhmann. Boston: Kluwer, 1994.
Husserl, Edmund. *Phantasy, Image Consciousness, and Memory (1898–1925)*. Trans. John Brough. Husserliana 11. Dordrecht: Springer, 2005.
Husserl, Edmund. *The Basic Problems of Phenomenology: From the Lectures*. Trans. Ingo Farin and James G. Hart. Husserliana 12. Dordrecht: Springer, 2006.
Husserl, Edmund. *Ideas for a Pure Phenomenology and a Phenomenological Philosophy, 1: General Introduction to Pure Phenomenology*. Trans. Daniel O. Dahlstrom. Indianapolis, IN: Hackett Publishing Co., 2014.
Husserl, Edmund. *First Philosophy: Lectures 1923/4 and Related Texts from the Manuscripts (1920–1925)*, Husserliana 14. Trans. Sebastian Luft and Thane M. Naberhaus. Dordrecht: Springer, 2019.
John of the Cross, *Collected Works*. Trans. Kieran Kavanaugh and Otilio Rodriguez. Washington, DC: ICS Publications, 1991.
Kafka, Franz. *The Collected Short Stories*. Ed. Nahum N. Glatzer. Harmondsworth: Penguin, 1983.
Kant, Immanuel. *Critique of Pure Reason*. Trans. Norman Kemp Smith. London: Macmillan, 1933.
Kant, Immanuel. *Critique of Judgement*. Trans. James Creed Meredith. Oxford: Oxford University Press, 1969.
Kierkegaard, Søren. *The Concept of Anxiety: A Simple Psychologically Orienting Deliberation on the Dogmatic Issue of Hereditary Sin*. Ed. and trans. Reidar Thomte in collaboration with Albert B. Anderson, Kierkegaard's Writings. 26 vols., vol. 8. Princeton, NJ: Princeton University Press, 1980.

Kofman, Sarah. *Comment s'en sortir?* Paris: Galilée, 1983.
Kofman, Sarah. *Smothered Words*. Trans. Madeleine Dobie. Evanston, IL: Northwestern University Press, 1998.
Klijn, A. F. J. Ed. *The Acts of Thomas: Introduction, Text, and Commentary*. 2nd rev. ed. 1962; Leiden: Brill, 2003.
Kojève, Alexandre. *Introduction to the Reading of Hegel: Lectures on the "Phenomenology of Spirit."* Ed. Raymond Queneau. Trans. James H. Nichols. Ithaca, NY: Cornell University Press, 1969.
Lacan, Jacques. "De la réalization du fantasme." *Magazine littéraire*, 424 (2003): 46–7.
LaCapra, Dominic. *Writing History, Writing Trauma*. 2001; Baltimore, MD: Johns Hopkins University Press, 2014.
Lacoue-Labarthe, Philippe. *Typography: Mimesis, Philosophy, Politics*. Ed. Christopher Fynsk and intro. Jacques Derrida. Cambridge, MA: Harvard University Press, 1989.
Lacoue-Labarthe, Philippe. *Heidegger, Art and Politics*. Trans. Chris Turner. Oxford: Basil Blackwell, 1990.
Lacoue-Labarthe, Philippe and Jean-Luc Nancy. *The Literary Absolute: The Theory of Literature in German Romanticism*. Trans. Philip Barnard and Cheryl Lester. Albany, NY: State University of New York Press, 1988.
Lacoue-Labarthe, Philippe and Jean-Luc Nancy. *Retreating the Political*. Ed. Simon Sparks. London: Routledge, 1997.
Lancaster, Rosemary. *Poetic Illumination: René Char and his Artist Allies*. Amsterdam: Rodopi, 2010.
Langbein, Hermann. *People in Auschwitz*. Trans. Harry Zohn. Foreword Henry Friedlander. Chapel Hill, NC: University of North Carolina Press, 2004.
Lanzmann, Claude. *Shoah: An Oral History of the Holocaust*. Pref. Simone de Beauvoir. New York: Pantheon Books, 1985.
Laporte, Roger. *Études*. Paris: P.O.L., 1990.
Lepetit, Bernard. Ed. *Les Formes de l'expérience: Une autre histoire sociale*. Paris: Albin Michel, 1995.
Leibniz, Gottlieb. *Discourse on Metaphysics, Correspondence with Arnauld, Monadology*. Intro. Paul Janet. La Salle: Open Court Publishing, 1973.
Levi, Primo. "*If This is a Man*" bound with "*The Truce*". Trans. Stuart Woolf. Intro. Paul Bailey. Harmondsworth: Penguin, 1979.
Lévy, Bernard-Henri. *Adventures on the Freedom Road: The French Intellectuals in the Twentieth Century*. Trans. and ed. Richard Veasey. London: The Harvill Press, 1995.
Lévy, Paul. *Journal d'un exile*. Paris: Grasset, 1949.
Lombard, Peter. *The Sentences*. Trans. Giulio Silano. 4 vols. Toronto: Pontifical Institute of Medieval Studies, 2007–10.
Londyn, Evelyne. "L'Orphique chez Blanchot. Voir et Dire." *French Forum*, 5, no. 3 (1980): 261–8.
Luther, Martin. *Luther's Works*, 55 vols., vol. 38: *Word and Sacrament*, vol. 4. Ed. Martin E. Lehmann. Gen. ed. Helmut T. Lehmann. Philadelphia, PA: Fortress Press, 1971.
Malamud, *The Fixer*. In *Novels and Stories of the 1960s*. Ed. Philip Davis. New York: The Library of America, 2013.
Malaparte, Curzio. *Coup d'État: The Technique of Revolution*. Trans. Sylvia Saunders. New York: E. P. Dutton and Co., 1932.
Mallarmé, Stéphane. *Correspondance, 1862–1871*. Ed. Henri Mondor and Jean-Pierre Richard. Paris: Gallimard, 1959.

Mallarmé, Stéphane. *Oeuvres complètes*. Éd. Bertrand Marchal. Bibliothèque de la Pléiade. 2 vols. Paris: Gallimard, 1998.

Mallarmé, Stéphane. *Collected Poems*. Trans. Henry Weinfield. Los Angeles, CA: University of California Press, 1994.

Mallarmé, Stéphane. *Divagations*. Trans. Barbara Johnson. Cambridge, MA: Harvard University Press, 2007.

Mandel, Naomi. *Against the Unspeakable: Complicity, the Holocaust, and Slavery in America*. Charlottesville, VA: University of Virginia Press, 2006.

Marion, Jean-Luc. *God without Being: Hors-Texte*. Trans. Thomas A. Carlson. Foreword David Tracy. Chicago: University of Chicago Press, 1991.

Marion, Jean-Luc. *Reduction and Givenness: Investigations of Husserl, Heidegger, and Phenomenology*. Trans. Thomas A. Carlson. Evanston, IL: Northwestern University Press, 1998.

Marion, Jean-Luc. *The Idol and Distance: Five Studies*. Trans. and intro. Thomas A. Carlson. New York: Fordham University Press, 2001.

Marion, Jean-Luc. *Being Given: Toward a Phenomenology of Givenness*. Trans. Jeffrey L. Kosky Stanford, CA: Stanford University Press, 2002.

Marion, Jean-Luc. "St. Thomas Aquinas and Ontotheology." In *Mystics: Aporia and Presence*, ed. Michael A. Kessler and Christian Sheppard, 38–75. Chicago: Chicago University Press, 2003.

Marion, Jean-Luc. *Negative Certainties*. Trans. Stephen E. Lewis. Chicago: Chicago University Press, 2015.

Marion, Jean-Luc. *D'ailleurs, la révélation*. Paris: Grasset, 2020.

Mark, Ber. *The Scrolls of Auschwitz*. Tel Aviv: Am Oved, 1985.

Mascolo, Jean and Jean-Marc Turine. *Autour du Groupe de la Rue Saint-Benoît de 1942 à 1964: L'Esprit d'insoumission*. Produit et realizé par Jean Mascolo et Jean-Marc Turine. Paris: Benoît Jacob Vidéo, 2002.

Maupassant, Guy de. *The Dark Side: Tales of Terror and the Supernatural*. Foreword Ramsey Campbell. Intro. Arnold Kellet. New York: Carroll and Graf, 1989.

McGinn, Bernard. "Love, Knowledge, and Mystical Union in Western Christianity: Twelfth to Sixteenth Century." *Church History*, 56, no. 1 (1987): 7–24.

Mehlman, Jeffrey. *Legacies: Of Anti-Semitism in France*. Minneapolis, MN: University of Minnesota Press, 1983.

Mehlman, Jeffrey. *Genealogies of the Text: Literature, Psychoanalysis, and Politics in Modern France*. Cambridge: Cambridge University Press, 1995.

Merwin, W. S. *The Rain in the Trees*. New York: Knopf, 1987.

Milon, Alain. "Maurice Blanchot, lecteur de René Char?" In *Maurice Blanchot, de proche en proche*. Ed. Éric Hoppenot et Coordonné Daiana Manoury, 209–20. Paris: Éditions Complicités, 2008.

Mosès, Stéphane. *System and Revelation: The Philosophy of Franz Rosenzweig*. Foreword Emmanuel Levinas. Trans. Catherine Tihanyi. Detroit, MI: Wayne State University Press, 1992.

Munier, Roger. "Expérience." *Mise en page*, 1 (mai, 1972).

Mounin, Georges. *Avez-vous lu Char?* Paris: Gallimard, 1946.

Musset, Alfred de. *Oeuvres complètes*. Ed. Philippe van Tieghem. Paris: Éditions du Seuil, 1963.

Nagy, Gregory. "Early Greek Views of Poets and Poetry." In *The Cambridge History of Literary Criticism*, 9 vols., vol. 1: *Classical Criticism*, ed. George A. Kennedy, 1–77. Cambridge: Cambridge University Press, 1989.

Nancy, Jean-Luc. *La Communauté désœuvrée*. Paris: Christian Bourgois, 1986.
Nancy, Jean-Luc. *The Inoperative Community*. Ed. Peter Connor and Trans. Peter Connor et al. Foreword Christopher Fynsk. Minneapolis, MN: University of Minnesota Press, 1991.
Nancy, Jean-Luc. *The Birth to Presence*. Trans. Brian Holmes et al. Stanford, CA: Stanford University Press, 1993.
Nancy, Jean-Luc. *La Communauté affronté*. Paris: Galilée, 2001.
Nancy, Jean-Luc. "The Confronted Community." Trans. Amanda Macdonald. *Postcolonial Studies*, 6, no. 1 (2003): 23–36.
Nancy, Jean-Luc. *Dis-Enclosure: The Deconstruction of Christianity*. Trans. Bettina Bergo et al. New York: Fordham University Press, 2008.
Nancy, Jean-Luc. *Maurice Blanchot: Passion politique, lettre-récit de 1984 suive d'une lettre de Dionys Mascolo*. Paris: Galilée, 2011.
Nancy, Jean-Luc. *La Communauté désavouée*. Paris: Galilée, 2014.
Nancy, Jean-Luc. *The Disavowed Community*. Trans. Philip Armstrong. New York: Fordham University Press, 2016.
Nancy, Jean-Luc. and Mathilde Girard. "Reste inavouable." *Lignes: Les Politiques de Maurice Blanchot, 1930–1993*, 43 (mars 2014): 155–76.
Nerval, Gérard de. "Aurélia." In *Selected Writings*. Trans. and intro. Geoffrey Wagner. Ann Arbor, MI: The University of Michigan Press, 1957.
Nietzsche, Friedrich. *Twilight of the Idols*, bound with *The Anti-Christ*. Trans., intro. and commentary R. J. Hollingdale. Harmondsworth: Penguin, 1968.
Nietzsche, Friedrich. *The Will to Power*. Trans. Walter Kaufmann and R. J. Hollingdale. Ed. Walter Kaufmann. New York: Vintage Books, 1968.
Nightingale, Andrea Wilson. *Spectacles of Truth in Classical Greek Philosophy: "Theoria" in its Cultural Context*. Cambridge: Cambridge University Press, 2004.
Oldenbourg, Zoé. *Le bûcher de Montségur: 16 mars 1244*. Paris: Gallimard, 1959.
Ong, Walter J. *The Barbarian Within and Other Fugitive Essays and Studies*. New York: Macmillan, 1962.
Origen. *The Song of Songs: Commentary and Homilies*. Trans. and ed. R. P. Lawson. Ancient Christian Writers. New York: The Newman Press, 1956.
Ormiston, Gayle L. Ed. *Transforming the Hermeneutic Context: From Nietzsche to Nancy*. Intro. Gayle L. Ormiston and Alan D. Schrift. Albany, NY: State University of New York Press, 1990.
Ovid, *Metamophoses*. Trans. Arthur Golding. Ed. Madeleine Forey. London: Penguin, 2001.
Pascal, Blaise. *Pensées*. Ed. and trans. Roger Ariew. Indianapolis, IN: Hackett Pub. Co., 2005.
Paulhan, Jean. *Choix de lettres*. 3 vols. Paris: Gallimard, 1992–96.
Paz, Octavio. *Alternating Current*. Trans. Helen R. Lane. London: Wildwood House, 1974.
Pine, Martin L. *Pietro Pomponazzi: Radical Philosopher of the Renaissance*. Padova: Editrice Antenore, 1986.
Plato. *Euthyphro, Apology, Crito, Phaedo, Phaedrus*. Trans. Harold North Fowler. Intro. W. R. M. Lamb. Loeb Classical Library. Cambridge. MA: Harvard University Press, 1914.
Plato. *Theaetetus, Sophist*. Trans. Harold North Fowler. Loeb Classical Library. Cambridge, MA: Harvard University Press, 1928.
Plato. *The Republic*. Trans. Paul Shorey. Loeb Classical Library. Cambridge, MA: Harvard University Press, 1935.

Plato. *Cratylus, Parmenides, Greater Hippias, Lesser Hippias*. Rev. ed. Trans. H. N. Fowler. Loeb Classical Library. Cambridge, MA: Harvard University Press, 1939.

Plotinus. *Enneads*. Trans. A. H. Armstrong, Loeb Classical Library. 7 vols. Cambridge, MA: Harvard University Press, 1988.

Poe, Edgar Allan. *Poetry and Tales*. Ed. Partrick Quinn. New York: The Library of America, 1984.

Proclus. *The Platonic Theology*. Trans. Thomas Taylor. Pref. R. Baine Harris. 6 vols. Kew Gardens, NY: Selene Books, 1986.

Proclus. *Commentary on Plato's "Parmenides."* Trans. Glenn R. Morrow and John M. Dillon. Trans. and notes John M. Dillon. Princeton, NJ: Princeton University Press, 1987.

Rahner, Karl. "Poetry and the Christian." In *Theological Investigations*, 23 vols., vol. 4: *More Recent Writings*. Trans. Kevin Smyth, 367–7. London: Darton, Longman and Todd, 1974.

Renan, Ernest. *Averroès et l'averroïsme: essai historique*. 3rd éd. Paris: Calmann-Lévy, 1867.

Rhees, Rush. *Discussions of Simone Weil*. Ed. D. Z. Phillips and assisted by Mario von der Ruhr. Albany, NY: State University of New York Press, 2000.

Robin, Léon. Ed. *Platon*, Édition de la Pléiade. Paris: Gallimard, 1944.

Robinson, T. M. Trans. *Heraclitus: Fragments: A Text and Translation with a Commentary*. Toronto: University of Toronto Press, 1991.

Rosenzweig, Franz. *Philosophical and Theological Writings*. Trans. and ed. Paul W. Franks and Michael L. Morgan. Indianapolis, IN: Hackett Publishing Co., 2000.

Rosenzweig, Franz. *The Star of Redemption*. Trans. Barbara E. Galli. Madison, WI: University of Wisconsin Press, 2005.

Ross, Kristin. *May '68 and its Afterlives*. Chicago: The University of Chicago Press, 2002.

Roth, John K. and Michael Berenbaum. *Holocaust: Religious and Philosophical Implications*. New York: Paragon House, 1989.

Sartre, Jean-Paul. *The Transcendence of the Ego: An Existentialist Theory of Consciousness*. Trans. and intro. Forrest Williams and Robert Kirkpatrick. New York: Hill and Wang, 1960.

Schelling, F. W. J. *Of Human Freedom*. Trans. James Gutmann. Chicago: Open Court Publishing Co., 1936.

Schelling, F. W. J. *The Unconditional in Human Knowledge: Four Early Essays, 1794-1796*. Trans. Fritz Marti. Lewisburg, PA: Bucknell University Press, 1980.

Schelling, F. W. J. *On the History of Modern Philosophy*. Trans. and intro. Andrew Bowie. Cambridge: Cambridge University Press, 1994.

Schelling, F. W. J. *Idealism and the Endgame of Theory: Three Essays*. Trans. and ed. Thomas Pfau. Albany, NY: State University of New York Press, 1994.

Schelling, F. W. J. *The Ages of the World*. Trans. and intro. Jason M. Wirth. Albany, NY: State University of New York Press, 2000.

Schérer, Jacques. *Le "Livre" de Mallarmé*. Paris: Gallimard, 1957.

Schlegel, Friedrich. *Philosophical Fragments*. Trans. Peter Firchow. Foreword Rodolphe Gasché. Minneapolis, MN: University of Minnesota Press, 1991.

Schmidt, Charles. *Histoire et doctrine de la secte des cathares ou albigeois*. Paris: J. Cherbuliez, 1849.

Simon, Martin F. A. *Friedrich Hölderlin, The Theory and Practice of Religious Poetry: Studies in the Elegies*. Stuttgart: Hans-Dieter Heniz/Akademischer Verlag Stuttgart, 1988.

Sobin, Gustaf. *Collected Poems*. Ed. Esther Sobin et al. Intro. Andrew Joron and Andrew Zawacki. Greenfield, MA: Talisman House, 2010.
Söderberg, Hans. *La religion des cathars: Étude sur le gnosticisme de la basse antiquité et du Moyen âge*. Uppsala: Almqvist and Wiksells Boktr., 1949.
Sokolowski, Robert. *The God of Faith and Reason: Foundations of Christian Theology*. 2nd ed. Washington, DC: Catholic University of America Press, 1995.
Sokolowski, Robert. *Introduction to Phenomenology*. Cambridge: Cambridge University Press, 2000.
Steenberghen, Fernand Van. *Thomas Aquinas and Radical Aristotelianism*. Washington, DC: The Catholic University of America Press, 1980.
Sternhell, Zeev. *Ni droite ni gauche: L'idéologie fasciste en France*. Paris: Seuil, 1983.
Stevens, Wallace. *The Collected Poems of Wallace Stevens*. New York: Alfred A. Knopf, 1954.
Stevens, Wallace. *Letters of Wallace Stevens*. Ed. Holly Stevens. New York: Alfred A. Knopf, 1972.
Suglia, Joseph. *Hölderlin and Blanchot on Self-Sacrifice*. New York: Peter Lang, 2004.
Surya, Michel. *Sainteté de Bataille*. Paris: Éditions de l'éclat, 2012.
Surya, Michel. *L'Autre Blanchot: L'écriture de jour, l'écriture de nuit*. Paris: Gallimard, 2015.
Surya, Michel. *À plus forte raison: Maurice Blanchot, 1940–1944. Suivi de deux lettres de Jean-Luc Nancy*. Paris: Éditions Hermann, 2021.
Syrotinski, Michael. *Deconstruction and the Postcolonial*. Liverpool: Liverpool University Press, 2007.
Tanner, Norman P. *Decrees of the Ecumenical Councils*. Ed. Normal P. Tanner. 2 vols. London: Sheed and Ward, 1990.
Taylor, Mark C. *Altarity*. Chicago: The University of Chicago Press, 1987.
Tolstoy, Leo. *On Insanity*. Trans. Ludvig Perno. London: C. W. Daniel, 1936.
Tsvetaeva, Marina. *Art in the Light of Conscience*. Trans., intro. and notes Angela Livingstone. Highgreen, Tarset: Bloodaxe Books, 2010.
Ungar, Stephen. *Scandal and Aftereffect: Blanchot and France since 1930*. Minneapolis, MN: University of Minnesota Press, 1995.
Valéry, Paul. *Reflections on the World Today*. Trans. Francis Scarfe. London: Thames and Hudson, 1951.
Valéry, Paul. *The Art of Poetry*. Trans. Denise Folliot. Intro. T. S. Eliot, The Collected Works of Paul Valéry. Ed. Jackson Mathews, 15 vols., vol. 7. Princeton, NJ: Princeton University Press, 1958.
Valéry, Paul. *Masters and Friends*. Trans. Martin Turnell. Intro. Joseph Frank. The Collected Works of Paul Valéry. vol. 9. Princeton, NJ: Princeton University Press, 1968.
Valéry, Paul. *Oeuvres*. Éd. Jean Hytier, Bibliothèque de la Pléiade. 2 vols. Paris: Gallimard, 1960.
Vetö, Miklos. *The Religious Metaphysics of Simone Weil*. Trans. Joan Dargan. Albany, NY: State University of New York Press, 1994.
Voragino, Jacobus de. *The Golden Legend or Lives of the Saints Englished by William Caxton*. Ed. F. S. Ellis. 7 vols. London: Dent, 1900.
Wahl, Jean. *Human Existence and Transcendence*. Ed. and Trans. William C. Hackett. Foreword Kevin Hart. Notre Dame, IN: Notre Dame University Press, 2016.
Weil, Simone. *Letter to a Priest*. New York: G. P. Putnam's Sons, 1954.
Weil, Simone. *The Notebooks of Simone Weil*. Trans. Arthur Wills. 2 vols. London: Routledge and Kegan Paul, 1956.

Weil, Simone. *Waiting for God*. Trans. Emma Crawford. Intro. Leslie A. Fiedler. New York: Capricorn Books, 1959.
Weil, Simone. *Écrits historiques et politiques*. Paris: Gallimard, 1960.
Weil, Simone. *Seventy Letters*. Trans. and ed. Richard Rees. London: Oxford University Press, 1965.
Weil, Simone. *Sur la science*. Paris: Gallimard, 1966.
Weil, Simone. *Poèmes, suivis de "Venise sauvée."* Paris: Gallimard, 1968.
Weil, Simone. *First and Last Notebooks*. Trans. Richard Rees. London: Oxford University Press, 1970.
Weil, Simone. *Oppression and Liberty*. Trans. Arthur Wills and John Petrie. Intro. F. C. Ellert. Amherst, MA: The University of Massachusetts Press, 1973.
Weil, Simone. *Lectures on Philosophy*. Trans. Hugh Price. Intro. Peter Winch. Cambridge: Cambridge University Press, 1978.
Weil, Simone. *Gateway to God*. Ed. David Raper with the collaboration of Malcolm Muggeridge and Vernon Sproxton. New York: Crossroad, 1982.
Weil, Simone. *Formative Writings, 1929–1941*. Ed. and trans. Dorothy Tuck McFarland and Wilhelmina Van Ness. London: Routledge and Kegan Paul, 1987.
Weil, Simone. *The Need for Roots: Prelude to a Declaration of Duties towards Mankind*. Trans. Arthur Wills. Pref. T. S. Eliot. London: Routledge, 2002.
Weil, Simone. *Gravity and Grace*. Intro. and postscript Gustave Thibon. Trans. Emma Crawford and Mario von der Ruhr. New York: Routledge, 2002.
Wiesel, Elie. *Night*. Trans. Marion Wiesel. New pref. Elie Wisel. Foreword Françoise Mauriac. New York: Hill and Wang, 2006.
Wilhem, Daniel. *Maurice Blanchot, la voix narrative*. Paris: Union Général d'Éditions, 1974.

Index

Adam 29, 193
Alain 84
Anselm, St. 2, 93
Antelme, Robert 108, 221-2, 224-7
aphorism 62, 67, 77, 111, 205
apophasis 219
Aquinas, Thomas St. 2, 40, 82, 131, 177-8, 180, 182, 189-90, 193, 199, 202
Aristotle 64, 137, 177-8, 182, 193, 199
Aron, Raymond 158
art 12, 25, 27, 52-3, 94, 109, 144, 159, 161-3, 191, 215
Ashbery, John 38, 55 n. 1
atheism 2-3, 36 n.38, 38-40, 56 n.5, 84-5, 94, 193, 205
Atlan, Jean-Michel 164
Augustine, St. 8, 9, 82, 127, 183, 189, 202
Auschwitz 11, 110, 114, 217-18, 221-2, 226-7; *see also* Shoah
Austen, Jane 162
Austin, J. L. 179
autrui 154, 167-9, 188, 190, 222, 224, 226

Bacon, Francis 134
Bailly, Jean-Christophe 88
Balthasar, Hans Urs von 38, 54
Barth, Karl 180
Bataille, Georges 21, 51, 64, 65, 77, 78, 89, 90, 104, 106, 113, 151, 179, 182
Beckett, Samuel 113
Bentham, Jeremy 9
Bernard of Clairvaux 81, 180, 181, 189-90
Biran, Maine de 84
Blake, William 208
Bloom, Harold 22, 34 n.4, 37 n.47
Blum, Léon 101, 104
Boileau, Nicolas 5

Bonaventure, St. 137, 182, 190
Bonnefoy, Yves 7, 13, 22, 54, 60, 67, 163, 219, 221
Brasillach, Robert 106
Breton, André 7, 151, 179
Briand, Aristide 101

Camus, Albert 103, 148
canon 14, 217
Carnap, Rudolf 179
Cathari 82, 83
Celan, Paul 11, 38, 162
Céline, Louis-Ferdinand 106
certitude 78-80, 83
Char, René 6, 14, 21, 38, 40, 60-71 *passim*, 113, 179, 216
Christ 54, 78, 81, 82, 92-3, 133, 193, 203
Claudel, Paul 63
communication 51, 65, 73 n.33, 112, 169, 182, 183
communion 89, 91, 93
communism 68, 89, 94, 95, 107, 111
community 88-96 *passim*, 169
Confucius 179
Conrad, Joseph 126-7
contestation 51-2, 80, 112
Cummings, E. E. 13-14

Da Vinci, Leonardo 163
death/dying 2, 9, 12, 13, 27, 28, 129, 134-5, 138, 147, 154, 215, 225
De Caussade, Jean-Pierre 82
De Gaulle, Charles 66-8
De Man, Paul 44-5
De Vega, Lopa 81
Deleuze, Gilles 21, 181
democracy 90-1, 96
Derrida, Jacques 3, 21, 67, 94, 96, 107, 112-13, 150, 163, 181
Descartes, René 64, 84, 134, 136, 137, 184

dialogue 6, 24
Dickinson, Emily 70
disaster 111, 198–209 *passim*, 214, 217, 219, 220, 227, 228
Doppelgänger 132
Dostoevsky, Fydor 126, 162
Drieu La Rochelle, Pierre 106
Du Bouchet, André 7
duplex veritate 202–3, 208
Duras, Marguerite 89

Eckhart, Meister 179
Eliot, T. S. 14, 45, 61, 162
Epictetus 147
Euripides 48
Evagrius Ponticus 179
everyday 15, 226
experience 26–7, 29, 50, 51, 66, 79, 85, 91, 96, 130, 138, 159, 169, 186, 218, 219

faith 79, 202-3, 208, 220
fascination 2, 15, 55, 69, 146, 159
Fénelon, François 82
Forêts, Louis-René de 60, 140 n.10
Foucault, Michel 21, 69, 110, 227
fragment(ary) 8, 13, 67, 111, 178, 198, 205–6
Frege, Gottlob 2
Freud, Sigmund 113

George, Stefan 38
Gnosticism 82, 85, 209
God 2, 6, 15, 27, 79–81, 84, 92, 181, 192–3, 199, 201, 209, 214, 222
Goethe, J. W. von 162, 216
Goncourt, Edmond/Jules 5
Gothic 12, 133
Grace 81–2
Gregory of Nyssa 181
Gundolf, Friedrich 39

Hardy, Thomas 124–5
Hegel, G. W. F. 7, 21, 27, 29, 38, 135, 136, 138, 145, 180, 181, 190, 199–201, 203, 214, 218, 221
Heidegger, Martin 6, 12–14, 21, 24–7, 38, 39, 44, 69, 70, 102–3, 123–4, 145, 147, 157–61, 164–5, 179, 181, 185, 187–8, 190, 220
Henry, Michel 184
Heraclitus 21, 45, 62, 64, 66, 68, 69, 123–4, 179
Herbert, George 79–80
Herder, J. G. 25
Herrick, Robert 11
Hill, Geoffrey 38
Hitler, Adolf 101–2
Hobbes, Thomas 161
Hölderlin, Fredrick 6, 14, 21, 22, 25, 38–55 *passim*, 63, 67, 69, 70, 113, 145, 148, 153
  "Brot und Wein" 47, 63
  "Der Einzige" 54
  "Mnemosyne" 53
  "Des Morgans" 46
  "Der Mütter Erde" 40–1
  "Patmos" 54
  "Der Rhein" 49–50
  Der Tod des Empedokles 46, 49
  "Wie Wenn am Feiertage" 42–8, 50, 63, 67
Homer 69, 162, 216
Hopkins, G. M. 13, 70
Husserl, Edmund 2, 3, 6, 7, 13, 136, 179, 182, 184–6, 215

"I" 10, 13, 26, 28, 31, 51, 65–6, 79–82, 84, 94, 107, 129, 135, 165, 188, 207, 215, 218, 220, 224, 227
idealism 131, 179, 199, 200, 203
Il y a 5, 146, 151, 160, 166, 171 n.25, 204, 211 n.33, 223, 226
image 25, 31, 52, 131, 134, 157–70 *passim*, 166, 216
impossible 26, 65, 84, 91, 111, 146, 169, 183
inspiration 26, 33, 71
interruption 168–9, 191

Jaspers, Karl 39–40
John of Ford 180
John of the Cross, St. 23, 40, 82, 179
Joyce, James 162, 179

Kabbalah 83, 201

Kafka, Franz   12, 14, 21, 22, 26, 28, 94,
    113, 145, 153, 216
Kant, Immanuel   21, 38, 50, 193, 200, 203
Karas, Vekoslav   31
Kierkegaard, Søren   12, 200
Klopstock, F. G.   38
Kojève, Alexandre   11, 138

Lacoue-Labarthe, Philippe   95, 96, 113
Lao Tzu   179
Laporte, Roger   108
Lascaux   61, 69
Lautréamont, Comte de   21, 24, 25, 33,
    113, 145, 148, 153, 179
law   149–50, 153
Leibniz, G. W.   177
Leiris, Michel   164
Levinas, Emmanuel   4, 5, 7, 8, 12, 21,
    22, 91, 92, 107, 109, 113, 114, 134,
    144–55 *passim*, 157–70 *passim*,
    178, 183, 184, 189, 191–3, 198, 204,
    207–8, 219, 223, 224
Lévy, Bernard-Henri   114, 221
Lévy, Paul   103, 106, 107
Loewenthal, Zalman   227
Lombard, Peter   82
Longfellow, H. W.   162
Luther, Martin   203, 211 n. 26

madness   144–55 *passim*
Malamud, Bernard   9–10
Malaparte, Curzio   101
Mallarmé, Stéphane   6, 14, 21–34 *passim*,
    40, 70, 113, 124, 145, 150, 162
    "L'Après-midi d'un faune"   32
    "Crise de vers"   28–9, 33
    Igitur   28
    "Sainte"   30–1
    "Le vierge, le vivace et le bel
        aujourd'hui"   32–3
Malraux, André   105
Marcel, Gabriel   148
Marion, Jean-Luc   14, 38, 50, 136, 186–8,
    193
Marx, Karl   7, 110, 113, 218
Mascolo, Dionys   95, 105, 182
Maulnier, Thierry   102–3
Maupassant, Guy de   126
Mauron, Charles   124

Mauss, Marcel   65
Merwin, W. S.   11
Messiah   206–8
Molière (Jean-Baptiste Poquelin)   162
Mondor, Henri   22–4
Moore, G. E.   179
Mounier, Emmanuel   100
Musil, Robert   4, 95
Musset, Alfred de   125

Nadeau, Maurice   105–6
Nancy, Jean-Luc   88–96 *passim*
Neher, André   63
Nerval, Gérard de   24, 104, 126
Newman, John Henry   78
Nietzsche, Frederick   12, 21, 27, 113, 179,
    181, 200, 215, 220
Novalis   43

Ong, Walter J   127
Origen   127, 180
Orpheus   25–6, 28, 33, 36 n.30, 65, 134
Outside   5, 7, 10–11, 12, 25, 55, 60–1,
    67–9, 129, 130, 134, 145–6, 150,
    153–4, 159, 166–8, 187, 191, 193,
    204–5, 211 n.33, 213–28 *passim*
Ovid   47–8

Parmenides   44–5, 147, 177, 183–4, 199
Pascal, Blaise   77, 80, 134, 179
Pasternak, Boris   63
Pater, Walter   4
Paul, St.   133
Paz, Octavio   45
Petrarch, Francesco   69
phenomenology   2–4, 6–8, 15, 124, 132,
    136–7, 145–6, 150, 160–1, 164, 168,
    185–8
Picasso, Pablo   31
Piccirilli, Furio   29
Pindar   38, 42–3, 54
Plato   41, 43, 60–1, 64, 66, 80, 82, 177,
    183, 199, 202
Plotinus   177–8
Poe, Edgar Allan   125, 139
Poincaré, Raymond   101
Pompanazzi, Pietro   202–3
Ponge, Francis   7
Pouillon, Jean   158

Pound, Ezra   61, 162
Proclus   134, 177-8
prophecy   61-3, 95, 206
Proust, Marcel   4, 162, 179, 216
Pseudo-Dionysius the Areopagite   178
Pushkin, Alexander   70

Rahner, Karl   45
reading   131-2, 230 n.12
religion   39, 41, 53, 189, 192
Renan, Ernst   202
responsibility   92, 107-9, 114, 158, 168, 170, 207-8, 221
Richardson, Samuel   179, 216
Rilke, R. M.   21, 22, 26, 145, 163
Rimbaud, Arthur   23, 51, 63, 65, 70
Ronsard, Pierre de   33
Rosenzweig, Franz   8, 198-209 *passim*
Rushdie, Salman   106
Russell, Bertrand   2

sacred   6, 39-40, 42-3, 51-2, 54, 55, 61-2, 64, 66, 70, 94
sacrifice   50-1, 53-5, 65, 93, 94
Sade, Marquis de   11, 21, 113, 145, 148, 179, 216
Saint-Beuve, Charles   5
Sartre, Jean-Paul   4, 5, 11, 84, 107, 111, 114, 148, 157-8, 160, 161
Schelling, F. W. J.   38, 49, 190, 199-201, 203
Schiller, Friedrich   38
Schlegel, Friedrich   205
Scotus, Duns   78
Sellars, Wilfred   179
Seneca   147
Shakespeare, William   27-8, 69, 139, 162, 216
Shoah   8, 198, 108-9, 204, 207, 213-28 *passim*

Sobin, Gustaf   38
Socrates   21, 61-2, 134, 179, 223
Sophocles   38, 47, 49, 53
Sosno, Sacha   164
Spenser, Edmund   14
Spinoza, Baruch   134
Sterne, Lawrence   216
Stevens, Wallace   21, 162
Stevenson, Robert Louis   126
suffering   84-5, 144, 147, 188, 219-20
Surya, Michel   99 n.58
Swinburne, Algernon   162

Tennyson, Alfred Lord   162
testimony   96, 152
Theōrós   43-4, 46, 47, 50, 55
thinking   13, 78, 123-4, 181, 191, 198-200, 209
third relation   7, 8, 111, 154, 169, 177-93 *passim*, 223
Tolstoy, Leo   148
Tout dire   179-80
tragedy   49, 51
transcendence   94, 144, 165, 189, 205, 228
truth   39, 111, 131, 158, 208
Tsvetaeva, Marina   63

Valéry, Paul   4, 11, 22-4, 100-1, 179, 191
Verlaine, Paul   25
Voltaire, François-Marie Arouet de   4

Wahl, Jean   8, 160, 188, 204
weariness   151-4, 178
Weil, Simone   7, 77-85 *passim*
writing   27, 61, 107, 139, 150, 159, 180, 186, 205